THE SOCIAL ECONOMY OF CONSUMPTION

Monographs in Economic Anthropology, No. 6

Edited by

Henry J. Rutz
and
Benjamin S. Orlove

UNIVERSITY
PRESS OF
AMERICA

Lanham • New York • London

Society for
Economic
Anthropology

Library of Congress Cataloging-in-Publication Data

The Social economy of consumption.
(Monographs in economic anthropology ; no. 6)
1. Consumers– –Developing countries. 2. Consumption (Economics)–
–Developing countries. 3. Households– –Developing countries.
4. Developing countries– –Social conditions. I. Rutz, Henry J. II. Orlove,
Benjamin S. III. Society for Economic Anthropology (U.S.) IV. Series.
HC59.72.C6S63   1989   339.4'6'091724   89–5447 CIP
ISBN 0–8191–7350–9 (alk. paper)
ISBN 0–8191–7351–7 (pbk. : alk. paper)

ACKNOWLEDGEMENTS

The papers appearing in this volume were presented on April 11 and 12 1986 at the sixth annual meeting of the Society for Economic Anthropology, hosted by Mahir Saul and his colleagues of the Department of Anthropology at the University of Illinois, Urbana-Champaign.

We wish to take this opportunity to thank our hosts and all the participants. There were twenty-two papers presented in the plenary sessions and an additional twenty-nine papers were discussed in a separate poster session. The authors benefitted from the lively spirit of discussion and debate that has come to characterize the Society's annual meetings. We owe a special debt of gratitude to Professor Gary S. Becker, who interrupted his own busy schedule to lend an economist's perspective to our proceedings. Finally, we thank the Editorial Board of the Society for its support. Francis Berdan, Frank Cancian, and Stuart Plattner encouraged us from start to finish and greatly expedited the appearance of this volume in print.

THE SOCIAL ECONOMY OF CONSUMPTION

Society for Economic Anthropology

Volume VI

Household Productive Consumption and Consumptive Production

THINKING ABOUT CONSUMPTION: A SOCIAL ECONOMY APPROACH

Benjamin S. Orlove and Henry J. Rutz

What To Think About Consumption

The broad goals of this article and this volume are to present and support two related claims: that consumption is a topic worthy of research by economic anthropologists, and that a promising way to conduct such research is to draw on several premises (here termed "the social economy of consumption") current in economic anthropology. These aims may appear as conventional tasks within a conventional sub-field of anthropology. Economic anthropologists tend to agree on the set of topics that are included within their subject matter, and virtually all are willing to place consumption within that set. As the following discussion shows, the social economy of consumption approach also falls within the range of approaches which may be applied to this subject matter. Nonetheless, we have organized this chapter in a different fashion from most review articles or introductory chapters. This choice reflects our earlier conversations about consumption with other colleagues. Some seemed excited about the notion of studying consumption, others thought (and some admitted to thinking) that this idea was not very promising, and still others had a more complex and less comfortable reaction: they were quite certain that consumption formed part of economic anthropology, they held strong commitments to a particular theoretical approach within economic anthropology, they realized that they believed that their approach was applicable to this topic, and they were troubled by the fact that they could not readily imagine how to carry out this application. Our organization stems from this nature of consumption: the difficulty in moving from the general and easily resolved question of its admissibility within economic anthropology to the more specific and less easily resolved question of the means and value of studying it.

If consumption were a more frequently studied topic, like the themes of entrepreneurship, households, marketing and development that other volumes in this series have examined, this chapter could have a more standard organization (a review of previous work, a discussion of current directions, an examination of current analytical concerns, a few issues of definition, a plan for the future). Instead, we have a set of interrelated sections. Counting this preamble as the first, the next section, which is the longest one in this article, examines one village in detail. The anthropologists who studied the village did not accord consumption much importance; we re-examine their material and show the dangers of such an omission. This case offers a concrete instance of the difference between an account which treats consumption carefully and one which does not. It appears early in the article, because we believe that its concreteness presents in clear fashion the significance of the themes that are discussed more generally later on.

1

The third section is the first of the three bundles of concepts that we present. It examines the location of consumption within economies as wholes, reviews the reasons for consumption always being placed at the end of the list that begins with production and exchange, and argues against the reductionist efforts which explain consumption in terms of production and exchange. The fourth section, the second of the conceptual bundles, lays out the social nature of our approach; we first argue that there is a set of the basic and rather general--if not trivial--assumptions which underlie the competing approaches within economic anthropology, and then apply these assumptions to consumption and give to this application the name "the social economy of consumption." (Stated in the briefest terms possible, we argue 1) that consumption is as much a part of economic activity as production and exchange are; 2) that consumption is as social in nature as production and exchange are; 3) that a view of economic change which incorporates consumption provides a fuller and more accurate account than one which does not; despite the apparently simple nature of these claims, they often have not been presented or examined systematically.) The fifth section reviews, with necessary brevity, other work on consumption that has been conducted in anthropology, economics, psychology, sociology and history. The sixth section is the third and last conceptual bundle: it suggests that the study of consumption has some significance for the examination of wider issues within the study of human society, particularly questions of historical change and of power. The three conceptual bundles present the three fundamental characteristics of our approach: its anti-reductionism in the first, its social nature in the second, and its emphasis on power and ideology in the third. Different readers may find themselves covering sections with varying amounts of attention and care. Some may focus on the ethnographic case, others on the three conceptual bundles, and still others on the review of other work. We believe that all these readings will support our initial claims, that none of the readings are contradictory, and that particular readers will find some readings to be more interesting, accessible, enjoyable, or persuasive than other readings.

When To Think About Consumption: A Case Study

Can consumption make a difference in Java?

Kali Loro, a pseudonymous Javanese village, offers an appropriate case to convey the difference between including and excluding consumption as a topic of study. This Asian setting is a familiar one to anthropologists: a dense population of peasants that relies on irrigated rice cultivation as their subsistence base and carries out a number of other types of gardening, craft production and marketing. Ann Stoler and Benjamin White studied this village in the early 1970s, at a time when the village had been influenced by the "Green Revolution," particularly by the adoption of high-yielding varieties of rice and of some simple new machines. The topics of their research were "production and exchange" (Stoler 1977:679), with an emphasis on labor. They analyzed economic activity on both an individual level (the responses of particular people and households to constraints) and an

2

aggregate level (the emergence of class differences between wealthy and poor peasants). Stoler and White drew on established frameworks in economic anthropology, particularly neo-Marxist approaches, in the treatment of class interests and exploitation, and decision theory, through the examination of individual variation in behavior and on the selection among alternatives. We offer a different analysis of social and economic structures and processes in Kali Loro, based on the articles by Stoler and White. Our analysis accords consumption as much importance as production and exchange, and it underscores the social nature of consumption activities. We place greater emphasis on ideology than Stoler and White do.

The two views of Kali Loro are quite different, as we will elaborate in the following pages. For Stoler and White, external forces--capitalism and its particular manifestation in the Green Revolution--bring change to Kali Loro. If one ranks different activities by the hourly returns which they offer, capitalism increases the differences between rich and poor peasants, offering the best options of cash-cropping only to the former, who have better access to markets and capital, and limiting the latter to worse options, typically ones with lower hourly returns. Changes in consumption are determined by changes in production and exchange; the rich can adopt luxuries, the poor are limited to subsistence. In our view, by contrast, the local people respond to capitalism as well as being influenced by it. We do not assume a single ranking of activities, but rather examine local debates over the relative valuation of options. In particular, consumption plays an important role; since the use of goods can both mark and change social relations, consumption forms an arena for other conflicts generated by changes within the local economy. For peasants, consumption serves as a means of making and weighing claims on one another on the basis of kinship, residence and ethnicity. Following through these two views, we arrive at a number of points of difference, in the arenas both of consumption (e.g., adoption of new goods) and of production and exchange (e.g., technological change, shifting patterns of labor relations). Phrased in simple terms, we argue that the study of consumption matters in Kali Loro, since it leads to a different picture of the village; by extension, we argue that it matters in all societies as well. We believe that the close analysis of a specific case can offer a strong sense of the importance of consumption. We therefore request the readers who agree with this belief to read the following eleven pages and those who disagree with it to turn to the next section, "where to think about consumption: its location in economics".

The non-consumptionist approach

White's work (1976) challenges the view that overpopulation is the cause of poverty and unemployment in Java. He shows that the area of irrigated rice land in Kali Loro would be sufficient to provide sustenance for the population as a whole, but it is unevenly distributed, so that three quarters of the population own less than the necessary minimum for household dietary needs. This land distribution limits the possibilities of earning a livelihood exclusively through agriculture. In order to generate income, peasants engage in a variety of activities, working an average of nearly 10 hours each day. White calculates the return in cash terms to different activities and shows that peasants generally choose the more remunerative forms of work available to them. Many economists, noting that a relatively small number of hours is spent in rice cultivation, had assumed that much of the potential rural labor force was idle.

Stoler (1977) also attacks a widely-held view of Java, that culturally-specific economic activities lead to "shared poverty," in which exchanges of labor and goods among peasants level economic differences. She examines *bawon*, the payment of women rice-harvesters with a share of the crop which they gather with an *ani-ani* or small finger-knife. The *bawon* shares are not fixed. Peasants give larger shares to women to whom they are more closely related, who live nearer them, or with whom they have participated in cooperative labor groups called *gotong-royong*. Individuals who are more distant cannot press as effectively for a high *bawon*. This system works to the advantage of the wealthier peasants. Such peasants receive larger *bawon* shares, because they harvest rice only for people to whom they are close in social and spatial terms; on the average they pay smaller shares, because they draw on a large pool of more distant individuals. The peasants with less land, by contrast, not only receive these smaller shares, but also must pay larger ones. Since their plots are small, they must give preference to close kin in recruiting harvest workers. Stoler terms this situation "exploitative" (1977:693). In other parts of Java, rich peasants have shifted the technology and social organization of the rice harvest by hiring middlemen, who bring in crews of male workers with sickles. The total harvest is slightly lower with sickles than it would be with the more technically efficient *ani-ani*; however, the landowners retain a relatively and absolutely larger amount. In Kali Loro, many of the better-off families have purchased rice hullers, retaining the rice that they had formerly given to the women who pounded it by hand; the advent of the sickle does not seem very distant. These technological changes further reduce what Stoler and White term the "bargaining power" of the poorer peasants, already weakened by their poverty. They note a shift from relatively egalitarian and reciprocal relations among peasants to more hierarchical and unequal exchanges between wealthy and poor peasants, resembling patron-client relations found elsewhere in Southeast Asia and throughout the world.

We argue that the inclusion of consumption as a topic of investigation expands the analysis of economic and social relations in Kali Loro. We term our approach the social economy of consumption perspective. We may now make explicit some of its constituting elements. Firstly, we do not separate consumption from production and exchange, but rather see them as composing a single system; activities which influence one will influence the other as well. To say, as Stoler does, that "new pressures encourage large landowners to use their wealth for outside consumption" (1977:694) suggests that large landowners first have wealth, and then spend it. We would argue that the consumption and the wealth are directly interconnected, and we also would consider the proposition that a desire for outside consumption encourages landowners to increase their wealth. Most importantly, we would not separate the analysis of income

4

generation and of expenditures; for well-off peasants who retain a strong orientation towards ties within the village, higher expenditure on ceremonies and higher *bawon* are linked directly through patterns of interaction in the village. An interest in consumption makes it easier to ask why peasants who own large amounts of land differ so much in their desire for higher income; one might expect all such peasants to share the wish to profit from the new opportunities which the Green Revoluton opened up. For most economists, it would not seem difficult to explain the efforts to increase income. They would be more hard pressed to come up with reasons, such as risk, information blockages or a high value placed on leisure, to explain why people would not seek a higher income. Many economic anthropologists would have similar difficulties with this diversity. A decision theorist might claim that income is a goal valued by many individuals in different settings around the world, and a neo-Marxist could argue that class interests would lead rich peasants to seek to monopolize land and employment opportunities. Both of these would not explain the rich peasants who shun these possibilities. Culturalists would tend to have a more normative view, and suggest that some cultures emphasize money-making while others do not; they would be hard-pressed to account for the sort of variability which is found in Kali Loro.

Secondly, we see consumption as being as social as production and exchange are. Village ceremonies such as *slametan* are merely one instance in which consumption directly involves a number of people. The communicative aspects of consumption strike us as particularly important. We wish to emphasize the point that consumption does not merely reflect social relations, in that it marks certain social statuses and ties, as White suggests when he speaks of fixed obligations. We argue instead that consumption can establish, maintain and change social relations, including those most directly involved in production such as *bawon*. In this way, consumption may be linked with power, much as production and exchange are. This view of consumption as dynamic rather than passive would seem to apply to Kali Loro even before capitalist relations of production appeared. Stoler offers one example of the sort of tensions marked by exchanges of labor and goods:

> the new bride of a small farmer, recently arrived from a hamlet about one mile distant, had to oversee the [rice] harvest for the first time. On the first day, she enraged her husband by giving *bawon* of one-fifth (more than was necessary). On the next day therefore, she determined to give shares of one-tenth (where the appropriate *bawon* would have been one-sixth or one-eighth) and compounded her *faux pas* by actually measuring out ten shares for herself and one for the harvester, that is, giving only one-eleventh share. Those harvesting said nothing, but in the evening, her close neighbors scolded her in public as she walked out of the house. On the third day the "proper" *bawon* was distributed. (1977:696).

Though this incident might reflect the woman's ignorance, the incompleteness of her socialization, or perhaps the differences in *bawon* between hamlets, it seems

5

quite plausible that the new bride's embarrassment demonstrates the tensions between different sorts of social ties that could have existed well before the Green Revolution ever arrived on Java. The different people voiced personal, and contradictory, criticisms, though couched in the same idiom; they told her that she failed to follow custom. In this way, consumption has an ideological character, in that it appeals to shared understandings and thus it allows for disagreement.[1]

Finally, a view that incorporates consumption provides a fuller understanding of historical change than a view which does not. We do not disagree with Stoler and White that capitalism has influenced Kali Loro in important ways; we would, however, see the changes not only as the product of capitalism entering the village, but also as the consequence of the village receiving capitalism. What seems to be at stake in Kali Loro is not merely the control over material goods, but over their evaluation as well. Since the conflicts seem to be partly within established patterns and partly about these patterns themselves, we do not adopt the term "bargaining power" which Stoler and White use. We acknowledge the importance of power issues, but find the notion of bargaining too narrow.

Non-consumptionists view consumption: an implicit analysis

For both Stoler and White, capitalism is the motive force in bringing change to Kali Loro; it drives both the individual process of decision-making and the aggregate dynamic of class conflict. Their analysis rests on production and exchange. However, they treat consumption with sufficient detail to offer a different view of this rural economy. Firstly, they discuss consumption as a topic or area of behavior. They note that the peasants of Kali Loro must assure themselves of the biological and cultural basic needs to life--food, clothing, shelter. As in other societies, the villagers have life-cycle celebrations and ceremonial feasts, known locally as *slametan*.. They also smoke cigarettes and chew betel nuts. Many, if not all, spend some money on the education of their children. Some wealthy peasants have begun to purchase new goods. On several occasions, Stoler and White mention fancy cloth, motorcycles and rice-hulling machines, and they make passing reference to other goods such as radios.

Secondly, and equally importantly, Stoler and White offer an implicit theory of consumption, in which expenditures on goods are divided into three classes: subsistence necessities, social investment and luxury. Although they do not offer an explicit categorization, they return on a number of occasions to the same set of types of goods. White speaks of subsistence when he mentions the "annual rice requirements" and "other needs in food, clothing, school fees etc." (1976:280) The notion that subsistence is fixed underlies his treatment of the lengthening of the working day to compensate for a fall in hourly earnings: "[a]s returns to labour decline, then obviously the number of daily hours of labour required to attain a given level of living must increase." (1976:280) The notion of social investment is also implicit. In the past, before a new irrigation canal permitted double-cropping, "[t]hose 'surpluses' that were produced by wealthier households were primarily used to buy more land and to fulfill a host of ritual and

6

economic obligations within the village." (Stoler 1977:693) By making these expenditures, they were "investing...back into the village economy for prestige and power." (Stoler 1977:694) This discussion treats expenditures on consumption for social purposes as fixed ("obligations"), as intentional ("investing"), and as having one purpose, that of creating hierarchy ("for prestige and power").

The term "luxury" appears in several ways. Stoler and White occasionally use the word ironically; for instance, they refer to time spent in non-work activities by saying "...idleness is a luxury which most of the population of Kali Loro cannot afford" (White: 281), to suggest that most people must work as hard as possible to achieve subsistence livelihood. Their main referent, though, is to the new goods that have come in from outside. Stoler mentions briefly the "new pressures [which] encourage large landowners to use their wealth for outside consumption (motorbikes, rice hullers, children's education, and so forth) rather than investing it back into the village economy for prestige and power" (1977:694). White's treatment (1976:283) is slightly longer. One paragraph describes the "opening up" of the Indonesian economy which brings "an influx into city markets of expensive and mostly imported luxury consumption items (Hondas, radios, luxury textiles and so on) and a concomitant wave of 'consumerism' which has not failed to affect many wealthy villages." He links this "opening up" to the "closing down" of political activity in the villages, trends that reduce the "bargaining power" of the poorer villages in labor relations. He concludes "[in] Kali Loro there are many wealthy landowners who still own no motorcycles or hulling-machines, who dress simply and give traditional harvest shares [*bawon*]...to those who depend on them; but there are larger numbers who spend more of their wealth than before outside the village and redistribute less than before to their fellow villagers." He notes a difference in the consumption patterns of two sorts of wealthy landowners, whom we could term "cosmopolitans" and "localists." The former, who buy fancy cloth, motorcycles and rice hullers, also seem to offer lower *bawon* and to spend less on ceremonies; they also send their children away to school. The latter continue the earlier pattern of sponsoring ceremonials and of dressing like other villagers. The former consume luxuries; the latter invest in social relations.

Stoler and White do not offer detailed reasons for the acquisition of new goods by the cosmopolitans. Once again, the use of language is significant. Consistent with both their actor-oriented framework and their implicit view of history as class struggle, they usually place economic actors as the subjects, rather than the objects, of verbs. The cosmopolitans, by contrast, appear as the object of verbs whose subjects are general economic forces: "new pressures [which] encourage large landowners to use their wealth for outside consumption" (Stoler 1977:694); "the 'opening up' of the Indonesian economy [. . . and] a concomitant wave of 'consumerism' which has not failed to affect many wealthier villagers" (White 1976:283). What are these economic subjects, which Stoler refers to merely as pressures and whose names White places within quotation marks? About all that we can deduce is that these subjects seem to be impersonal and to be located outside the village. This imprecision and vagueness is in striking contrast to the detail and specificity with which they examine production and exchange.

Consumptionists view consumption: an explicit analysis

We seek to examine directly this topic of consumption which White and Stoler sketch briefly. We expand rather than reject their work, accepting production and exchange as topics of study, but adding consumption as well. Although we find their use of neo-Marxist and decision theory frameworks to be appropriate, we also think that a careful examination of consumption entails closer attention to ideology than these approaches usually afford. This enlargement of topics and approaches will lead to a somewhat distinct analysis of the themes of social inequality and tensions on which Stoler and White focus.

A simple way to underscore the contrast is to examine households and disaggregate overall consumption into a series of expenditures, much as Stoler and White disaggregate overall production into a series of goods and income-generating activities. We use the word "expenditure" to include allocations of goods, such as home-produced crops, as well as of money. Stoler and White separate production and consumption more sharply than we do, and assign analytical priority to the first. We do not see the generation of income and the expenditures on consumption as two separate processes, but rather see that there may be close links between specific productive activities and consumption patterns.

1. Changes in the repertoire of goods.

One important type of goods is the items purchased from outside the village. Unlike Stoler and White, who attribute the introduction of these goods to impersonal forces from outside the villages, we note that these goods communicate present and future intentions to many people within the village. It seems likely that poor peasants will take the wearing of imported cloth by cosmopolitans to suggest a partial withdrawal from sponsorship of ceremonies and an unwillingness to pay high *bawon*. The motorcycles are in some sense an investment, in that money spent on a motorcycle reduces expenditures on transport and allows easier access to outside markets; they might well also be a source of individual pleasure, and they indicate to others an orientation beyond the village. They commit their owners to the future acquisition of monetary income beyond subsistence needs, for purchase of gasoline and spare parts. Mechanical rice hullers are also less simple to explain than they might appear; they not only reduce allocations of rice for women who hull with traditional equipment, but they also hint at the possibility of reducing or eliminating *bawon* by hiring in male harvesters with sickles. The localists are not merely individuals who unquestioningly retain an old way; instead, they offer a contrast with the cosmopolitans. Their wearing of traditional cloth bears messages as clearly as the use of fancy imported cloth by cosmopolitans. We do not wish to offer a neat typology in which individuals make some expenditures in order to invest (that is,

8

to increase future incomes), others to communicate and still others to satisfy personal desires; at this point, we merely wish to show that these aspects are interconnected and complex. We do wish to point out important historical dimensions of consumption, though. Stoler and White conducted their field work less than a decade after the political upheavals in which many thousands of peasants were killed. The lines of conflict were complex, partly following party affiliation, partly ethnic cleavages separating the more rural and subsistence-oriented Javanese peasants from more urban and commercial Chinese intermediaries. In this context, some peasants might have been identified with one group or another, not by their position in systems of production or exchange, but in systems of consumption--for being too linked to new urban patterns of use of goods rather than customary local ones. In this sense, consumption may become politicized, thereby serving as an arena for debating alternative systems of social and economic relations.

2. Changes in technology.

Although Stoler and White focus on technological change for the harvesting of rice, they also discuss the means for removing hulls from rice and making it fit for cooking. They mention mechanical rice hullers at several points. These machines were introduced in Kali Loro in the late 1960s (White 1976:282), and in about five years seemed to have displaced the practice of hiring women to pound rice by hand in exchange for shares of one-tenth. Stoler and White imply that the owners of these machines benefit in several ways: they retain a larger amount of rice, and they are paid more for machine-hulled rice, which stores better (Stoler 1977:694). These machines thus make the rich richer and the poor poorer, since the women who formerly worked in pounding rice for shares now must accept less rewarding activities, notably marketing. This increasing disparity in wealth supports their views of the effects of capitalist penetration. Although Stoler and White do not explain why rice production was mechanized first at this point, rather than at the point of harvest, the answer would seem simple: hulling takes place within the home, out of sight of the other villagers, so that the social cost is less.

With our interest in consumption, we speculated on the possibility that hand-pounded and machine-hulled rice might differ in other ways, particularly in cultural acceptability. (We also were interested in any contrasts between older traditional varieties and the newer high-yielding cultivars, but there was little information on this topic.) The examination of this point led us to prepare a simple chart (see next page) and to attempt to fill each of the nine cells with letters: U for unhulled, H for hand-pounded, M for machine-hulled, N for none. This effort led us to try to assess whether households were limited by the labor capacity of their members in the amount of pounded rice which they could offer. (We suspected that the poor and localists would pressure the cosmopolitans to serve hand-pounded rice at *slametan*, and that the cosmopolitans would offer machine-hulled rice instead.) We were surprised to find a direct disagreement

	home consumption	*slametan*	sale
poor			
localist			
cosmopolitan			

between the two authors on the hiring of women to pound rice. White states "[a]lthough many households still hand-pound their own rice for their daily needs, hand-pounding for wages ... has completely disappeared" (1976:282), but Stoler notes that "[a]lthough some large landowners still hire client women for daily pounding, this practice has been severely curtailed." (1977:694) We note that consumption preferences might influence production choices, even though we cannot resolve the contradiction between the two, one claiming that a practice is found and the other that it is not. Our interest in consumption leads us to pose some questions with greater emphasis than is the case with a focus on only production and exchange.

3. Changes in labor systems.

Stoler and White note that poor peasants dislike being paid in money to work for other peasants; they prefer to receive a share of the crop. They draw on an analysis of production and exchange to explain this fact: peasants seek higher incomes, and the cash value of rice which workers receive is usually higher than the cash wages (The data on returns to labor suggest that the cash value of lowest *bawon* --of one-twenty-fifth--are lower than certain wages, although the articles do not address this point directly.) Stoler and White claim that peasants reject wage labor as part of their efforts to maintain control of land and labor. We wish to add to these points an additional consideration based on an interest in consumption goods: a wage in rice and a wage in cash are different not only in amount but also in form, and that both are of importance. Peasants may value rice apart from its monetary or nutritional worth. (This practice does not seem to constitute an example of what other economic anthropologists have termed "limited spheres of exchange," because both rice and cash can be exchanged for nearly all sorts of labor).

In some instances, White and Stoler offer what appears to be an adequate account of economic action. To return to the rice harvest, they mention the difficulties of the simultaneous introduction in other villages of the sickle and of male harvesters from outside; in these circumstances, local women no longer work for *bawon*. White mentioned "the great distaste with which the . . . practice is viewed by most villagers" (1976:288). Landowners typically rely on middlemen known as *penebas* (Stoler 1977:691; White 1976:288); local opposition drives them to this measure, which entails some loss in income through payments to the middlemen. White refers to "a recent case of angry harvesters beating up a *penebas*"(1976:288), although he also mentioned that some landowners would use these middlemen only for a year or so and directly hire laborers in later years. It is likely that this "great distaste" reflects a concern over the loss of income in rice from harvest shares. It might go beyond the immediate loss in income, and demonstrate as well the concern for a reordering of social relations in the village as a whole. In any case, the *bawon* do not seem to be regulated exclusively by a desire to maximize income.

In other cases, though, a production and exchange framework is less satisfactory. Stoler notes that some large landowners "either pay farm laborers to prepare their fields, or if they wish to be freed from the burden of farm management, sharecrop out their land in exchange for one-half the crop -- the sharecropper bearing the risk, expense and work of cultivation" (Stoler 1977:681). Her discussion suggests that sharecropping works to the advantage of the landowners. In fact, it seems likely that large landowners would retain a higher proportion of the crop, and hence receive a larger income, if they hired laborers for field preparation, planting and other pre-harvest tasks. Furthermore, the returns for agricultural wage labor are several times greater than for other economic activities carried out by poor peasants, such as some handicrafts and food preparation (Stoler 1977:687). (It is this contrast that is relevant for the poor peasants, rather than the fact that sharecroppers receive more for their work than wage laborers.) It is puzzling why wage labor in rice cultivation is not more prevalent, since it would allow higher incomes for both worker and employer. Following a decision theory framework, Stoler suggests that landowners object to wage labor because it might bring them greater risk (1977:681), although this point is not supported by her qualitative discussion of fluctuations in rice harvests. She also states that poor peasants might find that agricultural wage labor would interfere with the scheduling of other activities (1977:687). This proposition seems unlikely, granted certain quantitative figures. White presents a detailed breakdown of income-generating activities into sixteen categories of work, and shows the number of hours worked per year by males and females of different age categories (285); he also indicates some differences between busy and slack agricultural seasons. It appears that poorer peasants, even in the busy months, allocate a considerable amount of time to activities whose returns are lower than his category of "wage labour (agricultural)" (285). (It is difficult to address these questions [of choice of activity and of form of remuneration] directly on the basis of the figures in the two articles, since White's category includes cash payments, shares in kind, and unpaid labor-exchange.) Our social economy of consumption view would read into Stoler's mention of "the burden of farm management" the opposition by some peasants to working in village fields

11

for cash, rather than for rice. The "burden" seems cultural and social, rather than logistical.

4. Other points.

We note a number of other differences between the consumptionist and non-consumptionist views. For example, Stoler and White portray the poor as being driven towards some level of biological subsistence. They work long days for low returns in order to assure that their needs are met. We do wonder, though, about cigarettes and betel--goods which contribute neither to biological nutrition nor to culturally-defined social reproduction in the way that weddings and *slametan* do. It seems likely that the use of these items is sufficiently structured that one cannot explain their consumption as the outcome of a physiological addiction. These goods may well play an important role in the etiquette of daily life. They might be a fixed need, in the sense that any particular individual could anticipate the quantities of each which he would have to provide to others, though it is more probable that the demand for them is flexible. To understand them, we would need to know more about the social connotations of their use, and about the social consequences of their unavailability.[2]

Our account might differ from Stoler and White on several other points as well, but these remain somewhat speculative in the absence of specific information. We can imagine empirical differences between these accounts. Shifts in the price of rice, for instance, might affect the *bawon* which wealthy landowners offer. A production and exchange view such as Stoler and White would imply that a rise in price would lead them to cut the shares, since the increasing value of their marketable surplus would give them another advantage over the poor, and would tempt them to acquire new goods. A social economy of consumption perspective might expect that localist landowners might increase *bawon*, since they would have relatively fixed needs for purchased goods, and might return some of the increased cash value of the harvest to poorer peasants in their efforts to strengthen their local social ties. (They might also choose to make this return through increased *slametan* sponsorship.)

We also are interested in the expenditures on education, since they have complex consequences. In part, they allow children to earn higher incomes later in life, so that they might represent investments of cash (for school fees, books, etc.) and of foregone children's income. They might also increase the possibility of migration to urban areas or other islands. This straightforward view of human capital formation may not be adequate, however. Hirschman (1982) distinguishes between preferences and metapreferences; the latter are patterns of evaluation of large categories of goods, and overall attitudes towards goods. Schooling may influence both of these. The patterning of expenditures by land ownership and by orientation (localist or cosmopolitan) might offer further understanding into the linkages between consumption and production. In any case, more information about the schools would be necessary for an analysis of the patterns of expenditures on education.

The differences which consumption can make

The social economy of consumption view differs from the approach of Stoler and White in several ways: in its elevating consumption to the same level as production and exchange, in its presentation of consumption as social, and in its view of consumption as an arena for debates over different ideological constructions of social and economic relations.

There are both weak and strong claims for the significance of this expansion. The weak claims make an appeal to the importance for social scientists of understanding the subjective meanings of human action; the analysis which includes consumption is better because it is richer and fuller, in that it provides a more detailed examination of the motivation of individuals. The strong claims make an appeal to the importance for social scientists of demonstrating systematic patterning of human behavior. We have deliberately chosen a relatively limited term, rather than more restrictive language about prediction or causation. The analysis which includes consumption is better because it is different and more accurate.

The weak claims, important in their own right, seem easy to support. A focus on consumption offers a broader view of the contestations between richer and poorer peasants. The issues include fundamental questions of the valuation of orientations towards the village and towards wider society, and thus go beyond efforts to increase income and to ensure access to land and employment opportunities. The more localist landowners--the ones who have not purchased rice hullers--wear simple traditional dress not only because their incomes from rice sale are lower, but also, we strongly suspect, because they use cloth to make ideological statements and to affirm certain social ties. They commit themselves to maintaining certain exchanges with kin and other villagers, and they may also be offering a statement on the relative valuation of Javanese and Chinese ethnic identities.

The strong claims may also be supported, although the evidence is not as clear. We could make a few minor points (the larger landowners who retain older patterns of both consumption and production may continue these practices, rather than shifting as Stoler and White imply that they will; the expenditures for stimulants seem to challenge White's discussion of "needs" [White 1976:280]). The best case, though, rests on the opposition in Kali Loro to agricultural labor paid in cash, rather than in rice, strong enough to lead poor peasants to seek other forms of work with lower returns; this point violates White's suggestion that "households would whenever possible choose the available combination of activities with the highest total returns to labour" (1976:280). In our view, the peasants are concerned, not only with the amount, but also with the form of the returns.

This point leads us to note certain difficulties in distinguishing between strong and weak claims. For instance, one could claim that the value of rice as a consumption good is not just its worth in monetary or nutritional terms, and that this importance is not surprising, granted its centrality to local production, the long history of its cultivation in the area, its presence in most meals, and the ritual elaboration of its production (Stoler 1977:683). This claim could be seen as weak, in that it provides fuller understandings of such features of daily life as the smooth working of *bawon* exchange relations. It could be seen as strong, in that it accounts for choices of work which are irrational in monetary terms.

This point also leads us to a second issue, of whether our claims are really based on consumption at all. We will offer a short treatment of this complex question. Although our alternative reading of Kali Loro was based on the notion of consumption, it could equally well have begun with the idea of interest. We would have noted that the actions of peasants were not solely guided by their individual and class interests as these are defined by labor processes; instead, they sought to shape and control social relations and the evaluation of social relations as well. The notion of ideology also might have provided a point of departure. The source of conflict in Kali Loro can be located in disagreements over the proper conduct of villagers to one another and to the outside world. In either case we might have drawn on some different examples, but we would have relied heavily on some of the same ones, such as the opposition to wage labor and the use of new goods. (These themes of ideology and interest occupy a large role in Stoler's recent historical and ethnographic research about Javanese plantation workers in Sumatra [1985].) Even if the differences between cosmopolitans and localists were phrased in terms of interest or ideology, the discussion would still have returned to consumption. It does not seem to be a unique accident of the case of Kali Loro that consumption holds such ideological importance. This significance stems from its links both to the material world of production and exchange and to the cultural realm of valuation. Consumption is a uniquely situated arena for debate over relations among peasants. After all, *bawon* allocation occurs only twice a year, during harvest periods, but the sounds of radios and motorcycles are a more continuous presence in the village.

Where To Think About Consumption: Its Location In Economics (conceptual bundle 1, in which we argue that the first fundamental characteristic of the social economy of consumption is its anti-reductionism)

The extended example of Kali Loro may help elucidate the nature of consumption as an object of study and its location within economies. The word "consumption" seems to have three closely related definitions. As noted by economists of a variety of orientations, consumption is the final phase of the cycle of economic activity which begins with production and moves through exchange, or, in a related version, through distribution and exchange. It is the last stage of both the social relations which are involved with objects, and of the objects themselves. (We acknowledge the production, exchange and consumption of

14

services as well, but we talk here more about goods.) A second definition focuses on types of activities in which individuals engage, rather than on cycles of activity linked to particular goods. It notes that consumption is a type of thing that people do, along with production, exchange and non-economic activity, and that consumption involves using things up rather than making them or transferring them. Finally, these cycles and types of economic activities can be linked into systems of economic and social relations. One can speak of a system of consumption, much as one can speak of systems of production or of exchange. The case of Kali Loro demonstrates that these definitions are easy to apply in some circumstances--motorcycles are produced in factories, exchanged for money in stores and markets, and consumed as they are driven. One can also point to examples which do not fall clearly either inside or outside the category of consumption; is the difference between payment in cash and payment in rice an example of consumption or of exchange? This difficulty in establishing boundaries, however, is not unique to consumption; for example, one could conceptualize sharecropping as relations of production or as exchange of labor for goods. These problematic instances seem less common than the simple ones, though, and it is unlikely that our overall view of consumption would change greatly as principles of definition shifted from broad to narrow. (For a justification of this blithely casual attitude towards definition as the root of meaning, please note Hacking [1983], especially Chapter 6, "Reference.")

Our claims to the significance of consumption are anti-reductionist. When we say that other authors have tended to give priority to production and exchange, and that we wish to give greater weight to consumption, we mean several things, since the different sorts of priority derive from the different definitions of consumption. Following the first definition of consumption given above, production has a temporal priority over exchange and consumption, as exchange does over consumption. Since it occurs last, it is shaped by earlier phases but does not shape them. Following the second definition of consumption, production and exchange activities are more important because they may be presumed to be more social and more salient than consumption activities. The economic lives of individuals are shaped by relations in the workplace and in the marketplace; consumption fits into spare time. Finally, some authors argue in terms of a causal priority when they categorize economic systems according to criteria of production or of exchange. To take only one example of many, some Marxists include in the notion of mode of production the idea that forces and relations of production determine other aspects of the economy at one moment in time and through history. Rather than becoming embroiled in disputes over the nature of causation in the universe or in society, we will pass on to a more general notion of priority, analytical priority: the general idea that knowing about systems of production and exchange is sufficient for understanding the structure and dynamic of economic systems as wholes, and the specific idea that knowing about production and exchange tells us virtually everything about consumption, but that knowing about consumption tells us virtually nothing about production and exchange. One might expect, for instance, that status goods would occupy an important role in consumption in economies which might be characterized by production (e.g., feudal mode of production) or by exchange (e.g., systems of redistribution). In such views, the three definitions of consumption tend to merge, and there is some intuitive appeal to this deprioritizing of consumption. The production and exchange of rice occupy a great deal of time and concern in Kali Loro; the eating of rice could seem less important. The wearing of a garment seems much more straightforward than the numerous steps carried out by farmer, weaver and tailor in producing it and the social ties of sale, barter or gift exchange. Nonetheless, as we have seen, this downgrading of consumption offers a less detailed and less accurate view.

We are not proposing to grant consumption priority over production and exchange. In the first definition, the temporal sequence of phases does not seem to offer obvious reasons for elevating one phase over another. In the second and third, we prefer to view as wholes the economic activities of individuals and economic systems, and to grant consumption importance within these wholes. (We shy away from talking about "equal" importance, for several reasons. Importance does not seem measurable as a continuous or discontinuous quantity. Even to speak of greater or lesser importance would require the notion of well-structured systems of explanation, whether deductive systems of more general laws and more specific hypotheses, or causal systems of antecedents and results.)

Several important advances in economic anthropology have consisted of simple schemes of classification. The analysis of systems of production has been advanced by debates over the nature of modes of production and over the categorization of subsistence types within cultural ecology. In a similar fashion, Polanyi's classification (1957) of reciprocity, redistribution and market exchange carried forward the examination of systems of exchange, as did Sahlins' categorization (1974) of positive, balanced and negative reciprocity. Despite the continued significance of these examples, we do not propose a similar classification of systems of consumption, not from an obtuse inability to invent such schemes, but from a basic difference in our definition of our task. We seek to end the relative neglect of consumption, not by erecting it as a distinct and exclusive object of study, but rather by demonstrating its importance and autonomy within economic activities and systems. Despite this claim, though, efforts to establish a typology of societies by their patterns of consumption. Weber (1987) offers a simple tripartite division into "societies of simple reproduction", "Asiatic and feudal societies", and "societies of accumulation", quite similar to the production-centered categories erected by Wolf (1982). Goody also engages in systematic comparison of systems of consumption. He carries forward his contrast (Goody 1976) between marriage patterns and kinship systems of Eurasian societies (with high population densities and plow agriculture) and African societies (with low population densities and hoe agriculture). In *Cooking, cuisine and class* (1982), he examines the consequences of these economic and social patterns for diet. He pays particular attention to the ways in which differences in control over labor and political centralization influence feasting in both regions and the restriction of an *haute cuisine* to Eurasia. Other chapters in the book offer different sorts of contrasts:

16

an examination of two Ghanaian societies (one a traditional state and the other uncentralized, in pre-colonial, colonial and independence periods), a number of local food systems before and after their contact with "industrial" and "world" food systems.

How To Think About Consumption: The Social Economy Perspective (conceptual bundle 2, in which we argue that the second fundamental characteristic of the social economy of consumption is its insistence on the social character of consumption)

The claims of the social economy perspective are simple; they consist of the notions, shared by virtually all economic anthropologists and in fact by virtually all social scientists, that economic action must be understood as social action and that economic systems are related to social systems. In our efforts to prepare an overview of the study of consumption, we kept talking about a number of themes: how consumption was often public in nature, how goods could be used not only to reflect but also to influence social relations, how a system of categories of goods could be linked to a system of social classification. These themes did not offer much promise of serving as the broad assumptions which we sought. We kept waiting to arrive at something that would feel like a theory in economic anthropology: a small number of interrelated general statements that would contrast sharply with another such theory or theories. It took us a while to arrive at the idea that the principles which the social economy perspective used were the assumptions which competing approaches within economic anthropology all shared.

Frustrated in our efforts at theorizing, we turned to a simpler and more familiar task, the literature review. We noted that economics and psychology provided an "individual economy of consumption" which examined rationality, decision-making, cognition and constrained choice. Some individuals interested in meaning and symbolism, such as Mary Douglas, use an approach which we term the "cultural economy of consumption"; they argue for a congruence among systems of classification of goods, of consumption occasions and of social relations. Marxists in a number of social sciences offered a "political economy of consumption", in which consumption patterns reflected class systems or overall modes of production. We then realized that these three approaches correspond fairly closely to the three dominant schools in economic anthropology. One of us has termed these decision theory (which "examine[s] the way in which cultural, social and material contexts influence the choice by individuals among behavioral alternatives"), culturalism (which examines the "correspondences between economic and social systems of particular societies") and neo-Marxism (Orlove 1986); Geertz (1984) calls them neoclassical, cultural and neomarxist approaches.

Despite the tensions among these schools, they share certain assumptions, which may be broadly divided into individual and aggregate levels. (If their basic conceptualizations of economic action and systems differed more sharply, they

17

would not be able to debate so readily.) At the individual level, they assume that economic action is at least partially social action; individuals are involved in face-to-face relations which influence, and are influenced by, their ties in activities of production, exchange and consumption. Decision theorists include a social dimension in their study of individuals and the choices which they make. However great an emphasis which culturalists and neo-Marxists may place on aggregate systems, they retain some notion of individuals as actors; the most extreme views within structural Marxism, such as the idea of individuals as bearers of structures, are quite atypical. At the aggregate level, they see that economic systems are also social systems in the sense of forming institutions and sets of categories. Few economic anthropologists, including decision theorists, would view a market economy as wholly impersonal, for instance.

These notions of social economy may seem obvious and trivial. One could hardly proclaim as a new approach a social economy of production or a social economy of exchange, since the debates have implicitly taken such approaches for granted. It does strike us, though, as worthwhile to propose the study on social economy of consumption. Much of the previous work has neglected this social dimension. As we discuss in the next section, the examination within economics of preferences tends to treat consumers as isolated individuals, even though it would be hard to deny the social nature of relations of production and exchange. Some culturalist discussion presents consumption categories as fixed and automatic, even though it would allow a wider range of action in production and exchange activities. In a similar vein, some neo-Marxist writers proclaim a capitalist logic of consumption which is simpler, more rigid and less mediated by social relations than the corresponding logics of production and exchange. In other words, the social dimension of consumption has often been lost. This social dimension is the second fundamental characteristic of the social economy of consumption perspective, along with the anti-reductionism discussed in the previous section. In the next section, we will trace this social dimension of consumption through several fields. Before we move to that section, we will present the social economy of consumption with regard to several types of goods. This discussion illustrates our understanding of consumption as social through an examination of different instances.

We begin by proposing to examine food, clothing and shelter as distinct categories. Each of them make fairly well-bounded categories of goods; there are few problematic cases of inclusion and exclusion. Certain differences emerge in the patterns of utilization of these goods, understandable in simple material and psychological terms. (Our appeal to psychology stems from the fact that all three types of goods are linked to the human body and to sensation in some immediate way.) The relations of these goods to different fields of inquiry and the possible methodologies for studying them influence the nature of the discussion of these goods.

Food is fairly well-bounded as the sphere of all things that go into the mouth and are swallowed; medicines, some of which are taken orally, are a related sphere. It is clear to all people, anthropologists and non-anthropologists alike, that food is a basic need. It is easier to relate specific diets to nutritional status and to health than it is to link the amount or quality of housing or clothing to well-being. Unlike housing or clothing, food is limited in the physical quantities which can be consumed by an individual, though not in the economic expenditures. Food comes closer to being entirely consumed than other goods. The consumption events in the case of food are distinct: meals are frequent, relatively short, and entail face-to-face relations. (To state the obvious, there are simple universals of food consumption events, in that all cultures have some degree of patterning of ingredients into a cuisine and of eating into a meal structure.) The features give to food and to meals a cultural and political importance which has been recognized, particularly in the case of ceremonial feasting, for a long time (Robertson Smith 1889). And food seems to have a psychological importance in many settings. Appadurai (1981b) points out the mnemonic quality of food. As Rozin (1987) notes, humans, like many other animals, have an apparently innate concern over objects that are placed in the mouth. This link to well-being, this universality and this psychological importance may each in part account for the importance of academic debates over food. One can take as an example the exchange between Marvin Harris (1979) and Marshall Sahlins (1979) in the *New York Review of Books* over Aztec cannibalism. It is difficult to imagine an anthropological debate over housing or clothing drawing an audience as broad or as impassioned. This link may also influence political debates about food, as shown by grain riots in many parts of the world (Thompson 1971, Tilly 1971, Arnold 1979, Wong 1982, Rogers 1987).

Housing is also a relatively well-defined sphere. Housing has a solid presence in several ways. In comparison to a plate of food or to a garment, a house is large and permanent. Because of this size and duration, work parties for construction often involve more people than agriculture or cloth production, even though more time is spent each year in most populations in making food and clothing than in building. As a consequence of these qualities, houses are easily observable, apart from the people who use them. Their enduring nature also renders them accessible to archeologists and to historians. This solidity makes it easy to think of a house as an entity; it may therefore be associated with other entities. There is more of a tendency to think of houses as associated with social groups, rather than food and clothing, which because of their more intimate links with the human body are associated with specific social categories. The permanent nature of housing does serve to mark off broad status groups or classes, as many authors have noted. The early classic work on slave society in Brazil, *The Mansion and the Shanties* (Freyre 1936), is one example.

Bourdieu's discussion of houses among the Kabyle in northern Algeria raises several general points. He demonstrates a high degree of coherence in the symbolic significance of housing, particularly in the spatial and temporal location of persons, objects and activities. Although such a view could be taken as a standard structuralist analysis, resembling Levi-Strauss' accounts of Australian

19

kinship or Amazonian myths, Bourdieu's perspective is somewhat different. He suggests that the repetitive nature of human activity within houses enriches the symbolic significance of the use of space within houses. Houses do not merely exist as metaphors; they provide metaphors which can be used to many ends, with varying degress of consciousness (cf. de Certeau 1984). An individual would be likely to repeat or to imitate a particularly apt location for an object or an activity; this sequence generates what he calls the "surplus of consistency" in the meaning of space and housing (Bourdieu 1979:143). The large literature on houses as texts and as metaphors (e.g., Appadurai 1986:759) reflects both this usage of houses by the people who inhabit them and the permanence of houses for the people who study them. (This region of the world also provides an important example of the difficulty of completely separating one type of good from another, as Hattox (1985) documents in *Coffee and Coffeehouses: The Origins of a Social Beverage in the Medieval Near East* .)

The existence of the profession of architecture also affects the discussion of housing. The conventional representations such as floor plans and architectural renderings facilitate the comparison of housing in different settings (Hillier and Hanson 1984). Partially as a result, a portion of the literature on housing contrasts vernacular architecture with conventional Western architecture. It discusses the use of local materials, the means for mitigating uncomfortable aspects of local climate, and the facilitation of local patterns of movement and interaction. It is perhaps in housing that folk wisdom can most convincingly be demonstrated to reside. In the minds of many, it is the igloo that most clearly demonstrates the aptness of the Eskimo response to the exigencies of their setting, rather than the consumption of the contents of caribou stomachs or the use of animal skins in making boots.

Clothing is also a fairly well-defined sphere, although there are other forms of adornment (hats, watches, umbrellas, jewelry, tattoos, hair styles) and other uses of cloth (rugs, sacks). The nature of clothing as visible to all marks off both individuals and social settings. The temporal quality of clothing is also important; particular garments may last for a long time, but individuals usually wear them for short periods before changing them. The salience of cloth in prestations also comes from the role of the weaver, who shapes a product more permanently than a cook and more individually than a builder. The relative permanence of cloth, the public nature of its display, and its amenability to long-distance trade create another aspect of clothing, what Schneider (1988) terms "esthetic dialogues" between types of cloth, between cloth and other objects, in which the subtle patternings of the use of cloth indicate relations between different systems of social classification. Turner's (1980) discussion of clothing as a "social skin" argues for its close association with the person of an individual, and hence its appropriateness for classificiation along broad dimensions: age, gender, sanctity. This kind of association with the person leads cloth to have many uses that are distinct from those of food and housing: mourning, transvestism. This power of marking categories leads to several directly political aspects of clothing. As Schneider (1978) has pointed out, prestations of cloth can constitute a link to authority that is both personal and relatively enduring. For this reason, cloth can become an important arena of political contestation. One example comes from efforts by elites to maintain control; sumptuary laws often focus on dress rather than on diet, housing or other aspects of consumption, for instance. Other examples come from the resistance to control. Clothing and nationalism are linked in a wide range of societies. Anti-colonial struggles in Peru (Rowe 1955), India (Bayley 1986) and Swaziland (Kuper 1973) involved conscious use of dress, even though the weaving traditions in all three areas were quite distinct.

Who Thinks About Consumption

The literature on consumption contains a diverse range of topics and perspectives. Questions of space restrict our examination of this literature to a brief overview. We have organized our review on the overlapping criteria of discipline and approach. We begin with the social economy perspective from anthropology, sociology and history, move first to cultural economy within anthropology and then to individual economy in economics and psychology, and close with the political economy view from several fields. We acknowledge the somewhat arbitrary nature of our division of the previous work as a whole into a small number of categories and of our assignment of specific works into particular categories. To an extent that varies with each article and book, we are imposing the notion of "literature on consumption" onto pieces of work that have been written for different audiences and that therefore do not constitute a field with a well-defined set of issues and of position on these issues.

The social economy of consumption

Eric Wolf offers some useful hints in the analysis of these issues of consumption in his short book *Peasants* (1969). He begins his general discussion of peasant economies with an analysis, not of production, but of consumption: peasant households allocate their income to expenditures in four conceptually distinct "funds." The first one, the caloric minima, meets needs of biological survival. The second, the "replacement fund" consists of "[t]he amount necessary to replace...minimum equipment for both production and consumption"; it includes not only saving seed for planting and repairing tools, but also "cultural necessities" of clothing, housing, eating utensils, and the like. The "ceremonial fund," for events such as weddings, stems from the fact that "[e]ven where men are largely self-sufficient in food and goods, they must entertain social relations with their fellows, ... [since] social relations of any kind are never completely utilitarian and instrumental [but are] surrounded with symbolic constructions which serve to explain, to justify and to regulate [them]." (1969: 7) These three funds exist in all societies; what distinguishes peasants from "the primitive cultivator" is the "fund of rent," the outcome of "a social order in which some men can through power demand payments from others, resulting in the transfer of wealth from one section of the population to another." (1969: 10) These

21

transfers, whether paid for rental, taxation, or unequal market exchange, are also a portion of the peasant budget.

Wolf presents these funds as having fixed boundaries but flexible volumes. Peasants may respond to new economic and social conditions by increasing or decreasing levels of production and consumption. These changes entail shifts in the size of some or all of these four funds. He discusses cases in which some peasants are willing to risk social sanctions that follow reductions in ceremonial expenditures or rent payments; others cut back on the culturally-defined subsistence standards in the replacement fund. Nonetheless, each fund is well-defined; his discussion seems to presume that any two observers would agree into which fund any specific expenditure would be allocated. These assumptions have been challenged by the anthropological and historical research of the decades which followed the publication of *Peasants*. It would be more difficult now to claim that one can readily distinguish between the ceremonial fund and the fund of rent, the former resting on consensus among "fellows" and the latter imposed by the greater power of another social "section." To take only one of many possible examples, recent research in highland Latin America (Rasnake 1986, Wasserstrom and Rus 1980) shows that village *fiestas* allow peasants to make claims on elites as well as to accede to their demands, and that *fiestas* address complex and conflicting issues of hierarchy and egalitarianism in relations of peasants to one another as well as to outsiders. Similarly, it is harder to draw a line between the replacement fund (of expenditures on tools and on goods used to maintain a material standard of living within the household) and the ceremonial fund (of expenditures on goods used to maintain social relations outside the household). One can see both a more material side of the ceremonial fund--a household might lose access to irrigation water if it did not participate in certain festivities, for instance -- and a more ideological side to the replacement fund--social ties require symbolic representation within households as well as between them. Even the notion of caloric minima can be challenged. It is difficult in practice to establish criteria which clearly distinguish undernourished individuals from those with adequate nutrition, and minimum requirements refer to a range, rather than a precise level, of dietary intake. One cannot claim that diets are entirely shaped by biological constraints, and that the realm of society and culture begins with the replacement fund. (Wolf might well acknowledge these points today, as shown by his recent comments [1986] on his earlier treatment of the concept of closed corporate peasant communities.)

For some readers of Wolf, these difficulties of putting into practice his scheme of four funds are minor; they stem from the preliminary nature of his initial statement of his framework. For others, these difficulties are major. They are a result of an excessively ecological and economistic view of society. The ordering of the four funds, it could be argued, is not casual or accidental, but reflects a sequencing of views of peasants, first as biological organisms, and then as members of three types of social groups, which, in order of priority, are household, village and class. This listing implies a layering of society--quite like Julian Steward's notion of the level of socio-cultural integration--which deemphasizes the complex historical links among these different types of social groups.

In any case, these difficulties in implementing Wolf's proposed scheme of the four funds do not reduce the value of the basic principles which underlie them. He directs us to examine simultaneously production and consumption--income and expenditure, in more narrowly economic terms. This examination links economic and social relations, and presents both as having practical and ideological content. Furthermore, Wolf insists on working simultaneously at several different scales: seeing households and villages as social systems and as parts of wider social systems, viewing these systems in one point in time and in the unfolding of history.

Schneider (1978) and Mintz (1985) also adopt the social economy perspective. The cases which they examine, the importance of European cloth and Caribbean sugar respectively, are well-known in economic history. It might be assumed that an examination of the forces and relations of production and the development of commercial systems could account both for the rise of the textile mill and the slave plantation, and for the existence of a broad market for cloth and cheap food. Schneider and Mintz grant consumption greater importance in two ways: they see it as having a certain degree of autonomy from production and exchange, and they view it as an active force in history.

Schneider traces the development of black cloth in Europe through the sixteenth century as part of the economic, political and religious resistance to Byzantium and other Eastern Mediterranean centers, where luxury polychrome fabrics were produced. She examines the production and distribution of cloth, and distinctive uses of black cloth first in monastic and courtly settings and later more widely. She concludes that:

> black dress was a 'key symbol' around which Europeans rallied at various points in their history, as they warded off, defended against, and ultimately reversed the hegemony of manufacturing centers, more developed than their own, that exported an array of brightly colored cloth . . . the use of black dress was an integral part of the evolution of a European civilization, separate from and independent of the great Mediterranean and Oriental civilizations to which it was heir. Not just a distinctive symbol, black also contributed in a substantive way to a reordering of trade relations, so that Europe could import primary products and export finished goods (ibid., 414).

In other words, the origins of industrial capitalism lie in the social bases of demand as well as in production and exchange.

Mintz examines another shift in European consumption patterns, the widespread use of sugar. He devotes particular attention to the English working class, the first major market for sugar. In addition to its value in terms of money and calories, sugar had significance linked to its previous history as a medicine and as an elite luxury good. All these aspects were treated extensively in debates over tariff policies for sugar. Mintz sees it as "closely connected to England's fundamental tranformation from a hierarchical, status-based, medieval society to a social-democratic, capitalist, and industrial society" (1985:185). As sugar diffused down from one class to another, its uses and meanings changed. The new patterns of daily activity which the Industrial Revolution brought to the working class included not only factory labor but meals in which sugar played a key role, both materially and symbolically, "to validate social events" (ibid., 153). Sugar both literally and figuratively sweetened the lives of working class families, helping make them able to work and to accept an exploitative social order. Like the acceptance of black cloth, the increase in sugar consumption does not signal the unambiguous triumphs of capitalism but rather indicates the complex economic, political and cultural interaction of European capitalism with non-capitalist systems in Europe and outside.

Another line of anthropological thought which has influenced our thinking about consumption stems from several early case studies in Africa and Oceania on what were formerly termed "tribal economies". Firth, in an early essay entitled "Economic Psychology of the Maori" (192*), argued that in order to understand the "industry" of the Maori it was necessary first to understand their motives. (340) To make his point, he analyzed in detail the relationship between bird-snaring and the satisfaction derived both from the labor process and the product. The reader gets a sense of the influence both of Malinowski (the paper was written for Malinowski's seminar on the psychology of primitive peoples) and of Veblen (see below) on Firth's thinking when he parses out satisfactions derived from bird-snaring: ". . . the provision of food . . . the joy of craftsmanship . . . the emulative impulse . . . the wish to contribute to community welfare." (361) Presumably, demand for birds is fuelled by desire, wants are generated by society as much as by individual tastes, and labor is guided less by efficiency in production than by socially necessary consumption. Firth makes three general points that reinforce a social economy of consumption perspective: 1) the non-reductionism of economic behavior ("But some economists, sticklers for the traditions of the classical school, may yet argue: notwithstanding all this analysis of motives, we are still left with the one fact, that the Maori . . . desire only to obtain the greatest quantity of birds with the least effort and sacrifice . . . all that is necessary for the economist to ascertain prior to his investigations is not why he desires them, but simply that he does desire them. But this attempted reduction of the motives for economic action to a minimum is quite inadequate, and definitely misleading." (359); 2) the social and institutional embeddedness of economic activity ("Sometimes these traditional forces are anti-utilitarian (358) . . . To obtain any clear perspective of primitive economy, any true conception of its nature, it must not be wrenched form its social setting." (361); 3) the non-privileging of production over consumption, efficiency of labor over aesthetic and other criteria such as the "joy of craftsmanship". In his classic study of *The Primitive Economics of the New Zealand Maori* (1929), Firth pays a great deal of attention to consumption through an ethnographic description of particular goods and their uses in social and cultural settings.

Mauss's classic exploration of the principle underlying "the gift" is important to a social economy of consumption perspective for several reasons. In addition to its path-breaking significance for the study of spheres of exchange in non-market societies, and its insistence that society be the intellectual point of departure for examining the motives of individual economic action,*The Gift* (1967) can be seen as an attempt by Mauss to contextualize the exchange of goods in meaningful acts of consumption. The principle of reciprocity in exchange is a conventional attribute of the good itself, a partial determination of its value in use and the satisfaction derived therefrom. Several case studies of tribal exchange systems and their transformation under conditions of an encroaching Western market economy have drawn on the insights of Mauss and Firth to provide us with further insight into the connections between exchange and consumption. In one of these case studies, Bohannon (1955) conceptualizes spheres of exchange among the Tiv of Nigeria as "based on a ranked hierarchy . . . of categories . . . of commodities." (60) Tiv make a distinction between "gifts" and "market" exchanges in their categorization and evalutation of goods. (cf. Gregory 1982) Tiv have several words for "gift" and "market" respectively, each of which contextualizes a finite number of goods with variable value. No goods classified as gifts, however, have exchange value. Bohannon discusses only those goods that enter into market valuations. The classification of these goods raises non-obvious questions and suggests cultural puzzles about how Tiv organize their socially necessary consumption. For example, goods such as yams, pepper, locust-bean sauce, chickens, and goats are assigned to the same category of social use; values in exchange therefore follow from the way in which Tiv conceive of their consumption. Another category of goods consists of slaves, cattle, cloth and metal bars. To a third category is assigned women and children (but not slaves). Bohannon lacks data on demand for various goods, how demand changes over time, what the actual uses of the various goods are, and how all of this relates to exchange value. His attention, rather, is on principles of exchange and investment. A consumption perspective would have led him to examine a much wider range of goods (he explicitly states that many goods have been omitted from his classification, e.g., weapons, special tools, certain services (63), because these did not fit his analysis.

Nevertheless, Bohannon does address several important issues pertaining to consumption. First, he asserts that Tiv ideas about the grouping of goods persist despite apparent radical changes in practice. This is a case in which the culture of consumption remains stable and provides a basis for exchange behavior in the face of new goods that have entered Tiv life. Bohannon suggests that an explanation for the survivial of the classification is that its basis is highly shared moral principles to which Tiv continue to adhere. Tiv organize demand hierarchically by assigning moral value to different categories of goods: subsistence goods are subordinated to prestige goods, and both are subordinated to dependent persons (excluding slaves). (64) It is "good" (and possible) to convert up the scale and "bad" to convert down. Consumption categories thus organize priorities in exchange and production. Furthermore, Bohannon discusses briefly how goods are "removed", i.e. consumed. Goods in the first category all share the characteristic that they are removed by being "used up". Goods in the second category are removed as expenditures (e.g., on cloth), by death (e.g., slaves), or through conversion (e.g., brass rods to jewelry to prestige). In other words, there is a diminution of the utility of the objects and a concomitant conversion in their value. The value of each, however, retains its own qualitative form. Goods in the third category are removed by death alone.

A final question that Bohannon addresses is that of new goods and the problem of revaluation and its role in social transformation. He mentions many new goods that have entered Tiv social life and several old goods (e.g., brass rods) that have all but passed from the scene. Apparently, Tiv have continued to hold onto their classification of traditional goods and their evaluation of goods in terms of a moral hierarchy. Perhaps this assertion is the most striking conclusion of his study because it implies a stability to culture in the face of a colonial history that destroyed much of the functional value of Tiv social consumption (62). Slavery was abolished by the colonial power in 1910. Brass rods were extremely rare by the time Bohannon did his field work. Even more significant was the abolition of exchange marriage in 1927. Nevertheless, Bohannon maintains that "even 25 years after official abolition of exchange marriage, it is this category of exchange in which Tiv are emotionally most entangled." (62) The category of subsistence goods was the only one intact in the 1950s when the Bohannons did their field work; (however, Bohannon does not address the impact of new goods on this category.) As for the question of how Tiv have categorized the new goods that have come through the encroaching market economy, Bohannon states that many Western goods have not been incorporated into the persisting consumption categories. And money has become a common standard for all goods. (Tiv elders tried, without success, to retain the existing classification and add to it a fourth and low ranking category of money and Western goods [68]. It would appear that Tiv view consumption as an arena for the exercise of power and the expression of ideology.)

In another case study of spheres of exchange, Salisbury (1962) explicitly viewed the social organization of consumption and cultural classification of goods as the driving force behind an autonomous pattern of transformation among the Siane of New Guinea: "The determining factors affecting what changes [as a result of technological change in the form of steel for stone axes] actually took place were those concerned with the nature of demand for products and services". (162) Salisbury, who was the first European to live among the Siane, and who held a virtual monopoly over the supply of Western trade goods during his stay, recorded Siane demand for various goods and changing demand over the period of his field work as the basis for establishing categories of consumption and Siane principles of evaluation. Unlike Bohannon, Salisbury had a controlled method for answering questions about the stability of the Siane cultural classificiation and their reaction to new goods over time. Salisbury pays a great deal of attention to the specific goods in demand by Siane, which ones were "acceptable" as substitutes, and at what exchange rates over time--for example, bangles, etc. for beads; newspapers, etc. for salt; matches, etc. for razor blades, cash only for soap; cash only (Siane would take cash in exchange for goods but not goods in exchange for cash). (171) By actually observing demand behavior, he was able to establish a Siane classification of consumption based on five categories of non-substitutable goods of incommensurate value. As in the case of the Tiv, Siane categories were highly shared and appeared to be stable over time, with variable exchange rates depending upon particular persons or groups.

Salisbury not only linked cultural classification of goods to aggregate demand behavior based on exchange rates, but he also addressed the question of standards of evaluation that seemed to underlie the classification. Siane economy is non-monetary and there "is not even an implicit unitary standard" (186) that can form a single system for evaluation of all the various goods in demand. He solves the question of utility, satisfaction, or wants in Siane society by exploring the social uses of goods related to various nexuses of Siane economic activity. By examining the ends of activity in which goods in various categories are used up, he employs a method that in economics has come to be known as "revealed preferences" as a behavioral basis for assesssing notions of utility. Salisbury, however, assumes that preferences are attributes of Siane social organization, not of individuals. He isolates three standards of evaluation used by individuals and groups: subsistence goods that maintain social status; valuables that enable individuals to seek "free-floating" power; luxury goods that enable individuals to circumvent social dictates. (194) Consumption in Siane is for social status, power, and insurance against excessive social rigidity. Exchange and production are organized toward these ends, which provide the system rationality for the way in which Siane culturally classify their traditional goods.

What happens to this system rationality when it is broached by new goods? Is there a revaluation of standards and a transformation of the classification itself? Salisbury employs the concept of elasticities of demand in response to supply of new goods to answer these questions. He observed the process at two levels. Initially, the Siane fit European goods into the category of luxury goods. But over time (the period of his field work) they shifted some goods into one of the other categories, revaluing them through exchange rates in the process. To understand these patterns, Salisbury asks whether there are qualities attached to goods that render them appropriate for assignment to one or another category: "Evaluation [of a good] in terms of one standard is merely a matter of culturally determined classification .. . In fact there are regularities relating the intrinsic nature of goods with the standards by which Siane evlaute them". (196) For example, subsistence goods comprise food, clothing, shelter, and tools--all goods the consumption of which results in the physical survival of the Siane population. Goods classed as power tokens imply the owner's ability to destroy utility or productivity. He concludes that the different classes of goods vary in their qualities of storability, portability, durability, etc. European goods find assignment in the Siane cultural classification according to their intrinsic qualities.

Thus, we see that we remain eternally indebted to anthropological traditions which, although their practitioners' attention was turned primarily to problems of production and exchange, nevertheless had the sensitivity and perspicacity to realize, however intuitively or implicitly, that a partial solution to their problems lay in an exploration of issues we have addressed explicitly as a social economy of consumption.

Sociologists and historians have also contributed to the social economy of consumption. Some writings in each of these fields study the topic, and tend to emphasize social processes rather than individual behavior. Within sociology, Weber (1922) addressed the topic of consumption in his treatment of class, party and status group. The members of a status group share a specific and social esteem, honor or prestige. They may often have a monopoly on the ownership and consumption of specific goods, and may be more loosely associated with a wider set of goods. Weber notes that specific status groups are associated with particular life-styles (this term may be included, along with charisma, in the list of concepts which Weber used with great effectiveness but have since become sadly debased). Veblen's work is well-known for its treatment of prestige and competition. *The Theory of the Leisure Class* (1895) links the notion of consumption as public display with an examination of status hierarchies; it explores the consequences of this linkage through a general discussion of the importance of expense, leisure, and waste in affirming status. Support for these views is drawn from a number of areas of consumption, such as dress and education, and from a wide range of societies. Veblen anticipated many diverse topics that would come to attract attention in the study of consumption, such as connoisseurship, time allocation and the social underpinnings of fashion. His phrase "conspicuous consumption" suggests the communicative aspects of consumption, and the significance of consumption for influencing social relations. By using this term, Veblen insisted on the relevance of an institutional framework for challenging an emergent rigorous neoclassical paradigm which relied on assumptions about consumption as reflecting a purely individual utility. Simmel also discussed consumption in his major synthetic work on sociology (1908). He applied his interest in the formal properties of interaction to the topic of parties. Parties do not merely illustrate the general human tendency of sociability, but also vary in regular ways. The character of the social interaction (and, of interest to us, the nature and quantity of goods which are consumed) depend on the scale of the event, the relations of the host and the guests, and the range of social statuses of the participants. His article bearing the laconic title of "Fashion" (1904) also establishes formal arguments for the widespread occurrence of emulation and downward diffusion of modes. Sombart's *Luxury and capitalism* (1913) presents similar links for the importance of consumption in marking and maintaining status hierarchies. He credits consumption of luxury goods in European courts with shaping the timing and direction of the development of capitalism in commerce, agriculture and manufacturing. Within the courts, it was the courtesans--the women who cultivated affairs with nobles--who shaped fashion. Although Sombart's claims on the relationships among sexuality, luxury, consumption, fashion and demand seem exaggerated and unsubstantiated, he raises a number of important issues on the social context of consumption.

The topic of consumption has recently attracted considerable attention within social history. We begin our brief summary with a mention of Braudel's contributions to the study of everyday life. His notion of the *longue duree* involved an examination of the material basis of society, including consumption as well as production. As his discussions of food, clothing and furniture show, he saw consumption as a system of socially and culturally constructed meanings.

Other writers (Weatherill 1986) have drawn attention to the importance of consumption in influencing the direction of the Industrial Revolution. In this way, they correct the predominant emphasis on production and exchange. In their book, *The birth of a consumer society: the commercialization of eighteenth-century England*, McKendrick, Brewer and Plumb (1982) present a series of propositions: that the early industrialization of England can be understood in part through an examination of demand, that the high demand for goods in England reflects the relative fluidity of the class structure and the use of goods in marking status, and that the demand for specific types of goods such as cloth and ceramics was influenced by the patterns of use such as balls, teas and the like. Although these propositions may seem reasonable, they do suggest a strong modification of the view that the trajectory of English industrialization can be understood exclusively through an examination of production and exchange (levels of capital, transportation patterns, technological innovations, and so forth). Biddick makes similar points about the earlier transition in England from a medieval to an early modern economy (1988). Williams' examination of the Parisian middle class (1982) in the nineteenth century focuses on the social and ideological dimensions of shifting patterns of consumption. She grants consumption far greater autonomy than would be expected from a more conventional view that would emphasize changes in aspects such as demography, occupational structure and political interests. Other works continue this sort of European national histories of consumption. Frykman and Lofgren (1987) examine the Swedish bourgeoisie and their consumption patterns from 1880 to 1910. *The embarrassment of riches: an interpretation of Dutch culture in the golden age* (Schama 1986) discusses the expansion of consumption throughout Dutch society in the seventeenth century and its consequences for ideology, politics and the path of the Dutch economy.

Other researchers apply this perspective outside the core industrial nations. An economist, Felix (1979), contrasts patterns of industrialization in Asia with those in Africa and Latin America by arguing that a greater retention of indigenous objects as "positional goods" in Asia favored the industrialization of that region. He explains this contrast by an examination of pre-colonial societies. Similarly, changing patterns of diet reflect not only production factors such as local agronomic conditions and exchange factors such as prices, but also relatively autonomous demand factors. To take only one example of many, Lindenbaum

(1987) shows that complex patternings of nationality, class and gender have supported the production and exchange forces which have led to a strong shift in Bangladesh from a reliance on local rice to the increasing importance of imported wheat.

The cultural economy of consumption

We have assigned some works to the category of the cultural economy of consumption on rather imprecise grounds which rest on our judgment of whether the authors focus more strongly on thought or on action. We have done so however much they insist that their particular view offers the most reasonable balance between the two, or that it posits the only correct relation between them (we offer no definitive resolution of these issues). We include within the cultural economy of consumption those works which emphasize the patterning of goods by shared symbolic systems rather than the social dynamics and organization of the use of goods.

Arjun Appadurai is a leading figure in this vein. He discusses the importance of eating in India not only in terms of the absolute scarcity and unpredictability of food supplies, but also in terms of the cultural understandings of persons and of food. In his view, the South Asian concept of the human self rests on the notion of a biomoral substance which must be protected from damage and destruction. The intimacy of food sharing creates the potential both for the strengthening of persons through proper attention to biomoral substance and to their weakening (1981b). Meals thus come to constitute a fundamental context for the creating, maintaining, displaying and transforming of social relations. Appadurai illustrates his points through an examination of daily household meals, wedding feasts and food distribution at temples. His affinities with Wolf, Schneider and Mintz are greater than might appear at first, though, because of his attention to consumption as a realm for conflict. In a recent paper (1988), he traces the tensions between a national cuisine in India and specific regional and ethnic traditions, and the specific forces which favored the emergence of a national cuisine after independence. In his term "gastropolitics" are the notions of disputation and negotiation. This work underlies his application of the concept of "entitlement," developed by the economist Amartya Sen, to famine in South Asia. Appadurai defines entitlement as "the capability, under a given social, legal, and economic regime, of an individual or group to obtain legitimately the means of subsistence" (1984:481). He shows that this cultural understanding of consumption helps explain both the extent and the patterning of famine in different periods and regions of South Asia, in contrast with views that would emphasize food production and marketing systems.

Despite their differences, then, these social and cultural approaches share generally related perspectives on consumption, including importance of consumption as an arena for the settling of competing claims to status and power. Other anthropologists within the cultural economy of consumption turn to consensus rather than contestation. The strong influence of Durkheim and Levi-Strauss can be noted in Mary Douglas' work. Her early articles on food prohibitions (1966,1975) show her concern with consumption as demonstrating patterns of thought, especially systems of social and cognitive classification, and in particular the universality of efforts to separate out ambiguous elements in classificatory schemes. Her more recent work on meals (1975) carries forward this interest in structure; unlike the other writers, such as Rotenberg (1988), she finds in meals the demonstration of collective agreement. Differences in consumption patterns (Douglas and Isherwood 1979) reflect the organization of social relations (her well-known distinction between "group" and "grid") and an established hierarchy. Sahlins offers similar structuralist accounts of consumption in a variety of societies, such as his discussions of meat consumption and of cloth and gender in the United States (1976) and of shifts in consumption in post-contact Hawaii (1985). Both Douglas and Sahlins offer important contributions to the study of consumption as a system of categories of goods, which can be related to social categories, and, for Douglas, to temporal and social periodicities.

Bourdieu might be seen as occupying a middle ground between Appadurai and Douglas, in part because his notion of *habitus* draws both from the ideological underpinnings of power of the former and from the interest in structure of the latter. His monograph *Distinction: a social critique of the judgement of taste* (1984) marshalls an impressive body of survey data and anecdotal interviews in contemporary France to demonstrate on the one hand the divergence in knowledge and opinions regarding a wide number of areas, such as food, music, sports, and clothing, and on the other the order within this patterning, reflecting an individual's social origins, education, occupation and residence, what Bourdieu terms "economic capital" and "cultural capital." He notes the differences which separate the young left-wing nurse who hitchhikes to Greece, the baker's wife who likes her big gray settee because it does not show stains, the wealthy lawyer who received as a wedding present "a [classical] Greek head in stone, authentic and rather beautiful" (274) and who thinks that "if you're going to eat smoked eel, it's more agreeable to eat it in the Amsterdam fish market than in some tacky restaurant" (277). These people would not find each others' homes attractive, but they would also not find them surprising; they all offer with confidence a large number of judgments of taste. These esthetic judgments reflect and maintain the divisions of the French into social classes and political tendencies, but they also validate each group as distinct, rather than as superior or inferior. Of particular importance for Bourdieu's France is the continued weight of aristocratic courtly definitions of "culture" and "taste" and their impact on bourgeois consumption.

Barnett offers a counterpoint to Douglas' structuralism. In his academic writings and in his column "Observing" published in Advertising Age, he examines the rapidly shifting styles in American dress, music and diet. His explanation of this fluidity rests on the notion of "serial substitution" (Barnett and Magdoff 1986:414) or changing surface appearances in style and in personal relationships. He notes consonances among the use of goods, the system of social relations and the moral order: all are unstable and rapidly changing. This view maintains the sociological identity between classification of persons and of goods, as well as the psychological identity between self and object. (Barnett draws on Marxist sources, and makes brief reference to "two other cultural and socioeconomic frames" (*op. cit:*.:413): the new fundamentalism, and an underclass locked into "entrenched poverty" (414). He notes that participants in "serial substitution" need certain levels of cash income and that they support a capitalist system of production.

Douglas, Bourdieu and Barnett may be taken, not only to demonstrate the diversity of the cultural economy of consumption in contemporary anthropology, but also the diversity of consumption in advanced industrial societies. Despite recent changes in England, some standard images retain considerable validity: the sharp cleavage separating middle and working classes, the domination of the political scene by two parties, the gap between the wealthier south and the poorer north. Douglas' work may thus reflect the greater importance in England than in France or in the United States of knowing one's place in a social order and of putting other people in theirs. Bourdieu's work draws not only on his theoretical commitments but also on unique features of French society: the centralized and hierarchical nature of education and state institutions as a whole, the greater diversity of class differences and political parties, the dominant position of Paris. In this sense, Barnett's work reflects American society: as economic historians have noted, the growth of the frontier and the incorporation of immigrant groups have shaped marketing patterns in the United States, and have led to the greater importance of goods in establishing personal identity.

The individual economy of consumption

The social and cultural economies of consumption stand in sharp contrast to what could be termed the individual economy of consumption, the perspectives from psychology and economics. We briefly review these fields for two reasons: to make more explicit our differences with them, and to indicate within them several lines of inquiry that we consider to be compatible with our approach and to be fruitful.

Contemporary academic economics is a relatively unified field. It comes closer than the other social sciences to having the elements which constitute a paradigm in the epistemological and sociological senses given that term by Thomas Kuhn (1962). The studies of consumption conducted by economists fit within this paradigm, as shown by a perusal of textbooks by Mansfield (1986), in more advanced treatments (Hicks 1965, Deaton and Muellbauer 1980, Michael and Becker 1973), in empirical studies (Stone 1966, Cubbin 1975) and more exploratory essays (Leibenstein 1976, Stigler and Becker 1977). This work rests on methodological individualism: the models of microeconomics and macroeconomics are simple in their basic forms, amenable to elaboration through established procedures, and interrelated through straightforward processes of aggregation of individuals into collectivities. At one time, the economic literature on consumption drew on the concept of utility, a presumed subjective state. Much of the current literature now rests on the notion of revealed preference, which may be linked directly to behavior without reference to psychological processes; this formulation dates back at least fifty years (Samuelson 1938). Although this shift in epistemological underpinnings might appear to be a radical one, the applications of the two notions are quite similar. In both instances, individuals are assumed to have rankings in which any particular set of goods has a position in relation to other such sets; for conventional economic analysis to proceed, to these systems of rankings must display some simple properties, such as stability and transitivity. For utility theory, these rankings reflect subjective value; for the latter, they merely demonstrate regularities in observable behavior. Both cases lead to the same equations which express aggregate demand, and to their more familiar representation in indifference curves and budget lines; economics lacks the tension between models which rest on the mind and those which are based on behavior (McCloskey 1985), a difference of critical importance in anthropology, psychology and other fields. Demand at the individual and aggregate level is determined by the conventional economic variables of price and income and by tastes, which economists assume firstly to meet certain principles of formal logic and secondly to be unchanging. These variables serve as the basis for the construction of other variables, such as elasticities and marginal propensities to consume. Some aspects of these microeconomic models are well-developed and widely used in empirical studies, such as income and substitution effects of changing prices on levels of consumption. In other cases, the notion of revealed preference serves as a basis for the establishment of other, more general, topics, such as the operation of markets or the effects of taxes and subsidies on consumer behavior. Consumption has also been studied from a macroeconomic perspective, in which disposable income can be divided between consumption and savings. Both of these can stimulate economic growth, consumption in the short run by providing demand and savings in the long run as a source of investment. When linked with demographic analyses, microeconomic models of individual patterns of consumption have been aggregated to study economic growth and development (Modigliani 1986).

A considerable body of literature in consumer economics addresses such questions as the effect on aggregate demand for one good of a change in the relative price of another, the effect of a change in income on marginal expenditures on a particular good, the determination of consumer's demand curves from objective prices and indifference curves. Many of the questions have to do with income and price effects on the substitution of one good for another on the assumption of diminishing marginal utility. Applications of consumer economics cover an increasingly wide range of consumer behavior, e.g., the price of leisure (Owen 1969), the price of information and the role of advertising in consumer choice (Nelson 1970, 1975), and the choice of modes of transportation (Bruzelius 1979).

There is much variety to the nature and strength of anthropologists' objections to economists' notion of a universally applicable principle of revealed preference. The relative valuation of beef and pork, for example, is not simply a matter of individual taste whose interactions with changing prices and incomes lead to shifting levels of aggregate demand, but whose origins, distribution and dynamics are beyond the realm of investigation. For the many anthropologists who understand objects to be socially and culturally constituted, these views are difficult to accept. Anthropologists are also often troubled by the lack of contextualization and ethnographic realism in economists' discussion of taste and by the lack of attention paid to non-monetarized or partially monetarized economies. We might add another objection: the sharp separation between production and consumption, in which obtaining income and spending it are seen as entirely separate.

Furthermore, the intellectual styles of anthropology and economics are quite distinct. We may take as an example one of the early results of the economics of consumption, Engel's Law, the observation that rich households, on the average, spend a smaller portion of their total income on food than poor households (Engels 1895). For economists, it is a strong result, because of its simplicity, of its applicability to a large number of economies, and of its linkage to basic concepts of income elasticity, tied to the ranking of goods into necessities and luxuries. For anthropologists, it is far less impressive: the simplicity might appear as oversimplification, its applicability to non-monetarized economies is questionable, and it lacks linkages to cultural influences on preferences. Many anthropologists seek more detailed theories to account for food consumption and would be dissatisfied with the gross association of total income and total expenditure on food.

Despite these differences, some areas of consumer economics address issues quite close to the social economy of consumption. Two Nobel prize-winning economists examined expenditure patterns at different stages of an individual's life cycle, by including the plausible assumptions that the human life span is finite and that the future is less certain than the present. They noted regularities of allocation to savings and bequests. Milton Friedman is known for the permanent income hypothesis (1957) and Franco Modigliani for the life cycle hypothesis (1986). Although the microeconomic work on expenditure patterns can be framed in terms of net expected utility, discount rates, and the like, it also can be linked to a more social analysis of the development cycles of domestic groups. Similarly, Becker (1976), Linder (1981) and others use allocational theory to account for variations between household members in spending time and capital on income-producing activities and on leisure; this research also leads quite directly to an examination of social process within households. Schram and Hafstrom (1988) use Becker's framework as a point of departure although they show that role expectations influence these patterns of allocation in ways that are not immediately congruent with his framework. Other related research examines the consequences of multiple income sources (Neary and Roberts 1980). If a set of households with identical incomes is divided into two sub-sets, one of which

34

receives a cash grant and the other of which received food stamps of equivalent value, what will be the differences in their consumption patterns? This topic is of considerable importance to anthropologists, since in many instances each one of a series of multiple income sources entail different social relations. Lorenzen et al. (1988) show the importance of such state subsidies for poor households in a number of Mexican cities; households which receive health benefits, in particular, are able to allocate income more readily to other categories, such as food and housing. The willingness of the state to tolerate squatter settlements also favors some poor households, which otherwise would be faced with substantial expenses for the rental or purchase of housing.

With characteristic originality, Hirschman (1982) discusses consumer disappointment to counterbalance the focus on consumer satisfaction. He contrasts disappointment with food, with consumer durables, and with services, and examines the role of disappointment in preference shifts (Elster 1979). These points have wide applicability to societies in which new consumer durables acquire importance, whether in Belize (Wilk 1988), Fiji (Rutz 1988) or Burkina Faso (Saul 1988).

At a level of considerable generality, psychological approaches to consumption are similar to economic approaches in that they examine the actions of individuals and that they draw on some simple, broad notions. Psychologists tend to separate individuals from the social and cultural context in which they are located, and to look at responses to particular situations. They have in common with economists an interest in information-processing, in the largely inferred movement from initial perception to final response. As is the case with economics, the discipline of psychology has well-established standards of appropriate support for claims; they often favor experimental situations, attempt to draw on natural experiments when using field data, and display considerable care in construction of samples and operationalization of variables. Though this concern with data collection makes psychologists different from economists, it produces a similar gravitation towards formal models. The greater difference between the two lies in the fact that psychology is a field in which different approaches compete for paradigmatic status, and, as a consequence, consumer psychology is less unified than consumer economics. Many consumer psychologists study purchasing behavior exclusively, although others also examine the use of objects after purchase as well. Some researchers examine cognition, the classification of objects along dimensions and into categories; other work, drawing on psychodynamic approaches, focuses on affect, the emotional responses to objects. In addition, some social psychologists include in their models a number of variables which describe social context and measure social relations. These different tendencies have given rise to a large number of differing models. One review finds twenty-eight basic models, all of them predominantly cognitive, which differ according to a number of features: whether they examine attributes of products or consumers, which situations they emphasize (exposure, deliberation, purchase, communication or consumption), and which sort of decision process they consider (rational, semi-complex or clue-guided) (Hansen 1972:434-437). Another review, which focuses on the more narrow topic of vehicle choice, also finds a wide range of models, including qualitative choice models, noncompensatory models, hierarchical models, diffusion of innovation models and purchase decision process models (Turrentine 1987).

As Hansen's terminology suggests, consumer psychology is closely tied to specific applications in marketing. If their theoretical background and applied concerns lead consumer economists to consider goods at a very general level, such as food and housing, consumer psychologists examine goods at a very specific level: the texture of the peanut butter, the color of the dishwasher. Because of the economic significance of this research to many firms, the field of applied consumer psychology is large and fairly secretive, particularly in the details of specific research. But even the relatively small proportion of this work which reaches publication is absolutely large. As consumer psychologists have sought new models by which they can persuade consumers to purchase new goods, some have moved in directions which contain ideas linked to the social economy of consumption: the role of objects in communication, the social construction of the meaning of goods, the link between social identity and the use of goods (Foxall 1983). A number of articles in recent issues of the *Journal of Consumer Research* and in the annual *Advances in Consumer Research* address these general issues of the use of goods in advanced industrial societies in ways that blur, in true post-modern fashion, the boundaries among individual, cultural and political economies of consumption (Belk 1985, 1987). The discussion of consumer psychology raises the issue of advertising, a topic that occupies a position for many anthropologists quite like that of tourism: it is seen as modern and unauthentic. Another similarity is the difficulty of studying it. One can link the general fact of advertising with a general sort of economy, and perhaps with the notion of "false needs"; granted the size of advertising budgets, it also seems possible to link specific advertising campaigns with the increase in demand for specific products. It seems quite tricky, though, to mesh these links with our other understandings of consumption. In any case, this ability of anthropologists to study use behavior, rather than purchasing behavior, may provide the basis for much of the applications of the anthropology of consumption, particularly in the instances for which corporate funding has been available. An article in the 4 September 1986 issue of the *Wall Street Journal*, entitled "'People watchers' seek clues to consumers' true behavior," places quotation marks around a specific technical term when it appears for the first time, presumably in order to alert the reader to its novelty; that term is "ethnography." This article describes the ethnographic activities of the staff of an advertising agency (observation of six families while they were eating ice cream) and the contributions to the client ("more effective advertising"). A similar article in the Sunday Business Section of the *New York Times* on 11 May 1986, "Casting an anthropological eye on American consumers," discusses observations of dish-washing and diaper changing, and suggests that this research contributed to the development of new products. (The *New York Times* appears to think that its readers do not require an explanation to understand the term ethnography.)

We may finally note that consumer economists and psychologists may both be seen as ethnographers of a small range of societies, industrial nations of the twentieth century. The broad budget categories of economists are not merely a universally applicable analytical construct, but also the product of state regulation and financial institutions, as shown by the experience of the individuals who pay taxes and use credit. Similarly, the distinction between income and expenditure reflects the high degree of monetarization and the relative lack of inter-household exchanges of goods and services. For a psychological perspective, we note an article in the 30 July 1987 *Wall Street Journal*, entitled "As a favorite pastime, shopping ranks high with most Americans" with a sub-head "They browse, buy to dispel boredom, find fantasy; economists are amazed."

The political economy of consumption

This discussion of the individual economy of consumption has focused on consumption in capitalist societies. A different analysis of such consumption, which we term "the political economy of consumption," stems from the work of Marx. This work derives in part from the references in Marx' writings to themes of consumption and in part from his more general perspective. As Preteceille and Terrail show (1985: 150-153), Marx conceived of consumption needs ("necessary wants") as being shaped by several factors, including human biology, climate, and historical development, but he did not discuss them in great detail. He developed certain concepts, such as reification and commodity fetishism, which directly addressed aspects of consumption in capitalist economies; other, broader ideas, such as alienation and the relation of subject and object, are also applicable to the analysis of consumption. Many of these ideas have been taken up by writers interested in broad themes of culture and ideology, including Benjamin, Lukacs, Adorno, Marcuse, and, as Philibert (1988) points out, Gramsci. We hesitate to offer any definitive list, and refer curious readers instead to Jay's *Marxism and totality* (1984), which offers a thoughtful review of such works, some of which provide some general critiques of Western consumerism. As Jay's title indicates, these works stem from what is often called the relations of base and superstructure, rather than other work which focusses more specifically on the base.

This portion of Marxist study drew more anthropological interest when it was combined with the semiology of the French post-structuralist Barthes,[3] whose witty essays (1957, 1965) showed the possibility of linking broad analysis (influenced by Brecht's attempts to demonstrate the historical concreteness of situations which dominant classes defined as natural) with examination of concrete details of everyday life. (Other analysts, more loyal to structuralism, have not found his work so appealing [Bourdieu 1984:76].) Baudrillard (1968, 1970, 1972) has offered the fullest application to consumption of a synthesis of semiology and Marxism. He grants consumption a privileged position as a fundamental underpinning of exploitation under monopoly capitalism, a point which Marx is alleged to have missed because his analysis centered on competitive capitalism. Under advanced capitalism, "[t]he contradiction of class is . . . redefined as a continuum of consumption," (Gartman 1986:172) so proletarians are unconscious of their true class position. Baudrillard also questions Marx' privileging of use value over exchange value, another error which allegedly stems from Marx' limited range of cases. Drawing in part on the study of exchange by anthropologists such as Mauss and Bataille, Baudrillard explores the liberating potential of exchange through the symbolic and ideological constitution of exchange value. Baudrillard's discussion of the political economy of signs has attracted a good deal of attention.

A second trend in the political economy of consumption stems from Marxist analysis of the base of the forces and relations of production. This work, predominantly written in English, draws on a different set of Marxist concepts, developed in *Das Kapital*--labor theory of value, reproduction of labor, and surplus value. It examines the notion of the reproduction of labor, which has been taken for granted in much of the work on the dynamic of capitalism, a large body of literature which also refers to these concepts in debates on the organic composition of capital, the inevitability of falling rates of profit, and the like. Aglietta's book (1976) on the American economy since the Civil War is an example of such studies. He assigns critical importance to the interplay between capital accumulation and competition among capitalists. This tension leads on the one hand to internal differentiation of both capitalist and proletarian classes and on the other hand to state regulation, ultimately expressing itself in crises which are intertwined with state intervention. For example, the state's role in collective bargaining expresses contradictory tendencies, one towards increasing concentration of production in many branches of the economy and the other towards a differentiation of the proletariat into unionized and non-unionized sectors. These sectors are characterized not only by different wage levels, but also by different types of consumption; at certain points in time, only some workers could own houses and automobiles. He integrates this discussion of consumption into his more general theme of the fundamental importance of financial crises in capitalist development, particularly in his section entitled "financial centralizations through the transformation of the mode of consumption". The political economy of consumption thus plays a role in his more general analysis of capitalist development.

Feminist writings have a major role in this trend in the political economy of consumption. They have tackled several major problems: the relations between systems of gender inequality and class inequality, the connection between personal life and political activity, the relations of ideology and domination. Of specific importance are Marxist feminist analyses of domestic work and the family wage (Himmelweit and Mohun 1977, Hartmann 1981, Barrett and McIntosh 1980, Brenner and Ramas 1984, Barrett 1984, Lewis 1985). Another related theme is the role of the state in assuring subsistence through welfare systems, labor legislation and other programs (Dickinson and Russell 1986).

38

These two trends, much like their origins in the writings of Marx, are not fully distinct. Preteceille and Terrail (1985), for instance, are struck by the fact that social movements in Western Europe and the United States center around issues such as environmentalism which are not directly linked to the interests of particular classes. They examine advanced capitalist societies through a discussion of needs, looking on the one hand at ideologies which mask exploitation and on the other at economic crises which led to cuts in levels of consumption, whether through unemployment or through declining budgets of state agencies. Although the final chapters of their book suggest a very concrete concern (the direction of French politics in the latter portion of Mitterand's presidency, as the sectors with ambiguous class positions and party loyalties continued to grow in number), they conjoin a series of issues which others have tended to keep separate.

Why To Think About Consumption: History and Power (conceptual bundle 3, in which we argue that the third fundamental characteristic of the social economy of consumption is its ability to address questions of power through its linkage of ideology and economy)

Our review leads us to propose several reasons for which the study of consumption could attract broader interest. We discuss these reasons briefly and then illustrate them with a few cases.

Consumption marks categories and relations in a way that at times is taken for granted by all participants, and that at others raises questions and presents ambiguities. To phrase this point differently, the use of a particular good by a particular individual may be seen as entirely appropriate, but, at some times, or in the eyes of some observers, it may represent an inappropriate claim to a status or relation, or even a challenge to a system of statuses and relations. Consumption also entails the use of goods that can refer in multiple ways to other sets of goods in varying locations and periods. Although quite similar points could be made about other areas of social life, such as language or ritual, they have a particular salience for consumption, for several reasons: the physical tangibility of goods, their links to human biological requirements, the great frequency of acts of consumption, the public nature of participation in consumption events, the connection of consumption to economic spheres of production and exchange. These reasons can give importance to consumption: it can powerfully affirm certain social orders and can be a key arena of contestation and change of others. Phrased differently, consumption is thus linked to the constitution and transformation of hegemony.

The link between consumption and ideology is strong. Our thoughts on this link tend to center on the nature of consumption claims. Individuals may refer to their rights to consume certain goods and to their preferences of some goods over others; as we have suggested for the case of Kali Loro, these references in certain contexts can become a major arena for disputing other social categories and relations. Clark shows the importance of consumption claims in structuring the domestic and marketing activities of West African women (1988) and Bennett shows that ritual meals are a context for debating issues of class and community (1988). In his examination of food policy in Nicaragua since 1979, Zalkin (1988) emphasizes the importance of the category of necessities (*articulos de primera necesidad*), and the limits which this category places on governmental agencies and major organizations. The ideology of consumption influences the activities of the state, already bound by the pressures of war, by limited budgets, and by the urgency of widening and deepening political support; for many Nicaraguans, their meals have a particularly strong influence in their sense of the contrast between the present and the period before the revolution. (Another general line of reasoning, which we will only mention briefly, examines the link between consumption and the constitution of the person. This alternative view would point out the immediacy of the connection between consumption and the human body, and would speak of needs where we speak of rights, of desires rather than preferences, of sensation rather than satisfaction. It would arrive at the ideological importance of consumption, and of discourse about consumption, through a different route.)

We link several disparate examples to suggest the importance of the social economy of consumption framework and the ideological significance of consumption. These examples suggest ways in which the social economy of consumption can expand our understanding of capitalism and of the state. In this way, we suggest that it can move from topics that, although engaging, may appear of limited significance to other topics of broader concern to social science. However much wage labor and centralized states are common facts of life for members of advanced industrial societies, they are more contingent for many of the people whom anthropologists study. In many instances, individuals who could withdraw into subsistence production work for wages or sell their crops. The reasons for this participation in the cash economy include the role of coercion, the material benefits which follow from this participation, the lack of alternatives, and the prevalence of ideologies which make wage labor legitimate. Similarly, in many historical and ethnographic cases, states receive support, despite their weakness and the ability of many individuals to successfully oppose or to avoid state rule. A number of arguments have been proposed to explain this support, of varying merit in different situations. These include the role of coercion, the benefits which follow from participation in the state, the lack of alternatives, and the prevalence of ideologies which make state rule legitimate. To these arguments in both cases we wish to add consumption.

With regard to the cash economy, we note that subsistence cultivators are often forced into working to earn money, either by selling their labor directly or by selling cash crops. Such external compulsion may take the form of taxation, vagrancy laws (Smith 1984), or the reduction of land base by loss of land to colonial authorities, commercial farmers, plantations and the like (Klaren 1970); demographic pressure also constitutes another form of compulsion. These cases all suggest that the erosion of subsistence economies makes individuals enter into the cash economy against their will. Instances of this process are numerous, important and compelling. Nonetheless, they do not exhaust the reasons for participation in the wage economy.

An interesting variant is forced consumption; Spanish colonial authorities in Mexico and Bolivia (Larson and Wasserstrom 1983) distributed unfamiliar and undesired goods, in large quantities through a "compulsory market" (op, cit.:153) to Indians, who then had to earn cash to pay for them. This policy benefitted the large merchants who imported goods and the Spanish mineowners and landowners who sought Indian laborers, although it also created resentment against the royal officials who enforced it. This case raises the issue of preference formation; it suggests that in certain instances, individuals will not seek to obtain goods which are purchased with cash unless they are coerced.

In other instances, though, the entry into wage labor stems from an uncoerced wish for such goods. The ethnographic literature contains a number of instances which may be roughly divided into utilitarian and decorative goods, for which steel axes and glass beads may be seen as the type cases. A Brazilian case shows that some metal tools are far more efficient than native ones made of stone and wood, so that Amazonian Indians seek cash to purchase them, simply because they are moved by the universal human tendency to allocate labor efficiently (Gross et al. 1979). Other studies suggest that many Western goods have an esthetic appeal, perhaps because traditional ornaments lack variety or color, perhaps because within the vast array of potentially available Western goods are some items which will happen to fit in with native esthetic standards; these are the items which Murphy and Steward (1956) refer to as "trinkets" and "gewgaws," in contrast with "utilitarian wares." Both of these cases presuppose rather simple psychological principles and thus lean towards an individual, rather than a social, economy of consumption.

Our social economy of consumption perspective leads us to view as more complex the reasons for which individuals involved in a subsistence economy might desire to obtain goods available only by purchase. In many Andean villages, for example, certain rituals require purchased food, drink, fireworks, and the like; these social needs have led peasants to work in plantations (Gonzales 1985:127) and mines (Godoy 1985). Other goods hold a more complex and ambiguous social significance. In many villages, where all the houses were formerly roofed with thatch, sheet metal roofs are becoming quite common. From the perspective of an individual economy of consumption, the metal roofs could be seen as superior, since they last longer and because they take less time to install. (They might also have been judged as more attractive, although utility and beauty may be less clearly distinguished in the Andes than elsewhere. The Quechua term *sumaq* which a peasant might use to describe a metal roof could be translated as "excellent" or "beautiful".) Peasants formerly used thatch, because they obtained cash in very small quantities, and at very low rates of pay; once expanding national economies offered them higher wages, metal became cheaper relative to thatch in terms of time. One could bring in a social economy of consumption perspective by making arguments along the lines that Simmel

41

proposes and speaking of a downward diffusion of urban styles into the countryside; to accord a certain degree of autonomy to social processes at the village level, one could examine the social relations that focus around house construction. Roofing bees hold significance for their participants, since social ties are renewed and maintained in them (Platt 1978); the size and organization of these groups differ according to the materials which are used. Since fewer individuals are needed to construct a roof of metal than one of thatch, when a household switches from the latter to the former, they also reduce and shift their set of reciprocal ties. Whatever the choice of roofing materials, the household would also be the object of comments by other villagers, comments that center around such a visible sign of greater material wealth. A similar shift from local materials to purchased manufactured items in Belize has a different social dynamic (Wilk 1988), as do other cases in Latin America (Costa Rica [Barlett 1982]) and the Pacific (Fiji [Rutz 1984]) and Vanuatu [Philibert 1988]). These cases suggest the difficulty of making comparisons between a subsistence and a cash economy; the facile measurement of costs and benefits presupposes a standard of value, although value is complex and often ambiguous.

The discussion of this comparison raises a closely related point, the patterning of the distribution of home-produced and purchased goods. Weismantel (1988) provides a dietary example from a highland Ecuadorian village, where home-produced foods such as barley gruel and purchased foods such as bread are eaten in different ways on different occasions. Debates over the reallocation of certain food items both reflects and heightens the tensions between participation in local subsistence production and in an urban wage labor economy.

With regard to the second case of the state, we note a number of examples in which elites make use of consumption to maintain their control and rule. Morris discusses the material remains of Huanuco Pampa, an Inca provincial capital in the central Peruvian highlands, from a period when the representatives of the Inca state were few in number, and surrounded by large masses of ethnic groups with whom they had recently been at war. Morris was "surprised" (1985:485) to find room after room which contained little else than sherds of broken jars used for *chicha*, a maize beer. He had come with "expectations of a more military and bureaucratic form of administration." Through what means could the locals' participation in "drinking bouts" and other ceremonies translate into their acceptance of tribute obligations and of a loss of autonomy? We may assume that the Inca rule rested in part on assent as well as on coercion, and that some part of the consent stemmed from consumption activities. For the locals, the offering of *chicha* not only held high value, but also implied a certain sort of treatment within the Inca state. We can at best speculate on the reasons for the significance of *chicha*--its links to longstanding traditions of feasting, its greater and wider availability under Inca rule, its reference to household and to courtly interactions, the simultaneously personal and public quality of drinking, perhaps even cultural understandings of liquids (Bastien 1985). Other sources also attest to a major role of *chicha* for the Inca, and suggest that it gave the control of maize lands a significance that went beyond their simple agronomic and nutritional potential

(Wachtel 1982, Orlove 1985). One may multiply almost endlessly other cases which show how common are the linkages between statecraft, prestations and consumption events, drawing on cases from Europe (Schneider 1978, McKendrick et al. 1982), Asia (Hamilton and Lai 1988, Appadurai 1981a) and the Pacific (Sahlins 1985).

To review our earlier discussion, the social economy of consumption makes anti-reductionist and non-exclusivist claims. We suggest that most writers have tended to view consumption in reductionist terms. Whether they examine consumption (in contrast to production and exchange) as one stage in the existence of objects, as one type of economic activity or as one systems of economic relations, their works suggest that consumption can be understood as an outcome of production and exchange, either singly or in combination. Some, but not all, have treated consumption as an activity which is conducted by individuals; by contrast, we emphasize its social and communicative nature. For many reductionists, consumption merely reflects or marks already-existing social relations; the wedding ring (or turban, or wig) indicates the shift in status from single to married, or, in more elaborate versions of the same argument, individuals seek certain goods to establish and maintain specific social relations. We see as problematic and ideological the relation between goods and social relations. In this view, consumption is an arena for the weighing of claims.

Our non-exclusivism stems from our anti-reductionism. We seek, not to supplant the study of production or exchange, but to add to it. If the goal of economic anthropology is taken to be the analysis of economic activity, relations and systems, then the study of consumption is an autonomous component of this field. We also do not find ourselves regularly joining up with decision theorist, neo-Marxist or culturalist approaches, but rather find different combinations of them useful in specific circumstances. Perhaps because our work has led us to examine other disciplines, we find our intellectual commitments to be with the field of anthropology as a whole rather than to portions of it, as shown by, in particular, our emphases on social communication, on the contextualization of economic activity and on the interconnectedness of specific institutions.

The social economy of consumption can be of interest, not only to specialists within economic anthropology, but also to wider audiences. In general terms, the study of consumption leads to the examination of daily life on the one hand and of broad systems of stratification on the other; it joins the material world of the production of objects to the ideological world of the evaluation of objects. In more specific terms, there are a number of historical and ethnographic topics within economic anthropology in which clearer analysis and more fruitful insight may be gained through a closer examination of consumption. The list of such topics is impressive: as we have already indicated, these include such broad themes as the transition from feudalism to capitalism, the origins of the industrial revolution in England, and the incorporation of subsistence agriculturalists into monetary economies. They also include topics of great importance which are located at smaller spatial, temporal and social scales, such as the distribution of wealth and power within households and the dynamics of stratification within villages. In some instances, these different scales are directly linked; Mintz' discussion of sugar includes both global trade and household meal patterns, Schneider's examination of cloth in Europe conjoins shifting lines of imperial control and tablecloths. It is on the importance of these topics and the significance of these linkages that we make our claims for the potential of the social economy of consumption.

Notes

We are very appreciative of the many people who offered useful comments and criticisms of earlier drafts of this article. In particular, we would like to thank Arjun Appadurai, Marc Blanchard, Russell Belk, Mary Douglas, James Griesemer, Peter Lindert, Eugene Lunn, Sidney Mintz, Stuart Plattner, Daniel Rancour-Laferriere, Jane Schneider, Steven Sheffrin, Robert Sommer, Thomas Turrentine, Jacques Weber, Richard Wilk and Eric Wolf for the suggestions, many of which we have adopted. We make a special note of our gratitude to Ann Stoler for her openness in discussing reinterpretations of her published material.

1. With our interest in consumption, some details of the *bawon* caught our attention. We note that in all cases which Stoler and White mention, the shares are always fractions that are the reciprocals of certain numbers (2, 4, 5, 6, 8, 10, 12, 25), all of which are divisible by 2 or 5. [Certain other numbers--7, 9--are never mentioned, and 11 comes up only in the instance of the chastened bride, who "compounded her *faux pas*" by offering one-eleventh. We suspect that the harvesters would rather receive shares of one-twelfth rather than one-eleventh.] This distribution "takes place at the home of the landowner" (Stoler:686). These aspects of payment lead us to consider the significance of rice in the totality of production, exchange and consumption, rather than to focus on rice more narrowly in terms of production and exchange. These issues of measurement are treated with great insight by the Polish economic historian Witold Kula, particularly in his book *Of measures and men* (1986). His work also leads us to suspect that there are debates over the manner in which the rice is divided out-- whether baskets are merely filled to the brim or heaped up, for instance.

2. These ideas about stimulants may have come to us from analogies with our geographical areas of specialization. In the Andes, coca leaf and a home-brewed maize beer, *chicha*, are important to certain sets of interactions, as *kava* is in Fiji. Although there may be major differences among these substances, it may nonetheless be useful to compare them. We note that economic anthropologists frequently make use of analogies between systems of production and exchange, and we suggest that they extend this practice to the area of consumption as well.

3.   What separates structuralism from post-structuralism is open to debate; Barthes represents an early transition, a progenitor of later efforts to get beyond the limitations imposed by structuralist logic.

References

Aglietta, Michel
1976   *Regulation et crisis du capitalisme.* Paris: Calmann-Levy.

Appadurai, Arjun
1981a *Worship and conflict under colonial rule: a South Indian case.* New York: Cambridge University Press.

1981b Gastro-politics in Hindu South Asia. *American Ethnologist* 8(3):494-511.

1984   How moral is South Asia's economy?: A review article. *Journal of Asian Studies* 43(3):481-498.

1988   How to make a national cuisine: cookbooks in contemporary India. *Comparative Studies in Society and History* 30(1): 3-24.

Appadurai, Arjun, ed.
1986   *The social life of things: commodities in cultural perspective.* Cambridge: Cambridge University Press.

Arnold, David
1979   Looting, grain riots and government policy in South India 1918. *Past and Present* 84:111-145.

Barlett, Peggy
1982   *Agricultural choice and change: decision making in a Costa Rican community.* New Brunswick, N.J.: Rutgers University Press.

Barnett, Steve and JoAnn Magdoff
1986   Beyond narcissism in American culture of the 1980s. *Cultural Anthropology* 1(4):413-424.

Barrett, Michele
1984   'Rethinking women's oppression': A reply to Brenner and Ramas. *New Left Review* 146:123-128.

Barrett, Michele and Mary McIntosh
1980   The 'family wage': some problems for socialists and feminists. *Capital and Class* 11:51-72.

Barthes, Roland
1957   *Mythologies*. Paris: Editions du Seuil.

1965   *Le degre zero de l'ecriture. Suivi de elements de emiologie*. Paris: Gonthier.

Bastien, Joseph
1985   Qollahuaya-Andean body concepts: a topographical-hydraulic model of physiology. *American Anthropologist* 87(3):595-611.

Baudrillard, Jean
1968   *Le* systeme *des objets*. Paris: Gallimard.

1970   *La societe de consommation*. Paris: S.G.P.P.

1972   *Pour une critique de l'economie politique du signe*. Paris: Gallimard.

Bayley, C.A.
1986   The origins of swadeshi (home industry): cloth and Indian society. in *The Social Life of Things*. edited by Arjun Appadurai, pp. 285-321. Cambridge: Cambridge University Press.

Becker, Gary S.
1965   A theory of the allocation of time. *The Economic Journal* 75:493-517.

1976   *The economic approach to human behavior*. Chicago and London: The University of Chicago Press.

Belk, Russell
1985   Materialism: trait aspects of living in the material world. *Journal of Consumer Research* 12(3):265-280.

1987   A modest proposal for creating verisimilitude in consumer information processing models and some suggestions for establishing a discipline to study consumer behavior. In A. Fuat Firat, Nikhilesh Dholakia and Richard P. Begozzi, eds. *Philosophical and radical thought in marketing*. Lexington, Ma: Lexington Books. pp. 361-372.

Bennett, Diane O.
1988   Saints and sweets: class and consumption ritual in rural Greece. in *The social economy of consumption*. Edited by Henry J. Rutz and Benjamin S. Orlove, pp. 177-210. Lanham, Md.: University Press of America.

Biddick, Kathleen
1988 The link that separates: consumption of pastoral resources on a feudal estate. in *The social economy of consumption*. Edited by Henry J. Rutz and Benjamin S. Orlove. pp. **. Lanham, Md.: University Press of America.

Bohannon, Paul
1955 Some principles of exchange and investment among the Tiv. *American Anthropologist* 57:60-70.

Bourdieu, Pierre
1979 *Algeria 1960*. Translated by Richard Nice. Cambridge: Cambridge University Press.

1984 *Distinction: a social critique of the judgement of taste*. Translated by Richard Nice. Cambridge: Cambridge University Press.

Brenner, Johanna and Maria Ramas
1984 Rethinking women's oppression. *New Left Review* 144:37-71.

Bruzelius, Nils
1979 *The value of travel-time*. London and Sydney: Croom Helm, distributed by the Bibliographic Distribution Center.

Clark, Gracia
1988 Money, sex and cooking: manipulation of the paid/unpaid boundary by Asante market women. in *The social economy of consumption*. Edited by Henry J. Rutz and Benjamin S. Orlove. pp. 323-348. Lanham, Md.: University Press of America.

Cubbin, J.
1975 Quality change and pricing behavior in the U.K. car industry 1956-1968. *Economica* 42:43-58.

de Certeau, Michel
1984 *The practice of everyday life*. Berkeley: University of California Press.

Deaton, Angus and John Muellbauer
1980 *Economics and consumer behavior*. Cambridge: Cambridge University Press.

Dickinson, James and Bob Russell, eds.
1986 *Family, economy and state: the social reproduction process under capitalism*. London and Sydney: Croom Helm.

Douglas, Mary
1966   *Purity and danger: an analysis of the concepts of pollution and taboo.*
       London: Routledge and Kegan Paul.

1972   Deciphering a meal. *Daedalus* 101(1):61-81.

1975   *Implicit meanings.* L;ondon: Routledge and Kegan Paul.

Douglas, Mary and Baron Isherwood
1979   *The world of goods: towards an anthropology of consumption.* London:
       Allen Lane.

Elster, Jon
1979   *Ulysses and the sirens: studies in rationality and irrationality.* Cambridge:
       Cambridge University Press.

Engel, Ernst
1895   Die lebenskosten belgischer arbeiter-familien frueher and jetzt.
       International Statistical Institute Bulletin 9:1-74.

Felix, David
1979   De gustibus disputandum est: changing consumer preferences in economic
       growth. *Explorations in Econoic History* 16:260-296.

Firth, Raymond
1925   Economic psychology of the Maori. *Journal of the Royal Anthropological
       Institute* N.S. 28:340-362.

1929   *Primitive economics of the New Zealand Maori.* London: Routledge.

Fitzsimmons, Vicki Schram and Jeanne L. Hafstrom
1988   Consumption of household production time: bridging the gap between
       theory and empiricism. in *The social economy of consumption.* Edited by
       Henry J. Rutz and Benjamin S. Orlove. pp. 281-296. Lanham, Md.:
       University Press of America

Foxall, Gordon R.
1983   *Consumer choice.* London: The MacMillan Press, Ltd.

Freyre, Gilberto
1936   *Sobrados e mucambos: decadencia do patriarchado rural no Brazil.* Sao
       Paulo: Companhia Editoria Nacional.

Friedman, Milton
1957   *A theory of the consumption function.* Princeton: Princton University
       Press.

Frykman, Jonas and Orvar Lofgren.
1987   *Culture builders: a historical anthropology of middle-class life.* New Brunswick, N.J.: Rutgers University Press.

Gartman, David
1986   Reification of consumer products: a general history illustrated by the case of the American autommobile. *Sociological Theory* 4(Fall):167-185.

Geertz, Clifford
1984   Culture and social change: the Indonesian case. *Man* 19(4):511-532.

Godoy, Ricardo
1984   Ecological degradation and agricultural intensification in the Andean highlands. *Human Ecology* 12(4):359-384.

Gonzales, Michael
1985   *Plantation agriculture and soical control in Northern Peru..* Austin: University of Texas Press.

Goody, Jack
1976   *Production and reproduction: a comparative study of the domestic spehre.* Cambridge University Press.

1982   *Culture, class and cuisine.* Cambridge: Cambridge University Press.

Gross, Daniel R., George Eiten, nancy M. Flowers, Francisca M. Leoi, Madeline Lattman Ritter, and Dennis W. Wener
1979   Ecology and acculturation among native peoples of Central   Brazil. *Science* 206:1043-1050.

Hacking, Ian
1983   *Representing and intervening: introductory topics in the philosophy of natural science.* New York: Cambridge University Press.

Hamilton, Gary G. and Chi-Kong Kai
1988   Consumerism without capitalism: consumption and brand names in late imperial China. in *The social economy of consumption.* Edited by Henry J. Rutz and Benjamin S. Orlove, pp. 253-280. Lanham, Md.: University Press of America.

Hansen, Flemming
1972   *Consumer choice behavior.* a cognitive theory. New York: the Free Press.

Harris, Marvin
1979 'Cannibals and kings': an exchange. *New York Review of Books.* 26(11).

Hartmann, Heidi
1981 The unhappy marriage of marxism and feminism: towards a more progressive union. in *Women and revolution.* Edited by Lydia Sargent, pp. 1-41. Boston: South End Press.

Hattox, Ralph S.
1985 *Coffee and coffeehouses: the origins of a social beverage in the medieval Near East* . Seattle and London: University of Washington Press.

Hicks, John R.
1965 *A revision of demand theory.* Clarendon: Oxford.

Hillier, Bill and Julienne Hanson
1985 *The social logic of social space.* Cambridge: University Press.

Himmelweit, Susan and Simon Mohun
1977 Domestic labour and capital. *Cambridge Journal of Economics* 1:15-31.

Hirschman, Albert
1985 Against parsimony: three easy ways of complicating some categories of economic discourse. *Economics and Philosophy* 1(1):7-21.

1982 *Shifting involvements: private interest and public action.* Princeton: Princeton University Press.

Ironmonger, Duncan
1972 *New commodities and consumer behavior.* Cambridge: Cambridge University Press.

Jay, Martin
1984 *Marxism and totality: the adventures of a concept from Lukacs to Haberrmas.* Berkelely: University of California Press.

Klaren, Peter
1970 *Haciendas azucareras y los origenes del APRA.* Institutos de Estudios Peruanos. Lima: Francisco Moncloa Editores.

Lindenbaum, Shirley
1987 Loaves and fishes in Bangladesh. in *Food and evolution: towards a theory of human food habits.* Edited by Marvin Harris and Eric B. Ross, pp. 427-444. Philadelphia: Temple University Press.

Linder, Staffan B.
1970 *The harried leisure class.* New York: Columbia University Press.

Lorenzen, Stephen A., Arthur D. Murphy, and Henry A. Selby
1988 Household budgetary strategies in urban Mexico: mediating the income-consumption nexus. in *The social economy of consumption;.* Edited by Henry J. Rutz and Benjamin S. Orlove. pp. 399-416. Lanham, Md.: University Press of America.

McCloskey, Donald N.
1985 *The rhetoric of economics.* Madison: University of Wisconsin Press.

McGee, T.G.
1973 *Food dependency in the Pacific: a preliminary statement.* Development Studies Center Working paper No. 2. Canberra: Research School of Pacific Studies, A.N.U..

McKendrick, Neil, John Brewer, and J. H. Plumb
1982 *The birth of a consumer society: the commercialization of eighteenth-century England.* London: Europa Pulbications Limited.

Mansfield, Edwin
1986 *Economics.* 5th edition, pp. 459-500. New York: Norton.

Mauss, Marcel
1967 *The Gift.* New York: W.W. Norton.

Michael, Robert T. and Gary S. Becker
1973 On the new theory of consumer behavior. *Swedish Journal of Econoics* 75:378-395.

Miller, Barbara Diane
1988 gender and low income household expenditures in Jamaica. in *The social economy of consumption.* Edited by Henry J. Rutz and Benjamin S. Orlove, pp. 379-398. Lanham, Md.: University Press of America.

Mintz, Sidney
1985 *Sweetness and power: the place of sugar in modern history.* New York: Viking.

Modigliani, Franco
1986 Life cycle, individual thrift, and the wealth of nations. *Science* 234:704-712.

Morris, Craig
1985   From principles of ecological complementarity to the organization and administration of Tawantinsuyu. in *Andean ecology and civilization*. Edited by Shozo Masuda, Izumi Shimada, and Craig Morris, pp. 477-490. Tokyo: University of Tokyo Press.

Murphy, Robert and Julian Steward
1956   Tappers and trappers: parallel process in acculturation. *Economic Development and Cultural Change* 4:**

Nearly, J.P. and K.W.S. Roberts
1980   Macroeconoic models with quantity rationing. *Economic Journal* 88:788-821.

Nelson, Phillip J.
1970   Information and cnsumer behavior. *Journal of Political Economy* 78:311-329.

1975   The economic consequences of advertising. *Journal of Business* 48:213-241.

Orlove, Benjamin S.
1986   Barter and cash sale on Lake Titicaca: a test of competing approaches. *Current Anthropology* 27(2):85-106.

1987   Stability and change in highland Andean dietary patterns. in *Food and evolution: towards a theory of human food habits*. Edited by Marvin Harris and Eric B. Ross. pp. 481-516. Philadelphia: Temple University Press.

Owen, John D.
1969   *The price of leisure*. Rotterdam: University Press and McGill-Queens University Press.

Paroush, Jacob
1965   The order of acquisition of consumer durables. *Econometrica* 33:225-235.

Platt, Tristan
1978   Symetries en miroir. Le concept de yanantin chez les Macha de Bolivie. *Annales* 33(5-6):1081-1107.

Philibert, Jean-Marc
1988   Consuming culture: a study of simple commodity consumption. in *The social economy of consumption*. Edited by Henry J. Rutz and Benjamin S. Orlove. pp. 59-84. Lanham, Md.: University Press of America.

Polanyi, Karl
1957   The economy as instituted process. in *Trade and markets in the early empires*. Edited by Karl Polanyi, Conrad M. Arensberg, and Harry W. Pearson, pp. 243-269. New York: The Free Press.

Preteceille, Edmond and Jean-Piere Terrail
1985   *Capitalism, consumption and needs*. Translated by Sarah Matthews. New York: Basil Blackwell Inc.

Raznake, Roger
1986   Carnaval in Yura: ritual reflections on ayllu and state relations. *American Anthropologist* 13(4):662-680.

Rogers, John D.
1987   The 1866 grain riots in Sri Lanka. *Comparative Studies in Society and History* 29(3):495-513.

Rotenberg, Robert
1988   Boundaries in time: the dynamics of schedule constraints on household consumption in Vienna, Austria. in *The social economy of consmption*. Edited by Henry J. Rutz and Benjamin S. Orlove, pp. 149-176. Lanham, Md.: University Press of America.

Rowe, John H.
1955   Movimiento nacional Inca del siglo XVIII. *Revista Universitaria del Cuzco* 107:3-33.

Rozin, Paul
1987   Psychobiological perspectives on food preferences and avoidances. in *Food and evolution: towards a theory of human food habits*. Edited by Marvin Harris and Eric B. Ross, pp. 181-206. Philadelphia: Temple University Press.

Rutz, Henry J.
1984   Material affluence and social time. in *Affluence and cultural surviival*. Edited by Richard F. Salisbury and Elisabeth Tooker. Washington, D.C.: American Ethnological Society.

1988   Culture, class and consumer choice: expenditures on food in urban Fijian households. in *The social economy of consumption*. Edited by Henry J. Rutz and Benjamin S. Orlove, pp. 211-252. Lanham, Md.:University Press of America.

Sahlins, Marshall
1974   On the sociology of primitive exchange. in *Stone age economics*. pp. 185-276. Chicago and New York: Aldine-Atherton, Inc.

1976   *Culture and practical reason*. Chicago: Chicago University Press.

1978   Culture as protein and profit. *New York Review of Books* 25(18):45-53.

1979   'Cannibals and kings': an exchange. *New York Review of Books* 26(11).

1985   *Islands of history*. Chicago: Chicago University Press.

Salisbury, Richard
1962   *From stone to steel*. New York: Melbourne and Cambridge Uiversity Presses.

Samuelson, Paul A.
1938   A note on the pure theory of consumer behavior. *Economica* 5:61.

Saul, Mahir
1988   Expenditure and intrahousehold patterns among the southern Bobo of Burkina Faso. in *The social economy of consumption*. Edited by Henry J. Rutz and Benjamin S. Orlove, pp. 349-378. Lanham, Md.: University Press of America.

Schama, Simon
1986   *The embarrassment of riches: an interpretation of Dutch culture in the golden age*. New York: Alfred A. Knopf.

Schneider, Jane
1978   Peacocks and penguins: the political economy of European cloth and colors. *American Ethnologist* 5(3):413-447.

1988   The anthropology of cloth. *Annual review of anthropology*. in press.

Simmel, Georg
1904   Fashion. *International Quarterly* X(October):130-155.

1908   *Soziologie, untersuchungen uber die formen der vergesellschaftung*. Leipzig: Verlag von Duncker and Humblot.

Smith, Carol
1984   Local history in global context: social and economic transitions in Western Guatemala. *Comparative Studies in Society and History* 26(2): 193-228.

Smith, W. Robertson
1889   *Kinship and marriage in early Arabia*. Boston

Sombart, Werner
1967   *Luxury and capitalism*. Ann Arbor: The University of Michigan Press.

Stigler, George J. and Gary S. Becker
1977 De gustibus non est disputandum. *American Economic Review* 67:76-90.

Stoler, Ann
1977 Rice harvesting in Kali Loro: a study of class and labor in rural Java. *American Ethnologist* 4(4):678-698.

1985 *Capitalism and confrontatilon in Sumatra's plantation belt, 1870-1979.* New Haven: Yale Univrsity Press.

Stone, J.R.N.
1966 Spending and saving in relation to income and wealth. *L'Industria* 4:1-29.

Thompson, Edward P.
1971 The moral economy of the English crowd in the eighteenth century. *Past and Present* 50:76-136.

Tilly, Louise A.
1971 The food riot as a form of political conflict in France. *Journal of Interdisciplinary History* 2(1):23-57.

Turner, Terence S.
1980 The social skin. in *Not work alone: a cross-cultural view of activities superfluous to survival.* Edited by Jeremy Cherfas and Roger Lewin. pp. 112-143. Beverly Hills: Sage Publications.

Turrentine, Thomas
1987 Towards a dynamic model of vehicle choice behavior. Consumer behavior and alternative fuels: New Zealand project, working paper no. 1, University of California, Davis.

Veblen, Thorstein
1899 *The theory of the leisure class. new York: Macmillan Co.*

Wachtel, Nathan
1982 The mitimas of the Cochabamba Valley: the colonization policy of Huanyna Capac. in *The Inca and Aztec states, 1400-1800.* Edited by George A. Collier, Renato I. Rosaldo, and John D. Wirth, pp. 199-236. New York: Academic Press.

Wasserstrom, Robert and Jan Rus
1980 Civil-religious hierarchies in Central Chiapas: a critical perspective. *American Ethnologist* 7(3):466-478.

Weatherill, Lorna
1986   Consumer behavior and social status in England, 1660-1750. *Continuity and Change* 1(2):191-216.

Weber, Jacques
1987   C=R-I. My god, my gold! Reflexions sur la portee du concept de consumation. in *Ecrits d'ailleus: Georges Bataille et les ethnologues.* Edited by Dominique Lecoq and Jean-Luc Lory, pp. 39-64. Paris: Editions de la Maison des Science de l'Homme.

Weber, Max
1922   *Wirtschaft und gesellschaft.* Tubingen: J.C.B. Mohr.

Weismantel, M.J.
1988   The children cry for bread: hegemony and the transformation of consumption. in *The social economy of consumption.* Edited by Henry J. Rutz and Benjamin s. Orlove, pp. 85-100. Lanham, Md.: University Press of America.

White, Benjamin
1976   Population, involution and employment in rural Java. *Development and Change* 7(3):267-290.

Williams, Rosalind H.
1982   *Dream worlds: mass consumption in late nineteenth-century France.* Berkeley: University of California Press.

Wilk, Richard W.
1988   House, home and consumer decision making in two cultures. in *The social economy of consumption.* Edited by Henry J. Rutz and Benjamin S. Orlove, pp. 297-322. Lanham, Md.: University Press of America.

Wolf, Eric
1969   *Peasants.* Englewood Cliffs, N.J.: Prentice-Hall, Inc.

1982   *Europe and the people without history.* Berkelely and Los Angeles: University of California Press.

1986   The vicissitudes of the closed corporate peasant community. *American Ethnologist* 13(2):325-329.

Wong, R. Bin
1982   Food riots in the Qing Dynastry. *Journal of Asian Studies* 41(4):767-88.

Zalkin, Michael
1988   National and internatonal determinants of food consumption in revolutionary Nicaragua, 1979-86. in *The social economy of consumption*. Edited by Henry J. Rutz and Benjamin S. Orlove. pp. 121-148. Lanham, Md.: University Press of America.

CONSUMING CULTURE:
A STUDY OF SIMPLE COMMODITY CONSUMPTION

Jean-Marc Philibert

Introduction

The term simple commodity consumption will no doubt amuse or annoy, depending on how punctilious one is towards Marxist terminology. This pseudo-Marxist concept is used first to suggest that insights into consumption can profitably result from a neo-Marxist approach and, second, to ask whether or not there is in the field of consumption an analog to simple commodity production.

It may not seem obvious at first that an approach considering production as the diagnostic dimension of economic systems has a great deal to contribute to an understanding of consumption. But it has, if one is willing to set aside for a moment the dimension of utility, the materialistic aspect of consumption as it were, and to examine it as a cultural act. One of the advantages of a neo-Marxist framework is that it highlights power relations in societies that anthropology has been content for too long to portray as integrated cultures.[1] Anthropologists have been lax in pointing out, on the one hand, that the "official culture" they described in any given society was not necessarily everyone's culture and, on the other, that knowledge is an important political resource. Crick (1982:303) makes the latter point simply but effectively when he writes, "One of the important aspects of everyday knowledge is that it keeps certain people in power and certain others in the dark".

Marxism has always had a critical attitude to knowledge, although, as we shall see, the role of ideology and culture was perhaps not fully appreciated before Gramsci. Though all Marxists (and some non-Marxists as well) believe that in the "last instance" economic factors are determinant, it is obvious that some writers reach this stage of final analysis sooner than others and are quicker to bring the economic base into play.[2] Anthropologists like myself who sit uncomfortably between the two stools of cultural anthropology and neo-Marxism put up with the tension inherent in the refusal to commit themselves exclusively to either paradigm because each tradition complements the other in important ways: Marxism offers a welcome corrective to the politically aseptic view of culture found in cultural anthropology; anthropology points to the 19th century materialism of Marxism and its subsequent failure to appreciate the role of culture. One way of applying the insights found in each tradition is to focus on the cultural content of intergroup relations. In this perspective, one believes there is more to class relations than mere relations of production. As Worsley (1981:234) remarks,

> ... Groups and categories of people are allocated to roles and
> sectors not just in the economic order but in a total societal and
> cultural division of rights and duties, division of labor, and

differential access to valued goods, including power and immaterial goods.

This brings us to a second reason for coining the term simple commodity consumption. The study of peasant societies shows that the capitalist penetration of pre-capitalist economies has not resulted in the predicted disappearance of non-capitalist modes of production; it has led instead to the emergence of complex social formations in which dominant (capitalist) and subordinate (pre-capitalist) modes of production coexist. The social groups studied by anthropologists often have social systems in which economic relations are commodified, except for labor power, and yet these groups have managed to retain a use-value perspective.[3] The analytical focus of neo-Marxist anthropologists concerned with the study of interclass relations of production is of course the maintenance of such non-capitalist labor systems.

Let us assume for the sake of argument that there are patterns of consumption occupying an intermediate position between pre-capitalist and capitalist forms of consumption in a manner analogous to the position held by simple commodity production halfway between pre-capitalist and capitalist modes of production. Such an assumption would naturally direct our attention to the ways in which the partial commoditization of social life in peasant societies affects the role played by consumption in the social and cultural ordering of social groups. At the risk of unduly testing the reader's patience, let us indulge for the moment in a tripartite model of consumption: pre-capitalist consumption; petty or simple commodity consumption; and commodity consumption.

How does someone interested in simple commodity consumption study interclass relations of consumption? First by acknowledging that capitalist penetration and domination are not simply of a material nature. To quote Worsley (1981: 245) again,

> Among the Third World mass, cultural nationalism, and even political ideology, has long been displaced by consumerist values . . . Workers are now psychically incorporated, not via a Protestant ethic work so much as via their transmutation into consumers . . . The atomization of society produced by consumerism is now countervailed by new forms of mass identity and solidarity (e.g.,World Cup soccer, Disneyland).

This capitalist penetration also takes the form of penetration of industrially produced goods. The borrowing of such goods (food, clothing, means of communication or transportation) is not entirely explained by their greater convenience or utility value. Underpinning such goods are classificatory schemes, sets of ideas and perceptions, which gave rise to these items being produced in the first place.

A symbolic, but all too real, capitalist penetration takes two forms: (1) that of status-giving goods and activities borrowed from a prestigious Western world in order to share in this highly valued state of modernity; (2) the largely unforeseen insertion of Western classificatory schemes in local symbolic systems when such goods and activities become accepted. These cognitive structures assert themselves through the process of utilization.[4] I am describing here a process that may appear to some as singularly anthropomorphic, something almost in the nature of a conspiracy theory, but no more so than the operation of any formal organizational context such as an educational system for example. A structure of recognition underpins the use of these goods and activities; once this structure is in place, it then frames and limits other alternatives. Perceiving such structures is of course more difficult than understanding the use of goods as status symbols, a well-known process.

Can peasants resist ideological penetration? Do they have the means to refuse, incorporate, or subvert foreign classificatory schemes? Is the end product necessarily cultural subjugation? These are the questions raised here according to a model of society in which social groups, classes and fragments of classes, not the individuals/households/firms of liberal economics, are the main protagonists and in which culture is the terrain on which group struggle takes place. The article is divided into three parts: in the first part, some models of consumption in pre-capitalist and capitalist societies are reviewed; in the second, the link between consumption and power is analyzed; and in the last, the idea of consumption as "silent production" and a form of hidden resistance is examined.

Models of Consumption

A good starting point is the valuable model of consumption developed by Douglas and Isherwood in their anthropology of consumption. According to these authors, objects create meanings. They are needed to make the categories of culture visible (Douglas and Isherwood 1979:74). Consumers choose goods as part of a process of "cognitive construction", as part of a "classifying project". Goods are markers, counters in a competition in which advantage accrues to those who are well-placed in the system. Knowledge is power, an anthropological commonplace if there ever was one. Going beyond the obvious level of utility, consumption for Douglas and Isherwood amounts to a ritual activity that has to do with social inclusion and exclusion. In this activity, one is called upon to give as well as to receive marking services. The consumer, "instead of being regarded as the owner of certain goods, should be seen as operating a pattern of periodicities in consumption behaviour" (1979:123). Throughout, the motivation of the consumer is to obtain as well as to control information about the "changing cultural scene" (1979:95). There is finally a feedback from consumption to employment as those who belong to the top consumption class obtain a higher rate of earnings than others (1979:181).

Douglas and Isherwood advocate the use of an information model to understand the rituals of consumption. In this way they attempt to go beyond a purely utilitarian approach to consumption. The fact that people eat for sustenance hardly explains how many meals a day they consume, the people they eat with, or the classification of appropriate food for different occasions. It is with food as it is with sex: the satisfaction of a biological need is encoded in a set of cultural prescriptions and possibilities.

Douglas and Isherwood contrast the meaning encoded in sets of objects in complex industrial societies (and in different consumption classes within those societies) with consumption in small-scale, simpler societies. This has been cited as both one of the book's strengths at the level of an illuminating analogy, and one of its greatest weaknesses (Rosman 1982:212). The root of the problem is that the authors have constructed no theoretical foundation for assuming that consumption is conceptually the same in industrial societies and in the Third World. This is crucial to their view that consumption is a system of meanings. Their conclusions are consequently equivocal -- "Where the argument leads is hard to see" -- and evasive -- "Anthropology is not the discipline for finding solutions to problems" (1979:202). "The next steps which should follow from this argument are in philosophy, in econometrics, and in sociology" (1979:204).

Moreover, although Douglas and Isherwood rely heavily on a notion of differential time, which varies in terms of usage and value between consumption classes, their conclusions regarding time and consumption are self-fulfilling consequences of their assumptions. They somewhat uncritically assume that time exhibits a conceptual unity as a commodity that can be saved, spent, or wasted, an assumption that leads to assertions such as "it seems that the poor always have time on their hands, and less things to do with it than the rich" (Ibid.:194). This, the authors claim, is because the poor are not fully involved in production, which in turn is linked to low levels of consumption. This is indeed a view from the top.

While Douglas and Isherwood concerned themselves with commodity consumption, some French sociologists have attempted to develop models of consumption in the Third World corresponding to our categories of pre-capitalist consumption and simple commodity consumption. (See *L'Homme et la Société*, No. 55-58, 1980). These authors propose to look at the agents of consumption, be they individuals, social classes or states, and at the categories of consumed objects, the factors stimulating various forms of consumption including conspicuous consumption, and the means of diffusion of new patterns of consumption (Lombard 1980:143).

In traditional societies, goods are often signs of an ascribed social identity expressed in, as well as delineated by, rights of residence and ownership, position in a kinship system, participation in networks of exchange, and custody of parts of a shared symbolic universe. As D'Haene observes, "The object has no [semiotic] value except as a sign of the relationship it memorizes" (1980:183,

62

my translation). The semiological value of an object, then, is as a sign of an underlying social identity; it is the signifier of a signified social reality. To ensure correspondence between signifiers of social status, conspicuous consumption is often regulated: the right to wear certain clothes, to display certain adornments, to live in particular places may be reserved for given categories of individuals. However, with the advent of capitalism and the commoditization of social life, social statuses are no longer fixed by custom but are acquired temporarily through convention. The symbols of such social statuses themselves become commodities that are now accessible to all through the medium of money. As Adam (1980:155) points out, this causes a true semiological displacement: the use of money that makes it possible to acquire the signs of a given function or status creates at the same time the illusion that the full function or status itself is acquired by extension. The object now comes ahead of what is signified: no longer a sign, it becomes an image or a dream.

As one moves from the logic of consumption found in traditional societies to the logic of consumption in Westernized societies, new images displace traditional symbolism. Following the privatization of social life, individuals and groups find themselves isolated and in competition with one another by means of object-signs. Acculturated individuals purchase objects in order to attain what their image suggests, but there is never enough behind the image. Their desire is forever renewed but never satisfied. Their quest for social identity requires that they spend more and more, yet the logic of consumption itself cancels the sign-effect of their acquisitions (D'Haene 1980:183). This is so because of the double function of consumption, that of social integration as well as segregation. People express or mark their status by manipulating objects to form a discourse, manipulating signs to signal membership in a reference group. Goods and wants thus filter down from a model group to those deemed socially inferior. Yet these desires and the means to satisfy them also maintain distance and exclude. As Baudrillard (1970) argues, objects that are commercialized and serialized derive their semantic value from a prototype that is the sign of high social status. However, when the objects become readily available, the impact of their ownership is diminished. This has happened in the West to reduce the *cachet* of television sets, video recording units, hi fi sets, calculators, digital watches, and even personal computers. In efforts to counteract this tendency, people pay thousands of dollars for a Swiss watch, now transformed into a jewellery item, that is no more accurate than an inexpensive Japanese quartz watch. Everyone but the very rich is always one step behind. Indeed, "the social paradigm is also the paradigm of consumption which first presupposes wealth" (Adam 1980:153, my translation).

In the Third World, the bureaucratic neo-bourgeoisie acts as a relay for the diffusion of the Western way of life. The ruling class often adopts a modernist stance, but members of this class do not simply mimic Western archetypes; the nationalist consciousness developed at the time of independence from former colonial masters leads to syncretism in this matter. One finds designer sunglasses but also traditional dress. A few years ago in Vanuatu[5], a rebel leader who advocated a return to traditional ways was sighted in a government building with his assistants. The leader wore khaki trousers with matching safari shirt and a French beret. His men were naked except for customary loincoths that proclaimed the traditional legitimacy of the movement, yet they also carried attache cases to show they were nonetheless sophisticated and not to be taken for local yokels. In effect, they were claiming equal competence in two cultural worlds through their consumption of clothes and accessories. This juxtaposition of symbols derived from the powerful West with those found in the weak, local culture, in other words, the simultaneous pariahization and brahmanization of a political movement represents a potent manipulation of cultural codes.

The desire for Western goods, not only consumer goods but also productive goods from mining equipment to oil rigs to medical and educational systems, is most clearly expressed by those in power. This elite has its own practice of objects based on Western models of consumption. Although the ruling elite does not share the position of the Western bourgeoisie, it may nonetheless have equivalent aspirations.[6] In fact, members of this group must state their legitimacy by using the required object-signs. Such an elite has often assimilated the values and way of life of Western society (D'Haene 1980:185).

Anthropologists will no doubt feel uncomfortable with a sociological model contrasting consumption in traditional and modern societies along the only too predictable lines of ascription versus achievement. While the general validity of this distinction is not disputed, it does not facilitate the task of anthropologists who must differentiate between "traditional" societies. Moreover, what does one find among those who are not members of a ruling elite or in those parts of the Third World where capitulation to capitalism does not seem either natural or inevitable? Consumption is fundamental to understanding those cultures in the Third World where petty commodity production for the capitalist market is well-established while at the same time the capitalist mode of production is kept at a distance.

If we start from the premises that, among other considerations, (1) consumption amounts to an appropriation of meanings symbolized in the use of particular objects; (2) people consume according to a code of recognition, a semiotic chain invested in a (bound) series of objects; and (3) people speak about themselves in their consumption choices, then we can begin to deconstruct the "texts" that consumers create. In other words, we can proceed beyond the utility value of objects to the messages inscribed with and within them in the Third World. As Hall and Jefferson (1976:55) put it,

> Objects and commodities do not mean any one thing, they "mean"
> only because they have been arranged, according to social use,
> into cultural codes of meaning.

Tweed jackets, corduroy trousers and Clark Wallabies do not naturally go together though they have now become as indispensable to the male professorial role as developing, early in one's career, a pronounced academic stoop. Compare the following "patterns of significance" from Vanuatu, one found in a "traditional" setting, the other in an urban context.

You can't trust people with trousers !

Some important social and cultural contrasts were drawn when, during the 1983 Vanuatu electoral campaign, a member of Parliament addressed his rural constituents on the radio in the following terms:

> If you vote for me, I know that I can look after your needs. I am a member of Na-Griamel party and I know your traditional culture well. I am a member of Parliament, but I am really on the side of traditions. During the electoral campaign, there will be much talk, many lies and a lot of different political signs. If you see someone who goes naked, this man is one of yours, naked people of Santo. Someone who goes naked you can vote for. Such a man will defend you, look after your needs, protect your land. You shall hold on to these for the rest of your life.

While the first reaction to this statement may be to ponder the disquieting implication that all politicians really sound alike in all societies, let us consider the sets of contrasts used to "speak" to rural constituents: on the one hand, a traditional notion of political legitimacy is expressed through the set of nakedness, truth, traditional knowledge, and land; on the other, people who wear trousers, lies, modernity (parliamentary nation-state), and land spoliators are grouped together. To belong means to possess natural rights to land by virtue of membership in a discrete group which has a culture of its own and is associated with tutelary spirits found in the local landscape. The term sometimes applied in this insular world to those without traditional land rights is drift wood, something that has lost its roots and is washed ashore on foreign land. This strong, dichotomous view of tradition and modernity informing rural political legitimacy contrasts with the code found in a peri-urban village.

On "good houses"

I have for many years been interested in the conspicuous consumption of Erakor villagers (Philibert 1981, 1984, 1986). There was only one concrete house in 1973 in this peri-urban village which then numbered some 800 inhabitants. The number grew to 20 in 1979 and 31 in 1983. The Villagers' understanding of what constitutes a modern house is surprisingly thorough. *Haos i kamplit*, a fully furnished house, means having all the specialized furniture/implements found in rooms with specialized functions (living rooms, dining rooms . . .) such as buffets, bookshelves, curtains in windows, tiles on the floor, plastic tulips in plastic crystal-like vases, and pseudo-traditional artifacts, of the sort bought by tourists, on the walls. This form of housing is very much at odds with the "traditional" design of a one-room hut made up of split palm trees with a thatched or corrugated iron roof (to catch rain water).[7]

As Baudrillard (1970) points out, objects organize themselves into panoplies, into collections. An object is not simply purchased for its utility value, but for its position in a series of objects with a signification of its own. Brand names play in our society an important part in imposing a coherent vision of the whole seen as made up of indissociable parts. It is a chain not simply linking single objects but signifiers as well. Together, they amount to a super-object yet more complex. Consider the matching green or almond appliances in our kitchens (refrigerator, stove, dishwasher, kettle, toaster, mixer . . .) which carry a more coherent message than the same implements in mixed colors or simply white, because the relation between each appliance and the user is now mediated through the whole. The merchandise becomes culturalized, its utility value becomes sublimated into "ambiance", a sort of neo-culture. We are familiar with this phenomenon in our society with objects of consumption reproducing our cultural frames, our map of understandings. Our own culture specifies various constitutions of social identity (sex, age, class), which are expressed in and through the social uses of commodities.

Wealthier villagers in Erakor living in concrete houses with all the modern amenities have recently started to build small thatched huts in their yard where they can sit on coral floors covered with mats, like the poor, to prepare and drink kava (*Piper methysticum*) with friends. The line between tradition and modernity is drawn differently in this example, emphasizing the open-ended way in which signifiers fit together in a commodity-based society. As Sahlins puts it, the code works as an open set. (1976:185).

Moving from objects to their underlying reality as signs, we are confronted by different classificatory schemes which are at the very heart of the cultural representations of social groups. Acculturation is in a sense the borrowing or the imposition of someone else's symbolic order. This brings us to relations existing between cognitive structures. Gramsci's notion of hegemony is useful to explore the cultural dimension of interclass relations and the role played by ideological domination.

On Ideology

Gramsci's thought, as jotted down in the form of notes in his *Prison Notebooks* written during his incarceration from 1926 to 1937, must be pieced together: Gramsci died before he could accomplish this task himself. Moreover, to add to the difficulty, what he wrote was censored and many ideas could not be expressed plainly. His thought has been submitted to a great deal of exegesis and, as expected, there exists more than one interpretation of his ideas. I am basing this brief presentation of Gramsci's ideas on Simon (1982) and Mouffe (1979).

Gramsci uses the term hegemony in a special sense and the following is the simplest exposition of it that I have come across:

> The starting point for Gramsci's concept of hegemony is that a class and its representatives exercise power over subordinate classes by means of a combination of coercion and persuasion . . . Hegemony is a relation, not of domination by means of force, but of consent by means of political and ideological leadership. It is the organization of consent (Simon 1982:21).

For some Marxists, ideology is closely associated with the interests of a particular social class and is dealt with as false consciousness, the result of mystification, when an already established class manages to impose its perspective and world view on other social classes which then accept them as their own. Gramsci believes that a class, in order to rule, must go beyond its narrow class interests to take into account the interests of other classes or fractions of classes in order to develop broad-based alliances. It must develop a role of national leadership by articulating popular aspirations so that its class' interests and world view appear to represent general interests and the general will. It is ideology which gives such varied social groups and forces their unity. For him,

> Ideologies are not individual fancies, rather they are embodied in communal modes of living and acting . . . they are the uncritical and largely unconscious way in which a person perceives the world . . . and are compounded of folklore, myth and popular experience (Simon 1982:25).

In other words, ideology has to do with the way individuals and groups phenomenologically construct and understand their reality, what has here been called classificatory schemes. For Gramsci, all men have a "spontaneous philosophy" made up of language, "common sense", "good sense", popular religion and "the entire system of beliefs, superstitions, opinions, ways of seeing things and acting... collectively bundled together under the name of folklore" (SPN:323). (See *The Study of Philosophy* and also *Critical Notes on An Attempt at Popular Sociology.*)

According to Gramsci, class relationships are located in the sphere of economic production (economic coercion) and in state control (political coercion), but also in what he terms "civil society", institutions such as churches, political parties, trade unions, mass media, educational systems, cultural organizations... His contribution as a Marxist thinker is to show clearly that civil society is one of the terrains of class struggle and that it is there that hegemony develops and is exercised.

Anthropologists will have no difficulty accepting the idea that "subjects are not originally given but are always produced by ideology through a socially determined ideological field, so that subjectivity is always the product of social practice" (Mouffe, 1979:186). It also implies, when consciousness is derived from ideologies and when such ideologies are the world view of "social blocks" (class alliances), that all forms of consciousness are in effect political. This means that the project of anthropology, like that of other social sciences, is by nature political: there is no neutral, ideologically-free terrain on which to stand, nor has there ever been any. This led Gramsci to consider seriously the role of the intellectual: the symbolic ordering of social life and the social ordering of symbols and ideas are part of the same process, albeit a very complex one which cannot be apprehended by such simple notions as projection from one level of reality to another. We must allow for a large amount of indeterminancy and contradiction here.

Bourdieu's (1977: 83) notion of *habitus* helps us to understand the social determination of consciousness. *Habitus* is

a system of lasting, transposable dispositions, which integrating past experiences, functions at every moment as a *matrix of perceptions, appreciations, and actions* and makes possible the achievement of infinitely diversified tasks, thanks to analogical transfers of schemes permitting the solution of similarly shaped problems . . .

Let us examine a practice of objects to try to see what the relationship between objects represents and how the objects are transformed, contrasted and consumed. The following example from Vanuatu illustrates the embedded quality of the metaphors with which people transform an anomalous object into something both new and familiar. At the end of World War II, a Small Nambas tribesman on Malekula Island received, as a parting gift from an American serviceman, a lipstick in a gold colored metal case inscribed with the word "Hollywood." Its new owner covered the case with spider webs, made the required incantations to give it magical power, and transformed the lipstick into a traditional means to transport himself instantaneously from island to island.

The mental reconstruction of the lipstick as a means of transportation occurs through a practice of *bricolage*. The statements constructed with the lipstick concern metaphors of value, efficacy and agency, at the very least. They assert that a lipstick is an object of value to be traditionally protected and concealed in spider webs; that a lipstick can be a magical vehicle; that the power to effect this transformation rests with the owner, the recipient of a gift. Clearly, this construction employs an established vocabulary and syntax: only the object itself and the event of categorizing it are new. The act of using the lipstick in a way its manufacturers never envisioned establishes a here and now that is fertile ground for analysis. This created present is highlighted for us by distance in time and space between the serviceman and the tribesman, between World War II with its aircraft as agents of global violence and magical flight in a tiny, insular world, between the meanings we associate with lipstick and Hollywood magic on the one hand and traditional magical objects that create magical movement on the other.

We would not presume that the Vanuatu tribesman experienced the same contrasts or that he structures his practice of objects according to our rules. But we would assume that categorizing this alien lipstick is a process that creates contrasts and requires a structuring that occurs in its use.

A second example of consumption practices from Vanuatu will illustrate some of the dialectical relations between hegemonic structures and allow us to reflect on the ways social consciousness is objectified in cultural action. Jolly (1982) has recently examined the relation between cultural traditions (*kastom*)[8] and modernity among members of a traditional society, the Sa speakers of South Pentecost. She describes the recent penetration of the cash economy and wonders what the commoditization of food practices will do to the Sa culture in which food production and consumption are constitutive of gender identity through a division of labor, food taboos, and mythical associations.

Jolly also believes that another threat to the Sa speakers' symbolic integrity lies in the performance for tourists of an important ritual, the *Gol* or Pentecost land dive.[9] The staging of this spectacular ritual for tourists is particularly tempting for the Sa speakers as they can earn hard-to-get money by doing what they do best, that is to say by being themselves. The question is, are they remaining themselves? Jolly expresses concern that "the selling of traditional life-styles converts lived practices into folkloric spectacles" (Jolly 1982:352).

We confront here the Sa speakers in their role of producer and consumer of a cultural web. We find a dissociation in their practice as they now produce two rituals: one for themselves which is deemed efficacious, and one for tourists which is a staged or empty ritual. A cultural phase displacement must occur: people do not theatricalize their lives for others without taking on, for at least the length of the representation, alter's view of themselves. If there is, as is often the case, contempt toward a public which does not know enough to be able to distinguish between the real performance and its simulacrum, some of this scorn is also heaped on the actors themselves for having to play to such a poor public. The ritual statements made in the staged *Gol* are grammatical, they follow the syntactic rules, yet the ritual *parle pour ne rien dire:* it is an empty discourse.[10]

At issue here is not the fetishization of a culture as against symbolic integrity: traditional societies are no more, and no less, natural than modern societies in this respect, as both state various constitutions of identity, place, gender, local politics, etc. What takes place is a code switch. Commoditization converts the land dive into a sign with a different meaning, and power attaches itself differently to commodities than to other sorts of signs. In commodity-based societies, one finds control of the code while constant supervision of signs is abandoned. Clothing provides an illustration of this. In our society, social actors (designers and consumers) are given a large amount of freedom "to make fashion statements", as the advertisers call it, using what appear to be endless permutations of fabric, color, cut and accessories to signify, for example, the respective qualities of masculinity and femininity. Some social groups may even challenge the cultural code by manipulating the signs, as in the unisex style. In pre-capitalist societies, both signs and codes are controlled.[11] Hence, in staging a ritual, it is not only the valence of the signs that is changed; a switch is also being made to a new, more open system, a sort of symbolic free trade system. As the principles encoding signifiers change, so does the signified.

The Sa speakers are also consumers of this ritual, and the act of consumption establishes a present relative to time and space. The presence of spectators, and European spectators at that, vastly increases the spatio-temporal referent, although it is hard to say how much actors and spectators take in of the "other". The symbolic interchange takes place between actors who do not know their public and spectators who do not speak the actors' language. A comedy of errors, Jolly would say. Yet we must be careful not to over-emphasize the cultural impact of the West on "simpler" societies. The lack of communication mentioned above, the intellectual equivalent of ships passing in the night, can be an asset as well as a liability. How is staging rituals for tourists different from manufacturing artifacts for sale in the capital, something most anthropologists would probably encourage because it maintains traditional craft production? In both cases, the makers, ignorant of the uses to which the product is put, are equally alienated from their product.

Meaning and Power

Commodities are cultural signs that reproduce the cultural frames, the sets of understandings, which gave rise to their being produced in the first place. What is the relationship between dominant and subordinate systems of classification? Let us turn briefly to the link between meaning and power. The work of members of the Centre for Contemporary Cultural Studies at the University of Birmingham (Hall & Jefferson 1982) is particularly useful in this respect.
According to them,

> . . . just as different groups and classes are unequally ranked in relation to one another, in terms of their productive relations, wealth and power, so *cultures* are differently ranked, and stand in opposition to one another in relations of domination and subordination, along the scale of "cultural power". The definitions of the world, the "maps of meaning" which express the life situations of those groups which hold the monopoly of power in society, command the greatest weight and influence, secrete the greatest legitimacy (Clark, Hall *et al,* 1976:11).

How classes gain a monopoly of social authority for their own definition of reality and how they are able to reproduce it is what Gramsci was on to.

A hegemonic cultural order tries to *frame* all competing definitions of the world within *its* range. It provides the horizon of thought and action within which conflicts are thought through, appropriated . . . obscured . . . or contained. A hegemonic order prescribes, not the specific content of ideas, but the *limits* within which ideas and conflicts move and are resolved (Clark, Hall *et al* 1976:39).

The underlying classificatory schemes are of course unconscious. As Bourdieu observes (1979:559), they are objectified only when they have ceased to work in a tacit, practical manner, when the guardians of the established order, rather in the way grammarians attempt to guide and order "proper" speech, believe such principles must be codified and explained. It then becomes the official system whose principles are clearly expressed in the hegemonic apparatuses of school, church, law and other social and cultural agencies. Durkheim's sociology was part of such an objectifying effort (Hobsbawm 1985:269).

I have documented in a recent article (Philibert 1986) the development of hegemonic discourse in Vanuatu. Members of the Vanuatu political elite are now socializing their fellow countrymen, without their knowledge, to a new political culture, that of the nation-state. They are attempting to develop a national identity by putting forward a generic, "no-name brand" of culture based on the invention of neo-traditions (see Hobsbawm and Ranger 1983). A bureaucratic neo-bourgeoisie is in the process of establishing its intellectual, moral and political role of leadership. In its hands, modern political culture has not only become metaphorised as culture itself, which has the effect of denying the existence of sectional interests, but what is more, it is presented as a collage of the best of what traditional culture has to offer. What is constitutive of Vanuatu social identity, the image of the past as well as that of the future, is now controlled, as never before, by one group of *ni-Vanuatu* (people of Vanuatu). Through various cultural policies, members of this incipient social class have become the arbiters of what tradition is; they now hold the seal that authenticates practices as traditional.

Cultural hegemony is not simply restricted to one's own society. Are the peasants importing Western goods not also importing cultural signifiers, and if so, does this necessarily lead to a self-inflicted cultural subjugation? The expected consequences of imported goods need not always be some form of consumerism. The tendency may be diverted by rejecting or altering the objects or by using them with respect to goals and contexts alien to the imposed system. Peasants may respond to encroaching capitalism by transcending or outwitting the dominant social order without necessarily leaving it. After all, this is what happened in the field of production. De Certeau (1984) considers consumption to be a kind of production, a "secondary, silent" production hidden in the process of utilization. De Certeau's objective is to evaluate the production of images and representations against the secondary production that occurs in their consumption. To expanding, more invasive systems of production "corresponds *another* production, called 'consumption'. The latter is devious; it is dispersed, but it insinuates itself everywhere, silently and almost invisibly, because it does not manifest itself

71

through its own products, but rather through its *ways of using* the products imposed by a dominant economic order" (de Certeau 1984:xiii).

Reading offers a prototype for rethinking other kinds of consumption in which the user has often been seen as passive but is in fact creative, appropriating the written text and "inventing" memories: "a different world (the reader's) slips into the author's place" and makes itself at home, transforming the borrowed space of the text like a tenant furnishing an apartment with acts and memories (de Certeau 1984:xxi). Readers wander through an imposed system helping themselves: "Readers are travellers: they move across lands belonging to someone else, like nomads poaching their way across fields they did not write despoiling the wealth of Egypt to enjoy it themselves." (de Certeau 1984:174).

This process of "poaching" can be subversive in reference to the ways products imposed by a dominant economic order are used. This is especially evident today in those parts of the Third World where an obvious contrast exists between a persistent traditional way of life and the capitalist mode. There, the concealed subversion that occurs through consumption can encourage the independence of the very people that capitalist production would co-opt.

De Certeau (1984:xiii) refers to South American reaction to the Spanish conquest in the following terms:

Submissive, and even consenting to their subjection, the Indians nevertheless often made of the rituals, representations, and laws imposed on them something quite different from what their conquerors had in mind; they subverted them not by rejecting or altering them, but by using them with respect to ends and references foreign to the system they had no choice but to accept. They were other within the very colonization that outwardly assimilated them; their use of the dominant social order deflected its power, which they lacked the means to challenge; they escaped it without leaving it. The strength of their difference lay in procedures of "consumption."

Not only in South America, but also in Oceania, the permeability of systems of ideas to foreign constructs in economic, political, and religious spheres may paradoxically also be a source of strength.

There are not, to my knowledge, a large number of studies of the semiotics of consumption in the Third World. In a recent one, Adam (1984) recants somewhat his earlier view of consumption as the direct *assujettissement consommatoire* (subjection through consumption) of the Third World, a self-imposed form of cultural alienation.[12] Though commodity consumption still amounts for him to an enormous social theater with individuals putting on, as if they were on stage, the very social statuses they lack in real life, he now feels one must not overestimate the impact of borrowed Western signifiers. Many semantic displacements occur when Western signs are borrowed to fit a symbolic grid foreign to their production. In order to express their upward social mobility, African consumers will imitate one of the prestigious local models (well-known musicians, wealthy merchants or upper cadres in the civil service), rather than the archetype derived from the European ruling class. According to Adam, sociocultural signs are never arbitrary in the manner of linguistic signs: they describe and stipulate the attributes of prestige-carrying tasks and functions in the social hierarchy (1984:7).

A successful example of the way a local culture is able to appropriate imported elements is found in Janglish or Japanese English. In a tongue in cheek article, the journalist R. Whymant reports cases of borrowed English such as "creap" for coffee creamers, a wedding hall calling itself "a green and human plaza", a beverage named "pokhari sweat", etc. Janglish is "cheap chic", meaningless English used for adding local color to commercial goods. According to Whymant, "Janglish makes the pushers of *Franglais* seem like small time crooks. The French have the decency to leave the pirated words more or less intact. Not so the Japanese... "(Manchester Guardian Weekly, March 30, 1986:9). Examples of language misappropriation are "tatchi gaymu" (petting games), "imejji-uppu" (to improve one's image) and "no pan kissa" (coffee shop with panty-less waitresses). Not satisfied with such mutilations, the Japanese further claim borrowed English words as their own: "sebiro" is Japanese for a suit, a term originally derived from the Japanese pronunciation of "Savile Row".

One feels duty bound to point out that there exist other cases of linguistic borrowing in which local cultures have contained with less success the penetration of their vehicular language, such as *Franglais* or various sorts of pidgin English. Moreover, the empirical evidence available to me of the ability of local groups to outwit the dominant cultural order is far from reassuring. I have for some years now studied an undeservedly neglected sociological type in Melanesia, the peri-urban village, because it represents a natural laboratory in which to monitor the ever-shifting boundaries of rural and urban life. Peri-urbanites are neither peasants, nor proletarians: they occupy a social world which inwardly remains a village, while outwardly it has taken on the appearance of a town neighborhood. Established on their own land, peri-urbanites are wage earners who have retained corporate solidarities in that some food, labor, forms of mutual help, and land circulate among villagers in an uncommoditized fashion; they have also preserved the sort of discourses consonant with this form of ownership of means of production. Moreover, the village studied is endowed with considerable natural resources so that villagers cannot truthfully be said to be driven to paid employment by the specter of poverty and famine.[13]

Up to the mid-1960s, Erakor had essentially a rural economy with its inhabitants relying on subsistence gardening and fishing for most of their food, while using copra making, the marketing of produce in town, and occasional wage earning to raise the little money needed for church, school fees, clothes, imported food items, tobacco and alcohol. A drastic fall in the price of copra allied to unprecedented economic development in the capital following the establishment of a tourist industry and greater spending by the two colonial powers led the villagers to abandon petty commodity production for paid employment over a period of little more than five years. By 1972, wage labor outside the village was accounting for about 90% of the cash inflow in the village. The increased disposable incomes were quickly invested in new houses, modern furnishings, means of transportation, small businesses, and increased leisure activities (dancing and drinking in town). However, this economic boom was short-lived and was soon followed by economic recessions: a first one brought on by the 1973 world oil crisis, and a subsequent one by political troubles surrounding the country's accession to independence in 1980. One would have expected Erakor villagers to react to a contraction in the labor market by reducing their consumption of store-bought goods and by relying to a greater extent on subsistence activities to achieve some measure of self-sufficiency.

But that is not what happened. The villagers' "consumerist" urge did not ease off between 1972 and 1983, as can be seen from the tables below, and this, despite the fact that acquiring such consumer items had become harder (Philibert 1984b).

Women fared better than men on the labor market during the period of recession: the percentage of women among wage earners increased from 37% in 1972 to 45% in 1983. However, these aggregate figures only tell part of the story, as not all women were equally affected. The proportion of wage earners among able-bodied women of the 25-34 age group jumped from 23% (1972) to 51% (1983); during the same period, the proportion of salaried workers among the 35-44 years old women fit to work also increased appreciably from 18% to 27%. These women are precisely those whobelonged to the 15-24 age group studied in 1972 and who, having moved to better paying semi-qualified and qualified work in the interval, remained employed after their marriage. For the first time in village history, a category of Erakor women, much like Western women, work outside their home and raise a family at the same time.

Village Population

	1972	1979	1983
Number of Residents	628	836	1006
Number of Households	92	123	154

Such changes in the occupational structure, made in order to preserve the earning power of households, have had an impact on family organization. It has already had distressing consequences for child-rearing practices: a 1982 national public health study has found evidence of malnutrition among children in Erakor, ironically one of the wealthiest villages in Vanuatu. It was found among the bottle-fed children whose absent working mothers could no longer nurse. Whoever was left at home to mind the children, either did not know how to prepare the milk formula or the formula was replaced by condensed milk to reduce expenses.

Some social costs have been incurred as well, although these will not be felt for a while. Women may play a pivotal role in loosening, if not severing altogether, the tie between some villagers and their land, in other words in transforming part of the next generation of villagers into proletarians. (See Philibert n.d. for an extended development of this argument.) Let us consider the likely outcome of these occupational changes for women's productive function before examining the effect on their reproductive role. Land owners in Erakor must exercise their rights to parcels of land if they wish to resist the yearly encroachment of neighbors on their garden land. Women normally carry out many of the gardening activities which become severely curtailed by wage labor outside the village. Wage earners are thus at a disadvantage in the long term as their rights to a

Commodity Consumption in Erakor

Consumer Items	Number of Households		
	1972	1979	1983
Refrigerators	2	24*	40
VCR and TV	N/A	N/A	5
Cars/light trucks	14	48 (19 late models)	44 (20 late models)
Concrete house	1	20	31
*Boys***	0	7	11

*Electricity and running water were installed in Erakor in 1979. Electric refrigerators then replaced costlier kerosene-run refrigerators.

**Boys* is the pidgin term applied to agricultural workers hired by wage earning villagers to garden for them. As labor is uncommoditized among villagers, these agricultural workers come from other islands. The employer-employee relationship is a highly paternalistic one.

valuable uncommoditized resource are left more or less unprotected. The solution is of course to use *boys*, but not every household can afford them. There are today households in Erakor which do not garden at all.

Work in town is indirectly related by villagers to a drastic change in family organization, a four-fold increase of consensual unions in the village between 1972 and 1983. There were, in 1972, 7 couples living out of wedlock in Erakor, a behavior much frowned upon by village authorities in this Presbyterian Christian village. Their number grew to 31 by 1979 and it remained at this level in 1983. In the majority of cases, one of the partners is not from the village. During the 11 year period studied, the failure rate of such consensual unions, in the sense that the unions did not result in an eventual church marriage, was 30 to 40%. Unless paternity is acknowledged by an Erakor father, the children born of these unions are unlikely to obtain rights to garden land in the village or, at the very least, their rights will be less extensive that those of children born in wedlock. Land is transmitted patrilineally in Erakor with sons obtaining the lion's share. Consensual unions literally bear the seeds of a class of landless villagers.

The increased participation of young women in the labor force is responsible for their going to town not only to work but also to live. Although Erakor is only 10 km from the capital, some young women cohabit in town with non-villagers. They seem to prefer other islanders to Erakor men: in 1983, of the 26 Erakor women living with men in town, married or unmarried, only 2 had an Erakor partner. Erakor women, who have the reputation of being urban sophisticates, are attracted to men with well-paid jobs: almost half of them hold white collar jobs. These young women, breaking away from the expectation of marrying in the village, soon enter the social networks of their partners and are drawn further away from Erakor social life. The children of these women will have no access to land in the village. The Erakor women living in town will produce the first generation of *de facto* proletarians in Vanuatu, the first truly urban ni-Vanuatu.

Villagers' response to the recession has been to maintain their living standards at their current level by making greater use of women on the labor market. Villagers then acquiesced to changes in subsistence activities and in the division of roles within the family, and to a new form of family organization in order to reach their objective. Women have now become the unconscious vector of change-for-the-worse in the village economy; they are the agency through which important social relationships will no longer be reproduced as they stood in the past. This will lead to the abandonment of a tried and proven Melanesian adaptation to the modern world, the refusal to commit oneself entirely to the market economy (Brookfield 1973). An atrophied subsistence sector will leave villagers with only one economic leg to stand on, thus destroying the very condition which allows them to participate in the market economy under largely favorable terms. What is more, land being absolutely central to the Melanesian notion of identity, the greater impoverishment will first and foremost be a cultural one.

An order (levels, patterns, norms, modes) of consumption is linked to a given order of production, though it would be naive indeed to reduce consumption in a mechanistic way to the functional requirements of a system of production. It would be clearly wrong to conceptualize the relation between the two as that of a plug and a wall socket. The two systems are mediated by the domain of culture, a semi-autonomous dimension between on the one hand the consciousness, and thus motivation, of social agents and the structural requirements of a society on the other. To make things yet more complex, there are also "deep disjunctions and desperate tensions within social and cultural reproduction", as Willis (1980:175) remarks.

The Erakor material does not call into question de Certeau's view of the power of the powerless to deflect a dominant social order: Melanesians also engaged in passive, and at times not so passive, resistance during the colonial period. It does however remind us that ideology cuts both ways, that it leads to acceptance as well as resistance. What permitted South American Indians to resist the Spanish cultural order while outwardly accepting it is also what is leading some Erakor villagers to embrace a capitalist political economy now that they have tied their modern-day self-image to the ownership of industrial goods (Philibert 1982, 1984a).

Conclusion

Whether or not there is such a thing as Simple Commodity Consumption, our assuming that there is has enabled us to focus on the process of cultural categorization revealed in patterns of consumption. It is perhaps not so surprising that consumption obeys a different logic or follows a different sort of social calculus in societies that are not yet fully incorporated into a capitalist political economy. After all, unlike ourselves, people living in peasant societies do not necessarily see themselves as equals facing a world of goods obeying its own impersonal laws, and their social experience, in this sense, is not always expressed the way our own is, through a reification of the economic domain.

The following points have been briefly, too briefly, touched upon here: the social role of consumption in pre-capitalist and capitalist economies; the link between consumption, as a type of social notation shaping consciousness, and Gramsci's notion of hegemony; the relation between meaning, in the form of social classification, and power; the notion of consumption as silent production and hidden resistance. In a rather discursive fashion, it has been an attempt to examine the consumption of goods as the consumption of signs that are the social product as well as the agent of capitalist penetration of Third World countries. I hope to have convinced others that each of the above-mentioned themes deserves fuller treatment in its own right and that to approach consumption purely in terms of utility, marginal or otherwise, leaves out some of its most significant dimensions.

A comparative framework appears essential here, not simply to help us understand the diversity of modes of consumption, but more importantly to remind us that consumption is no less culturally determined in our own society. Anthropologists should not let economists get away with a naturalised, unproblematical model of consumption deemed universally applicable. It is in societies located at the periphery of the capitalist system that this can be achieved, because it is there that the capitalist structure of comprehension underpinning our social theories is more easily apprehended, the way poor novels rather than good ones serve as unwitting pastiches of an era, encapsulating faithfully the ideas and values of their time.

Notes

I wish to thank the Social Sciences and Humanities Research Council of Canada for providing a leave fellowship which allowed me to spend six months in Vanuatu in 1983 researching consumption and later seven months at the Australian National University as a Visiting Fellow. Many thanks to the Australian National University for the offer of a Visiting Fellowship and to Professor Anthony Forge, Department of Prehistory and Anthropology, Faculty of Arts, at ANU for his generous hospitality. I am also indebted to Professors F. Manning, C. Creider, J. Cannizzo, M. Spence and M.E. Smith, and to Jane Philibert for their comments and suggestions. I am grateful to Erakor villagers for their benevolent tolerance of my never-ending curiosity about their life, the way one puts up with flaws of character in one's friends. Much credit for the ideas expressed here goes to Dr. Margaret Rodman, a fellow Vanuatu anthropologist, who, at one time, was a co-worker in this research on consumption in Vanuatu. She co-authored a first draft of this article and I gratefully acknowledge her contribution here.

1.   The notion that one group, one language, one kinship system equals one tribe is today seen by many as an administrative *cum* anthropological fiction, the product of 1920s and 30s colonialism (Ranger 1983). Applying the concept of tribe to the Third World populations studied by anthropologists is in some ways no less problematical than that of social classes.

2.   A sociologist with impeccable Marxist credentials, Peter Worsley, has recently written an anthropological critique of Marxism, not unlike Sahlins's (1976), in which he attacks the "myth" of superstructure and economic base, more precisely the validity of such a distinction. He is also highly critical of structuralist Marxists for having "codified this culturally-specific logic of capitalism and turned it into a universalistic, invariant schema of base and superstructure, the base being the mode (or

modes) of production. Having abstracted production from all other relationships, they then invest it with determinative significance" (1984:29). The debate that raged throughout the 1960s and 1970s among French neo-Marxists such as Meillassoux, Godelier, Terray and Rey about whether to place kinship, an indubitable ethnographic datum if ever there was one, in the superstructure, the base, in both at once, or even to dissolve kinship altogether, should have alerted anthropologists to the limited usefulness of such a model.

3. The tenor of the literature on simple commodity production (SCP) is unfortunately, though aptly, caught in the title of an article written by a participant in the debate on SCP. See Chevalier (1983) "There is Nothing Simple about Simple Commodity Production".

4. In a perceptive paper, Weismantel (1988) discusses the social, ideological and cultural implications of replacing wheat bread for barley gruel in an Ecuadorian village as part of a general transformation in the political economy of the region.

5. The Republic of Vanuatu is a South Pacific archipelago with a population of some 130,000 inhabitants situated between the Solomon Islands and New Caledonia. Prior to gaining independence in 1980, the group was known as the Condominium of the New Hebrides, a territory jointly administered by France and Great Britain. I carried out fieldwork in Vanuatu in the peri-urban village of Erakor from 1972 to 1973, and again in 1979 and 1983 for a duration of 24 months.

6. Consumption is significant with respect to class analysis. The economies of less developed countries (LDCs) far from match those of nineteenth century Western countries. As Rivière (1975) remarks, modernization in LDCs is to a large extent planned and controlled by those holding political power. In such an instance, the ownership of the means of production matters less than the effective control of those means. If there is a bourgeoisie at all, it is a politico-bureaucratic bourgeoisie and it is their control of the means of production allied to their control of the legal and political structures of the state that allows them to claim a larger share of the social income. Such a Third World bourgeoisie is well known for its propensity for spending, unlike the saving and investing bourgeoisie of nineteenth century Europe. With a generally limited agricultural and industrial production, the differential amount of privileges in such countries is expressed in consumption. Social differentiation is thus better expressed by the appropriation of consumer goods than by ownership of the means of production. Rivière feels that the Marxist problematic must be corrected in Africa where the ownership of the means of production does not necessarily overlap with the ownership of the means of coercion, where economic power may rest less with production than consumption, and where access to wealth is regulated primarily by politics. Another

factor that makes consumption crucial for the understanding of social classes is the enlargement of the tertiary sector following independence with the establishment of a national administration and a universal educational system. This leads to the emergence of a large number of public employees, those most concerned in LDCs with living standards and social position. Finally, as opposed to nineteenth century Europe, workers in LDCs are not to be considered a social class in the process of becoming impoverished, an emerging proletariat. Quite the contrary in fact, since wage labor raises the social status of an individual rather than lowering it.

7. Anyone interested in how houses speak of their occupants will read with profit Rodman 1985a, 1985b.

8. Traditional culture, called *kastom* in Pidgin throughout Melanesia, has seen a great deal of political service in such newly independent countries as Vanuatu and the Solomon Islands. See Keesing and Tonkinson (1982), Philibert (1986).

9. "The land dive is part of an ensemble of rituals performed in association with the yam harvest. There is an intimate relationship between the harvest of yams and the dive. The quality of the crop determines the safety and efficacy of the *gol*, and the performance of the *gol* simultaneously ensures the worth of the harvest in the next year. This identity is based on the metaphysical identity of men and yams . . . the ritual is seen as a powerful statement of the strength and sanctity of men . . . The rite celebrates a "hot" dimension of masculinity. . . It is a statement both of men's potency and of resistance to European domination." (Jolly, 82:352-353)

10. Anthropologists are divided on the effect of commoditization on "traditional institutions". See Greenwood and McKean in Smith (1978) for opposite views of this matter. For the effect on one's identity of alter's view, see the startling case of salvaged ethnic identity described by Smith (1982). Having "lost" most of a pre-contact culture over some 250 years, the 100 or so Hispanized remnants of an Amerindian settlement engulfed by the city of El Paso decided to become "Indian" again after discovering the economic advantages attached to that identity. The American Bureau of Indian Affairs helped them set up a "traditional" Indian village as a tourist facility from which they now derive their livelihood.

11. I am grateful to Monty Lindstrom for making this point.

12. The following reflects his earlier view: "The phenomenon of alienation in the Third World today takes the form of affiliation to a universal code of recognition. The fact that it is accepted as the language of communication

with prestigious partners means that the mechanisms of exploitation are self-sustaining, without the need to resort to external means of coercion. Thus it emerges as the ultimate stage of domination, one in which the victims are themselves desirous of their condition" (Adam 1980: 158, my translation.)

13. Erakor, the second largest village community in Vanuatu, is a modern, prosperous village located on the island of Efate, some 10 km from Port Vila, the administrative and commercial capital. The village land, which covers an area of 1,409 ha, is bordered on the northern and western sides by a lagoon where villagers find fish and shellfish. Village households are involved to varying degrees in subsistence gardening (slash-and-burn cultivation of root crops mostly), with a majority of them self-sufficient with regard to native produce. In 1983, 248 villagers were also employed in town or in the two international-class hotels located across the Erakor lagoon. Villagers showed themselves to be particularly entrepreneurial during the colonial period, often taking the initiative in establishing links with European newcomers. They were the first on their island to welcome Christian teachers in 1845. A Canadian Presbyterian missionary who resided in Erakor from 1872 to 1902 exerted a strong influence on the villagers. They renounced the use of magical stones, intertribal warfare, dancing, men's houses, polygyny, and the drinking of kava (*Piper methisticum*). In return, the villagers found in the Presbyterian mission a powerful ally willing to protect native rights in the frontier situation prevailing during the early phase of colonial history. The mission also provided a social and intellectual framework within which villagers could react effectively to the colonial situation (see Philibert 1982). In 1884, Erakor villagers ceded the village land to the Presbyterian mission in order to prevent further land alienation. Encouraged by the mission, they started as early as 1910 to develop their own coconut groves as an alternative to wage labor on European plantations. In the mid-1960s, the villagers were the first Melanesians to become involved in the nascent tourist industry in the country. Twenty years later, they were the first ni-Vanuatu to be part-owners of a small hotel and restaurant sited on village land. Erakor villagers like to think of themselves, at their best, as culture brokers for their whole island. This is how an informant put it: "When a large wave comes from far away on the sea, it must first break on Erakor reef. It has always been so".

References
Adam, M.
1980 La contre-culture coca-cola. Le mirage des objets et la dépendance du consommateur dans le Tiers-Monde. *L'Homme et la Société*, 56-58: 149-160.
n.d. Le développement comme Signe. To appear in *Tiers-Monde*.
Baudrillard, J.
1970 *La Société de Consommation*. Paris: Gallimard.

Bourdieu, P.
1977   *Outline of a Theory of Practice*. Cambridge: Cambridge University Press.
1979   *La Distinction. Critique sociale du jugement*. Paris: Les Editions de Minuit.

Chevalier, J.
1983   There is nothing simple about simple commodity production. *The Journal of Peasant Studies* 10(4):153-186.

Clarke, J., S. Hall, T. Jefferson and B. Roberts
1976   Subcultures, cultures and class. In Hall, S. & T. Jefferson (eds.) *Resistance through Rituals*. London: Hutchinson.

de Certeau, M.
1984   *The Practice of Everyday Life*. Berkeley: University of California Press.

Crick, M.R.
1982   Anthropology of knowledge. *Annual Review of Anthropology* 11:287-313.

d'Haene, S.
1980   Essai d'analyse du fonctionnement des modèles de consommation dans les pays sous-developpés. *L'Homme et la Société*, 56-58: 179-187.

Douglas, M. & Baron Isherwood
1979   *The World of Goods*. Harmondsworth: Penguin.

Gramsci, A.
1971   *Selections from the Prison Notebooks*. New York: International Publishers.

Greenwood, D.J.
1978   Culture by the pound: An anthropological perspective on tourism as cultural commoditization, in Smith, V.S. (ed.) *Host and Guests*. Oxford: Basil Blackwell.

Hall, S. & T. Jefferson (eds.)
1976   *Resistance through Rituals*. London: Hutchinson.

Hobsbawm, E.
1985   Mass-producing traditions: Europe,1870-1914. In Hobsbawm, E. & T. Ranger (eds.) *The Invention of Tradition*. Cambridge: Cambridge University Press.

Jolly, M.
1982   Birds and banyans of South Pentecost: <u>*KASTOM*</u> in anti-Colonial struggle. In Keesing, R.M. & R. Tonkinson (eds.) *Rethinking Traditional Culture: The Politics of Kastom in Island Melanesia*. Special Issue of *Mankind* 13(4):338-356
n.d.   From corporeality to commodity: food and gender in South Pentecost, Vanuatu.

Keesing, R.M. and R. Tonkinson (eds.)
1982   *Reinventing Traditional Culture: The Politics of Kastom in Island Melanesia*. Special issue of *Mankind* 13(4).

Lombard, J.
1980   Modèles sociaux et comportements de consommation. *L'Homme et la Société* 56-58: 141-148.

82

McKean, P.E.
1978   Towards a theoretical analysis of tourism: economic dualism and cultural involution in Bali. In Smith, V.S. (ed.) *Hosts and Guests*. Oxford: Basil Blackwell.

Mouffe, C. (ed.)
1979   *Gramsci and Marxist Theory*. London: Routledge & Kegan Paul.

Philibert, J-M.
1981   Living under two flags: selective modernization in Erakor Village, Efate. In Allen, M. (ed.) *Vanuatu. Politics, Economics and Ritual in island Melanesia*. Sydney: Academic Press.

1982   Vers une symbolique de la modernisation au Vanuatu. *Anthropologie et Sociétés* 6(1):69-98.

1984a   Vanuatu. In Salisbury, R.F. and E. Tooker (eds.) *Affluence and Cultural Survival*. The American Ethnological Society.

1984b   Adaptation à la récession économique dans un village péri-urbain du Vanuatu. *Journal de la Société des Océanistes*, Tome XL, No. 79: 139-150.

1986   The politics of tradition: toward a generic culture in Vanuatu. *Mankind* 16(1):1-12.

n.d.   Women as agents of proletarianization in a peri-urban village of Vanuatu.

Ranger, T.
1983   The invention of tradition in colonial Africa. In Hobsbawm, E. & T. Ranger (eds.) *The Invention of Tradition*. Cambridge: Cambridge University Press.

Riviere, C.
1975   Classes et Stratifications Sociales en Afrique noire, *Cahiers_Internationaux de Sociologie*, Vol. LIX: 285-314.

Rosman, A.
1982   Review of Douglas and Isherwood's *The World of Goods*. *American Anthropologist* 84(1): 211-212.

Sahlins, M.
1976   *Culture and Practical Reason*. Chicago: The University of Chicago Press.

Simon, R.
1982   *Gramsci's Political Thought*. London: Lawrence & Wishart.

Smith, M.E.
1982   The process of sociocultural continuity. *Current Anthropology* 23(2): 127-142.

Smith, V.S., ed.
1978   *Hosts and Guests*. Oxford: Basil Blackwell.

Weismantel, M.J.
1988   The cultural construction of consumption events: the substitution of wheat bread for barley gruel in the early morning meal in highland Ecuador. In Rutz, Henry J. and Benjamin S. Orlove (eds.) *The Social Economy of Consumption.*. Lanham, Md.: University Press of America.

Willis, P.E.
1980   *Learning to Labour*. Westwead: Gower.

Worsley, P.
1981 Social class and development. in Berreman, G.D. (ed.) *Social Inequality*. New York: Academic Press.
1984 *The Three Worlds*. London: Weidenfeld & Nicolson.

THE CHILDREN CRY FOR BREAD:
HEGEMONY AND THE TRANSFORMATION OF CONSUMPTION

M. J. Weismantel

Introduction

In this paper, I discuss the substitution of wheat bread for barley gruel in the early morning meal in Zumbagua, an indigenous parish of highland Ecuador. While at the macroscopic level such changes in consumption may appear to be part of an inevitable, unilinear progression from subsistence to market systems, they are experienced by households actually undergoing them as a contradictory and conflict-filled process in which ideological and cultural issues play an important part. Wheat bread for barley gruel in the early morning seems like an insignificant change, the substitution of one carbohydrate for another, but because bread enters the indigenous kitchen as part of a complex of cultural, ideological and social transformations, its significance can be greater than the effects on family nutrition or the household budget would suggest. In indigenous Andean communities today, there is a symbolic association of leavened white bread with the dominant culture; this association has historical and material aspects that relate it to general transformations in the political economy at a regional level.

Not only does purchase of breads by indigenous peasants raise social and ideological questions, but close study of this phenomenon highlights issues within the realm of economic analysis as well. As I hope to show in this paper, use of the household as an analytical unit of consumption and production can disguise very real differences between household members as economic actors. In Zumbagua, the household as a whole is involved in a combination of subsistence, commercial and wage labor activities, but the involvement of individuals in these spheres of activity is determined by their age and gender. Conflicts of interest between household members are frequently exposed and exacerbated by everyday consumption issues such as dietary innovations. These conflicts of interest between household members in turn reveal the contradictory pressures and forces at work in the nation as a whole.

Zumbagua is a rural parish of the province of Cotopaxi, in the western cordillera of the Andes. The parish today is relatively isolated and unimportant politically and economically, but this was not always the case. Zumbagua first entered the historical record as an Augustinian hacienda during the colonial period, at which time it was an important and lucrative landholding, where enormous flocks of sheep produced wool for the textile workshops of the intermontane valley. In the republican era, these Church-owned lands were taken over by the state, which used proceeds from the hacienda to fund social services in urban areas. Thus production within the parish has for several centuries been directed by national-level organizations that channelled profits from the zone into investments in the urban economy.

85

Because the hacienda of Zumbagua belonged to the state, it is one of the few highland areas which was directly and radically affected by the national agrarian reform law enacted in 1964. In the mid-1960s, the hacienda was dissolved and title to the land distributed among parish residents. Inequalities in land distribution quickly developed, with white[1] hacienda employees establishing themselves as an economic and social elite. However, some indigenous families have succeeded in challenging white control, although many then take on the trappings of ethnic whiteness themselves, and simply reproduce the existing system of exploitation once they attain elite status. Ethnic whiteness in Zumbagua, as in much of the Andes, is largely inseparable from integration into the cash economy. Storekeepers, busdrivers and schoolteachers are "white", even if the individuals who presently hold these jobs were "Indians" ten years ago.

At the present, most of Zumbagua's residents are both much poorer and much more ethnically indigenous in language, dress and custom than is common in Ecuador today. The population lives in widely dipersed rural housholds scattered over the parish's 10,000 hectares. Most of the parish is of an unusually high altitude for Ecuador, ranging from 3500-4000 meters in elevation, well above the upper limits of maize cultivation at that latitude. Residents of the parish utilize several production zones, the most important being high valley lands, used for barley, fava bean and potato cultivation, and the still higher paramo grasslands, used for sheep and llama pastoralism and as a source of grass fuel. But although the people of Zumbagua have a strong emotional commitment to farming, it is in fact impossible for households to support themselves purely through agriculture and pastoralism. Every household is also involved in a variety of other activities, which in fact tie them to the national economy to a far greater degree than is immediately apparent. One important strategy is to send some males outside the parish as temporary wage laborers. Older workers typically find employment in small sugarcane fields and mills located in the lowlands immediately to the west of the parish, but younger men tend to go to the capital city of Quito to find work, usually in construction.

The rapid change in the relations of production of the parish in the last several decades has had a profound effect on social relations at the household level. The biggest schism is between young adults, who have come of age since the dissolution of the hacienda, and an older generation who lived under the hacienda system. The problems revealed by the issue of bread and gruel, however, do not highlight this generation gap, but rather bring to light divisions within younger families.

The proletarianization of males is creating a gender gap among young adults, which does not exist in the older generation. Males typically begin work in Quito between the ages of ten and fourteen, so that by the time a man marries at the age of twenty he has had a very different socialization than his bride. He is at home in an urban environment, speaks Spanish, listens to the radio, knows something of national sports and politics, music and slang. She, in contrast, has rarely if ever left the parish, speaks only Quichua, wears indigenous clothing, and knows the mythology, songs and elaborate Quichua riddle games of indigenous culture. She is a subsistence farmer and pastoralist, having taken over almost all the agricultural duties of the farmstead, while he is a wage laborer. Since Andean marriage does not entail a merging of financial assets and earnings, there is frequently an economic disparity between the two as well: he has money and she does not.

There is also a generation gap within these young families, between parents and children. Unlike their parents, many Zumbagua children today go to school. The children thus are becoming accuturated to national Ecuadorian society: schoolchildren understand Quichua but hardly speak it, and spend their time tearing photographs of cars, airplanes and motorcycles out of any scrap of Spanish-language magazines they can lay their hands on. The lessons they learn in the classroom, which include the rule that white, urban and professional is good and Indian, rural and peasant is bad, hardly encourage them to learn farming from their mothers and grandparents. Although their labor is very important to the family farm, most children do not look to farming as their future, regardless of whether they attend school or not.

In the above description, I have presented the roles of male and female, adult and child as fixed and predictable. In fact, however, although these descriptions are not inaccurate, they not only gloss over individual variation but also fail to reveal the conflicting attitudes individuals often feel towards the social and productive roles they play. There are few individuals, of any age or sex, who do not feel the attraction of both agricultural and proletarian lifeways, and fewer still who have not cursed the inadequate livelihood provided by both economic strategies. The fact that men who work in Quito have had to adopt more "white" cultural traits than their wives does not necessarily mean that they value "whiteness" more. The glamor of urban life and purchased goods can appeal more to women, for whom they represent an exotic and unknown world, than for their husbands, who frequently characterize the time they spend in the city as a painful exile from indigenous life.

In hacienda days, ethnic identity and productive role were determined for the people of Zumbagua by forces beyond their control. Exploitation of this work force by the national economy was then made possible by a rigid caste system in which distinctive customs preserved social boundaries. Today a new political economy prevails, and national ideologies call for the rapid assimilation of indigenous peoples. But the issue of whether such assimilation is in fact desirable is one on which the parish itself remains divided.

In Zumbagua, where ethnicity is largely a matter of socially-recognized markers such as language, dress and custom, consumption choices become a major arena in which individuals and groups establish their ethnic identity. Consumption decisions thus involve a complex of issues beyond financial capacity and individual psychology. In the parish today, issues which are ultimately of a political and ideological nature, such as choices in productive strategy and cultural identity, are being argued not so much through overt debate, speechmaking and confrontations in the political arena of the parish, but rather through everyday consumption decisions being made at the household level. The pressure to assimilate does not remain at the level of abstract ideology, but pervades the textures of everyday life.

The people of Zumbagua are constantly bombarded from within and without by images of their cultural practices as being backwards and wrong. The imposition of these labels of inadequacy is part of a political and eonomic process which is hegemonic in nature. The erosion of the subsistence economy is inevitably occurring, an overdetermined process in which ecological degradation, overpopulation, and drastic changes in the national economy have all played apart. But the erosion of people's faith in the validity of the food and clothing, language and celebrations they grew up with is also the product of a multiplicity of forces. In an isolated rural area like Zumbagua, this message filters through in small ways, but the pressure is unrelenting. I refer to it as hegemonic because, to quote Raymond Williams, the impostion of a political order is hegemonic when it is not ". . . expressed in directly political forms . . . by direct or effective coercion . . ." but rather through ". . . a complex interlocking of political forms, and active social and cultural forms . . .What is decisive is not only the conscious system of ideas and beliefs but the whole lived social process as practically organized by specific and dominant meanings and values" (Raymond Williams 1977: 108-109).

The transformation of indigenous practice occurs not only when the schoolchild is taught to salute the Ecuadorian flag, but also when his mother hesitates over what foods to serve her family, fearful that there is something inadequate in a meal of homegrown foods unembellished by purchased foodstuffs or condiments. Even women who have little interaction with white outsiders, separated from them by the language barrier, learn the lessons of cultural and social inferiority. Children so young that they have scarcely ever left the farmstead have already begun to learn them too. These messages of inferiority color private consumption rituals within the household, as well as more public actions.

Food and Identity

My research in Zumbagua was directed towards uncovering the semiotic system that underlies the cooking of foods, a system that I refer to as cuisine. This study necessitated analysis of the relationship of Zumbagua ways of cooking to those of other Ecuadorians, the semiotic systems of people who, for the most part, are richer and whiter than those who live in the parish. For heuristic purposes, it would be possible to study Zumbagua cuisine in isolation from other cuisines that surround it, but the parish has never existed in such isolation. The cuisine of the parish has evolved as a system which, like its people, exists in a certain ethnic and class relation to other cuisines.

The people of Zumbagua are poor, rural, indigenous, and they live in the Sierra. In addition, they live above the zone of maize cultivation. All of these facts about them are reflected in their cuisine; in fact, as I discuss below, at times one food, *machica*, symbolizes all of these facts within its fan (Turner 1967) of referential meanings. Not only the diet of Zumbagua but its cuisine differs from that of the nation as a whole. Zumbagua people eat "Indian" foods in "Indian" ways: not only elements and techniques but the very syntagmatic chains by which they are combined into meals are not the same as even the stereotypical highland Ecuadorian cuisine. This difference is significant: it signifies not simply a particular way of life but one which is stigmatized.

Perhaps the quintessential *plato tipico* or traditional dish, in Ecuador is the kind of dish referred to as a *seco*. In the typical *seco*, the plate holds a piece of meat (beef, chicken, goat) cooked using one of a rather limited repertoire of techniques, condiments and vegetables. At the side are perhaps some fried potatoes and another vegetable, or a relish of marinated, finely sliced onions and tomatoes with lemon and *cilantro*. The dominant element on the plate, however, is the large, unseasoned pile of white rice.

In the full midday meal or *almuerzo*, the *seco* is flanked by a preceding soup and terminal sweet *colada*, dishes that evoke a meal structure descended from pre-Hispanic patterns. But as *caldo de pata* and other Ecuadorian soups are increasingly replaced by imports like canned cream of mushroom soup, and fruit *coladas* by a soft drink or a dish of canned peaches, the earlier heritage becomes less visible even though the sequence of courses still bears its mark. The sequence of meals also continues to resist North American influences: the light, continental-style morning *cafe* is followed by the main meal, the heavy, multi-course *almuerzo* in the early afternoon, and a light meal in the evening.

To wealthy Ecuadorians whose repertoire of foods includes European and North American dishes, the *seco* and the colada are nostalgic reminders of the past. For most Ecuadorians, however, these dishes remain standard everyday fare. For the well-to-do, *platos tipicos* such as *seco* remain important because they symbolize the country's heritage. Unlike pizzas or sandwiches made of Wonder Bread, American cheese and bologna (*pan de miga, queso americano y pastel mexicano*), the glamorous fast foods, processed foods and snack foods that are modish among the young and the nouveaux riches, students and professional classes, *platos tipicos* are substantial, solid: bland and starchy, they reach their full flower in the traditional *almuerzo*, the heavy midday meal at which the entire family gathers. *Platos tipicos* stand for the strength of the family, that primary virtue of traditional Ecuadorian society. The ideological importance of *platos tipicos* for Ecuador is problematic, however, in a way which characterizes an Ecuadorian dilemma in seeking an autonomous identity through emphasizing the nation's heritage. For *platos tipicos* carry other messages besides "family" and "nation". They also stand for the poor, the ignorant, and the non-white: people with whom the elite, for the most part, do not wish to identify.

This opposition between the full *almuerzo* and the fast-food snack, though real, obscures a more complex hierarchy of cuisines. Shrimps *ceviches* and tropical fruits like the *grenadilla* and *chirimoya* certainly stand on the Ecuadorian side of the two rival American cuisines, North American and national, found in Quito today. But although "Ecuadorian cuisine" appears as a unified entity when opposed to sandwiches or pizzas, Ecuador in fact contains many cuisines. For example, the long-standing rivalry between highlands and coast is symbolized by potatoes vs. rice, by *locros* (stews) vs. secos (dry meals), by blandness vs. spiciness. This is true even though the *seco* made with rice is found throughout Ecuador, including the highlands. The *seco* dominates Ecuadorian cuisine; this dominance reflects a certain historical relationship between coast and sierra.

The *seco* also evokes the provinces rather than the capital city. In small towns and even provincial capitals, the restaurants all serve the same fare: *churrascos* and *apanados, pollo dorado, seco de chivo* (all of which are types of *secos*) appear on every menu and all are assembled on the plate in the same way. But while for Quitenos such dishes signify provincialism and a native heritage being left behind by the modern world, to the people of Zumbagua the same menu represents that outside, urban, modern world from which they feel disenfranchised.

In Zumbagua cuisine, like that of white Sierrans, there are two basic categories of dishes, *sopas* and *secos*. But in contrast to the white *almuerzo*, where *sopa* and *colada* flank a central, validating *seco*, in Zumbagua the *sopa* has a clear predominance[2]. The role of the *sopa* in Zumbagua cuisine is similar to that which Mary Douglas describes when she speaks of the power of the familiar dish to arouse in people "the flash of recognition and confidence which welcomes an ordered pattern" (Mary Douglas 1971:80). There is no doubt that the presence of the *sopa* validates most Zumbagua meals. It is the most important and most typical syntagm (dish/meal) of Zumbagua cuisine. Generally speaking, most main meals eaten in the parish consist of *sopas*. Each person sharing the meal is expected to eat at least two bowls full of soup, and more is always offered. The heavy starch content makes it a very filling meal.

The basis of these meals is boiled water. The word for "to cook", *yanuna*, itself means "to boil". Boiling is absolutely central to Zumbagua cooking practice. The essential wetness of Zumbagua dishes, which are served in bowls and eaten with spoons, contrasts sharply with the *seco*; the word *seco* itself means dry, highlighting its opposition to the water-based *sopa*. There is a strong disinclination in Zumbagua against eating any foods during a meal that have not first been immersed in hot water. Raw or dry foods are snacks meant to be eaten away from home or between mealtimes; they should not be eaten during a meal.

Beyond this underlying process of boiling in water, it is hard to write a minimal definition of a *sopa*. Unlike most peasant cuisines, everyday meals in Zumbagua may be based on any one of a variety of starches; no single complex carbohydrate predominates. It is the manner of cooking, the "ordered pattern" used, that characterizes the Zumbagua *almuirsu* (cf. Mintz 1985:8-9).

Sopas can be divided into two basic categories, *colada* and *caldo*. The first are thick, the latter clear soups. (This distinction is not absent from our own cuisine, although it is not clearly distinguished linguistically. Cream soups, bisques, chowders and bean soups are *coladas*; consommes, broths, noodle and vegetable soups are *caldos*). Note that potatoes, while important, do not play the role of fundamental thickener in *coladas*. While North American cuisine frequently uses potatoes as the thickening agent for a *colada*-style soup, in Zumbagua potatoes are never allowed to cook long enough to disintegrate in this fashion.[3] Other starches are used as the base of *coladas*, potatoes never. They are present in both *caldo* and *colada*, but are the validator for neither. A *colada* is validated by its thickening starch food, a *caldo* by its broth.

Whereas a *colada* must have a flour or meal of some sort used to thicken it, *caldos* may be without any starch. It is possible to make a meat broth for the sick which contains no starches at all, or only potatoes. Sick people frequently decide that they have no stomach for one or another starch, aversions which are always heeded; the extremely ill may only be able to eat pure broths. These clear broths in fact represent the quintessential *caldo*. However, neither meat broth nor its substitute, small amounts of purchased processed vegetable fat dissolved in boiling water, need to be present to make *caldo*. Hot water, noodles and salt make a perfectly acceptable *caldo*, one which cash-poor people consider somewhat desirable.

Overall, *coladas* are more common than *caldos* in everyday cuisine. A good, substantial *sopa*, the kind of meal an average family eats on a regular basis, consists of hot water thickened with home-ground barley or purchased wheat flour, cooked with a spoonful of fat, some salt, and three to five chopped onions. On most but not all days, a *sopa* also contains some extras: pieces of mutton, perhaps, or cabbage. A *sopa* should always contain enough potatoes so that each bowl served contains several, although in many households it often does not.

If potatoes are beyond many household's budget today, rice, the staple element of small-town "white " cuisine, is a rarely-eaten treat. Like the sophisticated Ecuadorian confronted with emblems of popular culture from the U.S., the people of Zumbagua view dishes such as the rice-based *seco* with both hatred and desire.

Secos contrast with everyday meals in Zumbagua not only in ingredients and in their non-soup nature but in other ways as well. These include aesthetic principles about color, texture, temperature, and consistency. In the parish, it is held that to be appealing food should be liquid, thick, uniform, and barely lukewarm. This is an ideal which women strive for in their cooking. The contrast between this ideal and the norms found in "white" cuisine is clearest in the *almuerzo*, the largest and most important meal of the day, but it can be found in the lighter meals eaten in peasant households before dawn and after dusk as well.[4]

Bread and Hegemony

Throughout Ecuador, the early-morning meal is referred to as *cafe*. For most "white" Ecuadorians, *cafe* consists of a cup of hot water, served with a saucer and a spoon, into which the individual consumer mixes instant coffee and sugar. It is served with two bread rolls. This meal is familiar to indigenous residents of the parish, since it is served in the early morning in restaurants and market stalls in the "white" towns Zumbagua people frequent. In most households within Zumbagua, however, the early morning meal takes quite a different form. Although still called *cafe*, it does not contain any coffee at all. The main component is *machica*, finely ground toasted barley meal. This cafe, like the "white" one, involves the serving of hot water, but there are no cups or saucers in evidence. Like most other meals in Zumbagua, this one is served in deep enamel bowls.

Water is heated to boiling, and sugar is dissolved into the water. Each person is handed a bowl of this sugar-water along with a spoon. At the same time, a container filled with *machica* is placed on the ground within everyone's reach, and everyone is invited to have some: *chapuvay*, *chapuilla*, 'go ahead and mix yourself some'. There is some range in personal tastes, but most people put about an equal amount of *machica* to sugar water in their bowl. This is frequently done gradually, with leisurely actions interspersed with morning conversations. At first the hot sweet water is sipped, then bit by bit spoonfuls of *machica* are added, producing a warm sweet gruel. Sometimes a cooked gruel of sweetened, coarsely ground barley (*arroz de cebada*) is served instead of water and *machica*.

Although most households consider *machica* an absolute necessity, a substance one simply cannot live without, an alternative construction of *cafe*, familiar to everyone, substitutes bread for *machica*. Despite being a quite different form of a starch food than *machica*, in the actual consumption bread, a "dry" food which does not require immersion in water, becomes somewhat similar to other indigenous starches: as people drink spoonfuls of coffee, they break the breads into pieces and mash them into the cup, producing a sweet soupy mass not unlike a gruel.

This act of making "white" breads similar to "indigenous" gruels in the actual consumption does not negate the implied threat to indigenous identity that eating bread in the early morning contains. This threat is especially felt because of the intimate, familiar nature of *cafe*, a meal which is only shared by household members. There is a tendency in Zumbagua for special-occasion meals to be served and eaten according to rules borrowed from white cuisine, and some indigenous households self-consciously try to model even their everyday eating habits according to white forms, behavior which quickly earns them the criticism of their neighbors. But controversy over whether to adopt white forms for everyday use, such as eating *cafe* according to the white pattern where carbohydrates are eaten as dry breads, also exists within households.

Many of the early morning quarrels I witnessed in Zumbagua homes erupted over the question of bread. This conflict arises between young children and their parents. Pre-school children, especially, demand bread as their right, and refuse to accept *mishqui*, sweet gruels, or *machica* in its place. Refusal is difficult for parents, since young children, especially the youngest child, are commonly indulged a great deal. Quichua-speaking mothers mimic their children's Spanish cries for bread: "Sulu tandata munan pan,pan,pan,'nin. Sulu wakan." They only want bread [*tanda*, Q.]. 'Bread, bread, bread' they say. [*pan*, Sp.] They just cry.

In current practice, bread is definitely a member of the *wanlla* set of foods, which also includes bananas, oranges and other fruits, hard candies and cookies. It is a snack food, and is frequently given as a gift. As such, bread is a necessity in certain circumstances: it is included among the offerings to the dead on *Finados*[5], the gifts exchanged during marriage negotiations or when asking someone to be a godparent, or as part of the redistributive flow surrounding fiesta sponsorship. Unless they are very poor, most families also buy some bread on Saturday as a treat for the children and for gift-giving in the web of *wanlla* prestations. Some of this bread is stored in the kitchen for any special occasions that might arise during the week. Many battles of will take place as mothers struggle to dole out the breads bought on Saturday as special treats, while the children demand them as daily fare. Fathers who witness these scenes seem to feel shame at their own inadequacy, their inability to fill their children's hands with bread. They may react with anger towards the child for his unreasonable demand, or towards the mother for denying the request. Often men shout that they will buy more tomorrow, as though resenting the implication that they in fact cannot.

What seems to be taking place is a struggle on the children's part to redefine what had been a treat (*wanlla*), a luxury good which most families can afford to buy but not for every day, into a staple, a necessary part of the morning meal. This is the process which Mintz describes as intrinsic to the needs of capitalism: demand must be created, new foods must be ". . . transformed into the ritual of daily necessity and even into images of daily decency" (Mintz 1979: 65). The children desire bread as the validation of a meal, that which seals it and marks it as satisfactory. They are pushing to redefine the role of bread in the domestic economy, not as a snack or treat but as something without which a meal would be incomplete. This redefinition implies an enlargement of the role of purchased foods in the household economy, and a preference for masculine over feminine contributions to consumption.

The change being suggested here is not the introduction of a new food into Zumbagua. Bread is already well established as a *wanlla* food, a snack or luxury food which nonetheless is a necessity in certain social interchanges. The substitution being urged by the children simply implies a change in the particular role played by bread. The significance of this change becomes clearer if we examine the meanings surrounding bread and those surrounding *machica*, the food which bread may supplant. Although other starches are important in the diet, barley, and especially *machica*, is a kind of core cultural symbol for Zumbagua. It is referred to by terms such as *bien calienticu*, food that warms you up when you eat it or *abrigaditu*, warm and comforting; people say that it is as filling as meat (although they don't mean this literally, but are using the comparison to highlight *machica* 's positive attributes). Those who have listened to the public health nurses' lectures on nutrition use the phrase *Buena alimentacion* to describe its goodness, while others simply insist that it is *alli alli mikuna* [Q], a very good food. It is the food that is given to kittens and baby puppies, and the first solid food given to human babies. Mothers give little bags full of sweetened *machica* to their children when they send them off herding, and worry all day if a careless youngster leaves his behind.

Because it is the essential symbol of the home, *machica* is the quintessential symbol of hospitality. Some is always kept on hand to offer to visitors. It is not offered to formal guests, and certainly not to the white nurse, schoolteacher or priest, for whom, after much frantic searching, the crusty year-old jar of instant coffee is unearthed while a child is sent racing downhill to buy bread. *Machica* is for the familiar guest, for the *comadre* who always comes to help harvest or the neighbor who has come to castrate your pig. A woman loves to bring out the *machica* when her family visits from her *natal comuna*, or when sisters visit from the *comunas* into which they have married. It is as though with this single act she can recreate the disbanded family home.

The meanings attached to *machica* derive partially from the way it is made. Ideally, it is entirely produced on the farmstead. Cultural ideals demand that barley sown by a family be seed from its own stores, not purchased; the sowing, care, harvest and threshing of the crop is done by extended family members; lastly, the sifting, grinding and toasting of the grain to make *machica* is done by the women of the family. Mothers make *machica* for their children, and in-marrying women prove their allegiance to the family, and their obedience to their mother-in-law, by grinding barley in the cold hours before dawn. Where the traditional extended family is still maintained, daughters-in-law creep into their mother-in-law's kitchen at four in the morning to start making *machica*. In the newer family structure, where wage labor gives a young couple independence from parents and in-laws, couples may pay to have barley ground in the town mill. This is socially disapproved, however. Machine-ground *machica* isn't *mishqui*, sweet or tasty, people say, and older women cluck with disapproval over a house where dawn finds a cold hearth, that is, where *machica* is not being toasted in the morning. Because of this association of *machica* with female productive and social roles, women react very emotionally to their children's rejection of barley gruels. It is not only the demand for precious purchased food over abundant home-grown grains that troubles them. In demanding bread, children reject their mother's contribution to the household and reach for foods that their fathers provide.

Zumbagua adults do not feel that bread is appropriate for everyday meals because it is part of a class of food defined as *wanlla*. *Wanlla* is anything that is not part of a meal. In this sense, it could be translated as "snack", "treat" "junk food" or "dessert food", and *wanlla* can be all of these. But the second meaning of *wanlla* is "gift". All of the foods called *wanlla* are primarily purchased in order to be redistributed. The motivation is not so much altruism as the exercise of power: giving *wanlla* is a critically important social and political action in Zumbagua; no one can be a successful social actor without understanding how to give and to manipulate others into giving. Any food given as a gift can be called *wanlla*. Hence in certain contexts rice, onions, noodles, milk or any other food could be *wanlla*. Some foods, however, are always *wanlla* in nature: they do not form part of regular meals and their primary purpose, in Zumbagua eyes, is as gifts. Since eating in Zumbagua always takes the form of offering and receiving food, these goods are still *wanlla* even when bought by members of a household and consumed within that household.

Bread is the *wanlla* par excellence. It is the universally appropriate gift, the favorite treat. In Zumbagua minds, bread has none of the qualities of a staple. It is truly a *golosina*, a treat, a luxury. More so than perhaps any other food, consumption of bread is directly dependent on a family's disposable cash income. It is the one special food that everyone would like to have on hand all the time, while at the same time it is recognized that no one ever needs bread. Potatoes and barley are necessities; bread is for enjoyment.

In households where men are absent wage-workers, the relationship of husband and wife entails certain exchanges of food. Whatever the husband's job, one of the obligations of a wife is to have food ready for him when he returns home. In households where he comes home only on weekends, every other week or even only once a month, this offering on her part becomes increasingly important symbolically. She cooks the best food she has, and the form she uses is strictly indigenous, using locally produced foods like *machica* to welcome him back home. While she presents him with these boiled grain soups or gruels, he brings *wanlla*: raw foods and treats from the city. These may include noodles, flour, cookies, candies and fruit, but bread is an important component.

The relative importance of her contribution compared to his depends on the financial situation of the household. If the young couple is part of a large, landholding extended family, he may return bearing only treats and goodies. But if they are a relatively isolated, land-poor couple, she and the children may have been subsisting on nothing but *machica* and water awaiting his return, and he will then bring in a substantial supply of groceries. In treating purchased foods like bread as part of everyday meals, the children seem in some ways to be making a prediction that the latter kind of household will become more common as they grow up, a prediction that seems more likely than not. Whatever the future may be, they certainly are expressing a preference for a male-provided, purchased commodity, bread, over the female-produced complex of cooked grains. And in defining bread as part of everyday meals, they are proposing a substantial shift in the role bread plays in Zumbagua cuisine.

Gruel and History

This contrast between two starch food forms, one of which is produced by and represents the local economy, while the other is part of a state-level economy and so enters the local community with all the prestige and symbolic power of the state behind it, is reminiscent of the relationshop between maize and potatoes described by John Murra (1975) for Inca times. According to Murra, potatoes were the humble food of humble people, while maize, the cultivation of which necessitated systems of irrigation, was associated with the imperial power of the Inca state. The ability of the Inca state to make maize into a prestige item is suggested in the fragments of myths and stories cited by Murra in which the superiority of maize over potatoes is implicitly suggested.

According to Murra, the Spanish chroniclers were blind to the competition between maize and potatoes because, coming from a grain-based economy themselves, they never considered the possibility that tubers could be a staple. I find this observation to be very pertinent to the question of breads and gruels today, since our own prediposition towards bread as a basic food, as seen in its description as the "staff of life", can prevent us from perceiving the alien nature of leavened wheat breads to household economies based on boiled foods. As Americans, we all carry with us the mythic image of home-baked bread, but in areas of the world where fuel is precious, bread baking is beyond the scope of the individual household.

Our own predjudice towards leavened bread, which can be seen in the unpleasant associations that the word "gruel" has in English, is an artifact of what Raymond Sokolov (1984:108) has called "the inexorable march of wheat". As he points out, our disdain for boiled grain dishes is not just a matter of taste but is the product of specific political and economic processes in Europe and, later, in the Americas as well. The hegemonic nature of the contrast between gruels and breads played a part in the changes in taste that accompanied the spread of the Roman Empire, for example, where Tannahill says that "Bread . . . was established as being more desirable than grain-pastes and porridges" (Tannahill 1973: 57). According to Goody, "In Europe . . . the northern extension of bread from the Mediterranean was associated with its use by the conquering Romans and by the missionizing Christians, who sacralized this high-status food through its use in the Mass" (1982:180). In Zumbagua, the intonation by European priests during the Mass of "Give us this day our daily bread" has similar connotations of white validation of a high-prestige food to indigenous listeners.

Oats and barley, and the porridges and unleavened breads that are made from them, symbolized the provincialism of the Scots to the eighteenth-century writer Samuel Johnson. According to Sokolov, Johnson's jibes on the subject of Scottish culinary tradition, with its emphasis on such gruel-based dishes as haggis and flummery, are revealing of the relationship between London and the hinterlands of the British Isles. "[Johnson's] . . . complete insensitivity to the real situation that condemned the Celtic fringe (and the north of England) to oats and barley . . . is an unappealing, but, once again, typical expression of the imperial status of London" (1984: 110).

In this century, Goody cites the opposition between porridges and breads as one facet of the colonized/colonizer dichotomy in Ghana, where rising black elites, who previously made much of their familiarity with European culinary habits, have only recently begun to publicly eat porridge as an affirmation of their ethnicity (Goody 1982:177, passim). Goody's comments on the production aspects of this opposition are very relevant to the Andean case. He points out that the early success of bread among European foods introduced into the area can perhaps be attributed to the possibility of producing it on a small, localized scale (1982:180). In Ecuador, bread baking and sales figure importantly among the entrepeneurial possibilities open to the lower-class "white" and cholo populations whose livelihood is based on products which appeal to and are affordable for people from the small towns and rural hinterlands of the Sierra.

As Goody points out, the contrast between leavened breads and gruels or toasted grain products is one of technology; baking bread implies use of an oven, a technology which contrasts with that of the rural household where techniques are limited to boiling and toasting (1977:180-181). Because of the high energy input required for their use, ovens in turn require some type of commercial or communal organization of production in low energy consuming economies such as that of rural Ecuador.[6]

In conclusion, then, bread in Zumbagua has for some time now been a high-status food which contrasts with local products, although its specific role in local cuisine may be changing. Family arguments over the introduction of bread into the early-morning meal involve issues larger and more complex than worries over the family budget. In addition, the roles of children and parents, men and women in these conflicts indicates the heterogeneous nature of family members both as producers and as consumers, a heterogeneity which household-level economic analysis can overlook. As to the resolution of the conflict, it remains to be seen whether the children's cries for bread and the continued erosion of the household's ability to sustain itself through subsistence agriculture will succeed in transforming everyday practice.

Notes

1. Race and ethnicity in the Ecuadorian Sierra, as in much of Latin America, is determined primarily by socioeconomic class, "Indian" and "peasant", "white" and "elite" being practically synonymous. In Zumbagua, ethnicity for permanent residents is bipolar, *blanco* (white) referring to the small local elite and *longo/a* (a derogatory term similar in connotation to the English "nigger") labeling the indigenous majority. Zumbagua "whites" would not be considered white at all by urban or upper-middle class Ecuadorians, while the metaphorical nature of these terms is demonstrated by the presence in the parish of green-eyed, fair-haired, freckled "longos", the product of the institutionalized miscegenation of hacienda days, as well as by the membership among the parish "whites" of a family of coastal blacks. Terms for people of mixed blood, such as *mestizo, cholo*, or *misti* are infrequently heard in the parish and never refer to those who were born there. The word *cholo* identifies market sellers, while professionals such as the staff of the Catholic Church or the government-sponsored clinic are referred to as *gringos*, foreigners, even when Ecuadorian. Everyone born in the parish is categorized as *blanco* or *longo*, although local gossip identifies those who are "trying to be *blanco*" or "trying to be both".

2. I use terms--*sopa* and *seco, caldo* and *colada*--which come from Ecuadorian national cuisine, but are here applied to categories used within the parish. These are not words that people of the parish themselves use. Although more acculturated and Spanish-speaking residents of the parish may use these terms to apply to Zumbagua dishes, monolingual Quichua speakers do not. Soups are commonly referred to simply as *almuirsu*, from the Spanish *almuerzo*, lunch. I have borrowed these terms to label certain implicit categories used by Zumbagua women when cooking: they refer to specific types of syntagmatic chains I discovered in their practice. I use the Ecuadorian Spanish terms because they most closely approximate native categories, (not surprisingly, given the common cultural roots, European and Native American, of both cuisines) and to avoid meanings implicit in English cooking terminology.

3. Local farmers prefer varieties which retain form after boiling and consider those which break down (*deshacerse*) as inferior.

4. The Zumbagua sequence of meals is similar in concept to the typical Ecuadorian pattern, in that meals eaten after dark are light while daytime meals are heavy. As I describe elsewhere (Weismantel 1987) among current conflicts over cuisine in the parish is the issue as to whether to eat three times a day, the national pattern, or four (*cafe* {5 A.M.} , *almuirsu* {10 A.M.}, *almuirsu* {3 P.M.}, *cafe* {8 P.M.}). The latter meal structure is suited to the schedules of women who must both cook and herd sheep,

but it cannot be sustained if the children attend public schools that send them home at noon for a meal.

5. Finados is the November 1-2 celebration for the dead, observed throughout the Andes. Many of the rituals of the holiday, which syncretize indigenous and Hispanic elements, suggest the symbolic significance of food and eating, and especially of starchy foods; the *colada morada* or *yana api* is in fact a gruel, made of maize in maize-producing areas, but in Zumbagua it is more frequently made of *machica*. For food symbolism in Finados, see Weismantel 1983; Hartman 1973, 1974 provides the best data on contemporary Ecuadorian practice.

6. There are communities in the Sierra that have ovens, however; these are frequently owned as money-making enterprises by certain families who undertake the roasting of pigs or the baking of quantities of breads for weddings and other special occasions.

References

Douglas, Mary
1971   Deciphering a Meal. in *Myth , Symbol and Culture*. Clifford Geertz, ed. New York: W.W. Norton and Co. pp. 61-82.

Goody, Jack
1982   *Cooking, Cuisine and Class: A Study of Comparative Sociology.* Cambridge: Cambridge University Press.

Mintz, Sidney
1979   Time, Sugar and Sweetness. *Marxist Perspectives* 2:56-73

1985   *Sweetness and Power: The Place of Sugar in Modern History.* NY: Viking Press.

Sokolov, Raymond
1984   Oat Cuisine. *Natural History* 93 (4):108-111.

Tannahill, Reay
1972   *Food in History.* NY: Stein and Day.

Turner, Victor
1967   *The Forest of Symbols*. Ithaca: Cornell University Press.

Williams, Raymond
1977   *Marxism and Literature*. Cambridge: Cambridge University Press.

NATIONAL AND INTERNATIONAL DETERMINANTS OF FOOD CONSUMPTION IN REVOLUTIONARY NICARAGUA, 1979-1986

Michael Zalkin

Introduction

Food consumption is a key question for any society. However, in the context of popular and revolutionary social change, it becomes a critical concern. In the first seven years of its history, the Nicaraguan revolution experienced serious problems supplying food to its population.

The neoclassical theory of consumer demand suggests that consumption is a matter of constrained choice by the individual. While individuals always have choices, many determinants of consumption in Nicaragua tend to originate far beyond the individual consumer's domain. Food consumption, in particular, has numerous national and international determinants. Historically, internal social and economic transformations, as well as actions by the state, have altered Nicaraguans' access to foods. So, too, have foreign governments' food aid programs, and the investments of international merchant and productive capital. More recently, access to food was limited by the war of liberation. It is currently limited by the economic blockade and "covert" war efforts of the U.S. government as it attempts to put an end to both the Sandinista National Liberation Front (FSLN) and the revolution itself. An additional determinant of food consumption has been the macroeconomic policy of the Sandinista government and the FSLN's efforts to carry out a social transformation of Nicaraguan society.

These are all institutional or structural interventions which affect consumption on what the neoclassicals call the supply side. In a supply-constrained economy, market demand for food is insufficient to bring forth supply. Yet the social transformation now taking place in Nicaragua is not solely of an economic nature, nor is it determined only by institutions. For example, the changes in Nicaragua include new forms of political expression. The demand for food in Nicaragua is not limited to an event in which the individual confronts the market, purchasing power in hand. Rather, demand for food is a social process in which individuals united in mass organizations also confront individual and social (state and private) suppliers of food outside of the market mechanism. Consumers receive food through both individual and administrative processes. Demand for food is often expressed via popular organizations and mechanisms (neighhorhood meetings, for example) to the state. The supply of food is in part an outcome of the political and economic transformation of Nicaraguan society.

This paper specifies ways in which the nation-state, a hostile foreign government, and international political expression and alliances have influenced Nicaraguans' consumption of food. Three moments in Nicaraguan history will be drawn from: the decades prior to the 1979 victory of the revolution; the first years of the revolutionary period (1979-1983); and the rest of the revolutionary period (1984-1986). Most of the paper is focused on the supply side. However, the demand side will also be briefly considered as it exists under revolutionary conditions.

The examples used will suggest that exclusive focus on individual choice, in the Nicaraguan case, leaves out crucial factors determining consumption. The point is not to prove the relevance or irrelevance of consumer sovereignty as a concept for analysis of Nicaragua. It is clear, however, that a theory of consumption different from the neoclassical theory of consumer demand is necessary for the analysis of societies in revolutionary or socialist transition. Several steps are taken in this direction.

Consumption in the Pre-Revolutionary Period

Prior to 1979, consumption by Nicaraguans was strongly affected by the dominant model of socio-economic development. This model is referred to by some as the agro-export model (Nunez, n.d.), one in which Somoza and other leading families engaged in capital accumulation as the state directed the economy toward the production of agro-exports. This model did not imply a priori that food consumption would be affected, or affected negatively. However, the implementation of this model in the 1950-1979 period provoked serious and negative consequences for food consumption in Nicaragua.

The expansion of capitalist agro-export production involved the expropriation of peasant landholdings in the fertile Pacific regions of Nicaragua in the 1950s and 1960s. These peasants were mainly petty producers of grains and other foodstuffs. Their migration to the agricultural frontier or to the cities provoked problems of consumption. Those who stayed in agriculture were marginalized either as agricultural worker or rural semi-proletarians (engaged in both petty production and working in agro-export harvests). Living conditions for agricultural workers, including consumption, have been described by Nunez as both extremely poor and deteriorating in the pre-revolutionary period (Nunez, n.d., pp. 92-111).

Peasants who migrated to the frontier encountered lands that were of poorer quality than those in the Pacific. Lower productivity, rural to urban migration, and relatively low producer prices for maize and beans (a result of the power of the state and rural merchants, landlords and moneylenders) implied that less of their own food production remained with peasants. It meant less peasant income to purchase other foods and non-food consumption items. There was also a negative impact on production of certain foodgrains. Indicators of food production show stagnation in maize and bean production from the mid-1960s through the 1970s (FIDA, 1980, p. 38). Peasants engaged in full-time petty production declined. By the end of the 1970s, 35% of the rural economically active population (EAP) were semi-proletarians, and 31% full-time rural workers (CIERA, 1984b, p. 15).

Stagnation in food production did not mean that only small quantities of food were produced and/or available. A 1976 study by A.I.D. suggested that certain foods, such as fruits, plantains, maize, rice, sugar, and fats, were available on a per capita basis in sufficient quantity. Rice is an interesting counter-example to maize and beans, in that its production in the 1960s shot up as the result of state subsidies for large-scale capitalist rice growers. Other foods, however, were less available on a per capita basis--milk products, eggs, meat, fish, vegetables, roots, beans and wheat (CIERA 1983, p. 41). The economic marginalization of the rural population restricted its diet primarily to rice, beans and maize.

An economic indicator of rural marginalization was the distribution of income of the rural versus urban residents. In a 1974 study it was estimated that the annual cost of an adequate family diet was C$8,736 (CIERA, 1983, p. 41). The average income of the lowest 50% of the rural population was C$1,694. At the same time, the average income of the poorest 50% of the population of Managua was C$6,317 per year. The Managua average was higher than the separate rural averages estimated for each of Nicaragua's six regions.

Rural home consumption certainly augmented the paltry rural monetary incomes. It is difficult to estimate the size of this increase. As a rough example, consider the case of poor peasants, who engaged in petty food production on their own or rented land and sold their labor power during export crop harvests. In 1978, these peasants represented over 35% of the rural Economically Active Population (EAP) (CIERA, 1984a, p. 25). A 1980 estimate shows poor peasants to produce a yearly average of 2.2 manzanas of maize, of which 15 percent is marketed; 1.4 manzanas of beans, of which 25 percent is marketed; 2.1 manzanas of coffee (assume for convenience that all is marketed); and to have 2.8 head of cattle (Zalkin, 1986, p. 120). Using 1982-83 grain yields as a proxy, the average poor peasant would have produced about 37 quintales (hundred-weights) of maize and 15 quintales of beans, of which an average of 31 quintales of maize and 11 of beans would have been kept for home consumption. At official 1974 prices, the implicit value of this home consumption would have been 2385 cordobas, leaving poor peasants' average income well below the average for the urban poor. The new level of C$4079 is likely to be an overestimate, if, after adding to it for home consumption of milk and cheese, one subtracts for losses in grain storage and the gap between actual grain prices received by poor peasants and official prices. This estimate suggests that even with home consumption accounted for, the agro-export model tended to have a negative impact on both direct access to foods and on the income levels for the rural population.

Not unexpectedly, migration to the cities mushroomed. By 1980, over 30% of Nicaragua's population resided in the capital, and over 50% in urban areas (CIERA, 1984b, pp. 1, 7). Half of the urban EAP was involved in informal sector activity (CIERA, 1984b, p. 20). A 1977 study of Managua described the informal sector as composed of a much higher percentage of women (55%) than Managua's formal sector (32%), and as composed of persons with unstable work and income (CIERA, 1984b, p. 26). It was estimated that 58% of Managua's informal sector in 1977 earned less than 200 cordobas per week. By comparison, only 20% of Managua's formal sector earned as low a level of income (CIERA, 1984b, p. 28). Nicaragua thus produced a distorted model of consumption, with a sharp urban bias. In 1982, Managua, with one-third of the nation's population, consumed two-thirds or more of Nicaragua's supply of pasteurized milk, cheese, chicken, eggs, plaintains, tomatoes, and onions. Thus Managua developed as a kind of sponge, absorbing foods from all regions of the country. Yet the result was not simply that all urban dwellers were better off. Both rural peasants and members of the urban informal sector were limited by access to productive resources and ultimately income which in turn limited their access to food. This was paradoxical for both groups. Rural peasants produced food but were so poor that their access to food was not guaranteed year round. Urban informal sector employees were primarily involved in food sale or processing as merchants or domestic servants, yet unsteady work and income prohibited sufficient access to foods.

While the 1974 study showed the average income of the lowest urban 50% to be four times that of the lowest rural 50%, the urban average still represented only 72% of that necessary for a family to consume the recommended levels of foods. The average income of the urban poor was also less than one third that of the average of all residents of Managua. In the early 1970s, medium and large-scale property-holders represented 3.5% of the rural population, but received 63.1% of total rural income (FIDA, 1980, p. 2). Income was skewed within Managua, between Managua and the countryside, and in the countryside itself.

Income distribution was clearly related to consumption levels. There were significant differences in food consumption by income level in the capital. A 1982 study showed large variations in food consumption between the lowest and highest income strata. Not surprisingly, the lowest income stratum showed deficiencies with respect to the recommended daily diet, while the high income stratum showed surpluses in almost all foods studied (CIERA, 1983, pp. 88-89).

These outcomes, which were not to be easily altered in the revolutionary period, have been attributed to the pre-revolutionary development of a model of accumulation and the role of the state in that model:

The gap that existed between the urban and rural popular sectors reflected the Somocista policy of favoring the city with a series of measures that gave the urban sectors greater food purchasing power. In this context there existed, for example: a policy of relatively favorable salaries for the working class, giving it salaries that compared favorably with other Central American countries; a system of prices that permitted the urban sectors to buy foods relatively cheaply, due in great part to the low prices that the producer received, and a distribution network controlled by the state that also favored access to basic grains by urban consumers (CIERA, 1983, p. 42).

Finally, consumption levels were skewed within the peasantry. Different access to means of production by different peasant categories tended to be reflected in production and consumption levels (in volume and quantity) (CIERA, MIDINRA, 1980, and Zalkin, 1986).

The Initial Impact of the Revolution on Consumption (1979-83)

Data does not exist which would permit a direct comparison between consumers in the pre-revolutionary period and consumers in the initial revolutionary period. The only statement that can be made with certainty is that within Managua the relationship between family income and consumption was positive in both 1972 and 1982.[1] Lack of measurement prohibits any definitive conclusion as to whether or not the revolutionary government created increased opportunities for consumption among the least privileged of Nicaraguans. However, it is clear that the state intervened quite heavily in the food system so as to create opportunities for consumption for both rural peasants and urban dwellers. Here we will consider the nature of that intervention and its impact on consumption.

The intervention by the Sandinista state was not an effort to increase the living standards of all Nicaraguans. It would have been unrealistic to have expected increased living standards for the wealthy, given the consequences of Nicaragua's history of capitalist exploitation, the earthquake of 1972, and the revolutionary war. As a government publication stated,

One of the fundamental goals of the revolution is to satisfy the basic necessities of the people. To do this the state has prioritized the production of basic foods, and popular consumption; in this way changing the logic of the agro-export model that oriented the development of the economy below Somoza and transforming the patterns of consumption that were previously characterized by a high incidence of luxury consumption (CIERA, 1983, p. 58).

This commitment to "basic" consumption had numerous policy components and effects. One level of intervention targeted basic food production. It was hoped that production would have a direct impact on consumption. It would raise the levels of food consumption of the poorer rural peasants. This would result primarily from measures extending land, credit, inputs, technical assistance, marketing services and organization to poor and medium peasants (Austin, Fox, and Kruger, 1985; Barraclough 1982; Deere, Marchetti, and

Reinhardt, 1985; and Zalkin, 1986). Support for peasant and non-peasant food production was also counted on to supply foods to non-producers, and to raise per capita levels of food consumption for both food-producing and nonfood-producing families.

The second level of intervention was focused on the system of distribution. The idea was to guarantee a minimum level of access to *bienes basicos* (basic consumption goods) for the entire population. The first component was a system of *canales seguros* (secure channels) of food distribution: stores run by the state, commissaries in state institutions and large state and private businesses, and agreements with small private shopkeepers. A second component was price intervention. The state declared the prices of fifteen food items legally controlled: rice, beans, maize, sorghum, beef, pork, chicken, fish, eggs, milk, cheese, sugar, salt, cooking oil and coffee. These were chosen on the basis of being important components of the national diet, rather than on nutritional grounds (Utting, n.d., p. 10) (although liquid and powdered milk were included from a nutritional point of view). Another factor was the capacity of the state to control the flows and prices of these foods administratively. The basic foods were quite heterogeneous. For example, beans were consumed as is; cheese was processed in rural areas; chicken and eggs required a large quantity of imported inputs; and cooking oil was processed, for the most part, in urban areas. Inclusion of cooking oil in the list implied linkages with other foods, such as its use in cooking of maize and beans, items on the basic list, and the frying of non-basic foods, such as plantains. Prices of fifty other products (food and non-foods) were regulated.

Both controlled and regulated prices had legal maximums, the difference being that the latter were less actively watched over. The latter group included wheat flour and flour-based products such as bread and noodles; condiments such as tomato paste, ketchup and mustard; processed meats such as ham and salami; and soft drinks. Another group of foods and non-foods were left unregulated, such as the small quantities of imported canned goods that found their way into the national market, and fruits and vegetables, which fluctuated in price. Third, price subsidies were introduced for maize, beans, rice, cooking oil, milk and sugar. Again, this was based on a perception of the most important foods in the Nicaraguan diet. The state encouraged the use of maize and tortillas, not for nutritional reasons, but rather to reduce bread consumption (based on imported wheat). Other policies included the direct delivery of foods, and the expansion of employment (CIERA, 1983, pp. 58-70). During 1982 and 1983, the state created a quota system, using rationing cards to guarantee direct distribution of first sugar and then other items (rice, beans, salt, cooking oil, powdered milk, and an important non-food, soap) to the population.

The efforts of the state to supply a basic basket of food consumption items to the population had several interesting effects. First, while the distribution system was supposed to serve all areas, in the 1979-83 period it primarily served urban ones. This was the cumulative result of many factors: the state administrative structure, its personnel, the supply infrastructure, and the mass organizations were all concentrated in urban areas. The historical patterns, the relative ease of identifying problems in the urban areas, and the difficulty of operation in rural areas (not to mention combat) all contributed a strong urban bias to the state's efforts.

A second impact was a series of distortions created by the product selectivity of the new distribution and rationing efforts. The FSLN did not implement rationing to limit consumer access to basic foods. It rather wished to guarantee access by the entire population to sufficient quantities of foods. This was difficult in that the population did not have a history of sufficient access to basic foods. Now the population demanded their quota of foods as their right, and even per capita increases in some foods (see below) were insufficient to satisfy consumer demand. This effect was only strengthened by selective protection of food prices. With prices of some necessary goods uncontrolled and sharply rising, and prices of a small set of the most basic goods actively controlled and subsidized, it was normal for demand pressure on the latter to rise. Urban and rural salaries were strictly controlled from 1980 to 1983, based on the protection of the "basic" set of foods. Again, the rising prices of non-protected items pushed consumption over to the protected and subsidized foods.

Rural consumption did not fare well via this system in the first few years, for the above reasons. However, it should not be interpreted that rural food consumption suffered uniformly. In the first full year of revolutionary agricultural production, the state expanded its credit program to finance almost every peasant foodgrain producer. The flood of credit that was unleashed coincided with Nicaragua's access, in the first year, to hundreds of millions of dollars in international relief funds, much of which was used to import consumption items into the country. Thus, rural consumption levels for both home-produced foods and purchased foods probably increased dramatically during the 1980-81 agricultural cycle.[2] While this rural access declined after that first year, peasant access to home-grown production permanently increased. Prior to the revolution, coercive economic pressure from landlords, merchants, and moneylenders often forced peasants to sell or hand over an amount of grain that included part of that needed for family consumption. The new rental laws, land distribution, producer grain sale at guaranteed prices, and a very lenient credit repayment policy all now permitted peasants to satisfy their own consumption needs first. This affected maize in particular, allowing increases in peasant home maize consumption and forcing maize imports in order to satisfy urban demand.

The creation of the *canasta basica* (basic basket) led to some conceptual confusion with policy implications. "Basic" meant different things to different people at different times. At the beginning of the revolutionary process (see above), basic was not well defined but referred to those foods which formed the basis for the diet of the *sectores populares* (popular sectors) (productive and unproductive workers, informal sector population, and peasants), and which were necessary for their survival over time. Price controls redefined the basics into a smaller group, and the quota system reduced it to only the most elementary group of products. These choices did not reflect precise studies of consumption, but rather the stylized facts of Nicaraguan consumption as they were known to policy makers. Those foods protected and/or distributed by the state were also determined by product supply and the state's ability to control and distribute that supply.

Several problems resulted from these definitions. For example, the basic basket did not reflect regional differences in the Nicaraguan diet. It is true that the consumption of maize, beans, and rice were fairly generalized among the population. However, varied access in rural areas to other products meant different levels of dependency on grains, and therefore different levels of adequacy provided by the quotas. Where there was increased access to meat and dairy products, it tended to reduce the emphasis on grains. Starchy foods, an important complement to the basics, varied between regions. Managua tended to have greater access to bread and wheat products, given the greater historical impact of the U.S. model of consumption, as well as U.S. export programs for wheat, on the urban population and infrastructure. Rural areas with greater levels of irrigation or rainfall tended to have greater access than others to plantains, cassava and other starchy foods. These included the Pacific coastal plain (where ground water was more abundant) and the deep interior and Atlantic Coast (where rainfall averages around 100 inches per year). A basic basket that was fixed for all areas was inadequate to deal with geographic differences in food consumption.

The quota-related basics formed a smaller group of foods than that to which the population was accustomed to having access. This problem had different ramifications among different classes and groups. Wealthy members of society, such as capitalists and merchants, were used to consuming large quantities of meat and many imported food items, none of which was protected under quotas. However, the wealthy could outbid the poor for the smaller available supply of these foods. For the poorest urban groups, the consequences were more severe, in that they had regularly consumed at least some meat proteins and other supposed non-essentials. One such case involved soups based on imported chicken and beef consommes (Sopa Maggi, a Swiss product), a working class and informal sector tradition. A sharp decline in the supply of Sopa Maggi and a corresponding increase in price did not so much affect caloric consumption as it disrupted an established pattern of popular consumption.

The Sandinistas could not guarantee an adequate supply of these items. For example, the cattle herd had been drastically reduced due to increased slaughter and export by farmers decapitalizing during the revolutionary war. Unfortunately, the FSLN's definition of a basic basket under the quota system gave the impression that all necessary and/or customary foods were included. There was some tendency for policy statements to give the impression that the basic basket was available, sufficient nutritionally and acceptable to the majority of the population. While the Sandinistas were faced with many problems not of their own creation or choice, this confusion around the basics question in turn limited Sandinista capacity to make choices from the limited alternatives available. It also tended to create dissatisfaction when the public statements describing the population's access to food were not identical to the population's daily experience.

The Later Revolutionary Period (1984-1986)

During the first years of the revolution its leaders could reasonably argue that gains were being made in food consumption. A large infusion of external aid had allowed food consumption to normalize quite rapidly in 1979-80. Even with incipient hostilities from the United States and the ex-members of Somoza's National Guard in Honduras, the FSLN and the Nicaraguan people expected a fairly rapid reconstruction of a viable economy in a few years. The results might not include luxury food imports as in the Somoza period, but it was expected that basic foods would be provided for all Nicaraguans. This did not happen. By 1984, most non-essential food consumption items were scarce in Nicaragua, only available in small quantities through the black market (inaccessible to most Nicaraguans). For many foods such as fruits, vegetables and meats (not the most basic but certainly traditionally consumed by popular sectors), only limited and uneven supplies were available. Even items in the basic basket (maize, beans and rice) were at times in short supply.

The FSLN made its share of errors, some of which are mentioned above. As well, state production suffered from extremely poor management. Non-state production (peasant and non-peasant) of foods was characterized by a sizable flow of resources, but grains in particular suffered from falling real prices. Expected production increases did not come to fruition. A cap on rural salaries in favor of increased rural social services did not create an incentive for worker productivity. Also, workers on state and capitalist farms tended to interpret the revolution to mean a reduction in the length of the workday. In peasant production, particularly maize and beans, the state committed sizeable resources, but confronted problems of historic and massive proportions (such as the geographic dispersion of the peasantry, and the difficulty of organizing the state for such a large endeavor).

Blaming falling levels of food consumption on the FSLN's program, however, is a narrow and mistaken view. Much of Nicaragua's food consumption has depended on imports, which require the generation of foreign exchange via exports. Data on 1979-84 export crop production show significant increases in the quantity of cotton, sesame, bananas, sugar cane, and Havana tobacco. Data on world market prices from 1980-83 show sharp declines in cotton and coffee prices (Nicaragua's two most important exports). The declining international terms of trade wreaked havoc with Nicaragua's ability to import and produce consumption goods. Lack of hard currency affected, for example, imports of direct inputs for foods such as the raw material for cooking oil, containers for oil, milk and sauces, chicks for poultry production, and medicines and feed for beef, pork, and poultry. It also affected the numerous indirect inputs necessary to keep the food system functioning.

Opponents of the Nicaraguan revolution often mention the falling level of overall consumption in the 1984-86 period, which certainly has occurred. However, this ignores the problem with international prices for Nicaragua's exports and the fact that production of the most important internal consumption crops--rice, beans, maize, sorghum and red tobacco--all showed important production increases in the 1979-1984 period (MIDINRA 1984, pp. 16, 19-20). Per capita consumption levels for certain foods also rose during this period. A comparison of the 1976-1978 average with 1983-1984 shows per capita declines in maize, pork and beef, but per capita increases in beans, rice, flour, oil, sugar, eggs, chicken, and milk (CIERA, 1985, p. 44).

The problems of consumption in Nicaragua, however, are more complex than the international terms of trade. Another major factor, the U.S.-sponsored war against Nicaragua, must be taken into account. The destruction of infrastructure and the mining of ports has negatively affected food marketing within Nicaragua and food imports. The cost of repairing the damages and defending the country against the "Contra" (armed by the U.S.) has reduced resources available for food production. It draws large quantities of male labor power out of productive employment and into defense. The major part of the national budget must now be geared to defense efforts, instead of investments and imports to improve food and other consumption. The U.S. government's cutoff of bilateral aid, such as PL480 wheat shipments (1981), its maneuvers in international organizations to block loans, and its total embargo on trade (May 1985) to Nicaragua, are all public knowledge. The latter has meant a loss of markets for $47 million in Nicaragua exports, and $135 million in imports, affecting Nicaragua's capacity to obtain seeds and inputs for agriculture, and raw materials and equipment for agroindustry (CIERA, 1985 p. 60).

Maize and bean production has been particularly hard hit by the war. This production is carried out mostly by peasant producers in the deep, mountainous interior of Nicaragua, precisely in those areas of greatest Contra activity. Attacks on vehicles reduced marketing activity and decreased poor peasant willingness to travel to look for wage work. Attacks on production co-operatives decreased production, as did the need for peasant grain producers to participate in the defense effort (of the country and locally, of their own farms). A state program of peasant resettlement in the zones of greatest conflict increased the resources at the peasants' disposal; however, in the short-run it disrupted grain production.

The external aggression has limited the power of the revolutionary state to maintain consumption and reduced the policy alternatives available. There is a clear recognition in Nicaragua that a return to the pre-Contra war (and post-revolutionary war) levels of food consumption is impossible under the present circumstances. In spite of this, one set of state efforts is concentrated on guaranteeing basic food production. These include efforts to increase grain production on large farms to make them at least self-sufficient; support for community and family gardens; creation of irrigated state grain projects; continuation of supply of inputs and credits to peasant producers; the strengthening of the input supply and product marketing system; and the massive distribution of land to peasant cooperatives and individual peasant producers.

Another set of efforts involves improvements in the distribution system for foods (also affecting non-food products). Some factories and farms are now supplying 100% of their food output to the Ministry of Internal Commerce (MICOIN). An increased number of goods are controlled by the state; that is, the state no longer permits them to be sold for higher prices in the "parallel" market. Mass organizations--of neighborhoods, rural and urban workers, and peasants-- have a more important and more direct role in the functioning of the distribution system (CIERA, 1985, pp. 38-39, 62).

A third set of measures affected the number, kind and prices of products which the state controls. Subsidies were sharply reduced in 1985 for foodgrains. The strongest arguments for ending the subsidy were both the cost to the state and the state's inability to guarantee that subsidies reached consumers (particularly since grains were often inputs for other products). It was felt that real consumer purchasing power could be better defended by offering basic necessities for purchase at official prices in "secure" channels.

The latest measures (1985) divided products into four groups. The first group included cooking oil, sugar, rice, sorghum, and salt. For these products, considered essential, distribution was nationalized and a basic quota guaranteed. A state monopoly was established on wholesale and retail marketing. The second group--maize and beans--was also essential, and a quota guaranteed, but distribution was not nationalized. The state simply did not have the resources to continue to market grains from tens of thousands of peasant producers, and now proposed to share this task with private merchants. For these two groups, the state intended to assure fair distribution of the available supply, and to import if national production was insufficient and foreign exchange available.

A third group of products included foods such as eggs and powdered milk. In this group, distribution was nationalized but no quota guaranteed. The state would guarantee a fair distribution but would not guarantee imports. A fourth group consisted of those foods whose distribution was not nationalized and no quota guaranteed.

It is extremely unfortunate that in spite of a clear commitment by the FSLN to provide a minimum level of consumption for the population, the available supply of foodstuffs and the food purchasing power of non-farmers declined drastically. Reports during 1986 indicate that food supplies are tight, particularly in the capital.[3] This is a result in part of the Reagan administration strategy to create such difficult economic conditions that the Nicaraguan people will turn against the FSLN. While the U.S. government has so far been unable to achieve its goal (it has not broken internal support for the FSLN), the U.S. has been successful in contributing to economic difficulty for most Nicaraguans.

The Politics of Demand

This paper has focused on how pressures and policies have affected the supply of food. For foods distributed by quota and sold at official prices, the full quota is demanded by consumers, but the quotas are not always met and are not influenced by excess demand. For foods allocated by the market, the price mechanism eliminates would-be consumers. In Nicaragua's case, both controlled and free market food supply have not been completely determined on the supply side, nor completely determined externally. The role of consumer demand cannot be ignored. For example, price subsidies for certain basic foods in the early 1980s and rising prices and scarcity for other basics and non-basics helped to increase demand for the subsidized goods. So, too, has a 4% percent population growth rate since 1979.

Demand also played a role in food consumption as the result of changed social relationships in the countryside. Rents were decreased by decree, land redistributed on a large scale, and credit and inputs distributed by the state at negative interest rates and guaranteed prices, respectively. This eliminated many of the reasons for which peasants were required to sell a share of their grain. Traditional agricultural texts treat this marketed surplus as production minus consumption, the implication being that it is traded by the peasant by choice. However, from the viewpoint of class analysis, food marketing (or delivery, if payment in kind) may not involve a trade of equal value (measured in labor time embodied in the product). There may be involved a process of *redistribution* of the food producers' surplus labor time (defined as total minus necessary labor time). In the moment of its production, rural petty producers control this surplus. However, it can be argued that in the pre-revolutionary period the surplus was redistributed to other rural agents on the basis of their control over physical and financial means of production as well as means of circulation (such as the animals and vehicles necessary for rural marketing).

The redistribution of and increased access to farm resources during the revolution freed up grain for disposal by peasants. For some peasants, the marketed surplus had previously included grain they otherwise would have consumed. Pent-up peasant demand for their own grain resulted in increases in direct peasant consumption of food. Low producer prices for grain and low rural availability (and high rural price) of non-farm consumption goods added to this effect.

Demand also was expressed along non-market lines. The system of administrative mechanisms for urban and (less so) rural food supply were complemented by an administrative and popular system for transmission of the "political demand" for food to the state and for state decisions concerning food. This two-way process concerning demand was not always explicit. For example, in the first years of the revolution, the FSLN and state policy makers thought that the agricultural production program and the food distribution measures would solve urban and rural food problems. There was little sense that rural problems were not being solved until the FSLN saw some signs of discontent: peasant cooperation with the Contras, and lower attendance of peasants at agrarian reform ceremonies. While food was not the only issue, peasant demand for basic products that they did not produce (or did not produce enough of) was increasingly reflected in rural studies from 1982 onward and in the vocal complaints of the massive FSLN-allied peasant organization (UNAG). In response, the FSLN freed rural maize and bean prices to increase rural income (and allow peasants to compete in the market for scarce food and other items). It also increased the administrative supply of processed food items to the countryside through stores on state farms and cooperatives.

The initial urban bias of distribution policy was the result in part of the close presence of the industrial workers, state workers, merchants and members of the informal sector to the national, regional, departmental, and municipal state offices. Their demand for food was felt, sometimes implicitly (administrators had direct daily contact with the urban population) and sometimes explicitly, by way of the block associations (CDS) and the quite vocal urban merchants. The stronger political voice of the urban masses maintained for them a greater relative share of food supply. Over time, however, the increasing severity of the military situation in the countryside drew greater attention to the criticisms of rural food distribution made by UNAG and the Association of Rural Workers (ATC). By 1985, although first priority in food distribution was being reserved for soldiers fighting the Contras, increased attention was being given to rural food distribution. This meant a relative decline in attention by the state to urban consumption (although it likely continued to have a greater relative share).

The urban decline was not shared equally by all urban residents. Productive workers were given priority in the urban marketing system by way of distribution centers in workplaces. State workers were protected to some extent, with workplaces organized for regular and direct access to producers and/or distributors of certain foods (eggs, for example). Those with the least priority included members of the urban informal sector, whose contribution to national defense, material production, or organization of the revolutionary process was considered small. Professionals existing outside of the state or urban industry were also not specifically prioritized except for their households' inclusion in the basic quota system described above.

Conclusion

Four determinants of internal consumption have been discussed in this paper: the pre-revolutionary agro-export model, revolutionary state policy, the external aggression against Nicaragua, and political demand. In the revolutionary period, the hostility of the United States to the Nicaraguan revolution, the substantial efforts of the Nicaraguan state, and the mechanisms of political demand contribute substantially to the explanation of food consumption. Nonetheless, these factors are not the only influences on consumption policy. Much qualitative and quantitative work on consumption in Nicaragua remains to be done. For Nicaraguan policy makers, it is essential that a serious income-consumption study of both rural and urban areas be carried out. Such a study should take into account both income and class position of each person interviewed (the latter based on the process of production, appropriation and/or distribution of surplus labor in which each individual is involved), particularly since class transformation is an explicit revolutionary goal.

Tastes and preferences, even in the Nicaraguan situation, can have important consequences. Neoclassical consumer demand theory exploits certain very intuitive ideas which seem to hold in many circumstances: different persons have different tastes and preferences, and if given a monetary budget and a vector of prices they will express those preferences in the marketplace. In Nicaragua consumers are no different, and the classic case of tastes concerns beans, the most basic of staples. Until 1981, bean imports were necessary to fill shortfalls in domestic production. While imported beans had the same color as traditionally-grown beans, they were rejected or consumed only grudgingly by Nicaraguans. According to consumers, they were too dry, took too long and too much fuel to cook, did not retain their shape in cooking and had an unsatisfactory consistency and taste. Even when the state was marketing national beans, since its system tended to store the beans longer (in order to fill demand in non-harvest periods) some of the same problems were noted.[4] More recently, renewed bean imports have run into a similar problem.

The moral is that the quantity of food consumption is certainly the primary concern, but not the only concern. Both can cause political damage to a revolutionary alliance. Quality questions cannot be considered unimportant. The Nicaraguan government has experimented with different varieties of red beans and soybeans--the first grew with greater productivity, the second has greater nutritive impact. Although excellent from the farmers' point of view, the Nicaraguan consumers would not accept the new red beans. Consumer education programs have been small and so far, so has their effect.

In spite of the relevance of individual preferences to the bean question, it is inappropriate to analyze consumption in Nicaragua according to the neoclassical theory of consumer demand. It is also unlikely that many neoclassicals would attempt to do so. Neoclassical theory was developed in advanced capitalist countries. Although it has been applied to many Third World nations, the Nicaraguan economy and Nicaraguan society are undergoing so great a structural transformation that a neoclassical analysis might be reduced to a discussion of "externalities." Even if Nicaraguan society reached some semblance of "equilibrium" and "evolutionary" change, neoclassical theory still would remain challengeable by way of its analysis of consumers as isolated individuals consulting their individual preference orderings and the vector of market prices. Once social processes and institutions are introduced affecting and expressing the wishes of groups of individuals, then both the mathematical properties and the analytical entry point of neoclassical theory of consumer demand become suspect.

It might be that a different approach to food consumption is appropriate for Nicaragua. An alternative methdology would be one that is interdisciplinary, political and economic, social and cultural. For example, in a "food system" approach, consumption can be seen as the final phase of the food chain, one that begins with production, and moves through marketing, storage, product transformation, distribution, and finally consumption. In each of these phases, there are various actors: individuals, groups, classes and institutions. Within and between the phases, the actors and the products are involved in many complex circuits and relationships. Each actor is involved in the constant reproduction and alteration of the food system. Therefore consumption is a complex function with links to varied persons, products, and policies (Barraclough, 1982; Austin, Fox, and Kruger, 1985; and CIERA, 1984a and 1984b). All of these influences produce outcomes such as price, demand and supply of a product, individual income and preferences, and the choice of the consumer.[5] These outcomes are in turn partial determinants of the food system.

On a more general theoretical level, an alternative approach to food consumption could also begin by taking into account that Nicaragua is a case of socialist transition. Socialist transition can be defined as an alliance of classes (such as workers and peasants) and social groups (such as professionals, administrators and small merchants) who have as one of their goals the establishment of communal processes for economic, political, ideological and cultural decision-making. Communal goals--that of the body politic--might well include the right of each citizen to an adequate level of food consumption. This would replace the notion that an optimal solution can best be reached by leaving income exogenous and having consumption as an outcome of market processes. Instead, food consumption could be established on the basis of both collective and individual decision-making--collective in establishing basic rights to food consumption, and individual in allowing individuals input into social decision-making and choice for individual consumption purchases.

Such a theory is implicitly critical of both capitalist social formations and those undergoing socialist transition. The former often deny democracy in the economic sphere, thereby actually denying adequate consumption to a share (often large) of their population. Socialist countries have often provided sufficient food, but have paid little attention to the tastes and preferences of consumers. This is often a function of, among other things, the lack of participation of a large part of the citizenry in decision-making in general. Therefore a new theory of consumption might establish adequate consumption as a goal that would be part and parcel of an increasing democratization of social decision-making consistent with the definition of socialism presented above.

Choices on consumption in socialism often appear to be given less priority, behind such tasks as defense and the building up of an industrial base. In Nicaragua's situation, defense is certainly a legitimate concern, and may be for some time to come. Should their situation stabilize, the Nicaraguans may, like the Cubans, create an Institute for Research on Consumer Demand (Benjamin, Collins, and Scott, 1986).

For the moment, food consumption remains a challenge for revolutionary Nicaragua. Even in the middle of a war, a key question that is asked of Nicaragua's experiment is, "does it (or will it) deliver the material goods?" A key to the revolution's overall success and popular support will be its approach and achievements in dealing with the issues of food consumption. Until the United States government allows the Nicaraguans to focus on the construction of a viable economy, it is doubtful that great strides in food consumption will be made.

Table 1: Price Support Policies in the Revolutionary Period

1980:   Subsidies begun for maize, beans, and rice.
                 Official prices established for most basic foods

1981:   Subsidies begun for milk, cooking oil.

1980-81:   Network of state stores established to sell basic
                 foods at official prices.
                 Contracts established with small private shops to
                 distribute basic foods at official prices.

1982:   Subsidies begun for sugar.
                 Rationing system begun for sugar, through
                 existing stores and neighborhood organizations.

1983:   Rationing system expanded to include beans,
                 rice, cooking oil, salt, and powdered milk.

1980-84:   Subsidies for all products mentioned increase
                 sharply.

1985:   Subsidies drastically reduced for all products.
                 Devaluation of the cordoba (currency) increased
                 cost to consumer of food imports.
                 Prioritization given to working class in state
                 supply centers selling at official prices.

1984-85:   Price index for a basket of 12 basic foods and 3
                 non-foods rose by 462%.

Source: CIERA, 1983, Utting, n.d.; IHCA, 1986.

Notes

This paper is based on extensive collaboration by the author with the Center for Investigations and Studies of the Agrarian Reform (CIERA), Managua, Nicaragua. I wish to thank CIERA, its staff, and particularly its Director, Dr. Orlando Nunez Soto, for that opportunity. CIERA and its researchers deserve much of the credit for the work within; however, the views expressed (and any errors) are my own.

1. The author participated in the first study of consumption in Managua in the revolutionary period (CIERA, 1983). The only other study known to the author was undertaken from 1972-73. Aside from different methodologies, the changes in consumption in Managua due to earthquakes, wars, etc. are too great to make any significant comparison of the two studies.

2. The country was awash in external credits. At that time the supermarkets carried many non-basic imported foods.

3. The author confirmed this during a June-July 1986 research trip to Nicaragua. Reports on recent conditions include Julia Preston, Shortages, Rotting Meat Signs of Nicaraguan Strife, in *The Washington Post*, 25 July 1986, pp. 1, 24; The Quick Slide Down, *The Economist*, 23-29 August 1986, p. 36; and Jill Snolowe, Side-Tracked Revolution: Living with Breadlines and Block Committees, *Time*, 31 March 1986, pp. 2,24. For the most accurate overall view of the food situation in Nicaragua and its development over time, see Collins (1986).

4. These opinions were noted in group meetings with persons in charge of household consumption (generally women) in the popular barrios of Managua. See CIERA (1983).

5. Choice is irrelevant, for example, if products do not arrive at the market.

References

Austin, James, Jonathan Fox and Walter Kruger
1985   The Role of the Revolutionary State in the Nicaraguan Food System.*World Development* 13: 15-40.

Barraclough, Solon
1982   *A Preliminary Analysis of the Nicaraguan System.* Geneva: UNRISD (United Nations Research Institute for Social Development).

Benjamin, Medea, Joseph Collins, and Michael Scott
1984   *No Free Lunch: Food and Farming in Cuba Today.* San Francisco: Institute for Food and Development Policy.

CIERA (Centro de Investigaciones y Estudios de la Reforma Agraria)
1983   Distribucion y consumo popular de alimentos en Managua Managua: CIERA.

CIERA
1984a   *El funcionamiento del sistema alimentario. Informe final del proyecto estrategia alimentaria..* Tomo I. Managua: CIERA/PAN (Programa Alimentario Nacional)/CIDA (Canadian International Development Agency).

CIERA
1984b   *Managua es Nicaragua: el impacto de la capital en el sistema alimentario nacional. Informe final del proyecto estrategia alimentaria.* Tomo III. Managua: PAN/CIDA.

CIERA
1985   *El abc de abastecimiento.* Managua: CIERA.

CIERA, MIDINRA (Ministerio de Desarrollo Agropecuario y Reforma Agraria)
1980   Encuesta a los trabajadores del campo. Unpublished survey of 60,000 families involved in agricultural production.

CIERA, PAN, CIDA
1983   *Informe del primer seminario sobre estrategia alimentaria.* Managua: CIERA.

Collins, Joseph
1986   *What Difference can a Revolution Make? Food and Farming in the New Nicaragua.* 3rd. ed. Sa Francisco: Institute for Food and Development Policy.

Deere, Carmen Diana, Peter Marchetti, and Nola Reinhardt
1985　The Peasantry and the Development of Sandinista Agrarian Policy, 1979-1984. *Latin American Research Review* 20:3: 75 109.

FIDA (Fondo Internacional de Desarrollo Agricola)
1980　Informe de la mision especial de programacion a Nicaragua.

IHCA (Instituto Historico Centroamericano).
1986　Slow Motion Toward a Survival Economy. *Envio* 5:63 (September): 13-38.

MIDINRA
1984　*Estadisticas agropecuarias de Nicaragua 1980-1984.* Managua: MIDINRA.

Nunez, Orlando
No date　*El Somocismo y el modelo capitalista agroexportador.* Managua: Departamento de Ciencias Sociales de la UNAN.

Utting, Peter
No date　Limits to Change in a Post-Revolutionary Society: The Rise and Fall of Cheap Food Policy in Nicaragua. Mimeo.

Zalkin, Michael
1986　*Peasant Response to State Grain Policy in Post-Revolutionary Nicaragua, 1979-1984.* Ph.D. Thesis, University of Massachusetts, Amherst.

THE LINK THAT SEPARATES:
CONSUMPTION OF PASTORAL RESOURCES ON
A FEUDAL ESTATE

Kathleen Biddick

Introduction

Historians and anthropologists in search of a deep history of consumption in European agricultural development will find none. The chief models for historic economic growth implicitly conceptualize consumption as a derivative of production. A leading model based on supply and demand, formulated by Michael Postan in his classic essay for the *Cambridge Economic History* (1941) and more recently employed by North and Thomas (1973) assumes a medieval economy dominated by production for the market. The model leaves little scope for considering consumption and its links with production.

A developmental model of medieval economic development synthesized by Georges Duby (1974) does recognize that a gift economy rooted in consumption once throve in Northern Europe. A commodity economy driven by trade and the towns displaced it by the late twelfth century. The developmental model analyzes the gift-economy not for itself but retrospectively as "unproductive" practices undone by commerce.

A leading Marxist model of agricultural development (Brenner 1982) emphasizes the centrality of social reproduction. The access of feudal lords to extra-economic forms of surplus extraction and the access of peasants to subsistence plots structured feudal reproduction independent of the market. Brenner's model implicitly asserts the importance of consumption to the reproduction of people and things in the medieval economy. Unfortunately the Brenner debate over the origins of agrarian capitalism has not yet diverted Marxist empirical research from a one-dimensional concern with production in pre-capitalistic economies.[1] The problematic relation of consumption to the market therefore remains unexplored.

Witold Kula's much neglected study of Polish feudalism differs notably from universalizing models of Western feudal economies with their neglect of consumption.[2] A paradoxical relation of consumption to production, market exchange and reproduction binds the model at its core. "Costless" consumption of estate-produced cereals and fodder grains, meat, and animal products, resources such as timber and pasture, indeed peasant labor itself, enabled Polish nobles to use money received from their exports of wheat and rye to purchase those goods which money alone could acquire. Seigneurial struggles to conserve costless consumption in an export economy rendered peasant households particularly vulnerable to local markets. Kula insightfully notes that the supposedly variegated seigneurial economy which husbanded a combination of winter and summer grains and livestock was no multicrop system of agriculture, but actually a "multi-crop economy sustaining a single-crop economy" (Kula 1976: 40).

Consumption emerges as a central and empirically neglected dynamic of the feudal economies modeled by Brenner and Kula. To address such empirical neglect this paper constructs a local model of pastoral consumption on a middling-sized English medieval estate.[3] Specifically the paper analyzes how the Abbey linked consumption with production, distribution and reproduction for a set of "things", the Abbey's sheep flock and a cattle herd, at the high point of English seigneurial farming in the early fourteenth century. The choice of livestock for study responds to another neglected area in the literature of English agrarian development, that of pastoral husbandry.

A study of historic, pre-capitalist consumption presents unique problems of definition. How can we, used to thinking capitalistically of relative autonomous spheres of consumption and production, conceptualize consumption in a world where "there is no such thing as relatively independent spheres or circuits: production is immediately consumption and a recording process without any sort of mediation, and the recording process and consumption directly determine production, though they do so within the production process itself"(Deleuze and Guattari 1983: 4)? This study uses the metaphor of links and the paradox of the link that separates not to mystify but to sustain thinking back to the rebus of pre-capitalistic consumption.

An Introduction to Early Medieval Consumption on the Estate of Peterborough Abbey

The consumption practices followed by the Abbey at the turn of the fourteenth century had their roots in the early medieval period. The garbled stories preserved in later documentation of the Abbey recollect that its royal Mercian founders endowed the Abbey in the mid-seventh century with a territory of some 200 square miles that incorporated a large tract of low-lying summer pastures in the English peat fen, cultivated areas on the gravels of river terraces and woodland (Stenton 1970; Potts 1974). Recent work of archaeologists and historical geographers confirm that such extensive territories marked by the balanced access to large tracts of pastoral and woodland resources and cultivated areas supported chiefly lordship in seventh century England (Biddick 1984a; Hooke 1985; Williamson 1986). Evidence from later law-books, surveys, and the settlement groupings still discernible in the Domesday Book (1086 A.D.) shows that those people and places dependent on Dark Age lords provided their households with food, drink and the necessities of life on a seasonal basis (Barrow 1973; Jones 1984). Central to the organization of renders of goods and services was the extensive coordination of seasonal resources in a territory with the consumption needs of chiefly lordship, arrangements found in studies of other chiefly societies (Earle 1978). Consumption and not production served as the framework for constituting relations between social groups and resources within a territory.

The chiefly exercise of rights to "eat off the land" marks a separation of direct producers from full enjoyment of their labor. In consuming food and services, chiefs produced lordship. The intertwining of lordship and consumption modeled agrarian lordship in England for centuries. Remarkably resilient, the model of power only lost its meaning in the fifteenth century.

The following passage written in the tenth century recalls the chiefly exercise of right of consumption in a Welsh commote and also records how chiefs expanded and regularized that right to consume at a distance:

> Llywelan the Great and his son, Dafydd, came once a year into the Commote of Penllyn (in Bala) to hunt, bringing with them about 300 men. They exacted a feast--bread, butter, fish, and cheese-- but they took nothing when they did not come. Llywelyn (the Last) came which no previous Prince ever took, and he demanded money instead of food when he did not come. (Reese 1963: 156)

Details on the actual composition of Dark Age renders are very rarely preserved in written records of the eighth and early ninth centuries. A lease of land made by the Abbey of Peterborough in 852 A.D. sheds light on the system of renders at a more complex state of its development (Robertson 1956). In 852 A.D. Abbot Ceolred leased some land of the Abbey located in Sleaford, Lincs. for the period of two lives. In return, Wulfrid, the lessee, owed an annual render deliverable in three parts. First he rendered annually 60 wagons of wood, 12 wagons of brushwood, and 6 wagons of faggots. Wulfrid also owed the following food to the Abbey: 2 casks of clear ale, 2 cattle for slaughter, 600 loaves of bread and 10 mittan (a liquid measure) of Welsh ale. The Abbot as "lord of the church" collected a separate food render from Wulfrid which consisted of one horse, 30 shillings, and one day of food rent including 15 mittan of clear ale, 5 mittan of Welsh ale and 15 sesters of mild ale.

The details of Wulfred's food rent reveal how consumption linked processing and storage. First the lessee processed food at the point of production. The monastic household did not require storage space for unprocessed food or a large staff to process it. The lessee had to malt barley, grind grain and bake loaves of bread. Much of the render took the form of ale which can be viewed as a way of storing barley for consumption. Only the cattle seem to have been sent into the Abbey on the hoof. The monastery could then butcher the animals as it required.

Shortly after the Abbot of Peterborough drew up the lease with Wulfrid, the Vikings overwhelmed the Abbey (869 A.D.). When the English king refounded the monastery a century later it enjoyed access to a similar range of resources but controlled them no longer through a coherent territory but rather through a score of discrete manors dispersed in the landscape (King 1973). The Abbey managed its resources from the late tenth to the late twelfth century by relying on farmers who held manors from the Abbey on life-term leases in exchange for furnishing the Abbey with a set amount of food, or its cash equivalent, and some currency (Lennard 1959). The Abbey also collected wagons of firewood and fodder gathered by its peasants. Consumption persisted as the primary concern of the Abbey upon its refoundation.

No schedules for the monthly food renders collected by Peterborough Abbey have survived. Fortunately a schedule of monthly food renders preserved for the neighboring Benedictine Abbey of Ramsey, comparable to Peterborough in the worth of its landed endowment, offers some insight into the organization of consumption on English Benedictine estates in c. 1100 A.D. (Hart and Lyons 1893). A detailed itemization of the food renders and their cash values appears in Table 1.

The annual cash equivalent of the monthly food renders, including monthly renders in money, amounted to 4,981 shillings. Grain in the processed form of fine flour for bread, baked loaves, flour of second-grade, malted grain for drink, and oat fodder constituted 34 per cent of the annual value. Meat did not form a significant portion of the food render. This is as it should be in an observant Benedictine household (Knowles 1949). Secondary animal products (lard, cheese, butter, eggs) ranked second in their contribution (22 per cent) to the value of the annual food rent. Ramsey Abbey also collected a monthly cash payment which comprised 20 per cent (960/4,981 shillings) of the total annual value of renders. No contemporary figures exist for the size of the Ramsey household. Its neighbor, Peterborough Abbey, housed sixty monks and 44 servants in 1125 (Stapleton 1849).

The annual consumption of cereal and livestock products contained in the Ramsey schedule also provide interesting guidelines to the minimal level of demesne production required to feed a monastic household in the early twelfth century. Calculations for the acreage and livestock required to produce the food consumed by the Ramsey household are presented in Biddick (1986). To summarize, the farmers of the manors of Ramsey Abbey had to harvest between 878 and 1170 acres of grain depending on whether they used a two-course or three-course rotation in their fields. With 52 ploughs on its demesnes in the Domesday Book, Ramsey Abbey could have easily managed that level of arable production for consumption. To produce 17,280 pounds of lard Ramsey would have to herd 8,640 pigs (Biddick 1986). To produce the same weight of cheese the Abbey would have to herd 197 cows or 1,970 ewes or combinations thereof. Stock listed in a rare and early survey preserved for Peterborough in 1125 A.D. show that the \Abbey herded sheep and cattle on a scale sufficient to meet this high level of dairy production. The Peterborough statistics enumerating only 773 pigs contrast sharply with the 8,000 odd pigs required to produce the expected amount of lard. The heavy lard renders of Ramsey Abbey look back to an earlier period when the Abbey husbanded its woodland primarily for pannage. By 1125 A.D. the management of woodland by coppicing and its clearance for   agricultural purposes already conflicted with extensive pig management on the Peterborough estate (Biddick 1984b).

Such levels of consumption and production acquire more significance when compared to figures of two centuries later. At the turn of the fourteenth century Peterborough Abbey farmed 4,906 acres of cereal, over four times the acreage estimated for early twelfth century. The cattle and pig herd had doubled their numbers and the number of sheep and horses on the estate tripled. To understand this marked change in scale of seigneurial agriculture and its relation to consumption the political fortunes of the Abbey require some consideration.

In the late twelfth century the Abbey grafted on new methods   of production to its methods of consumption. The mounting fiscal demands of the English king, administratively the most powerful among his   European contemporaries (Hollister and Baldwin 1978), pressured the Abbey to produce more and more revenue.[4] To meet such demands, English agrarian lords contracted debts with foreign merchants who advanced them money for future payment in agricultural produce, especially wool (Jenkinson 1913; Dept 1926; Richardson 1960). Faced by the demands of the English crown coupled with structural indebtedness, English lordship had to expand production beyond consumption to reproduce its power. To do so lords took over direct production on their estates (Harvey, 1974). Over the period 1180-1220 A.D. the Abbot of Peterborough reclaimed arable and pastoral resources hitherto worked by his peasants and the farmers on his manors to produce the large plantation-like manors familiar from textbooks on medieval English agriculture.

A bureaucracy of accountants monitored agricultural production and the consumption of foodstuffs produced on manors; hence the unsurpassed (for Northern Europe) amount of written documentation for English demesne agriculture from the thirteenth to the fifteenth centuries (Harvey 1976). The thirteenth century also marked the heyday of dogmatic treatises on estate management (Oschinsky 1971). The handbooks make it clear that concern for consumption inspired the tremendous effort devoted to careful accounting. An excerpt   from Robert Grosseteste's treatise to the Countess of Lincoln (1240x1242 A.D.) on the governance of her lands and households offers an example of such reasoning:

> Here you will see how many quarters (=8 bushels) of corn
> you will be likely to use weekly in livery of bread and how
> many in alms; that is if you spend two quarters daily that will be
> fourteen quarters weekly, and seven hundred and twenty-eight
> quarters in one year. And if, to increase your alms you spend two
> and a half quarters daily, that will come to seventeen and one half
> quarters in the week and one hundred and ten quarters in one year.
> And when you have deducted this sum from the total amount of

your corn then you may subtract the amount for ale according to the customary weekly amount used for the brewing in your household. And then be careful with the amount which will remain for sale .(Oschinsky 1971:393)

By the end of the thirteenth century some lords began to add to their manorial accounts notes on the profit (proficuum) of the manor. In an important discussion of the perception of profit among English lords David Postles (1986) showed how they valued as profit items consumed on the estate, such as oats grown on the manor and fed to the manor horses. Such calculations show how important lords considered "costless consumption" in their logic of profit.

Historians call the thirteenth and early fourteenth centuries the period of "high-farming" for English agrarian lords and, as already noted in the introduction, commonly assume that production for the market and market-profit dominated lordly interests. A comparative model of the Polish feudal economy, the medieval handbooks for English estate management, and the profit calculations of English agrarian lords suggest something more complex, that issues of everyday consumption extensively shaped the strategies of seigneurial production and market exchange. Agrarian lords thus simultaneously reaped the advantages of what Braudel calls material civilization and economic civilization, because they carefully foreclosed their symmetrical linkage.

The following analysis of consumption of sheep and cattle and their secondary products on the estate of Peterborough Abbey will show how, in fact, the pressures of the Abbey's involvement with the market reinforced its model of consumption. To support these contentions I will analyze how the Abbey linked the consumption and reproduction of the estate herds of cattle and sheep with the production and sale of meat, wool, skins, hides, traction and dairy products. Such links illustrate the multidimensionality of consumption on the estate. They also show that consumption is undefinable without production and reproduction and unintelligible without consideration of the historical reproduction of agrarian lordship.

Sheep

By the late twelfth century Flemish merchants gained control over the English wool crop (Lloyd 1977). As they took over direct management of their estates, English agrarian lords entered the medieval world economy as exporters of wool. By the later thirteenth century the English king relied on customs on wool collected at English ports to secure loans from Italian banking houses. The position of sheep in the agrarian economy shifted from a subsistence animal relied upon primarily for its dairying and wool to a cash-crop animal requiring special management techniques to produce the volume of high-quality wool for export to the Flemish and later Italian textile industries (Trow-Smith 1957; Munro 1985).

With the pressures of cash-cropping wool (and they were great--England exported 46,382 sacks of wool, or just under 17 million pounds in 1304-05), it is interesting to study what consumption strategies, if any, the Abbey followed in its management of its sheep flock at a medieval peak of English wool export in the early fourteenth century. To begin the analysis of what choices the Abbey made about consuming and producing wool, mutton, milk, pelts and manure from its flock, which numbered between 4,000 and 9,000 beasts in the first decade of the fourteenth century, I will analyze first what products it chose not to consume, since it marketed them.

A guide to the Abbey's choices for the production and sale of meat and wool at the peak of high-farming in the early fourteenth century are set out in Table 2. At first glance the figures suggest that the Abbey produced both wool and meat for the market. When the purchase of sheep stock is compared, however, with sales in Table 3 the picture suddenly changes. Purchase of sheep stock usually exceeded sales. The Abbey either lost money or just broke even on buying and selling sheep. The sale of sheep for meat generated little revenue for the Abbey. The Abbey was not a market producer of lamb or mutton.

Further scrutiny of Table 3 shows too that the Abbey did not buy and sell its sheep at random. The Abbey opened up only certain cohorts of its flock to the market. Its deliberate strategy of buying and selling left intact the capacity of the flock to reproduce itself biologically. Lambs and yearlings, the reproductive future of the herd, were least open to the market. The Abbey purchased lambs just to compensate for losses of lamb to disease. The purchase of yearlings too was compensatory of their mortality. When the Abbey did sell yearlings, it sold only those too weak to merit investment to maturity, or those demographically superfluous to the strategy of flock reproduction. The Abbey thus used the market only to adjust but not to replace biological reproduction of its flock. The significance of this marketing strategy to consumption will be examined below.

The Abbey always lost on the exchange of wethers, the mature castrates of the sheep flock. It always sold more wethers than it purchased. The rough equilibrium between the number of wethers purchased and sold suggests that the Abbey steadily removed from the flock aging wethers whose productivity had declined and replaced them with more costly fresh stock. This strategy of culling aging wethers made the meat market, for which they were destined, a by-product of biological reproduction, but not the aim of production.

The fact that the Abbey bought mature stock on the open market also shows flexibility about mixing its wool types. The Abbey's attitudes toward breeding for wool do not reveal themselves in the accounts. The Abbey did not even bother to enumerate rams in their precise counts of sheep on its manor and of all the market exchanges of mature stock, the accounts record only one purchase of a ram on the manor of Kettering in 1307-08.

The Abbey bought and sold mature females, ewes, more erratically than the other cohorts of the sheepflock. When the Abbey wished to increase flock size in 1300-01, it purchased ewes to expand quickly the reproductive capacity of the herd. In 1309-10 it reversed this strategy and sold proportionately more ewes. Related to this sale of ewes was the purchase of more wethers than usual. The trade-off of 1309-10 made between sales of ewes and purchase of wethers suggests that the Abbey wished to make a faster gain on wool production than the biological rate of reproduction of the flock would allow. Wool prices rose over the first decade of the fourteenth century and the Abbey's choices made economic sense (Lloyd 1973). The Abbey turned to the market when it needed to supercede the biological growth rate of its herd. The Abbey used the market to adjust or accelerate production but it never let the market disturb the capacity of the herd to reproduce itself biologically.

The skins of sheep supplied much demanded raw material for lighter leather goods such as gloves in the medieval economy. The Abbey sold skins (Table 3) only as the by-product of biological reproduction of the herd. It sold only the skins of sheep which died on the manors. In 1300-01, 1309-10 the Abbey marketed the skins of dead sheep locally. In 1307-08 merchants who purchased the Abbey's wool clip centrally bought the woolly skins (*pellis grossa*) of sheep which died unshorn. The Abbey continued its policy of selling shorn skins locally that year.

Sheep also produce milk and manure. The Abbey milked its ewes regularly on the two nursing manors of the Abbey, Eye and Glinton, and sporadically on several other manors (Biddick 1986). Unfortunately the Abbey's accountants did not enter the yield of sheep milk; therefore, it is not possible to gage productivity. Other evidence shows, however, that the Abbey held only a minor interest in sheep dairying in the early fourteenth century. The Abbey spent one quarter of the total expenses of maintaining the sheep flock on the purchase of milk to nourish young lambs. In addition the lambs consumed between 50-60 per cent of the cow milk that the Abbey reserved from cheese production. The accountants failed to value manure on the Peterborough accounts, although medieval lords valued the manure of flocks highly (Smith 1943). The Abbey's practice of moving the cohorts of the flock in different circuits around its home and Northamptonshire manors ensured fairly even distribution of the manure.

Based on the study of production and exchange of the products of the sheep flock, it is reasonable to conclude that the production of wool dominated the Abbey's productive strategy, exactly what the pressures of the medieval world economy would lead us to expect. The production of meat and dairy were the by-products of this dominant production strategy.

How did consumption of the products of sheep husbandry on the Abbey's estate relate to these strategies of production and reproduction just discussed? An argument could be made that the Abbey did not emerge as a market producer of meat because it consumed rather than sold its own mutton. The statistics for sheep sent into the Abbey's Larder listed in Table 4 show, however, that the butchery rate for wethers was highest at the low rate of 2.7 per cent in 1309-10. The Abbey as a practice did not butcher the reproductive core of its flock, its yearlings and lambs, except for a few Easter lambs. The Abbey restrained its consumption of mutton at a modest rate in comparison to some contemporary ecclesiastical households whose annual consumption of mutton appears in Table 4. It could be that the Abbey's consumption of mutton would be higher, if its archive preserved its central household accounts. Central household accounts, only rarely preserved in English archives, recorded the purchases of meat made on the market. Without such central accounts, the historian can only make the important observation that the Abbey did not feed off its manorial sheep flocks. Or did it?

A chief source of estate revenue came from the Abbey's sale of its cash crop, wool. The Abbey sold its entire wool clip annually. What textiles it needed it bought on the market. The Abbey presumably used the money from wool sales both to protect and augment its household consumption through payment of loans, Papal and royal taxes and purchase of luxury goods such as wine and staples such as salted herring available on the commercial market. Central accounts preserved for other agrarian lords detail such activities (Dyer 1986). Unfortunately, the exact details of these expenditures for Peterborough Abbey cannot be reported without its central accounts whose purpose it was to record such cash outlays. The mentality guiding the Abbey's cash-cropping of wool can be gaged alternatively by questioning whether the Abbey "maximized" its wool production, a profit response which could override its usual concern that consumption should be as near to costless as possible.

The Abbey's sale of pastoral resources in the first decade of the fourteenth century show that it could have supported a much larger herd of sheep, if it had wanted to. It sold a total of 3,759 shillings of pasture in 1300-01; 4,038 shillings of pasture in 1307-08 and 3,848 shillings of pasture in 1309-10. These figures either exceeded or approximated the Abbey's income from wool sales (see Table 3). The bulk of the pastoral sales comprised peasant purchases of pasture which they grazed or mowed themselves. The Abbey still collected mowing services from its peasants in the first decade of the fourteenth century, which meant that the cut hay and forage it sold to peasants was also "costless" to the Abbey.

The production of wool did cost the Abbey money. First, the Abbey restrained to a minimum its consumption of mutton from its flock, a hidden cost of wool production. Second, the column "expenses" in Table 3 shows that keeping a flock for wool production cost the Abbey money. Ingredients such as imported mercury used in medicinal unguents to heal and protect fleece from the scab composed proportionately the largest of the cash outlays. Rather than expand its flock to match available pastoral resources and sell more wool, the Abbey stood by more familiar "costless" choices and sold its pastoral resources.

The Abbey could also have maximized its wool production by herding only wethers; they bore the heaviest and largest fleeces. To do so, however, would mean that the Abbey allowed the market to organize biological reproduction. The Abbey would then appear without choice as both a consumer and a producer in the stock market. Reproduction would cease to be costless, rather, the market would form costs involved. By herding a reproductive flock, the Abbey conserved its potential to reverse from cash cropping to subsistence. Once the market organized biological reproduction, the Abbey would become irreversibly caught in cash cropping. The Abbey's strategy of consumption, the link that separated it from a deeper involvement in the market, linked the reproduction of the Abbey's resources with the reproduction of its Abbey's lordship, since lords still consumed their subsistence needs as costlessly as possible to produce and reproduce lordship. When the links of consumption to production and reproduction broke in the fifteenth century, English agrarian lords also ceased to reproduce themselves.

The contrasts between the Abbey's flock management with that of early modern graziers in the same locale can help to illustrate the point I am making. The figures in Table 2 show that unlike the Abbot of Peterborough, the early modern graziers in Northhamptonshire expected to profit from both wool and meat production (Finch 1956). John Isham of Lamport enjoyed roughly equal returns from the sale of wool and meat from his herd. Robert Spencer reversed the proportions of his flock income by netting 59 per cent of his receipts from the sale of stock to the meat markets and 41 per cent from wool sales. The goals of production differed for the Abbey and the graziers. The Abbey ran an economy of scale devoted to wool production; the graziers ran an economy of scope with both meat and wool as chief products (Bailey and Friedlander 1982). More importantly each organized reproduction of their flocks in profoundly different ways.

The flow chart (Figure 1) helps to illustrate these reproductive differences. Even though the proportion of lambs, yearling, ewes and wethers in Spencer's flock looked similar to the Abbot's flock, the market, and not biology, reproduced the early modern flock. Spencer of Althorp bought and sold across all the cohorts of the flock. The market permeated the replacement of each cohort. Spencer sold his spring lambs to the meat market and then purchased lambs back in the autumn for shearing the following spring and then fattening for the meat market. Spencer bought juveniles cheap and sold them fattened at a profit, reversing the direction of gain and loss already observed in medieval stock exchange. Recall that the Abbey bought mature stock dear and sold off sickly and old stock cheap. The permeability of the early modern flock to the market meant that graziers could pursue a two-fold strategy of meat and wool production, since the market and not biology replaced the grazier's flock. If the Abbot of Peterborough had cycled so much meat into the market or his household, he would have soon undermined the biological capacity of the flock to reproduce.

Medieval lords staunchly resisted market penetration of flock reproduction. They preferred to appear on the market as a seller of pastoral products, especially wool. The control Peterborough Abbey exercised over pastures scattered throughout its estate enabled it to manage an elaborate local transhumance that seasonally coordinated the varying productive and reproductive needs of the cohorts of the flock with the pastures distributed over the landscape. Spencer of Althorp relied instead upon large compact tracts of enclosed pasture and enjoyed fewer options for coordinating space and time in flock reproduction. The slower cycles involved in biological reproduction of the flock and the pastoral diversity required to meet the demands of pregnant ewes and weaned lambs would have severely constrained Spencer given the resources he controlled and the production cycle he wished to follow.

The graziers let the market set the tempo for replacing cohorts of the flock within the concentrated tracts of pasture they controlled. The seigneurial lord's control over a grid of pastoral resources, control historically rooted in the methods of seigneurial consumption, enabled them to appear primarily as sellers of animal products rather than consumers and to protect biological reproduction of their herds. Exercise of control over the reproduction of "things" supported their control over the reproduction of their power as agrarian lords in medieval society. Consumption with its links to production and reproduction separated them from a widening chain of commoditization.

Cattle

The Abbey practiced comparable methods of consumption in its cattle husbandry. Cattle herds provide the products of traction, beef, milk, hides and tallow. The use of oxen to draw estate ploughs shaped the demography of the Peterborough herd which numbered over 1,200 beasts in the early fourteenth century. Oxen comprised one-third of the herd and their numbers correlated with the acreage the Abbey sowed with cereals. The Abbey used its herd to produce traction as a chief product. It "consumed" traction in its cereal agriculture, a good portion of the yield of which the Abbey and its horses consumed.

The Abbey could also choose to produce beef and dairy products. Table 5 lists the data for the Abbey's purchase and sale of cattle. The patterns found there generally conform to those already observed for the Abbey's sheep flock. The Abbey's sale of cattle, presumably to the meat market, did not compensate for purchases of stock. The Abbey used the cattle market as it did the sheep market, to adjust the biological reproduction of its estate herd. As with its sheep flock, its expectation that its cattle herd should function as a self-contained

131

reproductive unit meant that the cohorts most critical to biological reproduction were least open to market exchange. The Abbey sold stock from its mature cohorts as the by-products of biological reproduction: infertile and aging cows and aging oxen numbered among such stock sales.

The Abbey also consumed beef. Comparison of its consumption and marketing strategies of beef provide a fuller understanding of their influence on production of the estate's cattle husbandry. Table 6 lists the statistics for beef sent into the Abbey Larder along with comparative statistics selected from other ecclesiastical estates. The Abbey's consumption of beef conforms better to contemporaries than did its mutton consumption. The manors sent 66 beasts into the Abbey in 1300-01 and 129 and 203 beasts in the other accounting years. The Abbey culled cattle evenly across all the cohorts of its cattle herd except for calves which it tended to cull more frequently than oxen. Such an even pattern of culling shows how the Abbey kept the demography of its herd in an equilibrium that balanced traction, the chief product of the herd, with cereal production. At this joint consumption strategies in the cereal sector interlocked with cattle husbandry. To consume cereal as costlessly as possible the Abbey practiced a cattle husbandry which had the reproduction of draught oxen as its chief object. This suture of cattle husbandry and cereal agriculture enabled the Abbey to appear primarily as a seller but not a consumer on grain markets.

The Abbey also consumed half of the yield of its dairies (c. 6,000 lbs annually), mostly in the form of cheese; it marketed the other half. Even though the Abbey regarded traction as the chief product of the herd, it valued the production of cheese for home consumption and market sales. It sold dairy products on the market, but did not buy them there, with the exception of some liquid milk purchased in emergencies to sustain weaning stock.

The consumption needs of the Abbey organized its cattle herding. A comparison with early modern cattle husbandry highlights the importance of consumption as a strategy in seigneurial cattle husbandry. Surprisingly more is known about the buying, feeding and selling of medieval cattle than early modern cattle (Bowden 1967). The available literature for early modern cattle husbandry does show that immature cattle, the yearlings and two and three year-old cattle, were the cohorts most open to market exchange. The bones from these immature beasts comprise much of the faunal material in the early modern layers of many English urban excavations (Maltby 1979; Astill 1983). In contrast the Abbey conserved its juveniles for reproduction. The early modern grazier would buy young bullocks and heifers cheap, fatten them for a season or two and sell them at a cash surplus on the meat market. As with sheep graziers, early modern cattle graziers relied on the market to organize the reproduction of cattle stock. Long-distance exchange in cattle which connected breeding areas located in Ireland, Scotland, Jutland and Scandinavia with finishing and consumption areas in the North Sea zone made this early modern cattle husbandry possible (Alcock 1981; Dyer 1972; Edwards 1981; Everitt 1967; Pickl 1973; Skeel 1926; Trow-Smith 1957).

Methods of Consumption Transformed

The different relations between consumption and market exchange and herd reproduction among medieval lords and early moderng graziers have implications for our understanding of consumption in their respective economies. The right of a medieval lord to control resources coincided with the right to consume them. Agrarian lords abandoned rights to consume pastoral resources in the late fourteenth and fifteenth centuries when they leased out their manors for cash (Bolton 1980: 220). Such action broke up once and for all the coordinated use of resources on large estates which, since the seventh century, had structured their consumption and later their production strategies. In the fifteenth century lords entered the market as substantial consumers of animal foodstuffs rather than producers. With the demise of seigneurial methods of consumption the last link separating biological reproduction in the pastoral sector from its organization by the market unlinked itself. The early modern market relinked consumption and production through inter-regional specialization of livestock husbandry which spatially distributed the production of different cohorts of the life-cycle of cattle and sheep.

Early modern markets finished what medieval markets had begun among the peasantry. There is evidence that medieval markets had already penetrated the relations between consumption and production in the pastoral economy of the English peasantry. In a study of peasant cattle wealth based on tax records from the late thirteenth century I found that peasants specialized in managing different stages of the life-cycle of cattle depending on their geographical position in the regional economy (Biddick 1985). These findings suggest that the relations of consumption and production for the pastoral sector of the English peasantry of the Midlands resemble more closely the early modern economy than the relations just traced for their medieval lords. In other words the early modern pastoral market simply wrote the medieval pastoral economy of the peasants in capital letters.

Early modern relations of consumption and production not only reorganized biological reproduction of herds, it reorganized the reproduction of pastoral resources. The new relations of consumption to production unlinked boundaries between permanent pasture and arable through the widespread practice of convertible husbandry or more extensive and regular fodder rotations interspersed with cereal rotations (Bridbury 1974; Dyer 1981).

Economic historians have ascribed the supposed lack of technological innovation and stagnation of English manorial regimes to the lack of seigneurial investment (Postan 1975). If lords had been rational economic actors, they would have invested more. Recent research on the high productivity of medieval agriculture in the east county of Norfolk has recast the debate on agrarian innovation by emphasizing structural rather than technological differences (Campbel1983). Differences in the units of production, fields and farms, not technology, critically influenced agrarian progress and productivity. The links between consumption, production and reproduction outlined in this study of seigneurial consumption call for widening the debate on agrarian structure to include units of consumption and differences in consumption practices. This study urges rephrasing the questions "why was manorial agriculture so stagnant?" and "why was medieval agriculture in Norfolk so productive?" as follows: "how did lords and peasants model consumption in different locales and how did their model influence productivity"? The feathers and furs conspicuously consumed by English lords camouflaged the seriousness of everyday consumption of subsistence goods in their estate economies. Their decisions about consuming and marketing resources embodied feudal power, the link that separated them from the peasant farmers they lived among.

Table 1 Monthly Food Render-Ramsey Abbey c. 1100

Items	Value Monthly sh p		Value Yearly sh	% of Total	Yearly Amts
CASH EQUIVALENCES AND CASH RENDERS					
Cash Value	335	1	4021	80.7	
Cash Render	80		960	19.2	
RENDERS IN GRAIN (1)					
Bread flour	60		720		144qtrs
Grut	24		288		136
Malt	32		384		160
Oat fodder	12		144		80
loaves	13	4	160		24,000 lvs
(total)			1696	34.0	
RENDERS IN OTHER ARABLE PRODUCTS					
beans	1	4	16	0.3	24 treiae
RENDERS OF ANIMALS AND ANIMAL PRODUCTS					
LIVESTOCK					
Lambs	1	3	14		
Piglets	9		108		
(total)			122	2.4	
FOWL					
Chickens	1	8	20		
Geese	0	7	7		
(total)			27	0.5	
SECONDARY PRODUCTS (2)					
Lard	50		600		120 pensae
Cheese	30		360		120 pensae
Eggs	4		48		24,000
Butter	6	8	80		24 treiae
(total)			1088	21.8	
Honey	5	4	64	1.3	24 sextariae

Sources: Hart & Lyons 1893

[1] Bread flour measured in quarters (1 quarter=8 bushels). Other grain measured in mittae and converted into quarters. See Biddick 1986 for details.

[2] Lard and cheese measured in pensae. The regular pensae weighed between 144-168 pounds. For details on weight measurements and conversion see Biddick 1986.

Table 2 Comparisons of Medieval and Early Modern Income
From Wool and Meat
(in shillings)

SALES   WOOL MEAT & STOCK
Peterborough Abbey

1300-01	1873 62%	1130 38%
1307-08	4271 85%	737 15%
1309-10	3514 51%	3415 49%

Isham of Northamptonshire

| 1572-87 | 2840 53% | 2480 47% |

Spencer of Northamptonshire

| 1610-11 | 21347 41% | 30780 59% |

Source: Peterborough Abbey: Fitzwilliam A/C rolls 2388, 233, 2389 Northamptonshire Record Office. Isham and Spencer: Mary E. Finch,*The Wealth of Five Northamptonshire Families* 1540-1640. Northamptonshire Record Society 19 (1956).

Table 3 Buying, Selling, Expenses, Profits
Peterborough Abbey Sheep Flock
(in shillings)

PURCHASE AND SALE OF STOCK

1300-01	Wethers		Ewes		Yearlings		Lambs	
	sh	#	sh	#	sh	#	sh	#
BUY	1080	574	605	421	144	72	220	227
SELL	845	601	181	164	104	132	0	0
NET	-235		-425		-40		-220	
1307-08								
BUY	461	215	56	26	179	103	37	32
SELL	401	250	286	196	45	68	5	20
NET	-60		+230		-134		-32	
1309-10								
BUY	2333	893	219	103	172	89	174	110
SELL	2109	1400	1178	780	128	34	0	0
NET	-224		+959		-44		-174	

	NET STOCK EXCHANGE	SALE[a] WOOL	SALE PELTS	FLOCK[b] EXPENSES	NET INCOME
	sh	sh	sh	sh	sh
1300-01	-920	1874	199	966	187
1307-08	4	4271	323	1147	3451
1309-10	417	3514	233	718	3446

[a] Sale of wool based on number of fleeces multiplied by an average weight of 1.75 pounds per fleece multiplied by the yearly price average for wool as listed by T.H. Lloyd, The Movement of Wool Prices in Medieval England. Economic History Review. Supplement no. 6 (1973).
[b] Expenses include shepherds at average yearly wage of 4 sh., cost of folds, unguents, housing, feed (including cost of grain and milk), costs of washing, shearing, housing expenses including construction of a new bercaria (sheep house).

Table 4 Figures for Mutton Consumpton Contained in
Selected Household Accounts

(figures in parentheses based on yearly price
averages-all prices in shillings)

BATTLE ABBEY	1275	1278	1306	1319	1351
Mutton consumed					
number:	(155)	103	241	(117)	182 manors
					264-purchased
price:	182	113	282	275	238+307

BEAULIEU ABBEY	1269
Mutton consumed	
number:	523
price:	no price

DURHAM	1307	1317
Mutton consumed		
number:	232	343
price:	201	no price

BISHOP OF HEREFORD	1289	1300
Mutton consumed	carcasses	wethers
number:	94.5	29
price:	no price	no price

PETERBOROUGH ABBEY	1300	1307	1309
Mutton consumed	wethers	wethers	wethers
number:	29	30	117,3 lambs
			8 ewes
price:	sent in from manors-no price		

Source: See Table 6 for citation of sources

138

Figure 1. Comparative Flock Management

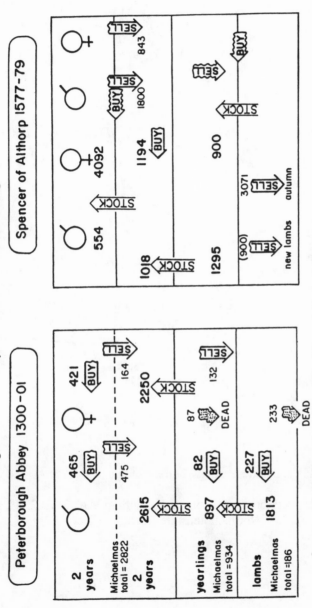

Source   Peterborough Abbey, Fitzwilliam A/C Roll 2388, Northamptonshire Record Office; Mary E. Finch, _The Wealth of Five Northamptonshire Families 1540–1640_, Northamptonshire Record Society, 19 (1956)

Table 5 Purchase and Sale of Cattle and Dairy Products
Peterborough Abbey Estate

	OXEN		COWS		JUVENILES[a]		CALVES	
1300-01								
Autumn #	367		253		427		231	
	#	sh	#	sh	#	sh	#	sh
Buy	36	387	4	26	0	0	2	3
Sell	9	114	10	35	4	15	5	5
NET (sh)		-273		+9		+15		+2
1307-08								
Autumn #	484		339		477		258	
	#	sh	#	sh	#	sh	#	sh
Buy	27	373	8	86	0	0	6	12
Sell	20	256	10	99	4	26	16	16
NET		-117		+13		+26		+4
1309-10								
Autumn #								
	#	sh	#	sh	#	sh	#	sh
Buy	18	266	13	197	0	0	1	1
Sell	40	472	33	475	11	78	8	9
NET		+206		+278		+78		+8

	Net Stock Exchange	Sales Hides	Sales Dairy
	sh	sh	sh
1300-01	-247	65	426
1307-08	-74	133	535
1309-10	+570	123	544

a Juveniles include bullocks, heifers and yearlings

Source: Peterborough Abbey, Fitzwilliam A/C Rolls,2388, 233, 2389,
Northamptonshire Record Office.

Table 6 Figures for Beef and Dairy Consumption
Selected From Household Accounts

(figures in parentheses estimated from yearly price average-all prices in shillings)

BATTLE ABBEY	1275	1278	1306	1319	1320	1351	
Beef consumed							
number:	7	16	72	77	52	40(m)[a]76	
Price:	92	193	909	820	795	380	339

BISHOP OF HEREFORD   1289
combination of live cattle and carcasses 102

BEAULIEU   1269
Beef consumed
number: 11 (manors) 1 (market)
Price: 59   2
Cheese from manors (in pounds)
consumed: 9,286
sold: 2,250

DURHAM   1307
Beef consumed
number: 228 (hoof)   60 carcasses
Price: 2101   300
Cheese (pounds)   1470
Butter (pounds)   266

PETERBOROUGH	1300	1307	1309
Beef consumed			
number:	64(manors)	119(manors)	146 (manors)
Dairy from manors			
cheese (pounds)	6531	5187	6593
butter (pounds)	307	945	858

[a] (m) cattle sent in from manors

Sources: (See references for full citation): Battle Abbey-Searle & Ross (1967); Beaulieu Abbey-Hockey (1975); Bishop of Hereford-Webb (1854); Durham- Fowler (1899); Peterborough-Fitzwilliam A/C Rolls2388,233,2389 Northamptonshire Record Office.

Notes

I wish to thank Henry Rutz and Benjamin Orlove for their support of this cross-disciplinary contribution and for their critical comments on earlier drafts. I am grateful to Stephen Gudeman for sharing helpful comparative insights.

1. Barry Hindess and Paul Hirst mention consumption on four pages of *Pre-Capitalistic Modes of Production*. In his effort to conceptualize consumption in pre-capitalistic economies C.A. Gregory reminds us: "The consumption sphere is very much a subordinate sphere under capitalism, and as such was not subjected to any systematic analysis by classical economists (Gregory 1982)."

2. For a discussion of universal and local models see Gudeman (1986). The French historian Guy Bois (1984) has drawn attention to the importance of Kula's work and its neglect.

3. This study draws on a book-length manuscript entitled The Economy Which Was Not One: Pastoral Husbandry on a Feudal Estate, Peterborough Abbey, 650 A.D.-1350 A.D. Manorial account rolls provide the primary sources used in the study. Archival references to the accounts appear in Table 1. For an introduction to account rolls as sources in medieval economic history see Harvey (1976). The archive of Peterborough Abbey is surveyed by Martin (1978, 1980). For reasons of space I treat only consumption of sheep and cattle. For a discussion of consumption and pig husbandry on the estate consult Biddick (1984b). I analyze consumption and horse husbandry in the monograph.

4. The issue of state consumption and its effect on seigneurial economies cannot be treated within the space of this paper. Henry Rutz asked me the important question: "If royal power is an exogenous force on consumption activities, isn't the Abbey similar to peasant households everywhere? If not, why not"? To answer this I would begin with a discussion of the capacity of English barons, through the corporate identity they forged over the late twelfth and thirteenth centuries, to disrupt the power of the king through civil war and parliamentary check. In a double move these same barons checked and excluded their peasants from the king's courts. Through exclusion of the peasantry and inclusion of themselves in a corporate identity, they created a minimal difference between themselves and peasant households vis-a-vis consumption and the state. The repression of the English peasantry in the twelfth and early thirteenth centuries has taproots in this battle over the high stakes of consumption.

References

Alcock, N.W.
1981   Warwickshire Grazier and London Skinner 1532-1555. *Records of Social and Economic History.* n.s. IV (1981). Oxford: Oxford University Press.

Astill, G.G.
1983   Economic Change in Later Medieval England: An Archaeological Review. In *Social Relations and Ideas.* T.H. Aston, *et al.,*eds. NY: Cambridge University Press. pp. 217-47.

Bailey, E, and A.F. Friedlaender
1982   Market Structure and Multiproduct Industries. *J. of Economic Literature* XX (September): 1024-1048.

Barrow, G. W. S.
1973   *The Kingdom of the Scots: Government, Church and Society.* London: Edward Arnold.

Biddick, Kathleen
1984a   Field Edge, Forest Edge, Early Medieval Social Change and Resource Allocation. In *Archaeological Approaches to Medieval Europe.* K. Biddick ed. Studies in Medieval Culture XVIII.pp. 105-18.

1984b   Pig Husbandry on the Peterborough Abbey Estate from the Twelfth to the Fourteenth Century. In *Animals and Archaeology: 4. Husbandry in Europe.* Caroline Grigson and Juliet Clutton-Brock, eds. British Archaeological Reports. 227: 161-77.

1985   Medieval English Peasants and Market Involvement. *J. of Economic History* 45 (4): 823-31.

1986   *The Economy Which Was Not One: Pastoral Husbandry on a Feudal Estate.* MS of monograph submitted for publication.

Bois, Guy
1984   *The Crisis of Feudalism.* New York: Cambridge University Press.

Bolton, J.L.
1980   *The Medieval English Economy 1150-1500.* Totowa, N.J.: Rowman & Littlefield.

Bowden, Peter
1967   Agricultural Prices, Farm Profits and Rents. In *Agrarian History of England and Wales 1500-1640*. J. Thirsk, ed. Cambridge: Cambridge University Press. pp. 593-695.

Brenner, Robert
1982   The Agrarian Roots of European Capitalism. *Past and Present*. no. 97: 16-113.

Bridbury, A.R.
1974   Sixteenth Century Farming. *Econ. Hist. Rev.* 27: 538-56.

Campbell, B.M.S.
1983   Agricultural Progress in Medieval England: Some   Evidence from   Eastern   Norfolk. *Econ. Hist. Rev.* 36 (1): 26-46.

Deleuze, G. and F. Guattari
1983   *Anti-Oedipus: Capitalism and Schizophrenia*. Minneapolis: U. of Minnesota Press.

Dept, Gaston
1926   Les   marchands   flamands   et le Roi d'Angleterre (1154-1216). *Revue du Nord* 12: 303-24.

Duby,   Georges
1974   *The   Early   Growth of   the European Economy*. Ithaca, N.Y.: Cornell University Press.

Dyer, Christopher
1972   A Small Landowner in the Fifteenth Century. *Midland History* I: 1-14.

1981   Warwickshire   Farming   1349-1520: Preparations   for   an Agricultural Revolution. *Dugdale Society. Occasional Papers 27.*

1986   The   Consumer   and   the   Market in Late Medieval England. Paper delivered at the Anglo-American Seminar on the Late Medieval Economy. Norwich, England, 25-28 July.

Earle, Timothy
1978   Economic and Social Organization of a   Complex   Chiefdom. *Anthropology   Papers. Museum   of   Anthropology. University of Michigan no. 63.*

Edwards, P.R.
1981   The Cattle Trade of Shropshire in the late 16th and 17th Centuries. *Midland History* 6: 72-93.

Everitt, A.
1967   The Marketing of Agricultural Produce. In *The Agrarian History of England and Wales*. IV. J.Thirsk, ed. Cambridge: Cambridge University Press. pp. 466-592.

Finch, Mary E.
1956   The Wealth of Five Northamptonshire Families. Northants. *Record Society*. XIX.

Fowler, S.F.
1899   Extracts from the Account Rolls of the Abbey of Durham. *Surtees Society*. 99.

Gregory, C.A.
1982   *Gifts and Commodities*. NY: Academic Press.

Gudeman, Stephen
1986   *Economics as Culture*. London: Routledge & Kegan Paul.

Hart, W.H. and P.A. Lyons (eds.)
1893   Cartularium Monasterii de Rameseia. *Roll Series*, 79. part iii: 230-34.

Harvey, P.D.A.
1974   The Pipe Rolls and the Adoption of Demesne Farming. *Econ. Hist. Rev.* 27: 345-59.

1976   *The Manorial Records of Cuxham, Oxon. 1200-1359*. London: H.M.S.O.

Hindess, Barry and Paul Q. Hirst
1975   *Pre-capitalist modes of production*. London: Routlege & Kegan Paul.

Hollister, W. and J.W. Baldwin
1978   The Rise of Administrative Kingship: Henry I and Philip Augustus. *American Historical Review* 83: 867-905.

Hooke, Della
1985   *The Anglo-Saxon Landscape. Manchester*: Manchester University Press.

Jenkinson, Hilary
1913   William Cade, A Financier of the Twelfth Century. *Eng. Hist. Rev.* 28: 209-27.

Jones, G.R.W.
1984   The Multiple Estate: A Model for Tracing the Interrelationships of Society, Economy and Habitat. In Biddick, 1984a: pp. 9-41.

King, Edmund
1973   *Peterborough Abbey.* Cambridge: Cambridge University Press.

Knowles, David
1949   *The Monastic Order in England.* Cambridge: Cambridge University Press.

Kula, Witold
1976   *An Economic Theory of Feudalism.* Atlantic Highlands: Humanities Press.

Lennard, Reginald
1959   *Rural England.* Oxford: Oxford University Press.

Lloyd, T.H.
1973   The Movement of Wool Prices in England. *Econ. Hist. Rev. Supp.* no. 6.

1977   *The English Wool Trade in the Middle Ages.* NY: Cambridge University Press.

Maltby, Mark
1979   Faunal Studies on Urban Sites: The Original Bones from Exeter, 1971-75. *Exeter Archaeological Papers* 2.

Martin, Janet D.
1978   The Cartularies and Registers of Peterborough Abbey. *Northants. Record Society* 28.

1980   The Court and Account Rolls of Peterborough Abbey: A Handlist. *Occ. Publication no. 2.* U. of Leicester History Department.

Munro, John N.
1985   Environment, Land Management and the Changing Qualities of English Wools in the Later Middle Ages. Paper delivered at the 20th International Congress of Medieval Studies.

North, Douglass C. and Robert Paul Thomas
1973 *The Rise of the Western World.* NY: Cambridge University Press.

Oschinsky, Dorothea
1971 *Walter of Henley and other Treatises on Estate Management and Accounting.* Oxford: Clarendon Press.

Pickl, Othmar
1973 Routen, Umfang, und Organisation des inner europaischen Handles mit Schlactvieh im 16 J. In *Festschrift Hermann Wiesflacher.* A. Novotny, *et al* eds. Graz. pp. 143-66.

Postan, M.M.
1941 Medieval Agrarian Society in its Prime. In *The Cambridge Economic History.* I. Cambridge:University Press. pp. 548-632.

1975 *The Medieval Economy and Society.* Harmondsworth: Penguin Books.

Postles, David
1986 The Perception of Profit before the Leasing of Demesnes. *Ag. Hist. Rev.* 34 (1): 12-28.

Potts, W.T.W.
1974 The pre-Danish estates of Peterborough. Peterborough Abbey. *Cambs. Antiquarian Society.* Proc. LXV: 13-27.

Rees, William
1963 Survivals of Ancient Celtic Custom in Medieval England. In *Angles and Britons: O'Donnell Lectures.* Cardiff: University of Wales Press. pp. 148-68.

Richardson, H.G.
1960 *The English Jewry under the Angevin Kings.* London: Methuen and Co.

Robertson, A.J.
1956 *Anglo-Saxon Charters.* Cambridge: Cambridge University Press.

Searle, Eleanor and B. Ross (eds.)
1967 *Accounts of the Cellarers of Battle Abbey* 1275-1313. Sydney: Sydney University Press.

Skeel, Caroline
1926 The Cattle Trade between Wales and England from the 15th-19th centuries. *Royal Hist. Soc. Trans.* 9: 135-58.

Smith, R.A.L.
1943   *Canterbury Cathedral Priory.* Cambridge: Cambridge University
              Press.

Stapleton, T.
1849   Chronicon Petroburgense. *Camden Society.* XLVII.

Stenton, F.M.
1970   Medeshamstede and its Colonies. rpt. In *Prepatory to Anglo-
              Saxon England.* ed. Doris M. Stenton. Oxford: Clarendon
              Press, 1970, pp. 179-92.

Trow-Smith, Robert
1957   *The History of British Livestock Husbandry.* London: Routledge
              and Kegan Paul.

Webb, J. (ed.)
1854   A Roll of the Household Expenses of Richard de Swinfield.
              Camden Society. old. ser. 9.

Williamson, Tom
1986   Parish   boundaries   and   early   fields: continuity and
              discontinuity. *J. of Historical Geography* 12 (3): 241-48.

BOUNDARIES IN TIME:
THE DYNAMICS OF SCHEDULE CONSTRAINTS ON
HOUSEHOLD CONSUMPTION IN VIENNA, AUSTRIA

Robert Rotenberg

Choice and Constraint in Household Consumption

When employed people win back time as a result of a legislated reduction in the standard work week, what do they do with that time? Do they use it for consumption activities, the expenditure of resources toward non-resource-producing ends? Do they trade it for more work time, or other resource-producing activities? Do they devote it to housework and childcare? These are the questions that faced the residents of Vienna, Austria as their work week shrank from 48 hours to 38 hours over the last 25 years. Their solutions to these problems in turn help us to understand how household consumption activities are organized in time.

The choices household members make in allocating their time have little to do with the relative efficiencies of their abilities, as suggested by microeconomic models of time allocation. Instead these choices appear to mediate between two sets of constraints. One set of constraints is a particularly urban phenomenon. It includes demands arising from powerful, public institutions, especially those on which households depend for income, provisions, and amusement. In urban society, the overwhelming majority of people earn the significant portion of their livelihoods from non-food-producing activities. Severed from the rhythm imposed on agriculturalists by plants and animals, the cycles of work, consumption and play in cities are based on tightly synchronized, conventional schedules for work, market and household activities. The schedules or calendars of work institutions, schools, markets, voluntary associations, religious organizations, public bureaucracies, and public transport systems are used to coordinate the activities of the many people involved. The schedules of the various public institutions constitute the state's efforts at regulating access to production and consumption.

The other set of constraints includes the demands on our time and attention by those with whom we have strong role-based relationships: our parents, siblings, spouses, children, in-laws, friends, and neighbors. Each relationship includes a varying amount of time that must be spent giving full attention to the other in order to maintain the relationship. Some of these role-time commitments are not predictable, such as the needs of a sick child. Only when we have satisfied the demands of the institutions and the people in our lives can we finally turn to consumption.

This paper illustrates how the state regulation of consumption activities, competing institutional and role-based demands, and culture-based priorities for consumption (i.e. the timing of mealtimes, shopping, and household recreations) have changed in Vienna. The timing of activities makes a difference in how people consume. Consumers are not entirely autonomous. Politically constituted schedules impose constraints on them. In the case of Austria, political ideals about equity in the duration and sequence of work shifts for all categories of workers standardized the rhythm of meals, marketing, recreational activities and entertainments within the city's households. This paper will explore how this standardization changed the way the Viennese eat, shop and play.

Looking at how schedules constrain activities is an effective way of studying consumption. Schedules are relatively easy to observe and describe. Standard work laws, shopping hours and school hours are publicly available. When people are asked to describe a day's events, the demands of public institutions are quite evident. I used 24-hour recalls of the previous day's activities to create a record of how individuals behaved toward these institutional demands. I assumed that social role responsibilities and the time required to fulfill them are sufficiently normative that interviews gathered within a small sample of households can reliably stand as models for households in general. I interviewed adult members of thirty households. These were selected by "snowballing" through three separate social networks. I reconstructed the household schedule by garnering 24-hour recall data from all household members.[1] Three separate time budget studies conducted by Viennese sociologists at ten year intervals provided a longitudinal perspective on household time allocations.[2] These surveys allow me to generalize with greater confidence from the sample of thirty households to the 391,300 households in the city (Magistratsabteilung 66 1983). Nevertheless, single-person households, pensioners, unemployed households, non-German-speaking households, and student cooperatives are under-represented in both my sample and the national surveys. Thus, the "Vienna" of this study really refers to the employed, multi-person households resident in the city. This constitutes only 43.7% of the total population.

Administrative Changes in the Public Schedule

The public schedule in Vienna impinges on far more households than one would expect based on the U.S. urban experience. Since the last decade of the 19th century, the city has elected a series of socialist municipal governments who have effectively reversed the tendency in industrial systems for local factory managers to define the work time of their employees (cf. Rotenberg 1987 for a comparison of industrial work discipline in Austria and the U.S.). The policy of the socialist governments has been to protect wage earners from losing control over the pace of work by taking away the workplace manager's ability to alter the length or position of work shift. In Vienna, control over work shift length is a priority issue in public forums.

While many industrial states have enacted standard work laws, the history of Austrian legislation in this area provides far fewer industry-specific differences and enforces stronger limitations on overtime and split-shifts. Collective labor contracts determine both the duration and sequencing of the work shift. These are negotiated by individual trade unions, but follow the standard policies set by the national trade union council. The effect of the trade union policies is a reduction in variation among work shifts across all work institutions. Since a much broader range of occupations in Austria are unionized, especially within small-scale work organizations, more people are affected by the standardizing pattern of the labor laws and collective contracts.

In those industrial states in which trade unions have failed to make the standardization of work time a matter of recurrent political debate, the public schedule retains a highly varied pattern of work times. This variation is the product of managers (and if they exist, trade unions) negotiating independently to set the work requirements for their employees. When union activity is only confined to large-scale work organizations, and unionizing of small-scale enterprises has not occurred, a standardizing pattern of work laws either fails to develop, or fails to affect enough households to dominate the life of a city.

An example of this difference between Austrian and U.S. cities is the differing treatment of shopping hours. In the U.S., shopping hours are regulated to suit local custom (the Blue Laws of East Coast cities), and protect public safety (restricting markets and fairs to times when sufficient fire and police personnel are available), as when a downtown merchants' association elects to open their shops on the same evening each week. In most cities, nothing prevents a store from staying open twenty-four hours if it is willing to supply its own security.

In Vienna, shopping hours are a matter of political debate because shop clerks, like all other workers, are thought to be entitled to protection from non-standard shifts. Even if a shop clerk wanted to work an evening shift, the trade unions would not tolerate it. An executive in the Union of Private Employees, the union that represents retail clerks of small shops, reacted to the suggestion of extending shopping hours for an extra hour in the evening as follows:

> . . . Once we start toying with [the shop closing ordinance] we won't be able to extract ourselves. And others, such as the tourist industry, would begin to pressure us for Sunday shopping hours. And so on . . . We fought very hard over the last hundred years for a forty hour week for all workers. And all that would go for naught over a small issue like this.

The shopping schedule in Vienna requires all non-food shops to close between 6:00 PM and 8:00 AM, and food shops to close between 6:30 PM and 7:00 AM on weekdays, and between 12:00 PM Saturday and 8:00 AM Monday on weekends (Kupka 1971: 94-100).[3] Such restrictive uniformity in the schedule of shopping hours would be impossible under the work shift policies of non-socialist industrial states. It works only because such a large proportion of the workforce is unionized that any challenge to union policies in one area of the economy is seen as a threat to union authority in all areas. Yet, as will become apparent below, the debate in Vienna over the merits of this restrictive schedule is by no means closed.

Beginning after the second World War, the federal government in Austria (at that time a coalition of conservative (oVP) and socialist (SPo.) parties) began a program of reductions in the length of the regular paid work week in all sectors of the economy. Figure 1 shows the sequence of legislative changes affecting employed people and retail shop hours. The changes in the regular paid work week initially involved freeing up time at the end of the week. The weekend in Vienna is a 20th century artifact. In the latter half of the 19th century, most workers worked seven day weeks. Only in the years just before World War I did the trade unions become powerful enough to insure free Sundays for all workers. The eight hour day was established in 1920. In 1948, 90% of all workers had a 48 hour, five and half day work week. In 1960, the reduction to 45 hours brought about a five day work week. By 1970, further reductions made four and a half day work weeks possible in some industries (Zeisel 1971).

While the work week was decreasing, the number of paid vacation days was increasing. The standard labor laws of the post-war period provided eight paid vacation days for entry level employees. By 1984, this had grown to 24 days for entry level workers. Workers with ten years seniority could acquire as many as forty-five vacation days in some industries. The number of paid federal holidays is thirteen.[4] Legislation extending the benefit of paid holidays to all workers was passed in the early 1950's. These long-term changes in the structure of work time have produced periods of free time which were never part of the pre- and proto-industrial life of the city. The new weekend has created opportunities for consumption and recreation which never existed before.

Household Responses

Given the opportunity to reallocate the newly won time evenly across the weekdays (freeing more time for weekday shopping), or to increase the size of the weekend by reallocating all of the time to the end of the week, households initially chose to increase the weekend. After 1970, these reductions were implemented by allowing each work institution or each industrial group to determine the reduction strategy that best suited their work conditions and the desires of their workers (Lamel 1976:92). Employed household members sought to reduce the length of their work days only after Saturdays were completely free of work demands. Prior to that, the work day for most workers averaged nine hours, eight and a half of which was paid and one half of which was an unpaid portion of the lunch break. By 1981, the work day averaged just over eight hours paid and one half hour unpaid. Commuting time adds on average an additional forty minutes at the beginning and end of the work segment.[5]

Figure 2 shows how the newly won time was re-allocated by comparing the distribution of time to activities in 1971 and in 1981. Over this decade, an average five hours of work time was returned to households per week. By 1981, consumption, play and sleep segments have increased slightly, but housework and child care increased by one-third. As the institutional demand loosened, the

152

role-time commitments increased, reflecting demands that were probably there all along. The magnitude of these percentages are somewhat misleading because they are based on averages across a variety of household situations. In the next three sections, the qualitative changes in eating, shopping and playing will be described, providing a more contextualized picture of the problems these households faced and how they solved them.

Changes in Mealtimes A meal is different from a snack. A meal is a period of time when people expect to eat socially. That is, they expect to eat with other people who are also eating, and with some attention to beginning and ending the activity together, as well as interacting through conversation during the activity. When snacking, people eat apart or together, but with no regard for the timing of the meal or to social interaction. Snacking is individually oriented eating; meal taking is socially oriented eating. Because of its social component, meal-taking requires people to coordinate their schedules with each other and has a conventional quality.

The number of mealtimes in a city can vary considerably from family to family. In Vienna, as Figure 3 illustrates, the number of socially recognized times for eating with others increased from four to five during the initial period of industrialization, and then declined to three during the last one hundred and fifty years.[6] The decline coincides with the period of greatest political and institutional conflict over the length of the work day. This conflict required managers and trade union officials to see the work segment as increasingly fixed, with rigid boundaries and with few distractions. Those categories of employed people whose work contracts were subject historically to the greatest level of conflict are the most constrained. These include primarily factory workers. The mid-day, mid-morning and mid-afternoon meals were either negotiated out of their work day entirely or greatly reduced in duration. Since workers had to rearrange their mealtimes away from home, the number and importance of the remaining meals in the household changed as well (Rotenberg 1981: 34-35).

Figure 4 compares the times actually spent eating among employed household members, housewives and pensioners in 1981. One can clearly see that employed people eat earlier breakfasts, later suppers, and fewer lunches than non-employed members of their households. The "fork breakfast" and "tea" have been squeezed out of the schedules of most workers. Among employed people, there is a strong possibility that supper, as well as breakfast, might not be eaten with the rest of the household. This alters the social meaning of food consumption. More and more people consume food through snacking. The coordination of effort required to bring the household together for a meal comes to be seen as unnecessary, except perhaps on weekends. The potential for a decline in nutritional quality is high since shared meals are more likely to be balanced and varied than individual snacking.

When we look at the eating times of employed people according to their work category (Figure 5), we find marked variation between factory, clerical and managerial workers, and, within these categories, between men and women.

153

These categories refer to three different degrees of control over the pace of work one finds in industrial work organizations, as well as differing levels of education, full-time versus part-time status, hourly vs. monthly methods of computing salaries, and the relative power and prestige in their work institution. Although the Viennese are highly conscious of these distinctions, to call them markers of class is to overstate the differences. While factory workers, office employee and administrators have different degrees of control over the pace of their work, all are subordinate to the institutions that hire and fire them. The differences are merely separate conditions under which an employee must adapt to the politically constituted schedule.

The lowest level of control over work pace is that of the factory worker whose rate is closely monitored by a foreman and who must keep up with various machines and other workers. The highest level of control belongs to the managers and executives, who set their own work agenda and calendar. Between them are the clerical workers who may be monitored by others, especially when consistently behind in the work, but who otherwise have some flexibility in setting their own pace. Once the routine is established, both factory and clerical workers evolve ways of reasserting informal control over the pace of work whenever possible. These two groupings of workers never attain the same level of control that is commonly available to their managers.

The factory worker can expect two morning meals. The first is at home between 4:00 AM and 7:00 AM. The early hour of this meal makes coordination with other household members difficult, but not impossible. The second is a work break, reminiscent of the old "fork breakfast" between 8:30 and 9:30. This meal is often eaten with co-workers, as is the mid-day meal. In the figure, the mid-day meal is a highly compressed one hour peak at noon. The compression is due to the heightened rigidity and standardization of the factory work routine. Also, the second half hour of lunch is unpaid. Workers sometimes trade this half hour for ending the shift a half hour earlier. Supper is eaten between 5:30 and 7:30.

Factory workers describe their household mealtimes as every bit as regimented as their work schedules. In this quote, a factory foreman describes how food consumption fits into his work day:

> At 4 AM I get up and by 4:20, I am on my way to work. At 9:00 AM, we take a breakfast break for fifteen minutes . . . We break for lunch at noon. It lasts for half an hour . . . There is no afternoon break, because everyone is interested in being able to leave early . . . My wife prepares dinner everyday at 6:00 sharp! Exactly when I come home, she begins. At exactly 6:00 PM the food is on the table. You could set your watch by it. This is the big meal of the day for me, and it takes about half an hour to eat it.

Of the three meals described here, two are eaten with co-workers. Only the evening meal is eaten with household members. His car-pool partner and co-worker at the factory has even fewer opportunities to eat socially:

154

I get up at 3:30 AM and make my breakfast. I even skip the morning break because there is so much to do... I eat supper as soon as I get home... I often skip lunch because I am trying to lose weight. For that reason I am quite hungry by 5:00.

He eats only one meal, supper. All of the other food taking is individual snacking. At the next highest level of work qualification, licensed service workers, there is a great deal less supervision and proportionately greater control over the pace of his work than factory workers. The effect of this increase in control on food consumption is immediately evident in this quotation from a gas appliance repairman:

I got up at 6:00 AM and made myself tea. That's all I eat for breakfast . . . It takes about ten minutes for me to drive to the office. I have to be there by 7:00, but I'm usually fifteen minutes early . . . Then I go out for a good fork-breakfast. I go somewhere were I can sit down, like a coffeehouse, and I have a good coffee and something to eat . . . At 8:30 or 9:00, I'm ready to start [work] . . . I go to lunch when I'm hungry. There is no fixed time. Yesterday I went at 12:30 for a quick one. Supper is the big meal of the day for me. Even so, sometimes I spend one and half or two hours at lunch. Yesterday, I spent only one and half hours. I like to have my afternoon light [work activities] so that I can have a coffee around 3:00 PM . . . When I get home, I eat supper, watch television and go to bed around 10:00 PM.

His early breakfast is only a snack. The mid-morning, mid-day, and mid-afternoon meals are taken with co-workers. Supper is again the only household meal. Thus, even though the total number of opportunities for social eating increases, the number eaten within the household remains small.

The mealtimes of an office worker are closer to that of the gas appliance repairman than to the factory workers. Some office workers enjoy daily coffee breaks. Lunch begins for many office workers at noon, but it could be delayed until 1:00 PM, especially among women office workers. Supper can take place anytime from 5:00 to 8:00, perhaps reflecting different commuting times. The differences between men and women in the height of the peaks is not as pronounced in this category. Here is how one secretary described her food consumption:

The day begins for me at 6:30 AM. By 6:50, I'm dressed and ready for a cup of coffee . . . At mid-day, I decided to shop for Christmas presents instead of eating lunch . . . We usually have two breaks, one at 10:00 AM and one at 2:30 PM. Since everyone was late yesterday, I didn't bother to make the morning coffee by myself . . . I finished work at 4:30 PM. I had an appointment with an acquaintance . . . Once home, I made myself a tea and ate some bread and butter in bed while watching television.

155

Ordinarily, this secretary eats four meals, three with co-workers and supper with her husband. Here, however, she indicates that these workplace meals are easily ignored. This interview reveals how variable the number of eating times in clerical work can be. Furthermore, this variability stems from the problem of coordinating her schedule with that of her co-workers, rather than structures imposed on her by the work pace, as was the case with the factory workers.

Managerial workers and executives reflect the greatest freedom of choice of when to eat during the work day and, perhaps for that reason, also the greatest differences between men and women. As Figure 5 shows, this group eats breakfast between 6:00 and 9:00, if male, and 5:30 to 10:30, if female. Lunch is lengthened and drawn out through the 12:00 to 2:00 PM time slot. There is more likely to be an afternoon "tea" among this group. Supper can occur anytime in the evening, reflecting, on the one hand, a very long work day, and on the other hand, variable commuting times. Female executives are likely to eat quite late, repeating a trend first observed in female office workers. Women in this category are more likely to eat meals than men, a reversal of the situation among factory workers. Here is the description of his food consumption by a trade union executive, whose wife is also an executive in a private firm:

> I got up as usual at 5:45. My wife made breakfast for us both . . .
> I usually skip lunch since I'm trying lose weight. But yesterday, I
> decided to have something for this head cold. I ate in the office: . .
> . At 4:00 PM, I had coffee and some pastry in the office . . . We
> [he and his wife] had dinner, which is usually the biggest meal of
> the day for both of us. This was at about 8:00 PM.

His two meals within the household and the absence of meals with co-workers are a decidedly different eating pattern from those described so far. Even the timing of the work segment snacks (mid-day and mid-afternoon) are unlike the food taking of the other workers. The coordination of eating times in the household, however, is particularly striking and demonstrate the heightened control over time, on and off the job, that managerial positions make possible.

From these Viennese, we learn that the choice of eating with other people, as opposed to by one's self, is limited by the person's relative control over the pace of work. Furthermore, this relative control over work pace affects the coordination of meals in the periods immediately before and after the work segment. Figure 5 shows that a greater percentage of clerical workers and executives eat before and after work. This heightened choice is represented by a series of peaks of extended duration. The differences in food consumption reflected in these graphs demonstrates that people with the lowest degree of control over their pace of work all eat their pre- and post-work segment meals at approximately the same time. People with greater control tend to eat their early and late meals at a variety of times.

In addition to the conditions of work, conditions within the household, too, can lead to variation in the choice of when to eat. The most important of these are gender-based role obligations. The greater variability of eating times among clerical and executive women demonstrates the impact of the household role-based time constraints.

Women in Vienna eat fewer meals per day than men for any number of reasons, including dieting, competing activities such as childcare, desire to leave work earlier, preference, part-time and split shift employment. Women consider themselves (and are considered by others) responsible for household organization, childcare, and meal preparation, in addition to their work responsibilities. The large number of these activities that demand attention before and after work postpones the opportunity to eat for many women. This feature of Viennese household role obligations can be seen in the shorter peaks and broader durations for food consumption among women in all three employment groupings.

The presence of children in the household not only implies that the household responsibilities of the adults will increase, but also that the schedules of more household members must be taken into account in planning meals. Like gender-based responsibilities and the conditions of work, multi-generation households create another set of conditions under which the employed and non-employed household members coordinate their food consumption. Younger workers of both genders tend to have larger households, often containing small children. These households are most likely to conduct joint meals serving as many household members at once as possible. These households account for the peaks between 6:00 PM and 8:00 PM. Managers and executives tend to be older people whose households are smaller. These households tend to eat later and more variably from day to day.

Changes in Shopping Time Shopping hours are another politically constituted constraint on consumption with which households must contend. As noted earlier, the Austrian government, like all states, regulates access to these shops for a variety of reasons. In the last thirty years, the primary reason for regulation has been the protection of nation-wide parity in the length of the work shifts of hourly wage workers including retail store clerks. Store closing ordinances have proved the most practical means for achieving this goal.

The ordinances create a pattern of shopping hours depicted by the background bars in Figures 6 and 7. If one considers the amount of time required to travel to the food store and actually shop, at least an hour before or after work is needed to shop on a daily basis. The situation is better on weekends. Even then, shopping is confined by law to the morning hours. Households must either shop on Saturdays or, if commuting times are short enough, late afternoons on weekdays.

Unlike the standard work week, the store hours can vary from place to place within the limits set by the store closing ordinances. Figure 8 displays the variations in store hours in four locations within and around Vienna. All four locations are dense residential areas. They differ primarily in the size of population served by the local market, and in the proportion of people who work and live in the same place, as opposed to those who commute to work (Rotenberg and Hutchison 1980). There is also a juridical boundary between the two mid-town shopping streets which are located within the city boundaries, and the border suburb and suburban county seat which are located in the Federal State of Lower Austria. This state surrounds Vienna, just as Maryland and Virginia surround the District of Columbia. The Governor of Lower Austria and the Mayor of Vienna are empowered by Federal law to set shopping hour ordinances, and can grant seasonal, or location-specific variances to those ordinances.[7]

Those places where fewer residents commute will have fewer store hours than places where a greater number of residents commute. This is because non-employed household members who are available to shop during the day tend to do so near their homes. These residential districts are identifiable because the number of potential customers drops at mid-day, as the residents return home to prepare and eat their mid-day meal. Subsequently, a greater proportion of shops in these districts close for an extended mid-day break. In areas which are a mixture of residential and business, the number of potential customers is relatively constant over the day, and may even increase during the lunch break.[8] For these reasons, there is variation in the actual number of hours stores will be open. The shortest shopping hours occur in the most homogeneously residential districts, as shopkeepers try to take advantage of their knowledge of the activity patterns of their potential customers to the maximum extent. The longest shopping hours occur in central business districts, as shopkeepers try to maintain maximum access for customers about whose shopping patterns they know far less.

Consumption time can only increase if there are no institutional constraints already in effect that channel or otherwise restrict the access of households to the various markets. These store closing ordinances are quite rigid. During the period when work time was being reduced, no significant redistribution of shopping time was possible. This was especially critical during the late afternoon. Instead, shopping shifted to a once weekly, Saturday shopping pattern.

On October 30, 1976, a long standing tension between shoppers and the store closing restrictions broke into public debate. A newspaper article reported on the shopping schedules of the wives of Federal and Municipal administrators. Most of these women were employed themselves and admitted that they too, like so many of the women they knew, had no time to shop. They complained that the store closing ordinance set unreasonable restrictions on shoppers, forcing them to rush around after work to buy fresh food for their family's supper. As for general merchandise, the early store closings made shopping for shoes or furniture a practical impossibility (Hammerl 1976: 3).

The municipal government refused to change the store closing ordinance. It argued that the restrictive hours were necessary to protect the quality of life of all retail employees, especially those working in small shops that were too numerous to effectively control, and often exploited clerks by demanding that they work extra hours. The problem was not in the central district, or with the big supermarkets. Rather, it lay in the small neighborhood shops employing less than five employees. They needed to have their time with their families in the evening protected, argued the government. The trade unions were even more militant in their refusal to budge on the restrictive store closings, as the quote from union executive cited in the opening section of this paper reveals.

In a poll published at the height of the public debate, 63% of the Viennese polled favored a liberalization of the shopping hours (Rabl 1976: 3). In spite of this pressure, the government, with the full support of the trade unions, remained firm. As of this writing, no variances have been made in the Viennese application of the federal store closing ordinance. Instead, the households adjust their shopping schedules. Those who wish to maintain the older lifestyle of daily shopping are taking the location of neighborhood food shops into account, as well as the location of work, when choosing where to live.

Many trade union officials wondered aloud in private why the eight hours which had been won for workers between 1960 and 1975 had not made the shopping schedules of households easier. The decision of how the work week would be reduced was left to the workers' councils in the different commercial and industrial groups. In smaller firms and factories, the workers themselves voted on how the time would be redistributed. What these people failed to consider was how their decision would affect their household schedules. The shopping schedule was established in 1959 at a time when people worked six eight-hour days. In 1965 when people were working either five and a half eight-hour days, shopping time could still fit into the after work period. In the 1970's, the work week shrank to four and a half nine-hour days and shopping after work became more difficult. This failure to consider the fit between shopping and work by the employees or their councils resulted in more weekend shopping. In this instance, decisions to decrease the work week resulted in an unforeseen pressure to shift the household shopping schedule to the weekend as well, ultimately reducing the total amount of free time.

Pressure to begin shopping on a weekly basis began with the first work week reduction in the 1960's. The 1961 time budget survey reports that 75% of the employed women and 21% of the men interviewed shopped on a daily basis. By 1971, the total number of daily shoppers had dropped to 17%. In 1961, people who shopped every day tended to shop each day in equal proportions. In 1971, daily shopping was clustered on Monday and Friday. These comparisons demonstrate a marked shift away from daily shopping and toward weekly shopping.

This shift had a deadly impact on the structure of the local markets, especially small food shops located in residential districts. From 1964 to 1974, the number of these small shops declined markedly. In the districts surrounding the central business district, where the households tended to be older, commercially employed, and declining in size as their children moved out, 30% of the total number of small food shops went bankrupt in ten years. Ten percent were lost in 1968 alone. In the middle sized districts with their higher population density and more affluent population, 36% of the small shops went bankrupt. In the large outlying districts populated by the most recent migrants to the city and large municipal housing projects, 29% of the small shops were lost.

With a decline in the number of small shops, shopping has also lost some of its social value. The newer, larger shops and supermarkets were organized for weekly shopping. They did not place the same value on establishing long-term relations with customers as did the small shops. Here is how one resident described the changing shopping conditions:

> The small shop, or as we call it, the *Greisler*, is a place to go when you have forgotten something. You cannot do your big shopping there. I don't know what will happen to the small shops. I hope they will always be there. They are so much more personal. You know the butcher and how good his meat is. You know the best baker in your neighborhood. I like to go to this greengrocer or that butcher in our [daily] farmer's market because I know they have good things. In a supermarket it isn't so personal. There is no relationship between you and the cashier. She doesn't care if you buy there or not. It's the same everywhere with these big shops. It's like a mass operation, insanely crowded and confusing. In a small shop, it's completely different. People thank you for coming and hope you'll come back. They do more for you. In large shops, the only encouragement to return is the price. In a small shop you are more likely to buy something because it is presented beautifully, regardless of what it costs.

The following resident points out the personal costs incurred by both the shopkeepers and their local customers as the small shops were squeezed out of the shopping strips.

> In the next apartment house there was a small food shop. The owners knew everyone and they would just write down the charges and you could pay every two weeks, or once a month. On Sunday, when all the other shops were closed, you could knock on the door and they would serve you because you were a neighbor. It was just like living in a village... But the owners made very little money. The whole shop was smaller than this room. When the supermarkets began to open, people often went there because the prices were cheaper. Only the very poor, who could only pay at the end of the month, continued to shop there and buy the more expensive food. The supermarkets would only take cash. Then came the value-added tax.[9] He [the shopkeeper] had never employed a bookkeeper. He always did the books himself. So he began to get into trouble with the tax office. It was

160

really terrible. In the end, he had a nervous breakdown and had to go to the hospital. They closed the shop and moved away.

These voices reflect the sense of a lost community in which shopkeeper and shopper shared common values as well as a common schedule. Households still manage to provision themselves in spite of the tight time conflicts. But the social meaning of shopping in the retail market is different as a result of the scheduling of those activities in time. One hears comments about a lower quality in the products purchased and a feeling of disinterest on the part of the shop clerks. Fortunately, a large number of small personalized food shops remain, protected by the restrictive store closing ordinances.

Changes in Play Times Play is the ultimate consumption activity, since none of the resources entailed or expended produce anything other than pleasure. Play activities are voluntary, superfluous and disinterested (Huizinga 1950: 4-13). Household play requires the coordination of the schedules of the various members. The single most important temporal artifact of household play in Vienna is the weekend, a period of time wholly dedicated to household play by the society.

When discussing the range of play activities, Viennese distinguish between *Erholungen* (recreations) and *Vergnugen* (entertainments). A systematic analysis of the kinds of activities that are considered exclusively *Erholungen* or *Vergnugen* reveals that the primary distinction between the two is how they are scheduled. Either of these can be active or passive. *Erholungen* are activities in which the participants determine when and for how long the play will continue. These include hiking, visiting a restaurant or wine garden, or taking a trip to another part of the world. On the other hand, *Vergnugen* are entertainments, such as sporting events, nightclub performances, or radio and television programs. To participate in such entertainments means once again engaging the public schedule of activities. To participate in recreations, on the other hand, means breaking with the institutional schedule, and choosing to play when and for as long as one likes.

Over the last two hundred years, the style of Viennese play activities has evolved more and more toward entertainments. In this regard, the Viennese are no different from urban populations in other parts of the industrial world. In the pre-industrial period, recreations dominated. A contemporary observer in 1792 notes that the middle of the day, from 11:00 AM to 2:00 PM in particular, was a favorite time for picnicing or conducting love affairs in the park lands immediately outside the city walls. At that time, too, Sundays were intended for taking long walks in the parks and woods with family and friends (Pezzl 1923: 217-223). In the 1830's, on the eve of full-scale industrialization, social evenings in private homes were the fashion. These would begin at dusk and last well past midnight. Parents and children would attend together, playing cards and making music (Gross-Hoffinger 1832: 124-135). The entertainments available to the pre-industrial Viennese, on the other hand, were limited to the theaters which required purchasing tickets in advance.

161

The process of standardizing the work segment during this century made the mid-day play period and weekday social evenings increasingly impossible to schedule. Social evenings on weekdays have become quite rare. A number of informants said that in general the practice of entertaining friends at one's home declined most dramatically after the second World War. Today, people gather primarily on weekend evenings. Even then, the preference is to entertain in pubs, restaurants and wine gardens rather than the home (Rotenberg 1984).

In contemporary Vienna, scheduled entertainments predominate during the work week, while recreations are reserved for the weekend. The weekday entertainment *par excellence* is television. In 1980, five out of seven households in the city had televisions.[10] Married men and women in their twenties and thirties, and retired people are the most loyal viewers. During the day, television programming is sparse. Only an occasional film or education program will be scheduled before lunch. Children's programming begins at 4:00 PM and continues until six. After the news at 7:00 PM, all evening programming is oriented toward adults. Radio, theater, concerts, cinema, and sporting events are also popular.

Vienna's theater, opera and concert performers are government supported. They are among the most prestigious entertainments in the world and draw substantial tourism to the city. For the Viennese themselves, these entertainments are expensive and very difficult to schedule within their work and household obligations.[11] Except for those managers and executives with greater control over their work pace, the Viennese attend their world class theaters and concert halls infrequently at best. Cinemas and cabarets are visited more frequently, but less often as income level and control over the pace of work decline.

Frustration over the difficulties in taking part in these wonderful entertainments broke into public consciousness in 1976. A group of young artists seized an old slaughterhouse district, St. Marx. The old buildings were being used for a theater festival at the time, but the city eventually intended to tear it down for an industrial park. The object of the occupation and the political confrontation that followed was to publicize dissatisfaction with the cultural policies of the government. The young activists demanded the creation of entertainment centers in the residential districts so that busy households could more easily take advantage of the city's musicians and actors. After a three month occupation, the government agreed to greater investment in scheduled entertainments outside of the central tourist district. Opportunities to visit what the occupiers of St. Marx called the "elite culture palaces" in the central district remains as difficult today as it was in 1976.

It seems to be the intention of the government to maintain a highly centralized entertainment district and to resist calls for investment in neighborhood-based, state-sponsored entertainments. Greater investment is made in the state-owned television networks and their productions. Reliance on public entertainments by households only offers the illusion of choice. In fact, these entertainments are scheduled so as to segregate people with different incomes and levels of control over their pace of work.

Contemporary recreations during the work week are most likely to take the form of meeting relatives or intimate friends at home. These meetings take place immediately after work. The coffeehouse is another place to meet friends in the late afternoon. Other active recreational activities that depend on the availability of specific facilities, like sauna bathing, swimming, bowling, and soccer, are maintained by the city as a public service. Access to these facilities is specifically scheduled for weekday evenings. Also, these facilities are more likely to appeal to individuals rather than households.

The weekend has a special place in households' play. Only on Sunday and Saturday are the work and role commitments sufficiently relaxed that the household can come together as a unit. These activities are most often long hikes in the wooded hills that surround the city. Family hiking as a weekend activity dates from the pre-industrial period. For some families the activity is so important that only heavy rain and snow keep them at home. These walks through the woods last as long as six hours and include a lunch stop at one of the many inns in the woods that cater to this favorite household recreation. The end of the hike, too, is likely to lead to a wine garden. There, the household may spend another two hours eating and drinking wine together. In summer, households may go to one of the nearby lakes or swimming clubs for the day. In winter, they may go skiing in the mountains a few hours south of the city. In 1971, a third of the respondents in the time budget survey had hiked in the woods on the previous weekend and a quarter had taken a drive outside of the city.

In the 1970's, the government sponsored a special mortgage program with subsidized interest rates (*Bausparen*) that provided households who otherwise could not afford a second home with the means to purchase summer cottages in the countryside. Weekend cottage estates were built in the agricultural towns located an hour or more from the city. Those who could afford the extra expense built their own cottages or rehabilitated old, unused farm buildings. The program lasted for approximately seven years.

Many of the households continue to occupy garden plots within the city limits which were originally distributed to the poorest workers during the depression to enable them to grow a portion of their own food. The gardens are rarely used for growing vegetables anymore. Instead, people have built tiny cottages and flower gardens on the 420 m^2 plots. Having a garden plot within the city is so popular that new garden settlements continue to be incorporated whenever the city makes the land available. These garden plots are popular because they provide a sense of community that many Viennese feel is otherwise missing in their weekday lives. The members of a garden settlement conduct activities throughout the year, administer the settlement's finances themselves, care for each other's children and grandchildren during work days in the summer, and treat each other to suppers and grill parties.

The desire to leave the city for natural surroundings on weekends reflects a consumption value I call the rural nexus in Viennese play. The object of this play is not merely to commune with nature. Instead, the urban household seeks to link itself with other households in non-urban settings. The goal is to recreate what the urbanites imagine rural community life to be like. It is not the work life of farmers and foresters that they seek to emulate, but the shared recreational life of rural villages and homesteads. Given the opportunity to spend a day together, Viennese households create idealized rural communities for themselves in quasi-agricultural settings. The effect is to symbolically invert the social and environmental conditions of their weekday urban lives.

The prevalence of the rural nexus in household play is responsible for the pattern of reallocation of time which occurred as the work week shrank in size between 1960 and 1975. Only on the weekend were the schedules of the various household members sufficiently open to plan common recreations. However, the very newness of the strategy contributed to increased frustration for some households. Even after the work constraints on weekends were removed, other constraints remained. The school schedule remained a half-day, six day week with classes on Saturday morning. Households with children protested that their children's schedules prevented the family from engaging in recreations together on Saturday, and thereby negated the social benefits of the work time reductions. The teachers' union blocked any changes in the six day schedule, declaring that the five day week could only be achieved by lengthening the school day. The teachers felt that the longer school day destroyed the highly productive homework period in the afternoon. Forcing the students to do their homework in the evening was also disruptive to family life, they argued. The conflict was resolved by having parents in each elementary school vote, as workers in each factory had voted over the work week reductions, for either a five day or six day week for their childrens' school. High schools, in which homework is a more important part of the curriculum, continued to hold the six day schedule.

Constraints on Consumption Time

We have explored three sets of consumption activities among multi-person households in Vienna. The data illustrate how state policy, competing institutional and role-based demands, and cultural priorities channel consumption into specific periods of the day and week. An extended discussion would show that a similar level of constraint based on the State mandated vacation and holiday schedule of the work year also exists seasonally. The timing of socially-based consumption activities can make a difference in how people consume. As these consumption activities compete among themselves and with work activities, the priorities of household-based versus individual-based consumption shift in time.

Household recreational activities have traditionally held the highest priority. The re-creation of community life which is otherwise unsatisfying or

164

undiscovered at work or within one's neighborhood is possible in natural surroundings.

These are available to the household only when the schedules permit. The conflict between children's school schedules and that of other household members on Saturdays shows how difficult it is to set aside time when all household members are free to play together. Creating a weekend period long enough for all household members to spend time together free of work and household responsibilities was a key element in the reallocation of time won back by workers. Indeed, the motivation for the trade unions to retain as much control over the work shift as possible, even if that meant increasing standardization of the work schedule for the entire society, derives from their understanding of the priority their members give to household recreations.

Eating, the ultimate expression of consumption, is constrained by the standardized work schedule whether one is actually at work or not. Historically, the number of conventional mealtimes per day is not constant in a city. They change to meet the demands of the work schedule. The greater the level of control over the pace of work workers enjoy, the more control they have over when to eat. People with the least control over the pace of their work are likely to eat fewer meals, while those with greater control are likely to eat more often. The trend is toward predominantly individual eating on weekdays with a higher priority for family-based eating on weekends.

Shopping activities are constrained by the standardized work hours. Additional constraints can be imposed locally as shopkeepers close their shops during times when customers are unlikely to shop. These shopping constraints are not directly tied to work hours legislatively, creating inconvenient situations where some households may have more time available to shop during a day, such as Saturday, and fewer shopping hours in which to do so. Nevertheless, households manage to adequately provision themselves, and the Viennese are not deprived of material goods and services by the inconvenience of their shopping hours. The desire to shop when it is convenient has had a disastrous effect on the smaller retail shops of the neighborhoods with a resulting decline in the role of these small shops as arenas for developing a sense of shared community in the residential neighborhoods.

Consumption is an ethical problem. It is accorded a high priority by the public agenda when it contributes to the overall growth of the regional economy, as in the consumption of recreational and entertainment products. It is seen in a less favorable light when it impinges on society's obligation to provide all its citizens with an equal opportunity to work and play. At that point, the opportunity to consume, even for the majority of citizens, gives way in Vienna to the higher value of equity in work shifts. On more than one occasion, Viennese have found themselves unable to gain access to a specific market when they wanted because of these shifting priorities. The effect of the public debate over these issues has resulted in a heightened consciousness of the trade-offs between the liberty to consume and the equality of working conditions.

Figure 1: Changes in Public Schedule, 1945-1985
Vienna, Austria

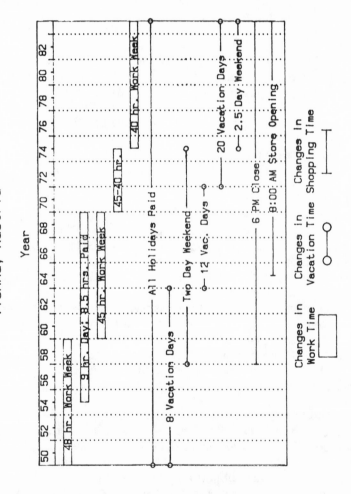

Figure 2: Redistribution of Activities Following Reductions in Standard Work Week, 1971 to 1981.

1971

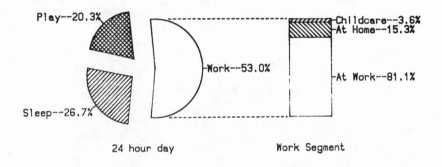

Play--20.3%

Sleep--26.7%

Work--53.0%

Childcare--3.6%
At Home--15.3%

At Work--81.1%

24 hour day

Work Segment

1981

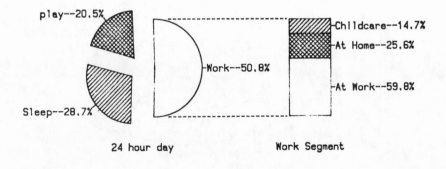

play--20.5%

Sleep--28.7%

Work--50.8%

Childcare--14.7%

At Home--25.6%

At Work--59.8%

24 hour day

Work Segment

Figure 3: Mealtimes in Vienna, 1792-1983.

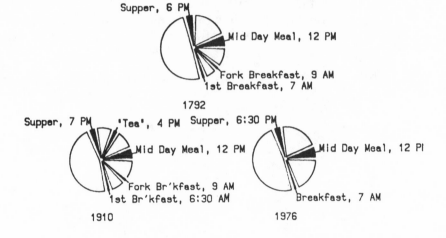

Figure 4: Food Consumption of Employed and
Non-employed Household Members in Vienna, 1981.

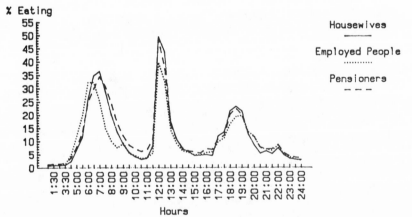

data: 1981 Mikrozensus, Oe S Z 1984

168

Figure 5: Food Consumption Times by Gender and Work Categories, 1981.

Men

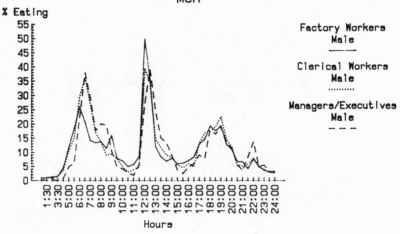

Women

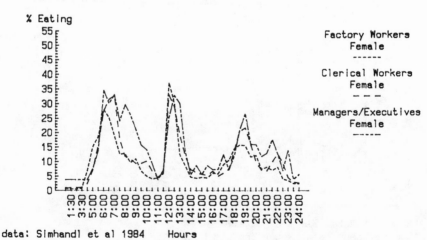

data: Simhandl et al 1984

Figure 6: Work Segment Constraints on Access to Retail Shops on Weekdays, 1980.

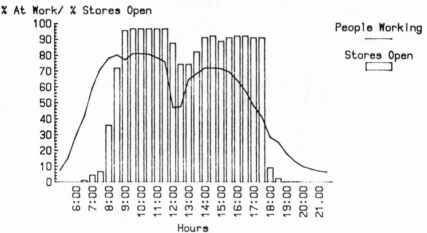

% At Work/ % Stores Open

People Working

Stores Open

Hours

Figure 7: Work Segment Constraint on Access to retail Shops on Saturday, 1980.

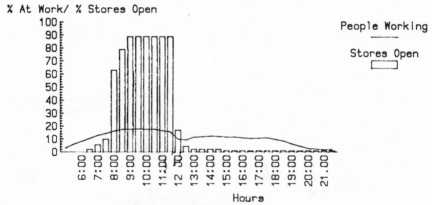

% At Work/ % Stores Open

People Working

Stores Open

Hours

'At Work' data: Simhandl et al 1984
'Stores Open' data: Rotenberg and Hutchison 1980

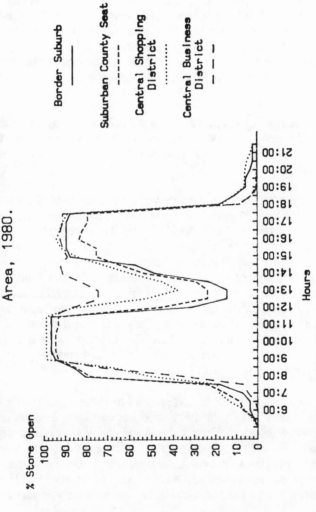

Figure 8: Access to Retail Shops on Weekdays in Four Locations within the Vienna Metropolitan Area, 1980.

Border Suburb

Suburban County Seat

Central Shopping District

Central Business District

% Store Open

Hours

data: Rotenberg and Hutchison 1980

171

Notes

The data considered here derive from my field research in Vienna in 1975 and 1976 (case studies), 1981 (archival research), 1982 (shopping hour survey), and 1985 (garden estate interviews). I would like to acknowledge the support I received from the University of Massachusetts Department of Anthropology European Studies Program for the initial research periods, and the DePaul University College of Liberal Arts and Sciences Faculty Research Grant Program for the 1982 and 1985 periods. I am indebted to Jola Zalud of Vienna for assisting in the translations of the interviews. Thanks also to Henry Rutz, Ben Orlove, and Mitra Emad for their comments on earlier drafts of this paper. This essay is dedicated to the memories of Theodore Prager and Fred Margulies, dedicated socialists and leaders of the post-war Austrian workers movement, who took the time to help me understand their vision of a just society.

1. This technique was pioneered in the mid-1970's by Thorsten Hagerstrand and the geographers associated with his school (Hagerstrand 1972). Carlstein has applied constraint models to temporal organization in preindustrial societies (1982).

2. The first two time budget surveys were conducted by the Kammer fur Arbeiter und Angestellte, a national research institute for work policy (Kammer 1961; Mundel et al. 1979). They were analyzed and published by the institute's staff sociologists. The third survey was conducted as part of the national census (Simhandl et al 1984). It was analyzed and published by the Oesterreichisches Statistisches Zentralamt, a federal agency. While the three surveys are not comparable in all respects, they have quite similar sample profiles and provide separate tables on the Vienna portion of the sample. They differ in the kinds of questions that were deemed important in the different decades, in the sophistication of the statistical analyses, and in the level of categorical specificity required in the respondents' answers.

3. There are a number of exceptions to these rules. For example, stores selling only bakery or dairy products can open as early as 6:30 AM for breakfast shoppers. Flower shops and candy stores have slightly extended hours. Stores in railroad stations selling products to travelers can stay open throughout the evening and weekend. On the four Saturdays before Christmas, stores are allowed to stay open all day. These exceptions aside, the retail market schedule is extraordinarily uniform.

4. Within Europe, only Italy has more federal holidays than Austria.

5. The average commuting time has dropped only a few minutes over the last twenty years. Times of ten minutes or less increased as times of 30-60

minutes decreased. This suggests a reversal of the trend of the first half of the century when people lived farther and farther from their workplaces.

6.   Breakfast is traditionally eaten in the household in the morning before leaving for work or school. Ideally a meal shared by the entire family, individuals who tend to leave the house at the same time tend to eat at the same time. It consists of coffee or tea, and bread or rolls spread with butter and jam. The fork-breakfast is traditionally a mid-morning meal eaten in cafes and bistros with workmates or colleagues. It consists of a soup and sausage, or a sandwich with beer or apple juice. For school children, it is almost always a sandwich and milk eaten during a mid-morning break from classes. The mid-day meal is traditionally the largest meal of the day. It can be eaten either at home (if home is nearby to work) with the entire family, or a restaurant, cafe, or cafeteria with workmates. It consists of at least two courses (soup and hot meat dish with starch) and sometimes a third (a sweet dessert). The mid-afternoon meal became popular among managers and professionals during the second half of the 19th century. It consists of pastry and coffee eaten almost exclusively in coffeehouses or pastry shops with friends or business acquaintances. It is rarely eaten on a regular basis today. Mothers and their school aged children sometimes eat this meal at home after the children finish their homework. Supper is traditionally eaten within the household among family and intimate friends. It is a cold meal typically consisting of bread, cold cuts and pickled vegetables.

7.   The survey on which this analysis is based took the state ordinance differences into account and excluded communities or categories of shops for which variances were in effect at the time the survey was conducted.

8.   This decision process can become quite complicated. For example, the potential customers for some shops may vary more than those for other shops. Restaurants, hardware stores, bakers and law offices may each reflect a different pattern of busy and slow periods. Also since some non-employed people are available to shop in all four districts, the day schedule of at-home household members plays a role in the decisions of some shops to close at lunch, especially those who sell food provisions.

9.   The Value Added Tax required retail owners to collect not only the portion of the tax that was created by their sale to customers, but also the tax that had been entailed by the sale of those products from producer to wholesaler and wholesaler to retailer as well.

10.   The observations in this paragraph are taken from a survey of the cultural life of the Viennese by the Institute for Empirical Sociological Research in 1974 (Institut 1974).

11.   In the 1971 time budget survey, differences in income and the related distinction between being in a responsible vs. a subordinate job position accounted for the differences in the responses to questions of how often people attended elite cultural entertainments, like theater, opera, cabaret and concerts (Mundel et al 1979: 283).

References

Carlstein, Tommy
1982   *Time Resources, Society and Ecology*. Volume 1, Pre-industrial Societies. London: George Allen and Unwin.

Ehmer, Josef
1980   *Familienstruktur und Arbeitsorganisation im Fruhindustriellen Wien*.Wien: Verlag fur Geschichte und Politik.

Gross-Hoffinger, Anton Johann (a.k.a. Hans Normann)
1833   *Oesterreich wie es ist. Erste Theil: Wien wie es ist*. Leipzig und Lowenberg: Eschrich und Comp.

Hammerl, Ernst
1976   Wann kauft Staris Frau: Politiker bestimmen den Ladenschluss--aber sie baden ihn nicht an. *Kurier* 10/30/76. p.3.

Hagerstrand, Thorsten
1972   The Impact of Social Organization and Environment on the Time Use of Individuals and Households. *Plan (International)* Stockholm.

Huizinga, Johan
1955   *Homo Ludens: A Study of the Play Element in Culture*. Boston: Beacon Press.

Institut (fur Forschung im Empirischen Soziologie)
1974   *Kultur in osterreich: Grundlagenforschung im Kulturellen Bereich*. 851/73. Wien: Institut fur Forschung im Empirischen Soziologie.

Kammer (Kammer fur Arbeiter und Angestellte fur Wien)
1961   *Freizeitgestaltung der Arbeiter und Angestellten Wiens*. Wien: Verlag der Kammer fur Arbeiter und Angestellte.

Kupka, Paul
1971   *Das Ladenschlussgesetz Samt Landes-regelungen*. Wien: Oesterreichischer Wirtschaftsverlag.

Lamel, Joachim
1975   Die Auswirkungen der Arbeitzeitverkurzung 1975 in der Industrie.
        Wirtschafts-politische Blatter (January). In Haas (ed.)
        Arbeitzeitverkurzung: Eine Dokumentation. Materialien zu Wirtschaft und
        Gesellschaft. Teil 3. Wien: Verlag der Kammer fur Arbeiter und
        Angestellte fr Wien. 1979 pp. 90-95.

Magistratsabteilung 66 (Statistisches Amt)
1983   Ergebnisse des Mikrozensus vom Juni 1982.*Statistisches Jahrbuch der
        Stadt Wien, 1982* Wien: Jugend u. Volk Verlagsgesellschaft m.b.H.
        Pp.29-30.

Mundel, Wilfred, Anton Auer, Hartmut Brachmeier, Franz Endlicher, Elizabeth
Hindler, Gerhard Jersabek, Oskar Nitsch, Manfred Pfiel, Emmy Scholl, Leo
Sejkot, Herwig Stage, Gerhard Stemberger, and Karl Weber,
1979   *Das Freizeitverhalten der Wiener Arbeitnehmer.* Wien: Verlag der Kammer
        fur Arbeiter und Angestellte fur Wien.

Pezzl, Johann
1923   *Skizze von Wien: Ein Kultur- und Sittenbild aus der josephinischen Zeit.*
        (herausg. G. Gugitz u. A. Schloffar) Graz: Lehkam Verlag.

Rabl, Peter
1976   Ladenschluss: Es steht 52:41. *Kurier* 12/4/76 p.3.

Rotenberg, Robert
1981   The Impact of Industrialization on Meal Patterns in Vienna, Austria.
        Ecology of Food and Nutrition 11:25-35.

1984   Viennese Wine Gardens and their Magic. *East European Quarterly*
        18(4):447-460.

1987   Community, Time, and the Technical Order. In C.R. Strain and S.
        Goldberg (eds.), *Technological Change and the Transformation of
        America.* Carbondale, Illinois: Southern Illinois University Press. Pp.
        133-144.

Rotenberg, R. and E. Ray Hutchison
1980   Social Organization of Time in a Small City: A case study from Modling,
        Austria. In Robert P. Wolensky and Edward Miller (eds.), *Proceedings of
        the Third Annual Conference on the Small City and the Regional
        Community.* Stevens Point, Wisconsin: University of Wisconsin Press.
        Pp. 345-354.

Simhandl, Gerhard, Richard Riess and Robert Riha
1983   *Tagesablauf: Ergebnisse des Mikrozensus September, 1981.* Beitrager zur
       Oesterreichischen Statistik, Heft 707. Wien: Oesterreichischen
       Statistischen Zentralamt.

Zeisel, Peter
1971   *Die Geschichte der Arbeitzeitregelungen.* Master's Thesis. Hochschule der
       Welthandel, Vienna.

SAINTS AND SWEETS:
CLASS AND CONSUMPTION RITUAL IN RURAL GREECE

Diane O. Bennett

Throughout Greece, households celebrate the annual feast days of saints for whom family members are named. These name day celebrations are consumption rituals. The core of the institution is a family receiving visitors and offering them refreshment. Whether the hosts provide a simple glass of ouzo or a multi-course meal, the type of refreshment, the manner in which it is served, and the way it is consumed are all dictated by local custom; adherence to a formalized pattern of consumption is necessary for honorable participation in the exchange of name day visits. The reproduction of the social system is an important function of name day visiting, and consumption is the principal mechanism through which this is accomplished. "In being offered, accepted, or refused [consumption goods] either reinforce or undermine the existing boundaries." (Douglas 1979: p. 72) The offering and acceptance of hospitality, reciprocated as the cycle of saints' days continues through the year, integrates the community, marks the boundaries of the important groups within it, mediates conflicts, and creates and maintains the network of ties that constitute the village social structure (cf. Gearing 1968, Gavrielides 1974).

On the Pelion peninsula, which extends into the Aegean off the southeast corner of Thessaly, the "proper" form of hospitality at formal name day celebrations, i.e., the form participants consider correct and traditional, is the serving of sweets; specifically, store-bought sweets, served in the wrappers in which they come from the bakery. The "proper" forms of consumption have changed over the last century; these changed forms not only reflect, but also help construct changing socio-economic boundaries. Residents of Lehonia, a prosperous village of 1400 on the inner slope of the Pelion, make several types of name day visits, each of which has a functional and symbolic place in the life of the community. These visits may be classified by the time the visit takes place, its duration, the food served,[1] the relationship of the participants, the form of invitation, and the room where the visitors are received. The general pattern is that duration of visit, quantity of food, and strength of relationship all increase as the day progresses. Figure 1 summarizes four basic types of visits observed in Lehonia. The morning visits, made between the end of mass and the beginning of the midday meal, are the only visits exchanged on a village-wide scale and the only visits suited to creating new social bonds; other visits cross neighborhood boundaries only in the case of pre-exisiting ties. These morning visits are the most formal, the most ritualized, and the most public. They delineate the bounds of the community and maintain morally-based networks among the participants. The focus of this paper is the role consumption has played in the evolution of the exchange of formal morning visits from an apparently egalitarian ideal to an arena for constructing social class.

Participants say that these formal morning visits are open to all and that any family will receive visitors if the female head of the household attends mass on the appropriate saint's day. In fact, formal visits mark a boundary between land and labor: a disproportionate share of the visits are made and hosted by women from households with substantial land holdings, while working class families very rarely participate in this reciprocal cycle of visits. This unacknowledged correlation between class and formal name day celebration raises several questions. First, why does participation follow class boundaries? Given that this difference in participation exists and that Lehonites acknowledge economic differences within the village, why has this boundary in name day visiting remained covert? Finally, how, in the absence of direct invitations, stated rules, or explicit limits on who receives formal visits, are working class families excluded? The thesis of this paper is that for economic and moral reasons, it has been advantageous to the upper class to covertly separate itself from working class families, and that consumption is the primary mechanism by which name day visiting has been used to mark and maintain class boundaries.

The first section of the paper discusses the practical and symbolic significance of name day celebrations, their relation to social structure, and their observance in Lehonia. The second section summarizes the nature and history of the class structure in Lehonia, and the following section considers the economic, social, and moral benefits of a covert division between classes. The fourth section of the paper examines how changing name day rituals have maintained this covert division. The concluding section considers what insights the interaction of class and cultural codes in Greek name day celebrations may provide into how consumption has entered into the maintenance of social boundaries during several decades of economic and social change.

Name Days and Social Structures

Name day rituals symbolize the central relationships in Greek society, including kinship and community ties, gender and age roles, and relationships of social and economic equality or inequality. Local practices combine the elements of family, food, and visitors in a variety of ways, modifying the basic cultural pattern of name day celebration to make different statements about important boundaries and the relations and solidarities that prevail within them. Most Greek communities appear to have at least one form of public celebration in which visits are exchanged on a village-wide scale and participation is at least nominally open to all (cf. Gearing 1968, Allen 1976: p. 194).

Even the simplest of public celebrations invokes the two most basic and enduring social groups in Greece: the nuclear family and the community. In opening its home to the community the family demonstrates its economic standing, proper housekeeping, knowledge of etiquette, and adherence to custom. By calling on a name day, visitors acknowledge the household's membership and position in the community; to pay a visit is to honor the celebrants. Gearing has

178

described name days as occasions on which the nuclear family performs as a team for an audience composed of the remainder of the community (1968: p. 66).

The position of the nuclear family as a solidary, independent unit and the fact that these are household, not personal, celebrations, is demonstrated in several ways by visiting practices in Lehonia. One member of the family receives guests on behalf of the household, and when paying visits, one member represents the family to other households. In Lehonia women fill the host and visitor roles at formal, public celebrations; as will be discussed below, this sets Lehonia apart from most villages. Traditionally a household celebrates only one saint's day annually, normally the name day of its male head.[2] If gifts are given, as is common at afternoon visits, they are gifts for the household, never personal items. The separation between the nuclear family and their visitors is emphasized by the location of the visit. Only individuals with intimate connections to the family, who call by invitation to share the evening meal, are entertained in the living rooms of the household. All others are received in the parlor (*saloni*), aptly described by Friedl as a ceremonial room in which the family presents itself to the world (1962: p.39). These are annual events for each household that give a current reading of its status in the community and relations with other households.

A visit also creates a morally-based link of practical economic and political significance between two households. In Lehonia, the way name day toasting is done emphasizes the dyadic nature of social relations that prevail within the community. Great formality is attached to serving the liqueur; the most correct form is for the hostess to offer the tray to one woman at a time. The visitor accepts a glass, rises, makes a toast, drinks, and replaces the glass on the tray. The heart of each toast is the phrase "many years (*hronia pola*)", may you live and prosper to celebrate this occasion for many years to come, but the speaker frequently demonstrates her close knowledge of the household by including specific wishes or compliments for the family's success in its current endeavors. Sometimes a hostess serves liqueur to an entire group without waiting for individual toasts. If she does this she always acknowledges the exception and demonstrates that she knows proper form by saying, "So you may drink it as you wish." On these occasions the guests never begin drinking together, but take turns rising and offering toasts. These formal toasts represent the community as a complex of household-centered networks, not a unified group.[3]

Name day rituals do, however, represent the community as a group whose members are united by shared custom and belief. The limits to participation in the formal exchange of name day visits mark boundaries inside which specific degrees of loyalty, trust, and good treatment can be expected. In smaller or more homogeneous villages the moral and geo-political boundaries of local community may coincide. Of a village in the Peloponnese, Gearing says that "all men stand similarly invited," that "attendance is almost compulsory at a family's observance of the name day of one of its members," and that by exchanging visits participants express their desire to keep competition between families within the moral limits set by tradition." (1968, pp.67-68) In Lehonia the moral boundaries have been redrawn inside the physical boundaries of the village. It is in this sense that I use the term moral community to refer to a subset of the local population. The participants in the village-wide cycle of morning visits compose the moral community.

In addition to representing and reproducing social structures, name day visits make symbolic statements about the nature of equality in the community: about actual differences in wealth, prestige and social resources; about how the villagers see these differences influencing their social and moral relationships; and about their ideological position on equality among community members. A comparison between the practices associated with public, village-wide visiting in Lehonia and in two other Greek villages will illustrate how the form of name day celebration may parallel socio-economic structure, and the role of consumption rituals in maintaining this symbolic correspondence.

In a small village in the mountains of western Thessaly, which I will call Mikrohori, name day visiting stresses equality within a moral community defined to include the entire village. This version of the formal name day celebration was described by a woman from Mikrohori who married a man in Lehonia. On the name day of her husband, a woman tells the priest if the household will be receiving callers. After mass the priest leads a party of the village men to each celebrating household. The men are received at the door and offered ouzo with which to toast the continued well-being of the household. A few locally grown nuts may be offered in a simple bowl, but no more. The role of the priest emphasizes the religious and moral nature of the occasion, and insures that all visiting families call on all celebrating families. The customary food is simple and inexpensive, so that no one is excluded from participation because of the cost, nor can any family use this as an opportunity to show off their wealth or taste. Because guests remain at the door and drink from the same glass, no attention is drawn to quality of household furnishings.

The second example is from the Peloponesian village of Fourni, described by Gavrielides (1974). In Fourni only the name days of male heads of households are formally celebrated with village-wide visits and it is the men who act as both hosts and visitors. From Gavrielides' description it appears that the entire village is included in the community that receives and pays visits, with the exception of the transhumant shepherds who winter there. Although the name day cycle does not serve to differentiate groups among the permanent residents, it serves as a public index of the status of the participants. Wealthier men serve more meat, and these men have more visitors; the wealthy and powerful may not return all visits they receive. Number and importance of visitors, time and duration of their visits, and amount of meat consumed all reflect and contribute to a household's prestige.

These villages can be taken as representative of two ideal structural types of rural community. Mikrohori has a small population, relatively homogeneous in all respects: wealth, religion, place of origin, and ethnic background. Its public visits emphasize this homogeneity and enforce a ritual equality among households. Fourni is representative of many Greek communities described in the ethnographic literature, stratified on the basis of wealth and prestige, but not differentiated into classes. Name day consumption rituals reinforce the prestige rankings, but emphasize vertical patronage ties rather than horizontal interest groups.

Lehonia represents a third structural type: a village differentiated into permanent, hereditary classes where visiting practices separate the participants into groups, but try to symbolize equality within the group. Within a given type of visit, the food served is equivalent in quality and quantity, and the length of time spent at each house is very consistent. This is especially true at formal morning visits when the ritual always begins with a wrapped pastry purchased from a bakery and served from a silver tray, continues with a liqueur, and concludes with the serving of a store-bought candy; the entire visit takes ten to fifteen minutes. As in Mikrohori, name day celebration is directly tied to church attendance, which is also linked to conceptual equality.[4] As the annual cycle progresses, participants take turns acting as host and visitor, offering and accepting hospitality (cf. Tapper and Tapper 1986 for a discussion of the ambiguous relations of superiority and dependency expressed in hospitality and commensality). Visiting relationships are symmetrical; visits that are not returned will not be repeated. Finally, the stated belief is that all families in the village can participate in these reciprocal visits.

In practice many families never participate, some vistors are not welcome, and the celebrations are egalitarian only within the group that participates. I was made aware of the discrepancy between what the Lehonites say about their celebrations and what they do when I saw women in church who were not at home to visitors after the mass. On one occasion I saw Popi, a woman whose husband is named Dimitrios, in church on Saint Dimitri's Day. This is an important name day in Lehonia; many families celebrate and there were many groups out making formal visits. As our group walked between houses there was protracted discussion of who had been in church and whom we should visit; passing the home of a Dimitrios or a Dimitra would jog memories and start a fresh debate. Many names came up and some were rejected: one woman hadn't been in church (her father-in-law was in the hospital); another woman celebrated, but rarely made reciprocal visits on the other families' name days; one of our group had quarreled with one of the hostesses. As is typical in village groups, we acted on consensus, making a visit only if all objections were dropped. At no time during these walks, or in parlors when notes were compared about who was visiting whom, did Popi's name come up, except when I mentioned it. My statement that Popi had been in church was met with expressions of mild surprise and immediately dropped without discussion. Midway through the morning I noticed Popi in the distance. She had changed from her church clothes to her work clothes and was headed in the direction of a farm where she often did wage labor.

One of the big complaints among village women is that you must attend mass to receive visitors, and conversely that you cannot go to church to be blessed on your name day unless you do want to open your home to callers.[5] Why then would a woman who had been in church and who appeared to meet all the criteria for celebration--a married woman with her own household in the central part of the village--receive no visits? Why would she not feel obliged to remain home to receive callers, and why would the women making visits fail (or refuse) to acknowledge her church attendance? The answer is that there is an additional, unstated basis for participation in formal name day visiting: class membership.

Observation of the actual pattern of participation shows that formal visits mark a boundary between land and labor. Although local families with substantial land holdings comprise only 10% of the village population, they hosted 45% of the formal visits tallied. Working class families rarely participate in this reciprocal visiting; they make up 44% of all households in the village but only 5% of the households that make and receive formal visits.

The patterns of speech and action associated with formal name day visiting in Lehonia accurately represent the socio-economy of the region, not only in the actual division between land and labor, but also in the ideal of conceptual equality that coexists with substantial inequalities in wealth and control of resources.

Classes and Categories: Land and Labor in Lehonia

In Lehonia differentiated classes exist within the village population. Some families control far more land than needed to support their households and more than they can work with family labor; other families with little or no land have to sell their labor to survive. At its peak, the wealthiest family in Lehonia owned 3000-5000 olive trees, as well as fruit trees, the silk factory, and a mill. Several families, both residents and non-residents, owned and own from 500-2000 olive trees. The poorest families did not even own houses. These are not merely wealth differences, but differences in relations to the means of production in the local economic system. These differences are not based on stage in the life cycle, but are hereditary and relatively permanent. Family histories show a continuity of class membership for at least three generations: father, son, and grandson have headed households as either wage laborers or landed proprietors.[6]

Although Lehonites do not speak openly about class differences among themselves, these economic differences have taken on social and cultural correlates and have formed the basis for unified action. Land owning and laboring classes have existed in Lehonia at least since the turn of the century. By 1875 a factory employed women, both local and migrant, in the production of silk (Kordatos 1960). While for some girls, from families with small land holdings, the accumulation of dowry by wage labor was a temporary stage in the life cycle, for others it was a lifelong occupation. Class relations in agricultural production were well- established by 1934 when an agricultural laborers' organization (*ergatiko somatio*) was formed to demand pensions and better wages. The social dimension of the division in Lehonia is illustrated by systematic differences in the celebration of name days.

Class structures are unusual in the Greek villages represented in the ethnographic literature. Many of the communities are, like Mikrohori, extremely homogeneous (e.g., Allen 1976, du Boulay 1974, 1976). In other communities the households differ in wealth and prestige, as in Fourni (e.g., Loizos 1975, Bialor 1968, 1976, Friedl 1962, 1976). There are a few cases where the existence, present or past, of classes is described or suggested (Schein 1970, 1974, 1975, Hoffman 1976: p. 330-331, McNeill 1978: p. 146, Campbell 1976: p. 72). The general picture, however, is of rural communities populated by a "peasant" class in which residents are stratified, partly on the basis of small economic differences and partly on the basis of non-economic variables (cf. Mouzelis and Attalides 1971: p. 182-183). It appears that even in villages where substantial variation exists in wealth and control of resources, this variation has not become the basis of permanent class differentiation among the residents, and does not form a basis for unified action.

Several features differentiate Lehonia from the other villages described: the magnitude of the wealth differences; the large number of wage laborers involved; the presence of a resident upper class which did not work its own lands; and consciousness, although not overt admission, of class differences. In 1982 the heads of 43% of all households living in the village supported their families by wage labor: 23% in agriculture and 20% in industry or menial jobs in the service sector. In 1958, 25% of the heads of households legally resident in Lehonia were laborers (*ergates*); by economic status 24% of the households on the legal roll were classified as landless (*aktimon*) and an additional 10% as poor (*aporos*). The landless and poor composed more than 34% of the real population of Lehonia in the 1950s. They are underrepresented on the roll because it includes only households legally registered in this village; many families have lived and worked in Lehonia for decades without changing their legal residence, and this group is predominantly working class.[7] (See Figure 3)

Another feature that sets Lehonia apart is the resident landowning class. These families are not simply wealthier peasants; they are proprietors running agricultural operations for profit and employing wage labor to do most or all of the work involved. A few of the largest owners can be called cosmopolitan proprietors: they have economic, social, and political ties that stretch to the borders of Greece and beyond. They hold themselves apart from local society and live outside the village for much of the year, but have played a critical role as large employers and in introducing urban culture in the village. The majority of the proprietor class, about 10% of the village population, are full-time residents. Their holdings are usually smaller, and their networks are less influential than those of the cosmopolitan proprietors, but these local proprietors are the leaders of local society and culture. It is they who take the leading role in name day celebrations. This differentiates Lehonia from those villages, including many on the Thessalian plain, where the tsifliks of Ottoman times became estates owned by non-resident Greeks or were broken up in distributions of land to the cultivators (cf. McGrew 1981). It is also different from the prosperous Cypriot village described by Loizos, where large owners labor on their own land and where the size of useful property is limited by what the family can work (1975: p. 316).

The unusual features of Lehonia's socio-economy are founded on its location, its agricultural wealth, and its specific history under the Turks. Lehonia is located on a small alluvial plain on the inner slope of the Pelion peninsula. Agriculture is the basis of the local economic system and land the critical resource. Industry and mercantile activities that have existed in the area have been based on local agricultural produce. Although village lands extend to the Bay of Volos, fishing has never been a major source of income, and only a few families are involved in tourism, primarily as a supplement to agricultural income.

Excellent soil, water, climate, and good transportation have contributed to making Lehonia a prosperous community. Residents insist that one *strema* of land (1/4 acre) in Lehonia is worth ten *stremata* on the Thessalian plain. The value of the land is due primarily to the availability of water for year-round irrigation which allows the Lehonites to cultivate a variety of profitable tree crops. Today the cycle of harvests, beginning in September with green olives, includes black olives, oil olives, green gage plums, plums, cherries, apricots, peaches, pears, quince, and apples. Tree crops are supplemented with truck crops such as tomatoes and beans. Leaf lettuce began to be added in the late 1970s as a source of cash in the winter months; it can be grown in orchards of immature fruit trees. Citrus products were a source of winter cash in the past, but after the last killing frost most of these lands were planted in truck crops and/or summer fruit.

Production is for export, and farmers specialize in the crops where they believe they will make the most profit, rather than striving for household self-sufficiency.[8] A variety of distribution channels is used. Olives are sold to the government-sponsored cooperative or local brokers. Fruit is marketed either directly or through brokers (*embori*) and truckers who act as middlemen (*mesites*), and sold primarily in Athens and Thessaloniki. Green olives, and occasionally fruit or beans, are sent to Eastern Europe; in the past fruit was shipped from the local port as far away as Egypt.

Fruit and olives have been such a reliable source of cash that by 1900 the Lehonites had given up planting wheat and concentrated on the cultivation of tree crops. Prior to the introduction of modern irrigation systems after World War II, few areas in Greece had enough water to support fruit crops, so that land on the inner Pelion with its natural irrigation networks was particularly valuable. The best parcels of land became concentrated in the hands of a few families and these families have required wage labor to work their holdings. Before World War II, the wealthiest family had 40 full-time employees working on its estate and in its silk factory, with an additional 60-70 hired for harvests. Profits from agriculture were such that even a family with much more modest holdings, e.g., parcels that could be worked with 4 or 5 regular laborers, could afford to hire people to do all its work--including a foreman to supervise and a maid for household work.

Such families were able to hire workers instead of using family labor because wages were very low in comparison to the market price of the goods produced. Even with the high demand for workers to cultivate labor-intensive tree crops, supply far exceeded demand due to a steady stream of permanent and temporary migrants to the area. Until opportunities for non-agricultural employment increased after the 1954-55 earthquakes and the opening of the job market in northern Europe after 1957, a man's daily wage represented less than 4% of the value of the olives he picked: about 2.5% between 1910 and 1920; 3.5-4% in the early 1950s. In the late 1950s the wholesale value of olives picked in a day was 5-6.5% of the daily wage. By 1980 the male daily wage for simple work such as olive-picking had risen to 1000 dr/day, roughly 30% of the wholesale value of the olives picked.[9]

The relation between land owners and agricultural laborers that prevailed in Lehonia until the late 1950s is described by some residents as exploitation (*ekmetalefsi*)--land owners were accumulating surplus profits at the expenses of the labor they employed. The living standard of laborers and land owners was dramatically different. Informants of every class agree that the workers lived at a very low level (*poli hamilo*) in past years. Proprietors in those days lived well. They built fine houses and imported their clothes from Paris. Sons were sent away to school, and it is said that a daughter could be dowered with one vat (*kade*) of olives, which could be filled with a single year's crop from a parcel with 50-100 trees. A worker could pick that amount plus his wage in 2-3 weeks.[10]

The magnitude of the differences in income and standard of living between proprietors and laborers in Lehonia is important not because it illustrates the wealth differences within the village, but because it shows the economic basis for the differentiation of classes. It is clear, among other things, that proprietors did not have to divide their estates to endow their children, and were able to accumulate wealth from generation to generation. This hereditary control of land acted as a foundation for economic, social, and political control within the village. Families with little or no land needed work, and to get it they did "favors" like hauling wood and water after their paid work day; they supported the political candidates of their employers; they stood aside as the wealthy filed to the front of the church on Sunday.[11] This is consistent with patronage systems observed throughout Greece and the Mediterranean, but in Lehonia workers got little in return besides their wage from most of the proprietor families: "Food?! They wouldn't even give us water." "He was sick for two years before he died, and his employer never even stopped to ask how he was." (There are, however, some wealthy families who are respected for their humane treatment of employees and their effect on both the quality and stability of village life should not be overlooked.)

185

The figures on standard of living also show how little working class households had available to spend on name day consumption. Families dependent entirely on wage labor were close to the minimum subsistence level, especially when it is remembered that even permanent employees do not have work every day. In the 1910-1920s, when the men's wage was 2 drachmes per day (women were paid half the men's wage) it cost about 86% of a man's wage to meet the caloric requirement for a couple with two small children for a single day (See Figure 2).[12] Even with both husband and wife working, 58% of their combined daily wage was needed for one day's food. In 1953 this cost 21.92 drachmes--88% of a man's, or 59% of a couple's income. This has, until recently, left working class families with little surplus to spend on social consumption rituals.

Wealth and class differences on the Pelion peninsula are not the result of post-war modernization or the recent intrusion of a capitalist mode of production in the area, but an evolved form of the system that existed under the Turks. An indication of the earlier wealth of the area can be seen in the buildings called *arhontika spitia* "houses of the leading families." That the wealth differences indicated by the houses reflected a class difference with social as well as economic dimensions is implied by the fact that the unmarried daughters of the leading families (*aristokratises*) wore silk caps, while other unmarried girls wore scarves.

Political ties, mercantile activities, and land ownership formed the basis of power of the upper class. The Peliorites enjoyed relative autonomy under Ottoman rule; only the Lehonia plain was directly occupied by Turks. The taxes paid by the other villages were collected and taken to the head village by a local elder, whose position permitted the accumulation of both wealth and political power. Wealth was also amassed through the export of agricultural produce and textiles. Ships from the Pelion were sailing as far as Egypt and the Black Sea during the 17th century. As the Ottoman feudal system weakened, trading and manufacturing flourished, reaching a peak in the early 19th century. The principal exports were olive oil, edible olives, fruits and nuts, silk thread, and finished textile products. As the struggle for an independent Greek nation spread northward, the Turks began leaving the area and land became available as a commodity in the Lehonia plain. Families in villages on the upper slope had cash to buy this land, and became the basis of the local proprietor class (Makris 1982, Kordatos 1960, Kizis 1979, Bjornstahl 1979). The Greek families who lived on the plain during its Turkish occupation have, for the most part, become part of the working class. The division between proprietors and laborers has become permanent and hereditary.

Since the 1950s the local economy has become increasingly tightly bound to the national and world economies, labor markets for Greeks have expanded in northern Europe, industrial development in the area has increased, and the economic importance of controlling land has decreased. By 1958 wages were up to 50 drachmes per day and the amount needed for daily food had dropped below 70% of the man's wage. During the 1970s wages in Greek manufacturing rose almost twice as fast as consumer prices (OECD 1983: p.70). By 1981 the daily agricultural wage in Lehonia was 1000-1500 drachmes for men and 700-800 for women. The same daily caloric requirement in bread and feta that took 88% of a man's wage in the early 1950s cost under 15% in the early 1980s. At the same time farm costs have risen and farm profits have dropped. The changing value of land and labor has also changed social relations between land and labor, but this change is still in progress. The social and moral structures of Pelion villages in the 1980s were influenced by the political economy of the earlier period; vocabulary, values, and boundaries associated with socio-economic classes reflect the earlier importance of land.

Differences in control of land and labor are an economic fact of life in the Pelion and are acknowledged by the inhabitants. In discussions of occupation and wealth, "laborer" (*ergatis*) and "landowner-proprietor" (*ktimatias*) are the two most commonly used terms in Lehonia. The terms *ktimatias* and *ergatis* classify household heads based on their source of income: land in one case, wages in the other. The larger landowners, until very recently, worked their properties with day laborers. Lehonites do not overtly acknowledge a class difference within the village, but the class nature of the relationship between the larger land owners and the agricultural wage laborers stands out clearly in the vocabulary of the working class as the distinction between "work-givers" (*ergodotes*) and "laborers" (*ergates*). These categories are mutually exclusive; a man with enough land to support his family would not do agricultural work for a wage, and if he did, he would no longer be considered a *ktimatias*. The categories do not, however, include the entire village population.

The division between the proprietor class (i.e., the *ergodotes*, who are all large landowners) and the working class is somewhat obscured by the existence of a middle group that neither buys nor sells labor. This "middle class" includes smaller farmers who use family labor or hire workers only at pear or olive harvests, fruit and olive brokers, shopkeepers, craftsmen, those who provide services such as trucking, and more recently, holders of white collar and civil service jobs. Like laborers, these latter are paid for the time they work, but they receive a salary (*mistho*) rather than the daily wage (*merokamato*) paid to both industrial and agricultural laborers. (This distinction is similar to that made between white-collar and blue-collar workers in the U.S.) Lehonites recognize the existence of households whose heads are neither proprietors nor laborers, but they have no traditional term to refer to them as a group. This is an accurate representation of their socio-economic structure, because those in the middle are not a class but a vaguely bounded category with no common relation to the means

187

of production and no clearly defined common interest. What the members of this "middle class" do have in common is that they do not do wage labor.

There are three groups in the population, divided in terms of relation to means of production: 1) Those who control the critical resource, land. In the past they controlled jobs, and did not do their own labor; today they hire labor regularly, but also do work themselves. 2) Those who work at their enterprises with family labor, making enough to support their families without doing wage labor; the enterprises may be farms, stores, produce brokerages. In a sense this group includes the entire spectrum normally described in Greek "peasant" villages. At the lower fringe of this group are the "skilled" laborers such as roofers or saddle makers, who speak and are spoken of as selling a service or a product rather than their time. 3) Those who have no control of the means of production, no productive assets, and only their labor power to sell. Patterns of participation in formal name day celebrations correspond to these groups. Figure 3 compares the percent of the formal visits hosted by each class with the percent of village households in that class.

The Peliorites focus on retaining control of one's own labor power. This distinction between those who labor for a wage and those who do not is the most striking point illustrated by the data on name day visits. Ninety-five percent of the formal morning celebrations were hosted by households in the proprietor and middle groups. Within this group of households headed by men who never labor for a wage, there is a difference in rate of participation in formal name day visiting between those households that regularly employ laborers and those that do not. The local proprietors who regularly hire laborers hosted 45% of the visits tabulated, although they represent only 10% of the households in the village. The "middle class" hosted slightly more visits, but this group includes 45% of the households in the village, so the frequency of participation by families that neither buy nor sell labor is far less.

Working class families, although they comprise 44% of the resident households, hosted only 5% of the formal morning celebrations recorded. It is significant that the working class households that participate in name day celebrations belong to the industrial working class, because those who do agricultural labor for a wage are generally poorer and lower ranked than those who have permanent industrial jobs, partly because of the job security and pensions of industrial workers and partly because these laborers are not directly dependent on their fellow villagers for their livelihood. The women from the two households that hosted visits were the only working class women who made formal morning visits to other households.

The circle of families symbolically united by the exchange of formal visits excludes the working class. This is not a case of separate circles for different classes. There is no community-wide visiting among the working class households, whose name day visits are limited to late afternoon and evening visits by their neighbors and kin. The visits shared by the middle and proprietor classes

188

form the only village-wide network based on the moral foundation of name day visiting.

The result is, therefore, to create and support moral- economic links within the upper classes, and to reduce the moral obligations of this group to the working class. This division is advantageous to the upper class, but to overtly construct a boundary along class lines is undesirable. It runs counter to egalitarian ideology, and if drawn sharply, can pose a threat to community stability.[13]

Advantages of Covert Separation of Classes

The ideology most commonly expressed by Lehonites is that purely economic differences are acceptable, and in fact honorable--they advance the family, and demonstrate cleverness and business acumen--but social and moral differences among community members are not acceptable. Social and moral equality, however, have economic costs: social networks, cultural superiority, and reputation are also economic resources; and moral bonds carry economic responsibilities.

Obligations to members of the community are rarely, if ever, spelled out unambiguously, but certain standards are implicit in the behavior of the Lehonites.[14] The existence of obligations that take precedence over straight economic interests is most clearly indicated by the fact that in the period of labor surplus, local laborers had better access to jobs at higher wages than non-locals. The going wage for local labor was not set by market mechanisms, and did not fall even when surplus labor was readily available. Prior to the expansion of non-agricultural job opportunites in the late 1950s, men seeking work gathered each morning in the clearing near the railroad station, or hung around outside the door of the coffeehouse begging for a job. Local laborers faced the same job shortage, but were more likely to be successful because "they knew somebody." Migrants were likely to be told, "There is no work; well...the wage is 2 drachmes, but if you are willing to work for 1 drachma I'll find something." This situation was based on the kind of patronage ties common in Greece--ties that can be created and maintained through name day visits--but it is important to note that both parties in these relationships are members of the local community, and that the local workers were afforded some sort of traditional protection.[15] There is no verification that locals got better and more frequent wages other than the recollections of informants, but even if their statements are not literally true, they indicate a sense of obligation to community members.

The range of proper behavior between community members is aimed at maintaining the basic dignity of both parties, providing a minimum level of economic well-being for all community members, and presenting the appearance of equality. The egalitarian value system of the Lehonites is a blend of several elements: the traditional basis of the redistributive economic obligations, the

189

modern influences of nationalism that stress the equality of all Greeks (cf. Herzfeld 1982), and universalistic values of capitalist, merit-oriented society that stress conceptual equality while encouraging the freedom of the nuclear family from moral obligations to the community (cf. Schneider and Schneider 1976). Display of wealth in houses and clothes is respected as a sign of economic achievement. It is, however, a bad thing to act better than others just because you have more money. Using a foreman to manage your laborers is also a bad thing, because it diminishes the laborer's dignity as an independent worker responsible for the success of the job, and because it establishes a barrier between employer and employee. All visible and formal barriers between classes are criticized. For example, the layout of the new cemetery with first, second, and third categories divided by concrete walks occasions frequent criticism--"Bury me in second class when I die; it's not right to be divided in death." It is the division, not the display of wealth in the elaborate grave markers in first class that is the cause of the criticism; an even wider disparity between massive granite monuments and crude wooden markers can be seen in the old cemetery, but they are placed side- by-side. The message seems clear: displaying your economic success is all right. Making formal divisions between classes or attaching moral correlates to them is not.

The ideal is conceptual, not economic equality; adherence is not intended to maintain equal distribution or prevent capital accumulation, but it entails some economic costs. These include charity, favorable terms on loans up to interest-free lending for medical or other emergencies, preference in hiring, paying a "fair" wage, and charging less than market price for services and home-grown products. Statements and actions by individuals in all classes indicate a belief that actions of this sort are proper between members of a moral community, and those who ignore these obligations are subject to criticism, gossip, and loss of respect.

Establishment of a social and moral division between economic classes is advantageous to the upper class because it reduces redistributive obligations. One reason that this division is covertly maintained is the idea of impropriety attached to making overt social distinctions. For people concerned with self-respect, grace, and honor, to make such distinctions is undesirable in itself. It is also undesirable because it would weaken the networks among the landed that are supported by the moral foundation of name day visiting. A second reason for avoiding overt distinctions is the desire to preserve social stability.

Stability of the community might seem too abstract an idea to figure consciously in the actions people take, but both the solidarity (or lack thereof) and prestige of the community, and the desire to avoid a recurrence of the open conflict of the civil war are topics of conversation. Conflicts within the community are minimized when the interests of the community-at-large are stressed over the interests of kin and other sub-groups, and when at least an appearance of equality and adherence to the moral system of reciprocal rights and obligations is maintained among community members. It is unlikely that more than a few villagers would trade direct economic benefit to the family for community stability, but they generally avoid explicit reference to current class distinctions, particularly any implication of social or moral status differences based on economic differences. During interviews men were reluctant to rank other men, or even occupations--"It isn't a good thing."[16]

To sum up, the dilemma confronting villagers is how to serve both interests of the family and obligations to the community, to balance egalitarian and hierarchical values, to simultaneously accomplish economic, moral, and social goals. Within economically homogeneous communities the economic costs of community membership tend to balance out over the life cycle or from generation to generation. The temporary imbalances are offset by moral gains. When class differentiation produces hereditary wealth disparities that outweigh variation over the life cycle, unchecked obligations to the community would become a continuous economic drain. Continued too far, sharing within the community can become a drain on respect as well, when donors are perceived to be squandering family resources. The problem is to limit moral obligations and increase economic gain while maintaining claims to respect and grace, and minimizing risk to the stability of the community. These moral-economic dilemmas fall more heavily on the rich, and formal name day consumption rituals have provided a mechanism to minimize their problem by covertly narrowing the boundary of the moral community to exclude the working class.

Changing Consumption Rituals and Changing Boundaries

Because of their traditional function in bounding and integrating communities, name day visits are a logical arena for creating a moral boundary between classes. Shared name day rituals give a moral basis to the separation between land and labor, just as they traditionally give a moral basis to cooperation and obligation within the community. Upper class Lehonites buttress the legitimacy of formal name day rituals by stressing their moral foundations. First, the dates themselves are designated in the Orthodox calendar, and only those who are named for Orthodox saints have name days.[17] These Saints' Days are celebrated in the liturgy, and on each of these occasions those who bear that saint's name are recognized during the mass when one of the church elders makes a circuit through the congregation sprinkling only those individuals with holy water. Attendance at mass is the only way to announce that you will be receiving formal visits. The prominent and unusual role of women in these public rituals may also be related to giving a moral basis to class division. The division of labor within the household delegates most activities involved with the family's religious obligations to the wife, including those related to funeral and mourning rituals, an important sphere for expressing egalitarian ideology. To have formal, community-integrating visiting done by women underscores the religious foundation of this institution.

Name day celebrations also gain moral significance through adherence to shared traditional rituals. Great importance is attached to following traditional forms and providing proper hospitality. Today wrapped sweets must be served off fine trays in a correctly appointed parlor with adequate seating capacity. This is uniform within the village, and the Lehonites treat the contemporary practice as if it were a timeless sort of form.

Name day hospitality was not, however, always as it is today. Sweets were first served sometime in the first or second decade of the twentieth century. One informant places the introduction of sweets in the upper village at about 1915; it was probably earlier in Lehonia. "When I was about fifteen years old they started serving sweets." "The rich families that is." (This was interjected by his daughter. She used the word *plousies*, i.e., rich, not merely well-off). "Before that it was very simple. You went to the door, and they had a table set up with figs, walnuts, maybe some raisins. You said 'many happy returns' and hit the road (*Hronia pola ke dromo!*). I used to beg my mother to go to the houses that gave sweets. Those who didn't know--the boors (*vlahi*)--thought the whole bowl was for them." His daughter now explains, "These were spoon sweets. In those days they put out one bowl and gave everyone a glass of water with a spoon on top. Each person was supposed to take one piece."[18]

This account indicates several things about name day hospitality. First, the apparently invariable practices are rather recent, as is the consumption of sweets. Seventy years ago people in the village were just learning the proper etiquette for eating spoon sweets. Since that time spoon sweets came to be regarded as the correct refreshments for formal name day visits, were later replaced by home-baked sweets, which have now been displaced by the even more costly sweets from the bakery. Second, serving sweets was a possible means to improve the family's reputation and even its honor. Sugar required cash expenditure, and was a link to the outside world. The civilized and cosmopolitan--the practices of the city--were and are valued in rural Greece. The urbane knew how to eat spoon sweets, the boors did not. Sugar was also a prized commodity (cf. Schein 1970: p. 111), and sweets a preferred form of hospitality. It would therefore be honorable to serve your guests sweets.

Consumption rituals with high cash costs divide the population on the basis of wealth, the display of which is accepted and even respected in Lehonia, without requiring any morally unacceptable overt statement about class boundaries. The serving of sweets was an ideal mechanism for creating such a division because sugar has historically been a luxury import into Greek villages, high-priced in relation to wages and prized for displaying hospitality. Adherance to these rituals may even suggest moral superiority based on success at provisioning the family and willingness to share your wealth through lavish hospitality (without requiring any economically or ecologically significant redistribution of wealth).

The result of the introduction and elaboration of this new form of hospitality, which has come to be regarded as the only correct way to receive name day visitors, was to limit the ability of the poor to participate. Figure 4 compares the cost of sweets with the daily wage throughout this century. Prior to 1910 no sweets were served and there was no cash cost attached to public, ritual visits. From calculations based on the retail price of sugar, recipes for sweets, and an estimate of 50 visitors, serving spoon sweets at its name day celebration would have cost an early 20th century household 1-2 drachmes, provided they grew their own fruit. The cost was much greater for landless laborers, who would have had to purchase fruit[19], bringing the cost of sweets for a single formal celebration to about 4 drachmes, or twice the daily wage for a male agricultural laborer--a prohibitive outlay for households spending over 86% of the man's wage (or 58% of the combined earnings of husband and wife) for a single day's caloric requirements.

In the 1950s, economic conditions for laborers began to improve. Wages rose in proportion to cost of consumer goods; by the end of the decade the cost of daily food had dropped under 70% of the man's daily wage. The cost of spoon sweets fell in relation to workers' income and they had slightly more disposable income which could be used for social consumption. In this period pastry replaced spoon sweets as the proper name day refreshment. In the early 1950s the cost of home-baked name day sweets was about 90 drachmes, 3-4 times the daily wage. Between 1955 and 1960 the cost of home-baked pastry fell back to twice the wage, but serving a wrapped pastry, liqueur, and a wrapped candy at a formal name day celebration cost 250 drachmes, the equivalent of 5 days' wages.

Serving the proper refreshments was the major cash outlay involved in name day celebration, but other costs also limited the ability of the working class to participate. Capital expenditures entailed in proper hospitality have increased throughout the twentieth century. From the plain table by the door, a glass, and a few bowls, the equipment necessary to receive formal visitors has come to include modern furniture, silver trays, and fine glassware. Handmade linens have been replaced by items purchased in Volos. Longer visits and larger groups require more chairs--it would be unthinkable for anyone to stand or to sit on the floor. Of course, the household must have a room for formal entertaining. From ethnographic descriptions of Greek villages it appears that every household had a parlor reserved for guests, but this was not the case in Lehonia. Not every family owned a home. Those who had to rent included the sons of some local farm families as well as migrants to the village. Some rental units built between 1910 and 1920 had two small rooms, one of which could have been fixed as a parlor if the family had the time and resources; others were a single large room. Houses built with government loans after the 1954-55 earthquakes had to follow an anti-earthquake design with one small room on either side of an entrance hall. The days when the entire family lived and slept in a single room are long gone. Demands for separate bedrooms, bathrooms, and an indoor kitchen apart from the living room compete with the parlor for use of space. To be able to set aside a room not required for everyday use, a family now needs a four or five room house. Housewives with less say that it is impossible to entertain properly.

A final cost was women's labor in preparing for and hosting the name day visits. If a family holds a formal celebration, one full day must be spent receiving visitors, with several previous days devoted to preparing the house and the refreshments. For a working class family, giving up a woman's wages would have been a grave hardship. When the silk factory was in operation, the jobs it provided to females were among the most permanent and stable in the village. In the past women in the landed families did not work, even on their own property, so this was not an expense for them.

It was never necessary for proprietors to explicitly exclude the poor from the group to which they honored the moral obligations of community membership. They introduced visiting practices consistent with traditional name day customs, desire for urbanity, and respect for providing hospitality and presenting the household in the best light. When this resulted in higher cash costs for participation, some families "voluntarily" excluded themselves from the exchange of name day visits and thus from fullest membership in the moral community.

Working class families had no choice about reduced participation in formal visiting and moral community. Either course of action would lead to a loss of respect and a lesser claim to mutual support: non-participation removes the moral basis for claims and networks provided by reciprocal visiting; to receive visitors without serving the proper foods in the proper fashion leaves one open to criticism or loss of honor for failure to follow custom or for inhospitality (cf. Dubisch 1972: ch.6, Herzfeld 1980: p. 343). This would provide a justification for hostesses from the landed families to stop returning visits. To continue to make unreciprocated visits would bring further criticism and loss of face. Either way the fault is with the poorer working class families.

By the 1980s local economic conditions had changed markedly. Location and climate are largely responsible for the relative prosperity of the Pelion, but outside factors have established the changing economic framework of Pelioritic class structures. Legislation regarding debt, taxation, land transfers, labor organization, and formation of cooperatives has influenced the economic situation, as have warfare and nationalist movements. The relative value of land and labor has been affected by externally controlled variables such as crop prices and markets, availability of non-agricultural jobs, reconstruction loans, and new irrigation technology that diminishes the competitive advantage of the region. Under current conditions labor has become more expensive and gained political power. Land has become less valuable as an economic and political resource, and local class structures have been absorbed into the broader national system (Bennett 1986).

The rituals and consumption associated with formal morning visits are currently losing their power to establish inclusion in and exclusion from the community. All the aspects that made village-wide visits special events are becoming high-frequency occurrences: sweets are consumed frequently, houses are being opened for more social occasions such as teas and tupperware parties[20], and more name days are being celebrated.[21] Nor can cash consumption requirements any longer limit participation; the cost of sugar and other consumer goods is falling relative to income, wages have risen dramatically in relation to farm prices, and many working class households have more disposable income than middle class farmers. As long as church attendance and proper hospitality are the only requirements, participation in morning visiting is open to anyone who has the cash.

In the past social class, wealth, and land ownership were highly correlated. The power of name day consumption rituals to delineate a boundary in the population depended on wealth differences, but the boundary between those who participated in this show of shared values and those who did not was (or became) more than a difference in level of disposable income. This is demonstrated by the response to changing economic variables.

The boundary between the group that participates in formal visiting and the group that does not has become relatively fixed. As the custom is practiced today, very few working class families participate even though rising wages have expanded their ability to afford such hospitality. The small number of women from this class who do participate in formal name day visits are from households headed by factory workers, not local agricultural laborers. Failure of working class wives to participate today is not just a matter of no free time. Women in this group who do not work, or who have retired, still do not receive formal name day visits. As agricultural labor has become expensive and hard to find, more women in the proprietor class are working with their husbands on their farms; these women make time for formal visiting, either by rearranging their schedules, or by hiring day laborers.

Some status-conscious working class women have begun to receive and pay morning visits, forcing the upper class women to return the properly paid visits or be guilty of a moral lapse. These are the households where the most friction occurred over visiting. These hostesses calculate and complain about who visited and who snubbed them. Visiting parties have difficulty deciding whether to pay a call, and sometimes break up before reaching these houses. Upper class women complain that "too many strangers" visit. Some of the landed families are no longer attending mass on name days; instead they are issuing word-of-mouth invitations for day-time visits. Name day celebrations are once again in the process of changing in response to new socio-economic conditions.

195

The Role of Consumption in Constructing the Social Economy

Social class differences, i.e., the social relations that prevail between and among members of the economic classes (based on differential control of land), are not based on purely economic factors, nor are they a simple reproduction of class relations that prevail in the larger political economy. In the village, disparities in wealth and control of resources exist in the context of face-to-face relations, shared history and values, and an integrated set of social, economic, and moral goals. When externally determined economic factors change, local social relations are reshaped through traditional cultural institutions.

This paper has examined one arena in which the construction and maintenance of social boundaries takes place: formal name day celebrations. The exchange of visits maintains social networks, and acts as a basis for trust and cooperation within the boundaries of the moral community, while excluding outsiders from its protection and benefits. By hosting a celebration a family proclaims its commitment to the system; by paying them the honor of a visit guests publicly affirm the family's good standing within the system. This is the traditional function of name day visiting, and this is how the institution functions in Lehonia. The only difference is that participation has been limited to the landed, thereby symbolizing and reproducing the social boundary created by differential control of land and labor. This gives the landed the benefits of a morally-based network among the well-off households, which may facilitate political favors, loans, credit in fruit brokerage, or joint ventures, including the pre-war marketing cooperative that purchased ships and fruit preserving machinery and set up its own retail outlets in Athens and Thessaloniki. The broadest benefit of the covert class boundary maintained by formal name day visits is, however, not the networks of the included, but the exclusion of the poor from the community of moral obligation.

Throughout Greece social and moral ties are established and maintained with consumption rituals. Sugared almonds are offered at weddings, brandy is served after funerals, and sweets are served on name days. If a glass of water is the only item consumed at a visit, it is still served, accepted, and used for toasting in a ritualized manner. Even before conspicuous and costly consumption became standard in Lehonia, display of wealth and worldliness in homes, gardens, and clothing was essential to maintaining a family's position in the community. Consumption of food and capital goods has been essential to the establishment of social and moral ties through formal name day visits. It was this inherent importance of consumption that allowed name day visiting to adapt so readily in response to the introduction of new economic conditions and new consumption goods.

196

Name day rituals make visible the social structure of the community and the current state of social relations between households. They are well-suited to this function because they are periodic, shared, and highly visible. The secular rituals which take place in the households of the community rest on a foundation of religion and tradition. This provides a moral basis for trust and cooperation between those who exchange these ritual visits. Three dimensions of variation in name day practices have been observed: between communities, through time, and among members of a single community. A difference also exists between what Lehonites say about their name day celebrations and what they do. It is suggested that all of these differences are best explained by reference to variations in socio-economic structures and to contradictions within local economy and ideology. In Lehonia, one of the salient features of social structure made visible in formal name day celebrations is the differentiation between classes. Consumption requirements with a high cash cost have been instrumental in maintaining this boundary, while permitting the participants to maintain a facade of egalitarianism.

TYPES OF NAME DAY VISITS IN LEHONIA			
	Morning	**Afternoon**	**Evening**	**Night**
Duration	10-15 min	20-30 min	45 min- 1 hour	2 hours or more
Food	sweets	sweets	appetizers	dinner
Relation	community member; no close tie	specific, but not close ties	friend; neighbor; kin	close kin and friends
Invitation	church attendence notifies	open	open	by invitation only
Place	formal parlor	formal parlor	formal parlor	everyday rooms

Figure 1

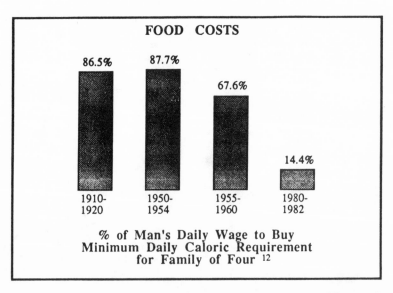

FOOD COSTS

86.5%   87.7%   67.6%   14.4%

1910-   1950-   1955-   1980-
1920   1954   1960   1982

% of Man's Daily Wage to Buy
Minimum Daily Caloric Requirement
for Family of Four [12]

Figure 2

FREQUENCY OF PARTICIPATION BY CLASS

CLASS	Formal Morning Celebrations Hosted number	% of total	Class as % of Village Population
Working Class	2	5%	43.6%
Industrial Labor	2	5%	20.0%
Agricultural Labor	0	0%	22.7%
Indigent	0	0%	0.9%
Non-working Class	36	95%	56.4%
Employer (hire labor)			
Cosmo Proprietor	0	0%	0.9%
Local Proprietor	17	45%	10.0%
Middle (labor neutral)	19	50%	45.5%

Figure 3

HISTORICAL COMPARISON OF WAGES AND COST OF NAME DAY SWEETS

	Estimated Cash Cost of Sweets	Daily Wage (Male, agricultural)	Daily Wage (Female, ag.)
pre1910	0 dr	N/A	N/A
1910-20	4 dr	2 dr	1 dr
1950-54	50-90 dr	25 dr	12 dr
1955-60	100-250 dr	40-50 dr	20-25 dr
1980-82	1500 dr	1000-1500 dr	700-800 dr

Figure 4

199

Notes

The field research on which this paper is based was conducted from January 1980 through July 1982, supported by a Dissertation Improvement Grant from the National Science Foundation and a University Fellowship from Washington University. Henry Rutz provided extensive comments that helped turn ideas originally presented in the poster session into a finished draft. Michael Herzfeld's critique was an invaluable aid in revising an earlier draft. Robert Canfield, David Browman, Patty Jo Watson, Adria LaViolette, and Becky Torstrick have read and heard many formulations of these ideas; their insights and their patience are appreciated. Michael Bennett learned Greek, talked with informants, typed field notes, exchanged ideas, loved the Lehonites, and prepared the illustrations. I thank these people and hope they will see their influence in the final product.

1   Gavriliedes (1974) notes the same correlation between food and distance. Cowan (1985) has pointed out a gender link in the type of food served: sweets/female, savories/male. Although there are signs of such a correlation in Lehonia, today they are overridden by the closeness of relationship, particularly in the case of name day visits. Although men may be offered ouzo instead of fruit brandy, if the relationship is formal rather than close or personal, they are given only sweets. Women as well as men are offered savory appetizers following the sweets if there is a closer relationship.

2   The prominent role of men in name day celebration emphasizes both their public importance and that these are celebrations of the household. The household is known by the husband's name and he represents it in its dealings with the outside. The most consistent element in descriptions of name day celebrations is that only males, usually adult heads of households but sometimes sons, have formal commemorations. Women and children celebrate informally, if at all (e.g., Aschenbrenner 1976: p. 219, Allen 1976: p. 194, Gearing 1968: pp. 67-68, Gavrielides 1974: pp. 56-57, du Boulay 1974: p. 14) The most visible difference in the way name days are observed in the Pelion, as compared to other places in Greece, is that women make and receive these formal visits. In other rural areas it is the men who pay formal, public visits, while in cities visits are typically made by man and wife together.

3   This contrasts with toasting on other occasions, e.g., in the coffee house or among a group sharing a table at the village festival, where the standard toast "to our health" (*ya mas*) stresses group membership.

4   Whether due to formal teachings of the church or ideas about the equality of all community members in the eyes of God, most Lehonites agree with the elderly agricultural laborer who said, "We were all equal in church."

This is in spite of the fact that divisions between landed at the front and laborers at the back are still visible each Sunday.

5   Complaints about name days practices are also class-related. The only working class women who complain about formal name day visiting are the few who now receive callers; they complain about the women who did not visit them. The rest of the complaints are from upper class women. The wealthiest complain that too many outsiders pay visits these days. The more modern and urbane complain about using church attendance to announce whether you are receiving callers; they want to put announcements in the newspaper as is done in the city, and say it's too much fuss to get ready and go to mass.

6   In talking about local class structures I have skirted three basic issues: the definition of class, the relation of the village to the world economic system, and the validity of studying class at a local level. Whether class is defined purely on the basis of relations of production or class consciousness is included as essential to defining a class situation, I feel that Lehonia has been demonstrated to meet the minimum criteria to be analyzed in terms of class. The relations of Lehonites to national and world political economies is indispensible for understanding their structures and their history. Several writings on the world capitalist system have provided a framework for my understanding local economic and cultural processes (Frank 1966, Schneider et al. 1972, Wallerstein 1974, Wolf 1982, Nash 1981). The focus here, however, is how local culture and economy were used to respond to changes in the total system, and how these changes took shape among the Lehonites. For a history of the national structures in which the Lehonitiko system has developed see Mouzelis (1978, 1986); for a study of the effects of the world economy on an area of Macedonia with early capitalist relations of production see Vermeulen (1976). While understanding the village as part of a total system, I believe it is also relevant to treat localized phenomena as class structures, as long as care is excercised in determining what aspects of the system remain localized and in separating the constituent elements of class relations and class consciousness, rather than treating class as a monolithic and reified structure.

7   Percentages for 1982 were calculated from a random sample of 110 households (25%) drawn from the list of the 440 occupied dwellings, compiled for the 1981 census of population. Assignment to classes was made on the basis of data collected through interviews and visits to the households between 1980 and 1982, and from key informants; the divisions and the designations are mine. Data for 1958 is from an official list of all legally registered households, where economic status and occupation were listed by the village officials.

201

8   The idea of the self-sufficient household is long gone from Lehonia. Since the 1920s only the wealthy houses with maids baked bread in their own ovens. There are three local bakeries, and in the past a few laborers' wives baked for extra income. Lehonites no longer make their own wine or cheese. The most graphic illustration of their market orientation is that two shopkeepers (*manavis, oporopolis*) make their living by selling fruits and vegetables to the Lehonites who make their living by growing fruits and vegetables.

9   Wage as a percentage of olives harvested is based on an average harvesting rate of 100 kg per day per person, using wages reported by informants and wholesale olive prices supplied by informants for 1910-1920 and 1980-1982, from the NSSG 1955: table 212 for 1950-54, NSSG 1963: table XXI:4 for 1955-59. Price for 1980-1982 is an unweighted average of black and green olive prices.

10   These vats contained 1000 *okades*, i.e., 1280 kilograms of olives. Olive trees, as they are pruned today, produce 20-30 kg every other year. It is said that the same trees yielded 100 kg in the past. Even at the rate of 20 kg/tree a single holding with 50-100 trees is enough to fill a vat from a crop.

11   These examples come from conversations with both proprietors and laborers. If the statements sound like a contradiction to the fact that Lehonites do not talk openly open class divisions, it is a contradiction representative of the ambiguity and ambivalence in the Lehonitiko social economy. One day a man says that workers never let their vote be influenced by their employer; six months later in the midst of a two hour conversation he says that in the old days the bosses made threats and even today a laborer has to worry about expressing his political ideas. Methodologically it is important to note that these statements never came up in response to interviews, or in groups; they are the result of long, private conversations where informants fall into monologues about their experiences and attitudes.

12   From the 1950s through the 1980s, feta cheese has been the most economical source of protein, in calories/drachma, for a family that purchases all its food. Two kilos of bread and one kilo of feta provide about 8700 calories, just under the daily requirement of 8900 for a couple with two children, aged 4-7 and 7-10 (Garrison and Somer 1985). Retail food prices are from the NSSG 1955: table 215, NSSG 1960: table XX:6.

13   I don't want to give the impression that this is a contradiction between an empirical situation of unequal control of resources and an ideology of equality. In the first place, the beliefs and values of the villagers are also empirical reality, albeit less visible than the economic situation. Second, contradictions between equality and hierarchy exist within the ideological

sphere. The egalitarian side of this complex set of beliefs and values is indicated by their attitudes on the cemetery and zoning, and by statements such as "it isn't right for some people to act superior just because they have more money." The hierarchical side of the value system is best exemplified by the competition between nuclear families and by the conviction that it is the right and the duty of every man to strive to advance his family above others, both in economic well-being and prestige.

14   Clearly, the degree of trust and reciprocal obligation within the nuclear family is much greater than that felt between members of the same community, but intracommunity trust and cooperation is apparently greater in Lehonia than in many villages. Campbell has said that among the Sarakatsani of northwestern Greece "unrelated persons view one another at all times with intense distrust." (1964, p.v) In a village in the Peloponnese "generalized moral obligations...are not taken very seriously by an adult." (Bialor 1968, p. 118) Campbell's generalization that the exclusive commitment to the interest of the family requires the exploitation of others (1983: p. 186) may need to be tempered to give a fuller picture of seriously felt obligations outside the nuclear family and outside the kin group. Campbell states that emphasis on honor via strict honesty in commercial dealings observed by Herzfeld (1976) on Rhodes is due to village endogamy. This is not the case in Lehonia, where kinship outside the nuclear family is not particularly strong, close kinship is not the only basis of moral obligation, and non-kin ties--based for example on neighborhood, friendship, or organizational memberships--are often stronger than those based on kinship outside the household.

15   Distinctions between local (*dopios*) and foreign (*ksenos*) that correlate more with class than with place of origin is one way the economic basis of inequality is camouflaged in Lehonia (Bennett 1985).

16   To explore the relation between prestige, wealth, and occupation I prepared two sets of cards: one set of names of village men, another of jobs available in the village and Volos. I asked informants to arrange each set in rank order, leaving the precise criteria for assignment open. When Silverman (1966) described using this technique in an Italian hill town, she said respondents were willing, because she was not asking them to do anything they did not normally do. Armed with the ethnographic knowledge that Greek villagers use a complex set of criteria to establish prestige rankings, and aware of stratification in Lehonia, I expected the same result, but I was met with a great reluctance to do any ranking. Even ranking occupations was considered not right, and not a good thing.

17   Naming practices also symbolize social relations, but here continuity of kin groups is the important element. A couple's first child of each sex is named for the paternal grandparent of that sex, the second son and daughter get maternal grandparents' names. Names are bestowed at

baptism by the godparent, and there is no apparent class basis to the choice. Not everyone has a name day. The most common exception to the practice of giving saints' names is the use of names from classical antiquity. This practice probably dates to the 19th century and would make an interesting footnote in the study of the interaction of politics and religion in the context of Greek nationalism.

18   Spoon sweets are pieces of fruit in a boiled sugar syrup. They are still commonly served in the village, but never on name days. They are no longer rare, a luxury, or particularly expensive, and have thus lost their power as boundary markers (cf. Douglas 1979). They are no longer associated with the innovative and cosmopolitan, but rather with the traditional and rural. When served today, each person is given an individual plate with several pieces of fruit (except in the case of bitter oranges, *neranzia*, where one piece is quite enough).

19   Informants say there were periods in the past when a day's wage for a laborer was equivalent to the wholesale price of 2 or 3 pears. In an apple-producing village higher up the slope, between 1910 and 1920 when the daily wage for a male was 2-2.5 drachmes, the price was 7.8 drachmes per kilo (10 dr/oka); the daily wage is equivalent to the price of 3-4 apples.

20   Tupperware parties were introduced in Lehonia c. 1981 and spread quickly through networks of kin and neighbors, at first as a social opportunity for women, and later because of the social pressure to sign up to give a party so that the current hostess would receive more prizes. Of the five parties I attended one was given by an upper class woman who invited about 30 upper class women from Lehonia, Volos, and other villages; two were given by middle class women, and two by wives of industrial laborers. At these parties, as at similar gatherings for the sale of embroideries and linens, the guests were relatives, neighbors, and neighbors of relatives, and were predominantly middle and lower class. Teas, coffees, and birthday parties are by invitation and appear to be held only by upper class women.

21   An additional factor in the rising cost of name day ritual is the change from celebrating a single name day for the household to celebrating for each individual. In part this change has been a concomitant of recent modernization and the rise of individualism; other anthropologists familiar with Greece have mentioned this shift, although it has not been examined in the literature. In Lehonia today the practice is being elaborated by the search for additional saints, from what they call the Catholic (*katholiki*) church or other localities, and expanded by celebration of birthdays.

References Cited

Allen, Peter S.
1976   Aspida: A Depopulated Maniat Community. In *Regional Variation in Modern Greece and Cyprus*, edited by M. Dimen and E. Friedl, pp. 168-198.

Bennett, Diane O.
1985   Class and Equality in a Greek Village. Paper presented at the 84th Annual Meeting of the American Anthropological Society.

1986   The Poor Have Much More Money: Changing Socio-economic Relations in a Greek Village. Paper presented at the 85th Annual Meeting of the American Anthropological Society. Ms. on file at the Department of Anthropology, Washington University.

Bialor, Perry
1968   Tensions Leading to Conflict and the Resolution and Avoidance of Conflict in a Greek Farming Community. In *Contributions to Mediterranean Sociology*, edited by J. G. Peristiany, pp. 107-126.

1976   The Northwestern Corner of the Peloponnesos: Mavrikion and its Region. In *Regional Variation in Modern Greece and Cyprus*, edited by M. Dimen and E. Friedl, pp. 222-235.

Bjornstahl, J. J.
1979   *To Odiporiko tis Thessalias 1779* (Travels in Thessaly 1779). Thessaloniki: Ta Tetradia tu Riga.

Campbell, J. K.
1964   *Honour, Family and Patronage*. Oxford.

1976   Discussion. In *Regional Variation in Modern Greece and Cyprus*, edited by M. Dimen and E. Friedl, p. 72.

1983   Traditional Values and Continuities in Greek Society. In *Greece in the 1980's*, edited by R. Clogg, pp. 184-207.

Clogg, Richard, ed.
1983   *Greece in the 1980's*. New York: St. Martin's.

Cowan, J.
1985   Going Out for Coffee: Everyday Sociability and Defining Female Personhood. Paper presented at the 83rd annual meeting of the American Anthropological Association in Washington, D.C.

Dimen, Muriel and Ernestine Friedl, eds.
1976   *Regional Variation in Modern Greece and Cyprus: Towards a Perspective on the Ethnography of Greece.* Annals of the New York Academy of Sciences, vol. 268.

Douglas, Mary, and Baron Isherwood
1979   *The World of Goods.* New York: Basic Books.

Dubisch, Jill
1972   The Open Community: Migration from a Greek Island Village. Unpublished Ph.D. dissertation, University of Chicago.

du Boulay, Juliet
1974   *Portrait of a Greek Mountain Village.* Oxford: Clarendon.

1976   Lies, Mockery, and Family Integrity. In *Mediterranean Family Structures*, edited by J. G. Peristiany, pp. 389-406.

Frank, Andre Gunder
1966   The Development of Underdevelopment. *Monthly Review* 18:4, pp. 17-30.

Friedl, Ernestine
1962   *Vasilika.* New York: Holt, Rinehart and Winston.

1976   Kinship, Class and Selective Migration. In *Mediterranean Family Structures*, edited by J. G. Peristiany, pp. 363-388.

Garrison, Robert H. and Elizabeth Somer
1985   *The Nutrition Desk Reference.* New Canaan: Keats.

Gavrielides, Nicolas
1974   Name Days and Feasting: Social and Ecological Implications of Visiting Patterns in a Greek Village in the Argolid. *Anthropological Quarterly* 47:48-70

Gearing, F.
1968   Preliminary Notes on Ritual in Village Greece. In *Contributions to Mediterranean Sociology*, edited by J. G. Peristiany, pp. 65-72.

Herzfeld, Michael
1976   Categories of Inclusion and Exclusion in a Rhodian Village. Unpublished Ph.D. disseration, Oxford.

1980   Honour and Shame: Problems in the Comparative Analysis of Moral Systems. *Man* 15:2, pp. 3398-351.

1982   *Ours Once More.* Austin: University of Texas Press.

Hoffman, Susannah M.
1976   The Ethnography of the Islands: Thera. In *Regional Variation in Modern Greece and Cyprus*, edited by M. Dimen and E. Friedl, pp. 328-340.

Kizis, Yiannis
1979   Timber Framed Houses of the Pelion, Greece.*Vernacular Architecture* 10:3-9.

Kordatos, Yiannis
1960   *Istoris tis Eparhias Volu tis Ayias.* (History of the Eparchia of Volos and Ayias. Athens: Twentieth Century.

Loizos, Peter
1975   *The Greek Gift.* New York: St. Martin's.

McGrew, William
1981   *Land and Revolution in Modern Greece, 1800-1881.* Kent State University Press.

McNeill, W. H.
1978   *The Metamorphosis of Greece Since World War II.* Chicago: Univeristy of Chicago.

Makris, K. A.
1982   Post-Byzantine and Modern Magnesia. In *The Story of a Civilization: Magnesia,* by G. Hourmouziadis, P. Asimakopoulou-Atzaka, and K. A. Makris. Athens: M. and R. Capon.

Mouzelis, Nicos
1978   *Modern Greece: Facets of Underdevelopment.* New York: Holmes and Meier.

1986   *Politics in the Semi-Periphery.* New York: St. Martin's.

Mouzelis, Nicos and Michael Attalides
1971   Greece. In *Contemporary Europe: Class, Status, and Power,* edited by M. S. Archer and S. Giner, pp. 162-197.

Nash, June
1981   Ethnographic Aspects of the World Capitalist System. *Annual Review of Anthropology* 10:393-423.

NSSG (National Statistical Service of Greece)
1955, 1960, 1963 *Statistical Yearbook of Greece.* Athens: National
    Printing Office.

OECD (Organisation for Economic Cooperation and Development)
1983   *Greece.* Paris: OECD Economic Surveys.

Peristiany, John G., ed.
1968   *Contributions to Mediterranean Sociology.* Paris: Mouton.

1976   *Mediterranean Family Structures.* Cambridge: Cambridge University
        Press.

Schein, Muriel Dimen
1970   Change and Continuity in a Greek Mountain Community. Ph.D.
        dissertation, Columbia University. Ann Arbor: University Microfilms.

1974   Stratification in a Greek Village. In *City and Peasant*, edited by A. La
        Ruffa et al., pp. 488-495. New York: New York Academy of Sciences.

1975   When is an Ethnic Group? Ecology and Class Structure in Northern
        Greece. *Ethnology* XIV:83-97.

Schneider, J., and P. Schneider
1976   *Culture and Political Economy in Western Sicily.* New
        York: Academic.

Schneider, Peter, Jane Schneider, and Edward Hansen
1972   Modernization and Development: The Role of Regional Elites and Non-
        corporate Groups in the European Mediterranean. *Contemporary Studies
        in Society and History*, June.

Silverman, Sydel
1966   An Ethnographic Approach to Social Stratification: Prestige in a Central
        Italian Community. *American Anthropologist* 68:899-921.

Tapper, R. and N. Tapper.
1986   "Eat This, It'll Do You a Power of Good": Food and Commensality
        among Durrani Pashtuns. *American Ethnologist* 13:62-79.

Vermeulen, Cornelis J. J.
1976   Development and Migration in the Serres Basin. In *Regional Variation in
        Greece and Cyprus*, edited by M. Dimen and E. Friedl, pp. 59-70.

Wallerstein, I.
1974   *The Modern World System.* New York: Academic Press.

Wolf, Eric R.
1982   *Europe and the People Without History*. Berkeley: University of
California.

CULTURE, CLASS AND CONSUMER CHOICE: EXPENDITURES ON FOOD IN URBAN FIJIAN HOUSEHOLDS

Henry J. Rutz

Cultural Classification and Rational Choice

Why do people want goods? The apparent naivete of Douglas's and Isherwood's (1979:15) question is intentional. The question leads in the direction of understanding the cultural logic that binds persons to things, the social uses of goods, and the polysemic value of goods. That is, all the interesting questions about goods point to an analysis of a social economy of consumption.

To economists, the answer is that people want goods to satisfy needs and desires. Through successive refinements over two centuries, the protracted debate over whether virtue or vice produce the greatest good, and the construction of a grand calculus of pleasure and pain, has come to mean precisely that individuals maximize their utility. However, for reasons of mathematical elegance and rigor, economists have found the subject of utility or preference formation to be relatively unproblematic, more or less a question of cardinal or ordinal ranking of preferences. More problematic are the market forces producing a change in the aggregate demand for a good, or the efficient allocation of income to expenditures that maximizes satisfaction for the rational consumer. Historically constituted tastes and the formation of culturally meaningful preferences fall outside the framework of such analyses. Nevertheless, two recent attempts to tinker with the neoclassical theory of consumer behavior, those by Lancaster (1971) and Becker (1965), deserve the attention of economic anthropologists.

Lancaster (1971) posits the notion that goods themselves possess no utility. Rather, goods have attributes or characteristics that are the object of satisfaction. Essentially, the problematic raises questions about the attributes goods possess that are consumed as the objects of utility, and how goods are grouped by consumers in order to make choices based on substitutions and complements. There are at least two reasons why the "characteristics approach" should interest economic anthropologists. First, the opacity of goods requires a discovery procedure that uncovers those attributes that underly consumer demand for goods; second, the classification of goods becomes a central problem in understanding consumer behavior. So far so good; but Lancaster also asserts that the physical characteristics of goods are the most important attributes. And he believes that, once discovered, these will prove to be universal. Anthropologists, working in other cultures and within an historical and comparative framework, are likely to begin with the opposite assertion, namely that the most significant attributes are conventional, i.e. their value is relative and arbitrary.

Becker (1965) introduces into the orthodox theory of consumer behavior (Michael and Becker 1973) the idea that households produce their own

211

consumption. Satisfactions do not derive directly from goods, either market or nonmarket. Instead, utility derives from using goods combined with household time to produce satisfactions, e.g., meals, cleanliness, health, and/or well-being. The problematic raises questions about the social contexts for household consumption. Becker (1976) has paid some attention to social interactions among household members, albeit within the neoclassical context of questions about maximization and efficiency in the allocative process. He also has taken pains to incorporate nonmarket goods and time in the analysis of how income and prices affect household production of consumption. In addition, the problem of substituting goods for each other and goods for time also is central to Becker's analysis. This leads us back to Lancaster and such questions as, What attributes of goods are the objects of consumer choice? Which goods are classified as substitutes and which are complements? How is the classification related to social contexts such as the consumption activities of household members? If these meanings are culturally constructed and shared, how are they reproduced and transformed? Together, then, Lancaster and Becker take for granted the discovery of attributes hidden in goods and the formation of preferences. The historical and comparative analysis of cultural logics and preference formation are of central interest to economic anthropologists and historians.

Consumption has to do with the using up of objects, whatever their source of production and however they are exchanged and distributed. Although we can conceive of a Robinson Crusoe engaging in acts of consumption that are totally private, even he was not outside history and society. His eating habits, to take one example, appear familiar to readers with similar cultural assumptions, and it was not long before his consumption of objects began to make sense in terms of his relations with Friday (who himself was an object of consumption in the relations of others before Crusoe intervened on his behalf). Consumption, it seems, is about the using up of objects in the production of social relations. "Consumption," say Douglas and Isherwood (1979:57), "is the very arena in which culture is fought over and licked into shape." Consumption is related to but distinct from both production and distribution and is fully contained by neither. People want goods in order to communicate values and meanings that make visible their social relations. The most important attributes of goods will change over time and vary from place to place.

An answer to the question of why people want goods leads along a path to other questions. What arbitrary meanings and characteristics do people assign to goods, and how are these given shared meanings in a system of classification? How are tastes or preferences formed and what relationship do they bear to the system of classification of goods? What is the relationship between shared meanings, preferences, and the choices of consumers? If consumption goods are also commodities, where do relative prices and incomes enter into an analysis of consumption activities? The original question is only apparently naive.

My purpose in this paper is to explore more general relationships between culture and consumer choice by examining in some detail one particular case, that of Fiji. The question to be addressed is prosaic: what accounts for patterns of Fijian household expenditures on food? The selection of a commonplace good, i.e. food, consumed routinely as an aspect of everyday life--meals--is intentional. Presumably, the very familiarity of daily routine has most to reveal about the uses of goods.

The Fijian case is apposite because a number of cultural, historical, and economic forces come together in a complex way. Fijians, by actively constructing their traditions (Rutz 1987), maintain a strong collective identity with important political and economic functions in a multi-ethnic state. Fijians, who are 46 percent of the population, are politically dominant over Indians, who are 49 percent and control the commercial life of the coutnry. Among Fijians a collective identity exists not only in the abstract, in such phrases as "the Fijian way of life" (*na sala vakavanua*), but more concretely in daily life where conversations about what it means to be Fijian are a part of ongoing social reality. Being Fijian is continually contrasted with and opposed to being Indian or European, "the money way of life" (*na sala vakailavo*). Eating "Fijian food" is a part of being Fijian. Although the household is a functional unit in which to observe meanings in social use, and for which data on expenditures on food can be collected, the household also is in many ways a microcosm of structured relationships reproduced in other forms of collective action in Fijian society (Sahlins 1976:32-35), activities in which food always performs an important material and symbolic function.

Fijian culture shapes consumer choice underlying expenditures on food in at least three ways. First, Fijians share a relatively simple classification of foods that provides the knowledge for determining which foods are substitutes and which are complements. This knowledge is necessary, in standard economic analysis, for making predictions about the effect of incomes and prices on consumer choice. Second, preferences for particular foods are not merely attributes of individuals; for broad categories, there is a general cultural ordering of preferences that lends stability to those of individuals without denying that variability exists. Anthropologists generally assume that cultures are stable entities. By linking the economists' assumption about stability of individual preferences to the stability of culture, while retaining the autonomy of the individual from culture, economic anthropology enters the debate between culture and rationality. Third, the cultural classification of foods is simple, but the meanings attached to foods can be complex and do vary by social context. To the extent that meanings in use affect consumer choice, there will be an effect on patterns of expenditure on food.

Cultural forces do not operate independently of market forces in determining urban Fijian household consumption of food. Urban Fijian households sell a portion of their labor and purchase some food on the market. Households produce their own consumption with different combinations of market and nonmarket time and goods (Becker 1965). Although most households engage in the home production of some food items, the total list of food items recorded in family budgets (see Appendix) can be purchased in retail outlets or at the marketplace. None of the urban households is without a money income and all purchase at least some of their food on the market. All informants have pricing information and are aware of changes in the prices of a wide range of goods. Their expenditures on food are constrained by income from both market and nonmarket production and subject to market prices. The greatest impact of market forces on consumer choice is the resulting inequality of household incomes and the appearance of distinctions of social class based on the possession of goods.

The next section expands the description of social class among urban Fijian households and its bearing on household expenditures on food. Then two questions about the Fijian culture of food are addressed. First, to what extent do households share a stable culture of food despite differences in class, and how does a shared classification enter into consumer choices underlying patterns of expenditure on food? Second, are there cultural preferences and, if so, how might they enter into consumer choice? Finally, two questions about change and transformation are addressed. First, the stability of culture notwithstanding, have there been long term transformations in food in the Fijian social order, a playing out of the confrontation between capitalist and precapitalist social formations? Second, can we trace the interplay between culture and consumer choice in effecting change by examining the pragmatic choices of today's consumers within the structure of the historical encounter?

Social Class and Urban Fijian Household Expenditures on Food

The class concept has received its sharpest definition in analyses of social groups that stand toward each other in different and determinant relations of production and that, because of those relations, have opposed and antagonistic interests. I have argued elsewhere (1987) that the commodification of urban land provides evidence for emergent classes within the Fijian component of the population. Although the data in this paper lend further credibility to a class analysis of cultural pluralism, determination of whether classes exist in Fiji, in the above sense, is outside the scope of this paper. I use the concept heuristically to describe and analyze differences in the economic conditions of households. It should be pointed out that Fiji is a multi-ethnic society, and that most analyses take the ethnic community to be the point of departure. There is some basis for doing so: a few thousand Europeans control most of the manufacturing, banking, insurance, and warehousing, either as owners or managers for overseas firms. Indians dominate the small business commercial sector and fill the professional ranks. Fijians are prominent in all areas of public life, but most especially in high government posts and permanent positions in the civil service. In rural areas, Indians predominate in the all-important sugar industry, while most Fijians continue to live in small villages and practice a mixed economy of subsistence cultivation and cash cropping.

But the plural society/dual economy model depicts the boundaries as being sharper in theory than they are in practice. And, perhaps more importantly, it always views ethnic communities as more homogeneous and solidary than warranted by the evidence. The majority of Fiji's population, both Indian and Fijian, are rural smallholding agriculturalists. A growing number of the population, both Indian and Fijian, are urban unemployed, underemployed, or unskilled manual and casual labor. A small but growing number of Fijians are entering commerce, while at the same time there are many Indians who occupy important positions in government. The poor wage earners of different ethnic communities increasingly have more in common with each other than with the well-off salaried or self-employed urban workers of their own respective ethnic communities. At the same time, those who have permanent employment and the prospect of some reasonable level of household accumulation beyond one generation, appear to be constituting themselves an urban middle class composed of skilled labor and managerial or professional services.

There are significant objective differences in the economic conditions of households. The greatest disparities exist within the Indian community, from hawkers through small businessmen to millionaire manufacturers. Economic differences within the Fijian community are less, but greater than communal ideologies would suggest. Especially in the urban capital of Suva, Fijians stand in relation to others as unemployed, casual laborers, poor wage earners, salaried employees, and a handful of private businessmen. For the purposes of this paper, the distinction I wish to make is between a working class settlement and an upper middle class subdivision. Disparities in household income are significant between these two adjoining neighborhoods in the Suva Urban Area, but income alone is insufficient to capture the class characteristics that affect consumption patterns. My purpose here is to describe the multiple criteria of social class that establish the conditions for consumption *as a class* while leaving open the question of whether social classes have begun to develop distinct cultural orders. This question is taken up in the next two sections.

Two samples of households were drawn from a larger socioeconomic survey conducted in 1982 in Suva, the capital and main industrial and commercial center of the country.[1] Three residential areas were chosen for the survey on the basis of their visible or objective differences in economic conditions and their articulation with the market and state. Households in two of these, Naivi and Lami, were sampled for more intensive time budget and family budget studies (Rutz n.d.).[2] What must be kept in mind is that households in the two residential areas differ in multiple criteria of class, income being only the most prominent marker of differences in household production and consumption, on one hand, and on the other differences in the way in which the household articulates with the state.

Naivi is one of many Fijian working class settlements in the Suva Urban Area. Of the total money income from all households, most of it is earned by skilled, semi-skilled, and casual laborers whose relation to capital is in terms of an hourly wage in return for labor. None earns significant income from other sources. Naivi is adjacent to the affluent subdivision of Lami, a mixed ethnic residential area in which many members of Fijian elites have purchased homes. Nearly all the income of Lami households derives from workers in salaried positions in the civil service. Consumption criteria are no less important than relations to capital for describing the shape that class assumes among urban Fijians.

Households in Naivi and Lami, respectively, have different linkages with market and state, with regard both to the sale of their labor and the purchase of consumer goods. Although there is little overlap in households with similar levels of income between the two areas, the few households that are at a similar level have different consumption possibilities. Households in Naivi fall outside the jurisdiction of local town councils, pay no rates, and have few urban services. Residents enjoy the use of land and housesites under customary tenure, which includes a complex web of reciprocal rights and obligations to native landowners (Rutz 1987). But Naivi residents pay no rent. In contrast, households in Lami look every bit like--and have the characteristics of--urban subdivisions in any capitalist country. Lami subdivision falls within the jurisdiction of Lami Town Council. Residents pay town rates and receive services such as electricity, garbage collection, paved streets, sewerage and drainage systems, and postal delivery. Residents of Lami have leased parcels for ninety-nine years and, for all intents and purposes, consider themselves owners of private property. They pay rents for their native land leases and their homes are mortgaged.

The one or two room houses made of wood or tin in Naivi stand in stark contrast to those of Lami, with their large multiple-bedroom European style houses made of concrete block and stucco. Naivi houses continue to imitate rural life, even as they begin to acquire some of the appearance of city dwellings. Whereas the inventory of household furnishings in Naivi is modest (perhaps an unused bed, a chest for clothes and one for dishes), households in Lami have tables and chairs, china cabinets, bedroom sets, floor coverings and wall hangings, and most of the appurtenances that mark bourgeois concepts of comfort. The food gardens that surround Naivi houses and give to it the appearance of a rural Fijian village contrast sharply with suburban landscaping in Lami used to demarcate property lines. Although food gardens are not absent on some Lami parcels, there are carefully kept lawns, border and foundation plants, and flowerbeds typical of suburban landscapes in capitalist countries. Both Naivi and Lami are situated on the perimeter of the Suva Urban Area, a short fifteen minute bus ride to Fiji's major industrial estate, to retail outlets and the main marketplace for food, and to administrative offices of the national government. Lami town also boasts an industrial estate of its own and has a small shopping center frequented by members of all households in both samples. In other words, households are articulated with the state in qualitatively different ways in Lami and Naivi, resulting in very different problems of household allocation. Mortgages, property taxes, property and life insurance, and utility bills link Lami households to state and market in a way that households in Naivi have circumvented.

Objective class differences between Naivi and Lami households are most apparent in differences in average income, but equally important for consumption patterns are differences in the composition and sources of income. Naivi households devote much more time to home production of food than those in Lami, while Lami households have more members engaged in wage labor, especially women. Because of the household division of labor, women's wage labor affects household allocation of time and goods more than men's. Income levels affect total expenditures on food, but the composition and sources of income affect expenditures on particular food items (Mintz 1979:68).

The effect on total food expenditures of differences in average household income is in the direction predicted by Engel's Law (Table 1).[3] The mean total household disposable income per week in Lami is over twice that of Naivi (Table 1, column 1). As household income increases, average total household expenditures per week increase (Table 1, column 2), but the average propensity to consume food decreases (Table 1, column 3).[4] The effect of income differences on total expenditures on food does not change appreciably when differences in household size and composition are taken into account (Table 1, columns 4-6).[5]

Composition refers to the proportion of total household income from money wages as opposed to income from home production (Table 2, columns 1 and 2). The mean household disposable income from money wages in Naivi is about a third that of Lami, while the disposable income from home production in Naivi is over eight times greater than that of Lami.[6] Since the figures for home production refer only to the market equivalent prices for food consumed during the week of the family budget--and not to market equivalent prices for all household production activities--they represent important differences in patterns of expenditure on particular food items.

The reason is that only a fraction of foods available through purchase in the market are grown at home (Appendix: Share of Home Production in Total Expenditures on Food: Naivi and Lami).[7] Because home produced foods are those labelled by Fijians as "Fijian food", the consumption patterns of working class Fijian households necessarily look more traditional than upper class Lami households, in which household production utilizes more market goods.

Differences in average household income between Naivi and Lami derive only in part from differences between wages of blue collar and salaries of white collar workers (Gounis and Rutz 1986).[8] A crucial aspect of total household income is the number of members employed per household (Table 2, column 4).[9] Multiple incomes per household offset poor wages relative to urban costs of living. Households in Naivi and Lami equally desire urban wage employment, but Lami households are much more successful in their search. The mean number of wage earners per household in both Naivi and Lami is greater than 1.0. Although a few households in Naivi have no wage earners, there are special circumstances that account for money income from sources other than the sale of household labor. For most households, their long term presence in the urban area depends upon a household's ability to find wage employment for a number of its members. The reason is not hard to find. The average wage for unskilled and semi-skilled labor was F$40 per week in Suva in 1982. Several Naivi households are at or below this functional urban poverty line and would be in difficult straits were it not for contributions of home production to income or, in a few cases, non-wage income from leases of native land. Additional wage earners, even when part-time or temporary, have a proportionally great impact on a household's ability to purchase market foods. In Lami, the primary source of household income derives from salaried workers who earn F$80-100 per week. Additional workers often earn F$60 per week. The class position of the Lami household therefore depends very much on the number of employed workers per household, not merely the salary of a single person. Multiple incomes increase greatly the range of choice in consumption and have an impact on patterns of expenditure on food.[10]

The working class households of Naivi tend to have at least one member who has permanent skilled employment and are able to find employment, part-time or temporary, for at least one other member. In all cases the primary wage earner is male and in most cases he is also head of household. There also is a pool of unemployed or underemployed labor for home production of food and other household production activities (Gounis and Rutz 1986). The upper class households of Lami have, in most cases, used social privileges, such as chiefly rank or close kin connection to a high level government official, to attain educational levels that secure opportunities in the labor market, mainly in public sector employment. Lami women, especially, have educational attainments well above their counterparts in Naivi, and many have skills which get them occupations that pay as well as those of men. In the Lami sample, several women are also heads of households. The result is that the mean number of wage earners per Lami household is over 3.0, and most earn wages higher than heads of households in Naivi. The threefold disparity between mean total household disposable income in Naivi and Lami is due, therefore, to sources of income as well as to wage levels for unskilled and skilled labor.

The importance of this difference in sources of income is that it affects patterns of expenditure on food in particular, and consumption activities in general, in several different ways. Problems of household allocation are simpler in Naivi because a household head who is also the primary source of income can control household labor and allocate income to the purchase of food. In Lami there exists complex arrangements for pooling different incomes, allocating household labor to various tasks, and allocating money income from various sources to different kinds of expenditures. There is more room for autonomy of the various income earners, and hence for bargaining and negotiating shared expenditures. Naivi and Lami share a formal similarity in the normative ideal of a strong male-headed household, one in which the "chief of the house" (*turaga ni vale*) is powerfully obligated to look after the welfare of all members in exchange for extreme deference and obedience. However, in Lami, greater market penetration is eroding the ideology of respect and obedience as well as actual ties of dependence. In Lami, issues of cheating with respect to shared expenditures, and negotiation over contributions, arise more frequently. Intra-household conflicts over allocation appear to be more intense when shared food expenditures are subject to appropriations from different sources of income (Rutz in press).

Differences in sources of income also affect patterns of expenditure on food through another means: time allocated to work outside the home and the social division of labor in the home. Here again, Naivi and Lami households share a formal similarity between household allocation of time to production and a normative ideal of a sexual division of labor. But pragmatic choices in Lami households lead to a rearrangement of the division of labor on both counts when women and/or junior members of the household work full-time at relatively high paying jobs. Such pragmatic choices in the allocation of labor have an impact on patterns of expenditure on particular food items. This issue is addressed below. First, however, we need to ask whether there exist shared characteristics of foods and stable preferences underlying consumer choice about allocation and expenditure.

Food in the Social Order

The class of goods Fijians term "food" (*kakana*) constitutes a structure of the *longue duree* (Braudel 1980: 27). True, a century of British colonial rule introduced many new foods--Indian and Chinese items as well as European ones. And sixteen years of independence have seen a steady increase in food imports and a growing food dependency (McGee 1975; Thaman 1979). But historical forces other than colonialism and market penetration have also asserted themselves. Despite plantation systems and cash cropping regimes aimed at the export market, Fijians have persisted in cultivating root crops within an enduring system of shifting cultivation (Rutz 1976; 1977). And "Fijian food" (*kakana vakaviti*) serves as one powerful material symbol of a social identity that has been forged, in part, by inter-ethnic competition with Indians. Nowhere is the maintenance of social boundaries more apparent than in Suva Urban Area.

The structural simplicity of the Fijian classification of food, shared by Fijians of all classes, is a type case of what Mintz (1985:146) and others have observed to be widely embraced by cultures in geographically separated areas of the world and for different periods prior to capitalist development. It consists of a "core" of root crops or cereals and a "fringe" of meats, vegetables, and seasonings. In the Fijian system, the core and fringe are defined in opposition to each other: "true food" (*kakana*) and "relish" (*i coi*). True food consists of root crops, especially taro, yams, cassava, and sweet potatoes, but also breadfruit and bread. Relish is everything else, including most fruits and vegetables, and meat and fish (see Appendix on Food Items).[11]

When total household expenditures on food in Naivi and Lami, respectively, are arranged by cultural classification, the cultural context for rational consumer choice is apparent (Table 3). For example, a formal economic analysis of the effect of income differences, or of changes in relative prices, on expenditures presumes a classification of goods. Goods classed together are thought to be close substitutes, while goods assigned to different classes indicate complements.Which goods are substitutes for each other and which are complements is an empirical problem. Cultural analysis shows that, at the most general level of analysis, the Fijian food system is dichotomized into two classes, each of which complements the other in the Fijian concept of a meal. Within a class, some food items are closer substitutes than others, comprising several sub-classes of food. The effect of a change in price for one item may increase or decrease household expenditures, depending upon whether it is a substitute for, or a complement of, that item.

Furthermore, a cultural analysis of the Fijian food system can make transparent the opacity of particular foods with respect to their valued or meaningful characteristics. Models of consumer choice in which incomes and prices are explanatory factors assume some knowledge of the characteristics of goods that make sense of utility or satisfaction. Lancaster (1971:10) states that "whether goods are close substitutes or not is shown to depend (as expected) on their characteristics, and, in principle, the closeness of substitution could be predicted from technical data concerning characteristics." However, the technical data to which he refers are the physical characteristics of goods. For example, Lancaster might group food items according to such characteristics as calories, vitamins, and proteins, arguing that each attribute, or cluster of attributes, predicts which foods will be substituted for each other when relative prices change. In effect, he views the selection of physical characteristics as culture-free. The error is in two directions: the revealed characteristics become universals, and the potential symbolic and social characteristics of goods remain concealed. His rational consumer is a nutritionist reduced to satisfying biological requirements devoid of soul and social being. In terms of the present analysis, the logic of table 3 is reduced to the question of whether Fijian household expenditures constitute a rational allocation of calories, vitamins, and protein, given incomes and market prices.

Lancaster's reductionism should not deter economic anthropologists from seeing his valuable contribution of providing a rationale for incorporating information about characteristics in formal models of consumer choice. It opens a door to synthesizing some of the theoretical concerns of the new consumer economics with developments in cultural analysis. Douglas and Isherwood (1979) have outlined some of the possibilities of an anthropology of consumption that take into account economists' interests, and Douglas (1971, 1984) has pursued a cultural analysis of selected consumption goods, food being among them. Sahlins (1976:169) probably is closest to echoing the received wisdom in anthropology when he expresses the view that a presumed universally rational and objective scheme depends on a cultural logic that is never the only one possible. The task, therefore, is not to reveal a structural constant in the indefinitely large variety of cultural contents, but rather to unmask the myriad cultural orders that make behavior meaningful. With respect to food, "Americans deem dogs inedible and cattle food" (1976:169). Sahlins points out that even in our own industrial culture, where the market has penetrated the farthest into our systems of meaning, incomes and prices do not fully encompass the "meaningful calculus of food preferences" (1976: 171). One need not agree with his polemic in which culture must account for choice and not vice-versa to observe that patterns of food consumption everywhere approximate poorly the nutritionist's conception of a rational diet (cf. Stigler 1945).

The very simplicity of the Fijian food structure accounts for its stability, enduring into the present in the face of over a century of capitalist development and the colonial creation of modern Fijian institutions. The characteristics of particular foods is a more complex problem for discovery and is related to issues of preference formation. Food is integral to all of Fijian social order. A household should provide food sufficient to meet its own daily consumption requirements, but households are made normatively interdependent by the obligation to give and receive food continually. Labor from outside the household for work on food gardens or housebuilding is formally reciprocated in meals (*oca*). As one moves from structure to meaning in use, symbolic complexity increases, mirroring the complex social relations of which food consumption is an integral part. The cultural characteristics of particular food items and their variable meaning in different social contexts is the stuff of Fijian public life, which is saturated with social rituals that reproduce the intricate and complex relations of rank and status (Hocart 1929; Walters 1978a, 1978b; Sahlins 1962, 1976). An example will serve to make apparent the importance of culturally meaningful characteristics for understanding food preferences and consumer choice.

Within the class of foods designated "true food", taro and yams stand opposed to each other in the Fijian cultural order (Figure 1). Within the established division of agricultural labor, yams are cultivated by men and taro by women. Yams are produced on dry elevated lands, taro on low lying wetlands. Yams are the necessary food offered to chiefs by commoners during the "first fruits" (*i sevu*) ceremony, a symbolic representation of chiefly powers of fertility and commoner control over land. In the Fijian conception, the fertility of land is

221

equated with the personal health of the chief, which in turn is equated with the well-being of the body politic (Turner 1984). Taro, however, is the more important crop, materially, in most of Fiji. Unlike yams, which represent hierarchical relations of male rank and power between chiefs and commoners, taro represents the egalitarian relations between men of different clans who exchange women. Taro is presented by women of a descent group on occasions when men make or reaffirm kinship alliances. As Figure 1 suggests, many other permutations of the opposition between taro and yams occur, making use of cultural characteristics of these food items. The problem being addressed, however, is household expenditures on food and how the characteristics of Fijian food items relate not only to classification for purposes of substitution but also to preference ordering for purposes of choice.

There are at least three ways in which culture enters into consumer choice. It already has been shown that cultural analysis groups foods into classes and sub-classes in meaningful ways for purposes of substitution. It remains to show how culture enters into a shared preference ordering of food items in both Naivi and Lami households, and how cultural meanings enter into specific consumption events such as meals. Cultural classification, ordering of preferences, and meaning of consumption events affect household total expenditures, proportional expenditures by class, and expenditures on particular items.

The cultural classification shared by households both in Naivi and Lami has built into it a general ordering of food preferences (Figure 2). Foods are not merely assigned to categories, they are ranked by cultural preference. For example, within the category of true food, taro and yams are preferred to all other true foods. Another root crop, cassava, is preferred to bread, which is preferred to potatos and rice. Within the category of relish, there is a definite preference for pork over beef, and beef over chicken in the sub-category of meats. Fijians consider the taste of prawns and fish to be superior to that of small land crabs and bivalve shell fish within the sub-category of fish and seafoods. Finally, there is a preference for young taro leaves over hibiscus leaves and both over ground ferns in the sub-category of leaf vegetables. The fact that eliciting a food classification produces an ordinal ranking of preferred foods within categories suggests that preferences are not merely the attributes of individuals. Certainly, individual preference orderings are sometimes expressed and could be elicited systematically. These would produce differences from the general cultural ordering of preferences and would reveal personal tastes. However, such preferences presumably would fall within the boundaries of the classification. The cultural ordering of preferences fits well Fijian conceptions of the social values of different crops and the origin of these values in the ecological adaptations of shifting cultivation to the island ecosystem (Rappaport 1963). Cultural stability in part rests on the origin and persistence of food production systems and the social relations these entail. The stability of the categories lends stability to preferences. Stability of preferences is one of the key assumptions made by economists in a formal analysis of the effects of relative prices on consumer choice (Becker 1976:5). If this analysis is correct, then the general preference ordering given in

Figure 2 can be presumed to underlie the pattern of expenditures by category in Table 3. It helps to explain why an analysis of expenditures based on relative prices alone is likely to be insufficient, leaving a residual category of "tastes" to account for what is not explained by prices alone in the orthodox theory of consumer behavior.

The cultural classification of Fijian foods also produces meaningful substitutes and complements. When Fijians say that they prefer taro and yams to cassava, and cassava to bread, and bread to potatoes and rice, they are saying that all these are substitutes for each other but none are substitutes for food items in other categories. The same is true for food items within other categories. If the price of one true food changes relative to others, consumers will choose to substitute relatively cheaper food items for more expensive ones. However, because preferences are ordinal, we don't know how a given change in price affects the amount of the substitution. Also, in this classification, taro and yams, and potatos and rice, appear to be perfect substitutes.

Strictly speaking, true foods are not always substitutes for each other. There are occasions such as "first fruits" ceremonies when only yams will do. There are other occasions, such as marriage ceremonies, when the social definition of the situation requires taro. Relational by definition, classifications fail to specify any rules for their application. Douglas (1984: 19) sounds an appropriate note of caution: "All human behavior is structured; there may be no end to the number of rules being observed by every individual every instant of the day. Consequently, the research that tries to compare structured behavior has to define a baseline, a time span, and the size of the mesh being applied to behavior across the board." Elsewhere Douglas (1979) has taken a more social utilitarian approach to the relationship between culture and choice. Without denying that goods represent a cultural order, she is more sensitive to the social uses of goods and their meanings in action. The social meanings underlying patterns of expenditure in Table 3 have as their social context the daily consumption of food by households. The class of consumption events of interest is "meals".

Fijians refer to a household "meal", simply, as *kana*, an idomatic term meal. The periodicity of meals has evolved in the urban area to fit the work-disciplines of the market economy and institutions such as church and school. Temporal rhythms of urban Fijian households are articulated with employers' demands, commercial hours for transportation schedules, and school routines. The flow of time is divided into work-days and weekends. Schedules and routines indirectly affect household expenditures on food by affecting meal-times and the time available to prepare and consume meals. Urban Fijians have adopted the European periodicity of eating meals thrice daily--morning, noon, and evening. Today meals are referred to as "breakfast" (*katalau*, derivation unknown), "lunch" (*vakasigalevu*, mid-day), and "dinner" (*vakayakavi*, early evening).

As consumption events, Fijian meals have a simple structure relative to, say, the bourgeoise conception of separate courses served in sequential order and culminating in dessert. True food and relishes complement each other and are served simultaneously. True food is more than symbolically central, it is materially the center of a meal, making up its bulk and quantity. Quantity of food alone is the criterion for a good meal. This contrast with bourgeois conceptions, which include a variety of aesthetic characteristics, bears emphasizing for two reasons. Unlike the bourgeois conception of a meal, diversity in menus from day to day is relatively unimportant. The total list of food items purchased by all households over the period of a week is rather short relative to working class or elite menus in the United States (Appendix: Food Items in Family Budgets, Naivi and Lami). Lami households on average do have a more diverse set of menus, but these remain well within the range of a recognizable Fijian culture of food.

A second reason for emphasizing the importance Fijians place on quantity is that the general well-being of a household is defined as much by its ability to serve a surfeit of food as by consumer goods that are used as social markers in industrialized countries. In other words, the important attributes of foods in Fijian culture, those which link consumer choice to utility or satisfaction, consist of implicit meanings of sociability and commensality, characteristics which enter into Fijian discourse about what distinguishes them from both Indians and Europeans, the other major ethnic groups in Fijian society. A comparative study of expenditures on food, which unfortunately does not exist, would be likely to show that Fijians spend proportionally more on food at comparable levels of income than either Indians or Europeans.

The discourse about meals contrasts with the meal as a consumption event. The casual conversation that takes place in social encounters always includes questions about where people have been, what persons they saw, and a story of some sort that often includes *how much* (not *what*) they ate or drank. It begins with the question, "Where have you been?" (*ko e lako mai vei?*). If the respondent has been at someone's house (visiting is frequent and obligatory), he/she describes the concrete setting and moves as a matter of form to compliments extended to his/her host/hostess. The respondent tells his/her listener(s) how much he/she drank or ate, always including a comment about how there was "too much" to eat or drink. It is obligatory to say that a host provided so much food or drink that his/her stomach was full and still there were quantities left over. If a respondent wants to slight a person, a standard way in which to do so is to suggest, ever so slightly, that great amounts of food and drink were not offered or served. The quality of dishes, their display, and other aesthetic characteristics are subordinated to the notion of surfeit.

In contrast to the discourse about food, there is little or no conversation during a meal. The most frequent comment during a meal is when someone, either a male head of household or an older woman who is in charge of serving the meal, tells another present to "eat more" (*kana vakalevu*). Adult Fijians often eat several pounds of true food at one sitting. Although menus might include Indian,

European, or Chinese food items and dishes, a frequent comment is that these foods and dishes "don't fill the stomach." No matter how much relish accompanies a meal, there is a feeling of hunger without sufficient true foods. Conceptions of the body and its social meanings fit these consumption practices. Adult Fijians tend to be large. A large stomach, especially, is used as a metaphor for a happy and contented household. Men will joke with each other that a man with a large stomach must be a "chief in his own household" (*turaga ni vale*), suggesting that his authority is certain and other members work together to provision the house with one of its most important social goods, food. Parallel comments apply to women as they have children, achieve a central role in the household division of labor, and acquire social standing with other women and through supporting men's consumption activities.

Consumer choice, then, takes place within a framework of intersubjectively constructed shared categories for grouping goods and consumption events that have social meaning. Patterns of household expenditure on food in Naivi and Lami are affected directly and indirectly by shared categories and social meanings for the daily consumption of food. First, the cultural classification is shared by all households and can be used to organize expenditures in Table 3. Second, the classification appears to be stable over a long period despite other changes due to a century of colonial history and the more recent period of capitalist development. The reason, no doubt, is that this colonial history ensured that the centuries old adaptation of village horticulture persisted into the present, despite permutations on the basic structure. Third, meaningful categories provide a classification of food items according to which ones are close substitutes and which ones are complements. Fourth, a shared and stable classification provides a basis for a general ordering of preferences that are also shared and stable, one whose attributes are attached to a social order of food and not to individuals. This in no way denies that preferences are also attributes of individuals. Fifth, the practice of a cultural order produces social meanings that affect consumer choice and resulting patterns of expenditure. The consumption of food within the routine of daily meals, the limited variability of food items in meals, the emphasis on true food and quantity over quality, and the character of the consumption event itself--all these factors affect the amount of total expenditure, the proportion spent on various categories, and the purchase of particular items.

If these preliminary conclusions are obvious to anthropologists, they are less so to economists, who have taken rationality to be culture-free and assumed that universal characteristics based on physical attributes can be used to group goods for purposes of analyzing choice. But anthropologists have become enamored of the beauty, elegance, and complexity of cultural classification to the point of denying the origin and functions of their structures. Culture becomes pitted against choice in an unnecessary struggle for survival of intellectual paradigms. Without social usage, there is no structure. Douglas (1979) and Mintz (1985), from very different perspectives, view the consumption of food in particular, and goods in general, as an arena in which interests are contended and categories and social meanings become reworked. Mintz examines historical forces that shape consumer choice over the long run by changing categories and shaping preferences. Douglas is more interested in how culture gets reworked through social usage in the short term. Both examine how culture is reworked by means of pragmatic choice.

New Foods, Preference Formation, and the Stability of Culture

Up to this point, certain cultural patterns have been treated as fixed constraints on consumer choice. Fijian households are free within the limits of their own resources and the range of food items available on the market to determine their level of expenditures on food and to choose what foods to consume. From the large number of different kinds of food available in supermarkets, Fijian households select only a limited range, suggesting that expenditures do reflect some domain bounded by a culture of food. That culture has remained stable over long periods and is shared among Fijians despite the emergence of social classes.

But Lami households not only spend more on food than households in Naivi, they spend on more different kinds of food (Appendix: Food Items in Naivi and Lami Family Budgets). The rise of class differences among urban Fijians is marked by the inversion of the cultural order that assigns root crops to true food and banishes meat to the periphery. Lami households spend significantly less on root crops and significantly more on meat, evidence for a "more European" and "less traditional" set of dishes. Root crops comprise 28% of total expenditures in Naivi, only 12% in Lami; meat/fish comprise only 29% of total expenditures in Naivi, 39% in Lami (Table 3).[12] If food is consumed within a social order, such that we must examine how that order constrains consumer choice, it appears also that consumer choice strains the boundaries of culture. Historical forces, at work for over a century, have had an impact on consumption and, by implication, the reworking of Fijian culture. New foods have been introduced, and along with them their social usages. Preference orderings have been reworked in the process. The extent to which new foods and their associated meanings are integrated into an existing cultural order or challenge its meaningfulness depends upon the particularities of history.[13] Three foods--cassava, bread, and beef--illustrate the possibilities for cultural transformation and preference formation.

Cassava was introduced to Fijian villagers by colonial officers of the Fiji Department of Agriculture in the first decades of this century. The root crop became widely diffused over a short period and entered Fijian consumption as a staple food. Widespread acceptance was due to several agronomic characteristics that allowed for its complete integration with the existing system of shifting cultivation. Cassava altered only slightly an ecological adaptation without in any way transforming it (Rutz 1976).

Cassava is a root crop that can be grown on soils too infertile for taro and yams. It required no new tools or exceptional investments, and yields were high for relatively low labor inputs. In other words, it was incorporated into an existing system of production without fundamentally altering it. To the contrary, its introduction probably increased the stability of the agricultural adaptation to the tropical rain forest (Rutz 1977). Integration in household production was accompanied by integration in household consumption. Fijians had no problem labelling cassava a "true food" and treating it as a near-perfect substitute for taro and yams in daily household consumption. The physical characteristics of the crop, including the fact that it was a tuber, that it could be prepared for consumption much as taro and yams were, and that it had similar tactile qualities and roughly similar appearance, no doubt helped it to become a "true food." The fact that cassava came with few, if any, social meanings, and that its physical characteristics were so similar to other true foods, is sufficient explanation for why it reproduced rather than transformed cultural classification.

The increasing consumption of cassava in daily meals is not explained by a shift in Fijian preferences away from taro and yams. Because cassava could be produced on poor soils with relatively low labor inputs, it was the perfect crop to provide calories for an expanding village, and later, urban Fijian population. Taro and yams, unlike cassava, carried heavy symbolic and social baggage. This was never transferred to cassava, which continues to rank a distant third when Fijians extol the taste of taro and yams and list the attributes of each variety with fine distinctions among them. What happened was that the culturally inferior cassava took its place in a cultural preference ordering behind the preferred root crops and was produced for daily household consumption. Daily consumption of cassava allowed for greater exchange and display of taro and yams on occasions of ceremonial exchange and consumption, where taro and yams remained obligatory and rewards of social prestige flowing from generosity ensured their higher value.

In the city, Fijians consume much more cassava than taro, and much more taro than yams (which are seasonal). Family budgets of both Naivi and Lami households show that nearly all of the total expenditure on root crops consists of cassava, including that of market equivalent prices for home production in Naivi households. The explanation for Naivi can be found in the same agronomic characteristics that make it the choice of village horticulturists. In Lami the explanation can be found in relative prices. The price of a basket of cassava in the Suva marketplace in 1982 was around F$2.50, compared to that of a bundle of taro, which fluctuated between F$3.50 and F$6.00. A basket of cassava is roughly equivalent to a bundle of taro and will feed a household of four for one meal.

Bread is another item that was introduced into the Fijian cultural order of food. Unlike cassava, bread came with important symbolic meanings and social usages in an alien culture. Bread also had little resemblance to the physical characteristics of root crops and could not be integrated with the system of tropical shifting cultivation. Whether bread transforms cultural classification, how it fits

227

into a cultural preference ordering, and what its social usages are can't be predicted from nutritional attributes. Bread probably was introduced by Methodist missionaries, whose diaries record its presence in their own diets as early as 1838 (Calvert 1858:19-20). Fijians have used flour to fry a kind of pancake for a very long time, but the consumption of bread in any quantity is premised upon the expansion of the market and capitalist development. Wheat is not grown in the tropics and bread is not produced in the home. Fijians must purchase bread at retail outlets supplied by one of only several large industrial bakeries that obtain their flour from a single importer and supplier, Flour Mills of Fiji, Ltd. The consumption of bread links Fijian households directly to the international grain market.

Bread symbolizes relations in the capitalist market. Wheat cannot be grown at home and households lack the technology for baking bread. Therefore the consumption of bread is predicated on the sale of labor for wages and the partial displacement of a household division of labor by an industrial division of labor. If import figures for wheat are any indication, consumption of bread and other wheaten products are increasing rapidly (Appendix: Wheat and Sharps Imports) in Fiji. The proportion of total expenditures on these items is high for both Naivi and Lami households (Table 3). Further evidence for the degree to which bread has penetrated the consumption habits of urbanites comes from reactions to increases in prices. The price of bread has risen faster than wages and has become an object of government price controls and consumer discontent. The price of a long loaf, the standard unit purchased by most Fijians, has risen from F$.08 in 1968 (Annual Statistical Abstracts:23), to F$.13 in 1973 (Fiji: A Developing Australian Colony), and again to F$.31 in 1981 (Fiji Times, January 22). Bread quadrupled in price over a period when wages tripled.

Fijians are not unaware of bread symbolism and its place in European culture. Fijian admiration for the achievements of that culture is surpassed only by their profound ambivalence toward it. As devout Christians for over a century, they are familiar with a host of biblical metaphors including bread as the body of Christ, the communal sentiments of "breaking bread" together, and bread as the "staff of life." Just as they associate civilization with Christianity, they associate bread with civilization. In Fijian history, civilization took the form of British colonial overlords and a white planter community that imported flour for making bread. Bread has in Fiji always been associated with urban life and its consumption symbolizes familiarity with and emulation of social groups that have held political and economic hegemony over the islands. In the context of the rural exodus of Fijians to Suva since independence in 1970, bread has taken on the significance of a key symbol in a new social order. One aspect of this order is the increasing differentiation between rural and urban kinsmen, and between social classes in the urban area. As one informant put it, "When my kinsmen visit from the village, they bring taro and want to eat bread." Bread marks the transformation from rural to urban life, from kinship to class, and from traditional ethnic identity to nationalism.

228

The increasing presence of bread in the daily meals of Fijians, especially urbanites, signals a more radical departure from the Fijian cultural order of food than does the consumption of cassava. Its assignment to a place in cultural classification, a cultural preference ordering, and social usage reflects these particular historical forces. Bread, like cassava, has entered Fijian cultural classification as "true food." However, it fits less neatly into a preference ordering and unambiguous social usage. As a true food, it is not as perfect a substitute as cassava for taro and yams because it is less dense and less filling, attributes of true foods that are central to Fijian ideas about health and contentment. It takes a large quantity of bread to satiate appetites. The long loaf, which most Fijians buy, weighs less than a pound and costs F$.31.[14] The relatively high cost of bread, combined with other charcteristics that make it a less than perfect substitute for "true food", precludes its use in the evening meal, the main meal of the day.

Bread has suffered the same fate as cassava with respect to its ceremonial function. Fijians do not consider bread an appropriate item for collective gift exchange and ceremonial consumption. Nor do Fijians prefer bread to taro or yams. Nevertheless, its symbolic association with urbanism, class consciousness, and nationalism lead to ambiguities about just where it does fit into the preferences of urban Fijians. New varieties of bread are constantly entering the urban market and Fijians have responded favorably to the opening of hot bread shops in the center of the city. A clue to the way in which a new item like bread can open possibilities for modifying the cultural order of food can be found in the pragmatic choices of households, discussed in the next section.

The introduction of beef presages an even greater potential for the influence of preference formation on the transformation of a Fijian culture of food. Fijian villagers have raised cattle in increasing numbers at least since the end of World War II. Like pigs, cattle are too valuable to butcher for daily consumption, especially without a household technology for storage and preservation of the meat. It isn't surprising, therefore, that cattle became substitutes for pigs in ceremonial exchange. The whole animal is displayed, presented, and divided for distribution exactly as the pig would be. In the 1950s, the Fiji Department of Agriculture began to encourage cattle-raising on a larger scale as a source of rural household income for a growing home market. Extension agents encouraged and helped with the expansion of pasture lands. By the early 1970s, there was a substantial home market for beef, especially in Suva and other urban areas. Government had invested directly in large cattle schemes and an industrial scale slaughterhouse. In 1982, independent Fijian producers had established a co-operative venture in retail marketing to compete with the growing number of private butchers. Refrigeration in retail stores, including freezers, solved the problem of storage and preservation. Also, refrigerators had come into demand as a major household asset wherever there was electricity. The price of beef relative to pork had declined steadily as a result of investment in a national beef industry and the near absence of a pork industry. Despite a cultural preference for pork, the origins for which can be discovered in the foraging habits of pigs within the village system of shifting cultivation, urban Fijian households began to consume an increasing amount of beef in daily meals. Urban Fijians had acquired a taste for beef.

Expenditure patterns in Naivi and Lami households reflect this trend (Table 3). Although meat/fish retain their cultural value as "relish" to a meal which consists centrally of "true food", in both Naivi and Lami expenditures on this category comprise the largest single proportion of total expenditures. And expenditures on beef are by far the greatest share of expenditures on meat/fish. In Lami households, the proportion of total expenditures spent on meat/fish (39%) is significantly greater than that spent on all true foods combined (29%). Given these market forces and the response of urban Fijian households, one can wonder whether, in the not too distant future, a more European culture of food will not displace the existing cultural order, at least with respect to daily household consumption.

In sum, the pragmatic choices of urban Fijian households, when confronted with capitalist developments in national markets for such food items as bread and beef, have resulted in patterns of expenditure on food that raise a prospect that cultural transformation is well underway. While the classification and general ordering of preferences appear to remain intact at present, social usage has shifted toward a more European pattern of food consumption. The emergent pattern can be seen clearly in a comparison of working class households in Naivi with those of upper class households in Lami. Bread (including other wheaten products) and beef (including other meats and fish) comprise 52% of total expenditures on food in Lami. And expenditures of Lami households on "relish" are 65%--nearly two-thirds--of total expenditures. Even in Naivi, where home production of true foods and fish ensures a continuance of a Fijian culture of food, expenditures on bread (including wheaten products) and beef (including other meats and fish) comprise 43% of total expenditures on food.

Pragmatic choices, based in part on market forces, and in part on a reordering of preferences along the lines of social class, are beginning to erode the centrality of true food as the core of a shared and stable cultural classification. It remains to be seen whether the emergence of objective social classes will invert the relationship between core and fringe, subverting the old classification and preference ordering. At present, Fijian culture, with its basis in an historically constituted form of social rank in a particular precapitalist formation, co-exists with the market and the formation of social classes. Patterns of food expenditure in particular, and consumption in general, are a counterpart of the co-existence of old patterns of work organized around home production and a sexual division of labor, on the one hand, and on the other, new work-disciplines organized around wages and an historically constituted division of labor. Of course, the co-existence of different divisions of labor, household and market, have persisted for over two centuries in industrialized countries.

New Work-disciplines and Problems of Household Allocation

Sahlins (1976:32) quotes a common Fijian aphorism that "every man is a chief in his own house." More accurately, every senior male head of household invokes the cultural model of chiefly authority to gain compliance from other members (Rutz n.d.). Household social structure is meant to be a microcosm of hierarchical and centralized political tendencies in Fijian society. The normative ideal is respect, obedience, and service to a senior male entrusted with the welfare of all household members. He commands cooperation for the prudent allocation of labor and goods in household production of consumption. Toward this end, the authority of a household head derives from the same legitimacy as that of a chief. Household members have the obligation to serve their head without comment or question.

From the standpoint of household allocation, the normative ideal describes a mature household as a single decision-making unit, pooling resources for cooperative household production of shared consumption within an established social division of labor. Authoritative allocation takes place within a social division of household labor organized by sex and seniority. A wife should serve her spouse, just as a sister should obey requests from her brother. Children are ranked by seniority along lines of sex, with the oldest son in a favored position as heir apparent to the father.

The ideal can be observed most easily in rural villages. Slightly older children take care of slightly younger ones down to the youngest, with older female children carrying the burden while older male children oversee the work. Older male children clear land and prepare gardens, which adult women then weed, maintain, and harvest. A wife oversees domestic chores of feeding infants, washing clothes, preparing and serving meals, cleaning up after meals, and general housekeeping. She directs older daughters who help her in all these tasks. The obedience husbands expect from wives can be illustrated in the preparation and serving of meals. It is a wife's duty to prepare all meals and to serve them at her husband's convenience. Ideally, wives serve husbands their meal first, waiting until afterward to eat their own meal. Should husbands come home hungry late in the evening, wives should awaken to prepare and serve a meal.

There are many factors that intervene to create discrepancies between the normative ideal and actual household allocation, but what must be stressed is the potency of chiefly authority in the household and the strength of principles of sex and seniority governing the division of labor. Circumventing authority, speaking out against it, and disobedience are not uncommon; nonetheless such conduct is viewed by Fijians as morally reprehensible and taken seriously by the wider community.

Both Naivi and Lami households participate in the urban economy of wage labor and the consumption of market goods, but they do so differentially. To summarize these class differences discussed earlier, working class households in Naivi, on average, have smaller households, fewer wage workers per household, fewer women wage workers per household, lower total disposable incomes, and devote much more time to home production of food than their upper class Lami counterparts. Naivi households look more like the households of their rural kinsmen despite their greater participation in the temporal rhythms of the urban market economy. Problems of household allocation are simpler in Naivi than in Lami because the male head of household also tends to be the primary wage earner and there are fewer sources of income to pool. In Lami, also, the relative absence of home production of food removes a major support for the household division of labor.

The result of all these differences is that household allocation in Lami is subject to more bargaining and negotiation than in Naivi. Differences in social class resurface in differences in the structure of households, which in turn have implications for household allocation. The question is whether these processes of intra-household allocation can be discerned in patterns of food expenditure. To illustrate the possibilities of such analysis, consider the effect of wage work and new work-disciplines on household allocation of female time to the production of meals. The market value of female time is greater in Lami than in Naivi, and the total amount of female time in Lami is more scarce relative to Naivi. Because the production of meals involves inputs of female time and food items, patterns of expenditure on food are closely related to decisions about time allocation. Furthermore, household production of meals within the Fijian social division of labor concerns not only the amount of time but its temporal location, i.e. a problem of articulating household temporal rhythms with those of the urban market economy.

A standard temporal location refers to the occurrence of an activity at a similar time over time (Zerubavel 1981:7-9). Because of the articulation of the household with the temporal rhythms of urban life, including set durations for work hours, school attendance, and transportation schedules, the point of greatest time constraint and most time pressure is around the morning meal on weekdays (Table 4). Breakfast is a time when all members of the household are present and no prior activities constrain the standard temporal location. Weekday limits to breakfast are set by sunrise and clock-time for the start of work and school. Both wage earners and children travel to school by bus, so bus schedules become important constraints on the standard temporal location for breakfast. In both Naivi and Lami, the average standard temporal location (STL) for the start of breakfast is around 6 AM, with a modal STL of 6.30 AM. The duration of breakfast in both Naivi and Lami is about 30 minutes on weekdays (Table 5). Wage earners and school children have left the house to catch buses by 7 AM. Personal hygiene and preparation for the day leave little time to extend the duration backwards, and set schedules for bus transportation leave little time to extend the duration forwards. The "sandwiching" of breakfast therefore leaves little room for choice about standard temporal location and duration.

The preparation and serving of breakfast, together with cleanup afterwards, present no particular problems for women who do not work outside the home. The major tasks of starting a fire with wood or lighting a fuelled stove and cooking root crops, combined with boiling water for tea, take about an hour. Cleanup, including washing dishes, add about a half hour to female tasks in the morning. The time between sunrise and the start of the meal is sufficient for these tasks, provided that women can adjust the STL for personal hygiene and allocate time to these tasks when wage earners and school children have left the house. However, women wage earners are precluded from these options. Given their own time pressures and those of other household members, a morning meal with root crops as the "true food" presents definite time allocation problems. One way around them is to serve cold root crops leftover from preparation of the evening meal on the day before. But another is to substitute bread and other wheaten products, especially dry biscuits, for root crops in the morning meal. These food items are market goods which require virtually no labor to produce a meal.

The strain toward allocative efficiency in consumer choice can be seen in a comparison of Naivi and Lami household expenditures on wheaten products as a proportion of total expenditures on true food (31% and 43%,respectively). A full analysis would have to take into account the total pattern of household allocation of time and goods. The argument here is mainly suggestive and emphasizes a "strain" toward efficiency, not strict maximization. Many other factors intervene between household behavior and consumer choice to affect household efficiency, the culture of food and sexual division of labor being only two of them.

Naivi household allocation is characterized by a double substitution. Underutilization of labor is greater in Naivi than in Lami, and the value of labor is correspondingly less. In addition, fewer women per household in Naivi work outside the home, and their average income is less than women's in Lami. In Naivi, households substitute relatively inexpensive male time spent in home production of root crops and female time spent in home production of meals for relatively expensive purchases of market foods, including bread and wheaten products. Theirs is a relatively time intensive pattern of food expenditure and consumption. Nevertheless, some women do work for wages in Naivi, and the overall working class aspects of this urban settlement fit the notion that consumption of bread is important and, no doubt, increasing.

In contrast, the higher proportion of expenditures on bread and wheaten products by Lami households is evidence for a relatively goods intensive pattern of household production and consumption, one that substitutes relatively inexpensive market foods for relatively expensive male and female time. More men and women are employed on average per household in Lami than in Naivi, and the market value of both male and female time is higher for Lami workers than for their gender counterparts in Naivi. Lami men spend little time in home production of food compared to Naivi men. The result is that a large proportion of root crops consumed in Lami households are now market foods. Whether Lami households consume taro or bread, the choice is a substitution of market goods for household time. Here, also, the substitution is a double one because women also substitute easily prepared foods for ones that are time intensive. Bread or dry biscuits at the morning meal frees women's productive labor from the standard temporal location and duration of preparing the morning meal. For women who work outside the home, bread is a pragmatic choice over root crops at breakfast.

What the above example shows is that patterns of food expenditure can provide evidence for a process of household allocation. Substitutions of time for goods, goods for time, or goods for goods require adjustments among all household members' time spent in production and consumption. Where there is pooling of resources and standard meanings and social usages in distribution and consumption, such reallocations are unlikely to be made solely by one person. Even in the Fijian household, where there are strong cultural underpinnings to authoritative allocation, the realities of multiple sources of income and pressures from outside the household on individual members' expenditures disrupt what otherwise might be an efficient allocation of household time and goods. This is particularly apparent in Lami households, where women and younger male wage earners, especially, attempt to negotiate or bargain for shares of income contributed to the household pool or for meeting specific expenditures. A household with many working sons will share unequally in monthly mortgage payments while their working mothers and sisters will pay for food. One member of the household will be responsible for utility bills while another will pay for school fees, and so on. While limitations of space prevent further exploration of bargaining and its effect on intra-household allocation of time, including expenditures on particular food items, there is evidence that, for Lami households, such pragmatic choices have begun to affect the sexual division of labor. For example, in households with working women but without surplus labor, men share more in household tasks assigned by the normative division of labor to women. These include preparation of meals and washing clothes.

Conclusion

This chapter began with the notion that one of the properties of cultures is stability. It used that notion to explore the relationship between culture and consumer choice, on the assumption that stable cultures underlie the economist's notion of stable preferences. It also explored the relationship between cultural classification and the economist's notion of substitutions. In both cases, the conclusion is that cultural analysis is not opposed in any fundamental way to a formal economic analysis, but rather that the one presupposes elements of the other.

The second half of the chapter departs from the position that culture is stable and sets limits on pragmatic choices which, in turn, lack the force to effect transformation. It explored the colonial historical and market forces that have reworked the Fijian culture of food. It also examined the way in which household allocation affects the cultural order of food when material conditions of existence are altered. In both cases, the conclusion is that the market as a material and ideological force can and does rework apparently fixed and stable classifications, meanings, and preferences, but it does so in historically specific ways that are difficult to predict. The formation of preferences rests on a system of symbolic relationships between goods and their meanings, the arbitrariness of which ensures a secure place for historical and cultural analysis outside the formal rigor of neoclassical economics.

Table 1 Engel's Law and Income/Expenditure Comparisons Between
Naivi and Lami Households

	(1) Household income (xDI/wk) F$	(2) Household expenditures on food (x$/wk/hh)	(3) APC	(4) Income (xDI/wk/CU) F$	(5) Expenditures on food (x$/wk/CU)	(6) APC
Naivi n=11	105.09	59.76	.57	17.30	9.84	.57
Lami n=15	228.64	98.17	.43	31.42	13.47	.43

APC= average propensity to consume food=E/I, column (2)/(1); DI= disposable income; in 1982, $1.00 Fijian=$.88 U.S.; CU=consumption unit

Table 2 Size, Composition, and Source of Disposable Income in Naivi Settlement and Lami Subdivision

	Composition		Size	Source		
	(1) xDI	(2) xDI	(3) Total	(4) x number of incomes per household		
	(wages/ salaries) F$	(home production) mep	household xDI F$	M	F	T
Naivi n=11	87.64	17.45	105.09	1.36	.45	1.81
Lami n=15	226.27	2.68	228.94	1.80	1.33	3.13

DI=Disposable Income; mep= market equivalent prices

Table 3 Comparison of Household Expenditures on Food in Naivi and Lami

Cultural classification	Naivi			Lami		
	$	%	%total	$	%	%total
Core (true food)	**228.59**	**100**	**47**	**221.61**	**100**	**31**
root crops	141.75	62	29	91.47	41	13
wheaten products	71.87	32	15	96.42	43	13
rice-potatos	13.97	6	3	33.72	15	5
Fringe (relish)	**264.07**	**100**	**53**	**495.51**	**100**	**69**
vegetables	33.20	13	7	64.89	13	9
meat/fish	150.59	57	30	300.12	61	42
dairy products	21.23	8	5	54.80	11	7
other	59.05	22	12	78.68	16	11
Totals	**492.66**	**100**		**717.12**		**100**

Source: Worksheets on family budgets for Naivi and Lami expenditures on food

Notes: 1) See Appendix: Food Items in Naivi and Lami Family Budgets
2) amounts include market purchases and market equivalent prices for quantities listed in family budgets, April-May 1982 prices
3) largest single expenditure in category "other" is for sugar

Figure 1 Symbolic Oppositions Between Yams and Taro

	Yams	ː	**Taro**	ːː
Gender	male	ː	female	
Division of labor	male labor	ː	female labor	
Production	dry land	ː	wet land	
Polity	chiefly	ː	lineage and clan	
	hierarchical	ː	egalitarian	
Ceremonial exchange	gifts from commoners to chiefs	ː	gifts between clans	
	asymmetrical alliance	ː	symmetrical alliance	
	"first fruits" ritual	ː	marriage and death ritual	
Reproduction	elongate fruit/penis	ː	ovate fruit/womb	
	fertility of land	ː	fertility of people	
Consumption	contribution to diet small relative to symbolic value	ː	contribution to diet great relative to symbolic value	

Note: The list of oppositions is partial; the permutations are incomplete (especially for gender), and implications for practice remain insufficiently explored.

Figure 2 Cultural Ordering of Food Preferences

Cultural Classification (selected foods)	Rank Ordering of Preferences (ordinal ranking)	
Core (true food)	1.0	
taro and yams	1.1	
cassava	1.2	
bread	1.3	
rice/potatos	1.4	
Fringe (relish)	2.0	
meats	2.1	
pork		2.1.1
beef		2.1.2
chicken		2.1.3
sea food	2.2	
prawn		2.2.1
fish		2.2.2
small land crabs		2.2.3
bivalve shell fish		2.2.4
"Fijian" leaf vegetables	2.3	
young taro leaves		2.3.1
hibiscus leaves		2.3.2
ground ferns		2.3.3

Table 4 Standard Temporal Location of Weekday Meals in Naivi and Lami

	STL Breakfast		STL Lunch		STL Dinner	
	mean	mode	mean	mode	mean	mode
	am		am-pm		pm	
Naivi						
start	5.57	6.30	11.49	12.00	6.38	6.30
finish	8.36	NA	2.41	2.30	9.58	8.30
Lami						
start	6.13	6.30	11.44	12.00	5.46	6.30
finish	9.52	NA	2.13	2.00	10.09	NA

Source: Time budgets for Naivi and Lami households
Note: numbers refer to clock-time; NA=no modal time

Table 5 Household Allocation of Time to Meals in Naivi and Lami

	Weekday		Weekend day	
Meal	Naivi	Lami	Naivi	Lami
	(mean minutes per person per day)			
Breakfast	29	30	34	33
Lunch	51	42	39	41
Dinner	42	38	43	34

Source: Fiji Data Form, taken from time budgets of Naivi and Lami households.

Appendix: Share of Home Production in Total Expenditures on Food
Market Equivalent Prices for Naivi Households

HH NAIVI	CORE Root Crops			Vegetables			FRINGE Meat/Fish			Miscellaneous		
	MEP	$	total	MEP	$	total	MEP	$	total	MEP	$	total
203	10.00	0.00	10.00	1.10	0.60	1.70	0.75	8.25	9.00	0.30	2.00	2.30
205	10.00	3.00	13.00	0.40	0.85	1.25	0.00	9.34	9.34	0.24	2.17	3.41
207	16.00	0.00	16.00	2.40	2.70	5.10	0.00	1.89	1.89	5.90	1.88	7.78
209	27.50	0.00	27.50	1.05	0.00	1.05	0.00	5.58	5.58	1.50	1.96	3.46
210	10.50	0.00	10.50	1.20	1.86	3.06	0.00	14.97	14.97	0.00	11.83	11.83
214	8.00	3.00	11.00	0.80	0.35	1.15	0.00	9.50	9.50	0.00	3.15	3.15
217	2.00	2.00	4.00	0.00	1.40	1.40	0.00	6.67	6.67	0.00	4.40	4.40
218	11.00	2.00	13.00	0.80	0.00	0.80	2.25	1.98	4.23	0.00	2.61	2.61
219	11.50	3.00	14.50	6.70	3.70	10.40	12.80	27.12	39.92	9.08	8.62	17.70
228	15.25	0.00	15.25	2.70	1.05	3.75	18.50	5.20	24.00	0.25	0.80	1.05
231	0.00	7.00	7.00	0.40	3.14	3.54	1.00	24.49	25.49	0.00	1.66	1.66
Tot.	121.75	20.00	141.75	17.55	15.65	32.20	35.30	114.99	150.29	17.27	41.08	58.35

Notes:
1) Market Equivalent Prices taken from Department of Agriculture price quotes of various commodities at the Suva marketplace during the week of the family budget exercise, May 5-12, 1982. Prices are quoted in the Fiji Times column, "To Market . . . To Market . . . ."
2) The table shows the share of home production for all foods recorded on the appropriate section of the family budget, with a separate column for market purchases of those same foods. It does not show the share of home production as a proportion of total expenditures on food (see textfile NAIVIEXP).

Appendix: Share of Home Production in Total Expenditures on Food
Market Equivalent Prices for Lami Households

HH LAMI	CORE Root Crops			Vegetables			FRINGE Meat/Fish			Miscellaneous		
	MEP	$	tot	MEP	$	tot	MEP	$	tot	MEP	$	tot
311	0.00	15.00	15.00	0.00	5.22	5.22	0.00	28.52	28.52	0.00	5.87	5.87
312	0.00	9.00	9.00	0.30	3.58	3.88	0.00	26.37	26.37	1.92	5.68	7.60
313	2.40	1.00	3.40	0.40	3.40	3.80	0.00	18.05	18.05	0.24	1.82	2.06
314	0.00	2.00	2.00	0.00	4.40	4.40	0.00	14.80	14.80	0.00	9.89	9.89
303	7.50	0.00	7.50	1.20	2.80	4.00	0.00	25.67	25.67	1.40	4.17	5.57
304	3.00	2.00	5.00	2.05	1.10	3.15	0.00	3.96	3.96	1.05	1.20	2.25
306	1.75	0.00	1.75	0.00	13.50	13.50	0.00	7.97	7.97	0.12	8.69	8.81
307	5.00	0.00	5.00	0.00	3.50	3.50	0.00	26.70	26.70	0.00	8.81	8.81
318	0.00	5.50	5.50	0.00	0.84	0.84	0.00	21.52	21.52	0.00	3.08	3.08
320	6.00	0.00	6.00	0.40	2.50	2.90	0.00	20.40	20.40	0.00	3.95	3.95
326	2.00	7.00	9.00	0.80	3.73	4.53	0.00	33.08	33.08	0.50	2.53	3.03
327	0.00	2.00	2.00	0.00	7.05	7.05	0.00	10.49	10.49	0.00	1.38	1.38
330	0.00	1.50	1.50	0.00	3.50	3.50	0.00	5.42	5.42	0.00	7.07	7.07
332	0.00	6.00	6.00	0.00	0.80	0.80	0.00	25.00	25.00	0.00	8.60	8.60
335	0.00	7.00	7.00	0.40	1.10	1.50	0.00	10.55	10.55	1.70	1.56	3.26
Tot	27.65	58.00	85.65	5.55	57.02	62.57	0.00	278.50	278.50	6.93	74.30	81.23

Notes:
1) Market equivalent prices are taken from Department of Agriculture
price quotes on various commodities at Suva marketplace during the week
of the family budgets, July 1-7, 1982. Prices are quoted in the Fiji Times
column "To market . . . to market . . . ."
2) The table shows the share of home production for all foods recorded
on the appropriate section of the family budget, with a separate column
for market purchases of those same foods. It does not show the share of
home production as a proportion of total expenditures on food (see textfile
LAMIEXP).

242

Appendix: Food Items in Naivi and Lami Family Budgets

Fijian term	English term	Traditional food	New food
kakana dina	true food		
dalo	taro	x	
uvi	yam	x	
kumala	sweet potato	x	
uto	bread fruit	x	
vudi	plantain	x	
tavioka	tapioca		x
raisi	rice		x
pateta	potato		x
madrai	bread (made from wheat)		x
sikoni	scones		x
visiketi	biscuits		x
bani	buns		x
Weetbix	cereal (brand name)		x
corn flakes	cereal		x
kena i coi	relish		
rourou	young taro leaves	x	
bele	hibiscus leaves	x	
ota	ground ferns	x	
duruka	(Saccharum edule)	x	
dovu	sugar cane	x	
ika	fish (generic)	x	
vivili	shellfish (generic)	x	
kaikoso	(Lamelli branchiata)	x	
lairo	land crab	x	
mana	small land crab	x	
ura	prawn	x	
vuaka	pig	x	
toa	chicken	x	
bulumakau	cow		x
uro	dripping		x
masima	salt	x	
yaloka	eggs	x	
vuana	fruit (generic)	x	x
bini	green beans, tinned bake beans, peas		x
baigani	eggplant		x
tomata	tomato		x
varasa	onion		x
kaveti	cabbage		x

karoti	carrot		x
rokete	hot pepper		x
kari	curry		x
soia	soy sauce		x
suvu	soup	x	x
pinatibata	peanut butter		x
?	tinned peaches		x
?	tinned tomato sauce		x
?	Nestle cream (brand name)		x
?	margarine		x
?	honey		x
waiwai	salad or cooking oil		x
saimoni	tinned salmon, tuna, pilchards		x
bata	butter		x
suka	sugar		x
vakatubu	yeast		x
jami	jam, preserves		x

gunu	drink		
ti	tea		x
kafe	coffee		x
sucu	milk (cow)		x
waimoli	orange juice	x	x
?	cordial		x
jusi	Jucy (brand name)		x
?	Ovaltine (brand name)		x
?	Bongos, Monster Much, Twisties (brand names)		x
?	Topsy (brand name)		x
sweet	Indian sweets		x

Notes: the distinction between 'traditional' and 'new' reflects current usage (1982) in Naivi and Lami, confirmed by my observations; Fijian terms are in Bauan dialect; the list is inclusive of items recorded in the Family Budget study; many more new foods are recorded in Lami than in Naivi family budgets.

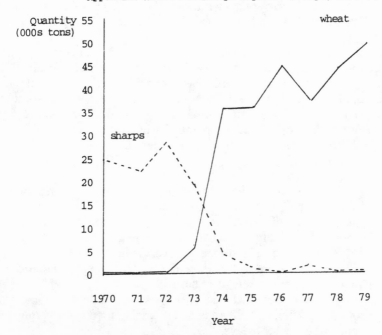

Appendix: Wheat and Sharps Imports to Fiji, 1970-79

Quantity (000s tons)

Year

Source: Parliamentary Paper 37, 1975, Table 3.2
Parliamentary Paper 50, 1978, Table 3.2

Notes

The following persons commented on all or part of earlier drafts of this paper: David Gray, for improving the overall style and organization; Hy Van Luong, for clarifying the argument; Stuart Plattner, for strengthening the discussion of social class; Manju Parikh and Victoria Bernal, for their skeptical approach to rationality; Ben Orlove, for clarifying the distinction between efficient allocation and negotiated arrangements; Nancy J. Pollock, for commenting on Fijian food culture and habits; George T. Jones, for helping with quantities. None is responsible for errors that remain. My continuing debt is to Mary Osborne, who was instrumental in the collection of data, to Doris, who can check the ethnography against our shared fieldwork, and to those in Naivi and Lami who participated in the Suva Fijian Study Area Survey and the time and family budget studies. Field research was conducted during 1981-82 with the support of NSF Grant BNS No. 8120354 and a Hamilton College Faculty Fellowship.

1. The Suva Fijian Study Area Survey questionnaire included demographic, economic, and social indicators for 92 primary variables. Residential areas were selected for observable differences and a convenience sample of Fijian households was taken for each area (an urban village, n=20; a working class settlement, n=38; a suburban subdivision, n=36.) For a more detailed description of samples and the sampling universe, see Gounis and Rutz 1986: Table 5. Data were collected by interviewing household heads and "housekeepers".

2. Two small samples were drawn from the SFSA population for the purpose of collecting time allocation and expenditure data (a working class settlement, n=11; an upper middle class subdivision, n=15.) Next-day interviews were used to collect time budget data. Activities from a 62 item activity code were recorded for every household member over 24 hours for a period of 8 days. Family budget data were collected by means of self-reporting diaries kept by all adult wage/salary workers in a household and an appointed "housekeeper" for each household. Data included daily market expenditures, home produced food consumed daily, and outgoing and incoming food gifts. Family budgets were collected daily for 8 days.

3. The panel data are suggestive but remain inadequate as a basis for capturing changes in total expenditures on food as incomes rise. Engel's Law refers to *changes* in income and expenditure for the *same* households over time, controlling for household size and composition. Longitudinal data are not available. The comparison between Naivi and Lami is based on multiple factors accompanying changes in income and expenditure.

4. For the difference in weekly total mean disposable income between Naivi and Lami households, t=2.9, .005>p>.0005 for a one-tailed test; for the difference in weekly total expenditures on food between Naivi and Lami households, t=2.3, .025>p>.01 for a one-tailed test.

246

5. For the difference in weekly total mean disposable income per consumption unit (>14 years of age=1.0 CU; >7<14=.7 CU; =<7=.4 CU) between Naivi and Lami households, t=1.54, .10>p>.05 for a one-tailed test; for the difference in weekly total mean expenditures on food per consumption unit between Naivi and Lami households, t=1.51, .10>p>.05 for a one-tailed test.

6. For the difference in weekly mean disposable money income from wages and salaries between Naivi and Lami households, t=2.31, .025>p>.01 for a one-tailed test; for the difference in weekly mean disposable income from home production of food (in market equivalent prices) between Naivi and Lami households, t=2.95, .005>p>.0005 for a one-tailed test.

7. The total number of food items in Naivi and Lami family budgets is a small fraction of the total number of food items available in large urban supermarkets, which continue to cater to European tastes.

8. While most Naivi and Lami households retain strong ties to rural villages of origin, they are firmly committed to urban life. Nearly a third of those employed in Naivi have found steady work as unskilled or semi-skilled laborers, and slightly over a third work in lower echelon service occupations. In Lami, over half of those employed work in professional, administrative, or managerial occupations in the public sector; another fifth work in clerical and other lower echelon service occupations (Gounis and Rutz 1986: Table 9). Occupational differences are correlated with educational levels. In Naivi, a quarter of the population has attained some secondary education but none has gone on to university. In Lami, over forty percent of the population has attained some secondary education and five percent have gone on to university (Gounis and Rutz 1986: Table 10).

9. Despite the fact that more than a third of the population of each residential area is under 15 years of age, the average number of years a person has been resident in the Suva Urban Area is 23 for Naivi and 16 for the subdivision (Gounis and Rutz 1986: Table 8). Naivi and Lami residents are not, for the most part, recent rural emigres, but a number are first generation urbanites. For the difference in the mean number of total incomes from wages and salaries between Naivi and Lami households, t=2.99, .005>p>.0005 for a one-tailed test; for the difference in the mean number of incomes from males between Naivi and Lami households, t=.63, and the hypothesis that there is no significant difference is accepted; for the difference in the mean number of incomes from females between Naivi and Lami households, t=1.29, .15>p>.10 for a one-tailed test.

10. The focus throughout this paper is on consumption characteristics of class. Household relations to capital are discussed more fully in Gounis and Rutz 1986. Suva Urban Area has three major industrial estates. Light

manufacturing industries include food processing, brewing, boat building and ship repair, chemicals, cement, ironworks, and many others. There are no massive assembly line or machine tending industries to produce proletarianization on a large scale. Nevertheless, industrial work conditions, wages and benefits, and time-disciplines pertain to workers in Suva Urban Area. There is a growing trade union movement, and in 1985 a Labour Party was formed to compete with the ethnically based Alliance and National Federation Parties (Lal 1986).

11. Pollock (1985) examines the semantics of Fijian food, in which she translates the Fijian term *kakana* as "edibles" and juxtaposes it to the term *gunu* or "drinks". Within this classification, Fijians eat tobacco but drink soft fruits or sugar cane (1985:197). In other words, the classification in this paper is meant neither to be exhaustive nor to be applicable to all areas of Fiji in all particulars. Regional differences in preference ordering and meaning obtain (Pollock: personal communication.) Pollock also discusses consumption of food items in non-meal categories (1985:200), which are excluded from the present analysis.

12. For the difference in weekly total mean expenditures on root crops between Naivi and Lami households, $t=1.50$, $.10>p>.05$ for a one-tailed test; for the difference in weekly mean consumption of root crops from home production (at market equivalent prices) between Naivi and Lami households, $t=3.11$, $.005>p>.0005$ for a one-tailed test; for the difference in the weekly mean money expenditures on root crops between Naivi and Lami households, $t=1.11$, $.15>p>.10$ for a one-tailed test. For the difference in weekly mean total expenditures on meat/fish between Naivi and Lami households, $t=.80$, $.20>p>.15$ for a one-tailed test; for the difference in weekly mean consumption of meat/fish from home production (at market equivalent prices) between Naivi and Lami households, $t=1.21$, $.15>p>.10$ for a one-tailed test; for the difference in weekly mean money expenditures on meat/fish between Naivi and Lami households, $t=1.58$, $.10>p>.05$ for a one-tailed test.

13. Stigler and Becker (1977) argue, to the contrary, that preference formation is stable over time and across cultural and class boundaries, and hence relatively unproblematic for purposes of economic analysis.

14. Bakeries sell a wrapped and sliced loaf for F$.47-F$.51. The price is prohibitive, but "taste" is also at issue. In contrast with the standard "long loaf", which is broken or cut into chunks and served ungarnished with tea, the sliced loaf is more suited to "refined" taste in small and more delicate sandwiches with a thin layer of filling--not hardy fare for people whose cultural preferences are for filling their bellies with quantities of true food. In Lami, some households will eat bread with butter, jam, or even peanut butter, and the sliced loaf can be seen occasionally.

References

Annual Statistical Abstracts, Fiji 1968
1970-71 Suva: Government of Fiji.

Becker, Gary S.
1965 Theory of the Allocation of Time.*Economic Journal* 75 (299): 493-517.

1976 *The Economic Approach to Behavior*. University of Chicago Press.

Braudel, Fernand
1980 History and the Social Sciences: The *Longue Duree*. in *On History*. trans. Sarah Matthews. New York: Harper and Row.

Calvert, James
1983 *Fiji and the Fijians*. Volume 2. Suva: Fiji Museum.

Douglas, Mary and Baron Isherwood
1979 *The World of Goods*. New York: Basic Books.

Douglas, Mary
1971 Deciphering a Meal. in C. Geertz, ed. *Myth, Symbol and Culture*. New York: Norton. Pp. 61-81.

Fiji, A Developing Australian Colony
1973 North Fitzroy, Victoria, Australia: I.D.A.

Fiji Times
1982 *Bread, Tea Cost More*. January 22.

Gounis, Konstantinos and Henry J. Rutz
1986 Urban Fijians and the Problem of Unemployment. in Christopher Griffin and Michael Davis, eds. *Fijians in Town*. Suva: University of the South Pacific. Institute for Pacific Studies.

Hocart, A.M.
1929 *Lau Islands, Fiji*. Honolulu: Bishop Museum Press.

Lancaster, Kelvin
1971 *Consumer Demand*. New York: Columbia University Press.

McGee, T.G.
1975 Food Dependency in the Pacific: A Preliminary Statement. *Development Studies Center Working Paper No. 2*, Research School of Pacific Studies, A.N.U., Canberra.

Michael, Robert T and Gary S. Becker
1973 On the New Theory of Consumer Behavior. *Swedish Journal of Economics* 75: 378-395.

Mintz, Sidney
1979 Time, Sugar, and Sweetness. *Marxist Perspectives.* Winter, 1979/80:56-73.

1985 *Sweetness and Power.* New York: Viking.

Pollock, Nancy J.
1985 The Concept of Food in a Pacific Society: A Fijian Example. *Ecology of Food and Nutrition 17*:195-203.

Rappaport, Roy
1963 Aspects of Man's Influence on Island Ecosystems: Alteration and Control. F. R. Fosberg, ed. *Man's Place in the Island Ecosystem.* Honolulu: Bishop Museum Press.

Rutz, Henry J.
1976 The Efficiency of Traditional Agriculture, Phases of Development, and Induced Economic Change in the Waidina Valley, Fiji. David C. Pitt, ed. *Development From Below.* The Hague: Mouton.

1977 Individual Decisions and Functional Systems. *American Ethnologist 4* (1): 157-181.

1987 Capitalizing on Culture: Moral Ironies in Urban Fiji*Comparative Studies in Society and History* 29 (3): 531-555.

n.d. Units of Time Budget Analysis. Manuscript.

in Fijian Household Practices and the Reproduction of Class. Richard Wilk,
press ed. *Studies in the Dmoestic Mode of Production.* Boulder: Westview.

Sahlins, Marshall
1962 *Moala.* Ann Arbor: University of Michigan Press.

1976 *Culture and Practical Reason.* University of Chicago Press.

Stigler, George
1945 The Cost of Subsistence. *Journal of Farm Economics* 27 (2): 303-414.

Stigler, George and Gary S. Becker
1977 *De Gustibus Non Est Disputandum.. The American Economic Review* 67 (2): 76-90.

Thaman, R. R.
1979   Food Scarcity, Food Dependency and Nutritional Deterioration in Small
       Pacific Island Communities. Paper presented at the 49th A.N.Z.A.A.S.
       Congress, Auckland, New Zealand. 24th January, 1979.

Turner, James
1984   True Food and First Fruits: Rituals of Increase in Fiji. *Ethnology 23:
       133-142.*

Walter, Michael A. H. B.
1978a Analysis of Fijian Traditional Social Organization: The Confusion of Local
       and Descent Grouping. *Ethnology* 17 (3): 351-366.

1978b An Examination of Hierarchical Notions in Fijian Society: A Test Case for
       the Applicability of the Term "Chief". *Oceania* 49 (1): 1-19.

Zerubavel, Eviatar
1981   *Hidden Rhythms.* Chicago: University of Chicago Press.

CONSUMERISM WITHOUT CAPITALISM: CONSUMPTION AND BRAND NAMES IN LATE IMPERIAL CHINA

Gary G. Hamilton and Chi-kong Lai

Introduction

In late imperial China, under both the Ming (1368-1644) and the Qing (1644-1911) dynasties, marketplaces across the country contained commodities that were distinguished for buyers by means of identifying labels, or what we now would call "trademarks" and "brand names." Chinese consumers, from peasant to official, routinely made informed distinctions about the kinds of products they would buy in the marketplace. That they made such distinctions is the topic of our paper.

We define brand names as any visible signs or devices used by individuals to identify their products or services (Cole, 1949). The signs must be ones that distinguish one line of goods or services from others similar in nature. These signs may consist of descriptive words, names, pictures, figures, numbers, symbols, or packages labels. These may be used individually or in combinations. These brand names may be a merchandise mark, a manufacturer's mark, or a dealer's mark. A trademark is the legal counterpart of the brand, and the two terms in the United States are essentially synonymous. [1]

Many researchers believe, as we discuss below, that the appearance of such product labels is usually associated with the development of capitalism. Although relevant, if not totally accurate for Europe, this generalization is, however, clearly inappropriate for China. Imperial China developed nothing like the capitalistic economy that formed in Western Europe by the eighteenth century. [2] Nonetheless, as early as the Sung dynasty (960-1279 A.D.), the imperial economy was extensively commoditized, so much so that Chinese economic historians (e.g., Fu, 1980; Lai, 1984; Lui, 1979; Peng, 1983; Wu, 1985) refer to the late imperial economy as being a "commodity economy" (shangpin jingji). A large number of these commodities--ranging from rice and tea to cloth and metal products-bore some type of product label (Lai and Hamilton, 1986).

In this paper, we discuss two aspects of this commoditized economy. First, we analyze product differentiation, emphasizing in particular the use of brand names. We show that these product labels were used as aids in marketing products, rather than as a means to regulate the activities of producers and merchants, which is the role that merchant and guild marks played in Medieval Europe. Second, we argue that the use of brand names is a production and marketing strategy directly related to the circumstances of Chinese social structure. Late imperial Chinese society was not rigidly stratified into fixed, hereditarily determined classes. Instead the class structure was fluid and a person's or a family's location in this structure, relative to others, was, at best, ambiguous and open to interpretation. We argue that this ambiguity allowed products to be used as status markers, which encouraged both the commoditization of the Chinese economy and the use of brand names in that economy to differentiate products. To establish the significance of this interpretation, we must place our observations within a comparative perspective. To this end, we will begin our discussion with a summary of the use of product labels in Western Europe.

Brand Names in Western Economies

Researchers usually do not study, or even mention, the presence of commodities bearing brand names. What little has been done is found primarily in marketing and advertising research (e.g., Borden, 1947; Coles, 1949; Davis, 1967) and in historical studies of patents and trademark laws (e.g., Schechter, 1925; Dutton, 1984). Recently, however, a few historians and social scientists have started looking more closely at patterns of consumption in Western societies (e.g., Jones, 1973; Ewen, 1976; McKendrick, Brewer and Plumb, 1982; Fox and Lears, 1983; Marchand, 1985). A uniform characteristic of these studies is that analysts regard the origin and widespread use of brand names as being an aspect of capitalist development.

Two types of studies are particularly important in this regard. First, several scholars mention the absence of brand names in medieval Europe. The seminal study is that by Schechter (1925). Schechter explains in his history on trademark laws that merchant and artisan marks were not brands names in the modern sense of the term. Instead,

the characteristics of the typical craftsman's mark of the Middle Ages were: (1) that it was compulsory, not optional; (2) that its purpose was the preservation of gild standards of production and the enforcement of gild or other local monopolies rather than the impressing on the mind of the purchaser the excellence of the product in question and thereby the creation of a psychological need for that product; (3) that, consequently, while the modern trade-mark is distinctly an asset to its owner, the medieval craftsman's mark was essentially a liability. (1925:78)

Schechter explains that the difference between modern and medieval commodity marks results from differences in production and distribution systems between the two eras, particularly in the relations between producers and consumers. For the majority of people in medieval society, "wants were comparatively few and unchanging." People "were supplied by neighboring craftsmen; consumer and producer stood in direct relation with one another." Each town of any size had its own merchants and artisans, who in turn organized guilds through which they sought to monopolize production and trade. The guilds "strove by every means at their disposal to prevent 'foreigners'--as the merchants coming from a town five miles away might be described--from competing with their gild" (1925:41-42).

Merchant and artisan marks were the devices by which guilds sought to exclude outsiders and to control the economic activities of insiders. Although Schechter's thesis is dated and too simple at times[3], historians of marketing and advertising (e.g., Borden, 1947;Coles, 1949; Davis, 1967), based largely on references to Schechter's study, argue that brand names start only in the modern era.

This thesis largely coincides with recent scholarship on patterns of consumption in modern society. A growing number of studies discuss the appearance, in the eighteenth century, of differentiated consumer products and the importance of these products for the success of Western capitalism. Mokyr (1977), Jones (1973), and most recently McKendrick, Brewer and Plumb (1982) argue that the eighteenth century English economy became commoditized in response to changing patterns of consumption. An expanding middle class, according to their analyses, began to require affordable items of fashion and comfort in order to emulate the accouterments of the elite. McKendrick (1982: 13) believes that this shift in demand is of such importance as to proclaim a "consumer revolution" in eighteenth century England. "[C]onsumer behavior was so rampant and the acceptance of commercial attitudes so pervasive that no one... should doubt that the first of the world's consumer societies had unmistakably emerged by 1800." This demand for fashionable products created an opportunity for manufacturers to explore ways to streamline their production and to market their products. Accordingly, such individuals as Josiah Wedgwood, the mass producer of English porcelains, began to create and to advertise brand name products designed to distinguish their wares from similar lines produced by competitors (Jones, 1973; McKendrick, 1982).

Research on later periods of Western capitalism (e.g., Ewen, 1976; Fox and Lears, 1983; Marchand, 1985) uniformly emphasize the interrelations of mass consumers markets, the growth of large corporations, and advertising and marketing based upon products having brand names. Consumerism and brand names, so the theory goes, went hand in hand to produce capitalist production as we know it today.

Even though their significance can certainly be debated,[4] that brand names are an important feature of modern Western capitalism can hardly be disputed. We doubt, however, that England was the world's first consumer society and that consumerism only occurs under conditions of capitalism.

Brand Names in Pre-industrial China

The appearance of brand names in late imperial China suggests the presence of a highly developed economy and of a large group of people interested in consuming for whatever reason. A brief summary of this economy and of the potential consumers is in order before we turn to product differentiation.

According to Albert Feuerwerker (1984:321-2), "late imperial China-- from the tenth century to the nineteenth--experienced in world perspective a remarkable millennium of premodern economic growth...[But] neither the direct nor the indirect influences of the state on the economy were major factors determining the nature and rate of this premodern economic growth." What explain the growth and everyday conduct of the the economy, concludes Feuerwerker (1984:322), are "the dynamics of the dominant private sector of the economy." In another location, Feuerwerker (1985) estimates this economy, from the Sung dynasty (A.D. 960-1279) on, had much higher flows of commodities in absolute and probably in per capita terms than any other society in the world before the nineteenth century, with the possible exception of Western Europe in the eighteenth century.

What was this dominant private sector like? G. William Skinner (1964-5; 1977) has shown that the late imperial economy was interlinked through hierarchies of marketplaces. Skinner's research shows that the Chinese marketing structure began at the bottom, in the standard market towns. Complex distribution systems, taking in ever larger urban centers, built up from those local systems. By late imperial times, Skinner (1977; 1985) believes that China lacked an integrated national marketing system, but nonetheless contained ten major marketing systems and within those ten systems, many, many markets of all sizes. According to his calculations, in 1893 the economic centers of China could be enumerated as follows: "standard market towns (27,000-28,000), intermediate markets towns (ca. 8,000), central market towns (ca. 2,300), local cities (669), greater cities (200), regional cities (63), regional metropolises (20), and central metropolises (6)" (1977: 286).

So many markets of so many different sizes and mostly outside of regular government control implies a very lively commercial world and many interested buyers, and that is what we find. Wu Chengming gives us the best estimate of the volume of the major items going through these markets, as is shown in Table One.

Table One

Estimates of the Important Commodities in 1840

Commodity	Volume	Value (1,000 Taels)	% of Total Value
Grain	24.5 Billion Catties (JIN)	16,333.3	42.14
Cotton	2,555,000 Piculs(DAN)	1,277.5	3.30
Cotton Fabric	315,177,000 Bolts (PI)	9,455.3	24.39
Silk	71,000 Piculs (DAN)	1,202.3	3.10
Silk Fabric	49,000 Piculs (DAN)	1,455.0	3.75
Tea	2,605,000 Piculs (DAN)	3,186.1	8.22
Salt	3.22 Billion Catties (JIN)	5,852.9	15.10

All of these items, with the possible exception of silk, were not luxury goods. Rather they were daily necessities, which were produced, by peasants and artisans, on a massive scale for sale in the marketplace. In addition to these items of great volume, there were, of course, many other commodities for sell in lesser volumes. Some of these products can be classified as luxury goods, most as simply "consumer products."

What groups served as the major consumers? If one disregards social structure for the moment, the urban population alone probably provided a sufficient number of buyers to account for the presence of brand names. In late imperial China, as late as 1820, only around 7 percent of China's 350,000,000 people (about 25 million) lived in urban areas above standard market towns, but even such a low percentage constitutes a slightly larger figure than that found in Europe during the same period. A high estimate for the population in all of Europe in 1800 was 205,000,000 persons, of which a little over 12% (around 24,600,000 persons) lived in urban areas (Hohenberg, 1985: 84). For China, however, confining consumers to the urban population results in a figure that is far too low, because the extensive and comparatively wealthy members of lineage groups, who made up the gentry class and who we know consumed many luxury products, were primarily based outside of major urban centers until fairly late in the nineteenth century (Ch'u, 1962: 168-199). This local elite made up a significant percentage of the total population. Undoubtedly the rural based portion of this group and the wealthiest segment of the peasantry constituted the primary consumers in the countryside, which gave standard market towns in China their extraordinary vitality.

Now let us look more closely at product differention in the marketplace. Our research to date turned up the same general types of commodity labels that are found in modern Western societies. First, many products, particularly foodstuffs, were divided into subtypes (lei) that in principle differentiated among generically different commodities[5]. For instance, Qing consumers could choose from among many different kinds of rice, teas, drugs, liquors, and wines (Chuan, 1979; Chen, 1984; Lin, 1985; Zeng, 1980). As in the West, this type of commodity label need not constitute a brand name. Second, many products, especially handicrafts, were differentiated by explicit brand names (biaoji) that identified the producer (either a firm or individual) or the area of production. Third, many products were differentiated by brand names (hao) that specifically identified the sellers (a firm or group of merchants). Like contemporary Western brand names, some biaoji and hao labels identified the name of a firm or person, and others identified qualities associated with the product.

Although clear in principle, in practice these three types of identifying labels are difficult to distinguish from each other. For instance, types of tea were finely graded, and, like European wines, their distinguishing characteristics were known to differ qualitatively depending upon the area of growth and the time of harvest[6]. Choosing from among many grades of a certain type of tea was further complicated by the fact that tea was marketed under both producer and seller labels. What applied to tea also applied to cotton and cotton cloth and to a considerable range of other commodities.

In fact, we (Lai and Hamilton, 1986) have verified the use of brand names in a wide range of commodities. Taking the most restricted definition of brand names, we have found either biaoji or hao labels on the following late imperial products: cotton cloth, items of clothing, porcelain, boots, tea, wine, medicine and herbs, scissors, needles, copper locks, copper mirrors, gold and silver bullion, hair ornaments, jewelry, jade items, writing brushes, writing paper, ink sticks, ink stones, lacquerware, books, and bank drafts. In no case was the brand name a signature affixed to a one-of-a-kind product; instead it was the means of differentiating an entire line of products from that of competitors. And in all cases the brand names were on products that were distributed interregionally for sale.

Many of the earliest brand names were related to the regional origins of the commodities. Examples of famous products widely available in major urban markets include Shaoxing wine, Jianzhou tea, Luchou silk piece goods, Xiangxiu (Hunan embroidery), Yuexiu (Guangdong embroidery), Shuxiu (Sichuan embroidery), Suxiu (Suzhou embroidery), Shujin (Sichuan cotton cloth), Huizhou ink stones and brushes, Fuzhou paper, Suzhou New Year prints, Yixing teapots and cups, and Jingdezhen porcelains (Deng, 1926:6-10; Quanguo Mingtechanpin, 1982). Such regional distinctions are not simple area designations. These products were widely available in most large urban centers, and in the richer regions of China, many could be found even in small markets[8]. For instance, one source for late Ming (cited by Fu, 1957:15-16; Li Renpu, 1983:199) lists 42 different kinds of cotton cloth available in the market of Yanshan, a small town in Jiangsu.

These regional labels functioned as brand names because the distribution of such products was normally controlled, in a specific location, by particular merchant groups. These merchant groups typically promoted their monopolized regional products through the use of signboards. These signboard advertisements can be readily seen in paintings as early as the eleventh century (Lai and Hamilton, 1986). Because of the merchant control of distribution channels, regional and even generic qualities of products acted as forms of brand name identification. They were devices used to promote sales.

A clear indication of the widespread promotion of differentiated products is found in the many lists of famous products that were published in late imperial times. Many of these lists contain products known by the firm names or by honorific labels symbolizing the product. Local gazetteers usually have a section devoted to famous local products, including manufactured products. For example, the 1817 edition of Songjiang fuzhi (6,19-23) lists different kinds of famous local commodities, such as cloth, blankets, shoes, papers, lanterns, and wine in addition to agricultural products. Besides supplying information about agricultural conditions, government officials frequently reported to the throne on the variety of products available in local markets, in addition to the price of

258

different kinds of rice (Chuan and Kraus, 1975). One can also find descriptions of locally available products in the "notes" and diaries of traveling scholars. But by far the most important of such lists were the ones complied by the imperial household (Zheng, 1979:62-3; Qingshi ziliao, 2,190-236). These lists contain those products judged fit for imperial consumption, and thus to be purchased by the imperial household itself (Pan, 1758: 41-42). To have a product on this list assured success and prosperity for its manufacturer, as it did for those manufacturers in England who could place upon their products the words, "by special appointment to H.M. the King." That so many lists were compiled certainly suggests that the availability and diversity of available commodities was an important fact to the Chinese of late imperial times.

Brief case studies of three different types of commodities will help clarify the market dynamics that underlay product differentiation. The first case, that of apothecary shops or drugstores, exemplifies brand names identifying the sellers of natural products. Chinese drugs and medicines, including pills, sticking plasters, and herbs come in a wide variety of subtypes (lei), but many also have explicit brand names. For example, "Lei Yunshang ciushenwan" (Famous pills of Lei Yunshang's drugstore) were favorite pills in Shanghai around 1700, and they are still favorites there today (Lei, 1984:230-1).

There are many other examples of brand names for drugs, but perhaps the most famous is that of the drugstore in Beijing, the Tongrentang (Yue, 1980:152-174). In the Yungzheng period (1723-1735), the Tongrentang became the seller of drugs and medicines for the imperial household. Capitalizing on imperial endorsement, the owners of the drugstore would invite all the candidates for each civil service examination held regularly in Beijing to the drugstore and would give them free samples. The owner hoped that, when these candidates returned to their home provinces, they would spread the word that the quality of the products from this store exceeded the quality of that available at other drugstores. Because of its fame, the store eventually opened independent branches in other large cities in China.

Most Chinese medicines are natural products, but even so the *hao* of the firm selling the products become an important indication of the quality and reliability of the products being sold. The identification of the selling firm was also important for manufactured products, as the following examples of the manufacture of metal products show.

The oldest brand name that we could unambiguously identify is the merchant mark, recorded in the Northern Sung (A.D. 960-1126), of the Liu family's needle shop in the city of Jinan in Shangdong province (Liu Guoji, 1982). The firm used a picture of a rabbit as its *hao*. This label appeared on the firm's signboard outside the shop, along with 28 words describing the excellence of the workmanship (gongfu) and of the high quality steel that went into the needles sold in the shop. The needles became known for their label.

Many other kinds of metal products were also made and sold on the basis of brand names. Such a case was that of scissors. In the Shunzhi period (1644-1661) of the Qing dynasty, Wang Mazi established a scissors shop in Beijing. Besides manufacturing scissors, this shop also bought high quality scissors made by other workshops. Everything he sold in his shop he marked with the shop name, which was his own name. Because of the high quality of the shop's scissors, Beijing residents, including the emperor, preferred to buy scissors that had been marked "Wang Mazi" (Pan,1758: 42).

Equally revealing is the case of the "Zhang Xiaoquan" scissors. In 1663 Zhang Sijia established a scissors shop in Hangzhou, and used "Zhang Dalong" as the name on the signboard outside his shop, as well as on the scissors themselves. Zhang's scissors were so well made that the brand became an item of popular consumption in Hangzhou and beyond. By the time Zhang Sijia died, there were many imitations of Zhang's scissors being sold that bore his brand name. Zhang Xiaoquan, Sijia's son, wanted to stop the pirating, so he decided to change the firm's name. Accordingly, he remade the firm's signboard and marked his scissors with his own name. He maintained and supposedly even improved the quality of his product, so that the "Zhang Xiaoquan" scissors became well known not only locally, but also throughout the country (Zhu, 1983: 22-25; Xiao and Zheng, 1982: 29-34).

In these examples, the brand name identified both the name of the firm manufacturing and selling the products and the name affixed upon the products themselves. Brand names for cotton cloth show other variations. Cotton cloth is a particularly important case because it occupies, by Wu's estimate, almost 25% of the total domestic trade. (See Table One)

The cotton fabric production was mostly centered in Songjiang prefecture, which is located in the Yangzi delta. According to Ye Mengzhu (1981: 157-8), a native scholar of Songjiang living in the seventeenth century, Songjiang cloth was classified into three categories by width. The widest cut of cloth, called biaobu, was shipped to Shaanxi, Shanxi, and the capital, Beijing. The middle category of cloth, labeled zhongji, was made for markets in Hunan, Hubei, Jiangxi, Guangdong, and Guangxi. The narrowest cut, measuring about one foot (chi), was called xiaobu, and it was marketed only in Raozhou and other districts in Jiangxi.[8] Besides being classified by width, Songjiang cloth was also differentiated by various types of woven patterns and by merchant seals. Even in remote areas, such as Guizhou, some cloth included advertisements (e.g., "A fine product circulated in Beijing.") woven directly into the fabric itself (Lai and Hamilton, 1986). According to 1512 edition of Songjiang fuzhi, the prefecture gazetteer, "As for cotton cloth...every [manufacturing] village and market town has its own varieties and names; the list is inexhaustible" (quoted by Nishijima, 1984:49). The edition goes on to list, in a special section on cloth, 15 different types. Within the distinctions made by producing regions, there was also an additional variation based upon the quality of weave. The most expensive cotton weave was known as "three shuttle cloth." One bolt of this cloth could be exchanged for one bolt of silk, both of which sold for about two taels per bolt. Ordinary cotton cloth sold from .3 to .4 taels per bolt (Wiens 1976; Nishijima, 1984).

In addition to these distinctions made by manufacturers, there were also those made by distributors. Cloth merchants, usually buying from producers in local market towns, were known by the quality of cloth they handled. To certify the cloth they would sell, in turn, to long distant merchants, they made a mark, known as a jitou (loom-head), at the end of each bolt of cloth they collected for resale.

The importance of these jitou brand names, and how they worked, can be gleaned from a late Qing novel, Sanyi Bitan (1827). In the story, Wang Yimei was one of the largest cloth distributors among the famous Xinan merchants (i.e., merchants from Huihou, Anhui Province). On his firm's signboard, he used his given name, Yimei, and he paid jihu (families involved in textile production) to place "Yimei" at the end of each bolt. Using this method, Wang developed a national market for his product and sold one million bolts annually. Although fictitious, the example is backed up by stone inscriptions showing that for the late imperial period, long distance cloth merchants made their decisions about which cloth to buy based upon merchant marks; firms having a reputation for honesty and quality would have their mark accepted above those of uncertain reputation (Shanghai beike: 84-88). Undoubtedly, because cloth marked with certain merchant chops would bring higher prices, the stone inscriptions also record complaints that some merchants using fraudulent marks would try to sell inferior cloth (Shanghai beike: 202-3).

In each of these three cases--herbs, iron products, and cloth--brand names were the chief means by which products were distinguished from each other. The forms of these brand names, however, were not consistent. As with brand names in the West, some identified sellers, some producers, some distributors, and some the heroic attributes of the products themselves. Consistent or not, their widespread use suggests that brand names were very important.

It seems likely that the use of brand names facilitated the widespread distribution of products, by creating within a product area needs and desires for a range of differentiated commodities. For instance, Songjiang cottons, which a 1534 gazetteer (cited by Nishijima, 1984: 30) called "finer than brocade," was distributed throughout all of China and, according to Chao Kang (1977: 50) and Wu Chengming (1985: 232-4), was an important export item in the nineteenth century that went to Japan, Southeast Asia, Europe, and the United States. Wu (1985: 232-4) estimates that the Songjiang merchants sold 20 million bolts of cotton fabrics during the Ming period and 30 million bolts during the Qing.

There are indications that many products bearing brand names were purchased by ordinary people all over the country, most of whom probably lived in urban areas. Brand names almost certainly served to differentiate commodities within a product sector, so that once obtaining a reputation for quality or even simply prestige, a product could be sold at a higher price. A good example of this process is the spreading demand for tea brought on by tea books. By late imperial times, over one hundred books on consuming tea had been published (Lai and Hamilton, 1986). These books discussed various types and brand names of tea and advised readers, for instance, which brands were most suitable to present as gifts for officials. These brands became famous throughout China, were widely circulated in most large urban areas, and sold for prices far above lesser known or less prestigious brands. Much the same situation prevailed for brands of wines, silks, and fine cotton cloth.

Brands names, therefore, created subclasses of goods within product areas, some of which sold at prices that only the rich could afford. The finest rhinoceros horn from Tongrentang and "three shuttle cloth" are examples of consumer products purchased by those, as the saying goes, who care to have "the very best." In premodern economies, luxury goods have typically been those commodities consumed only by the upper class, those who had the privilege and wherewithal to have what was denied to others. But in late imperial China, product differentiation allowed products to be judged along continua of price, quality, and desirability, so that people could buy according to their means and status, even according to their aspirations for the future. This kind of product differentiation is the mark of a consumer economy.

The Structural Sources of Consumerism

It was not until the beginning of the eighteenth century that the English economy began to be oriented towards consumer classes, as opposed to individual patrons. By contrast, the Chinese economy had become a consumer economy several centuries earlier. As mentioned above, many economic historians correlate consumerism and capitalism, but for China this correlation is clearly inappropriate. Although a generation of Mainland historians have searched for the "sprouts of capitalism" in China's "feudal" past, there is every indication that no such sprouts existed. Commodity manufacture remained tied to peasant-based handicraft production. Merchants continued as merchants only until they became successful; then they would become landlords. Handicraft and merchants firms were family based, were usually quite small in size, and represented discrete economic operations; each step in the economic process remained organizationally separate from every other step. China's premodern economy was not moving in a direction that would lead to an independent origin for industrial capitalism; on that score almost all Western analysts now agree.[9]

If Chinese consumerism is not caused by "capitalist sprouts," then what is its explanation? Alexis de Tocqueville (1969: 466-467), one of the few nineteenth century theorists to recognize the profound influence of social structure on the conduct of everyday life, provides a structural explanation of consumer oriented production that very useful in understanding the Chinese case.

> Craftsmen in aristocratic societies work for a strictly limited
> number of customers who are very hard to please. Perfect

workmanship gives the best hope of profit. The situation if very different when privileges have been abolished and classes intermingled and when men are continually rising and falling in the social scale...(The fluctuation in family fortunes creates) a crowd of citizens whose desires outrun their means and who will gladly agree to put up with an imperfect substitute rather than do without the object of their desire altogether. The craftsman easily understands this feeling, for he shares it. In aristocracies he charged very high prices to a few. He sees that he can now get rich quicker by selling cheaply to all. Now, there are only two ways of making a product cheaper. This first is to find better, quicker, more skillful ways of making it. The second is to make a great number of objects which are more or less the same but not so good. In a democracy every workman applies his wits to both these points....Craftsmen in democratic ages do not seek only to bring the useful things they make within the reach of every citizen, but also try to give each object a look of brilliance unconnected with its true worth.

Tocqueville is quoted here at length, because his analysis is helpful in understanding the complex institutional differences between the economies in Europe and China. The structural explanation he offers requires that economic activity be seen holistically, as embedded in a social order. More specifically, in this passage, as elsewhere, he argues that the causal relationship between production and consumption is only indirect. It is indirect because both are linked to one another through particular sets of social relationships; both result from the situational logic arising out of structural configurations. In this citation, Tocqueville contrasts, in an typological fashion, two strategies of commodity production, one found in societies with aristocratic class structures and the other in societies without clearly defined classes.

These two strategies of commodity production help to illuminate the large structural differences between China and Europe. In medieval Europe, there existed a clearly delineated class structure with very limited mobility between classes; this is an aristocratic class structure in Tocqueville's terms. The important aspects of this structural configuration in regards to the situational logic of participants are (1) the rigidity of class boundaries and (2) large differences in wealth and privilege between classes, which results in clear sumptuary distinctions between social groups. This situational logic favors a society in which patterns of consumption are class specific. Wealth being concentrated in a small, relatively stable group of nobles, the finest artisans produced exclusively for this group. What they produced was of such quality and expense and was so exclusively designed for people of that level that these artisans served no other class. One need only remember the accounts in Benvenuto Cellini's Autobiography to be convinced what a "master's piece" consisted of and to whom it was sold. To be sure, other artisans served other classes, but the other classes did not consume the same types of goods. In general, it would seem that an aristocratic class structure encourages personalistic strategies of commodity production, with craftsmen attempting to produce for people whom they personally know (Hilton, 1985).

Class specific consumption patterns continued throughout much of Europe until very eve of the French Revolution (Sabel and Zeitlin, 1985:166). To some extent, England and perhaps the Lowlands are the exception here. In these nations of shopkeepers, the rising level of living among non-nobles created a demand for affordable luxuries (Jones, 1973; McKendrick, Brewer, and Plumb, 1982). This demand was less obvious in most of the rest of Europe (Sabel and Zeitlin, 1985). Even in England, however, before this middle ranked group reached sufficient numbers and a sufficiently high standard of living to influence production, the artisan economy was still largely located in urban centers, was directed towards wealthy patrons, and had its structure rooted in powerful urban guilds that had the support of the king's laws (Berger, 1980; Hilton, 1985). As Braudel (1982) describes, by the seventeenth century, the increasing volume of interregional and international trade fundamentally altered this artisan economy. It was only with the expansion of interregional marketing networks that upper class demand reached beyond local producers, which in turn enlarged the middle class and promoted rural handicraft production[10.] It is at this point that brand names in the West begin to take on their modern meaning.

In China, the system of stratification was quite different from that found in Europe. Of course, China was not democratic, even in Tocqueville's broad meaning of that term. But the structural similarities between Tocqueville's America and late imperial China are nonetheless striking. In both locations the situational logic produced by social structure was similar enough to result in similarities in the practice of production and consumption.

Late imperial China and nineteenth century America were fundamentally decentralized societies, both in terms of politics and society. In the more market-oriented northeast, the main political and social unit in nineteenth century America was the township. In these small to medium sized cities that dotted the American landscape outside of the South, the predominate stratificational pattern was one of gradations in wealth, stretching from the very poor to the very rich, ambiguous class divisions, and a belief in, as well as the fact of, mobility up and down the social scale. According to Tocqueville, and largely substantiated by numerous studies documenting life in America (Taub, 1974; Lockridge, 1985), what one consumed--the location of one's house, the style of one's clothes, the denomination of one's religion--invidiously marked one's station in life. Moreover, at least since Tocqueville's time, both foreign and American observers have believed the United States, sometimes in rather crass terms, to be the epitome of a highly commoditized, consumer society. It became a society in which brand name differentiation was one of the chief strategies of the capitalist production (Ewen, 1976; Chandler, 1977).

Like America, late imperial China was fundamentally decentralized; its class structure formed ambiguous continua based on levels of wealth, power, and status; and people's location within this structure, to use Ho Ping-ti's (1964) term, was "fluid." Overlapping authority structures--village and lineage councils, temple and fellow regional associations, merchants guilds, formal and informal gentry organizations--dominated local society and reduced the impact of the Chinese state. In the Qing dynasty, state officials, numbering around 20,000, governed a population that reached 400,000,000 (Bastid, 1985:70). Furthermore, most officials were rotated every two or three years and were forbidden to serve in their native province, both measures preventing them from establishing roots in local society. The relatively light supervision of the state and the intertwined and coercive networks within local society generated a largely self-regulating and self-determining society.

This local society had ambiguous class divisions. By late imperial times there were no landowning classes in the European sense (Wiens, 1980; Rowe, 1985). In northern China, most landowners were peasants who farmed their own land. In central and southern China, where there were much higher percentages of tenant farmers, landlords could not claim the right to the topsoil of their own land. The size of even the largest landowners were generally modest, especially by European standards. Moreover, the land owned was not consolidated into a manor-like estate, but rather was in scattered plots. Accordingly, most landlords had very little to do with making agricultural decisions. Tenants and free-holding peasants made the critical economic decisions about what to grow and how to grow it. Most landlords were absentee, living in nearby cities. Partible inheritance patterns, in which all sons equally divided their father's estate upon his death, continually divided land ownership, tenant topsoil rights, and all other forms of wealth. The partible inheritance created the proverbial pattern of a three generation cycle marking the rise and fall of families.

Gaining and maintaining wealth and status was a preoccupation of most Chinese (Ho, 1964). Families developed diversified strategies; some sons studied for the examinations in order to become officials, while others became merchants. Families and lineage segments would compete with one another over access to lineage resources (Baker, 1979), and lineages would compete, sometimes violently, over area resources (Lamley, forthcoming).

The constant rise and fall of family wealth and position and the uncertainty of one's family's status at any one point accentuated the use of material symbols to mark status (Hamilton, 1977). The Chinese, being extremely conscious of the accouterments of daily life, developed mass consumerism to a fine art. One indication of mass consumerism is found in the widespread use of brand name products, as we have discussed above. But other examples abound[11]. One of the most striking examples of conspicuous consumption is the practice of footbinding. Beginning in the Sung and becoming widespread in the Ming and Qing dynasties, the practice of footbinding spread down the social scale to encompass daughters of rich peasants, of anyone who hoped to get their daughter married to a man of even modest means (Levy, 1967:37-63).

In this atmosphere of status competition, the Chinese economy was oriented toward a strategy of producing for a largely anonymous group of potential buyers. A more artisan-like strategy of serving an aristocratic class gradually disappeared in the Sung dynasty as this class itself began to disappear[12]. By the late imperial times, one finds an economy quite different from the European medieval and early modern economies. In late imperial times, we find an economy, as we have shown in our discussion of brand names, more like what Tocqueville suggests would occur in a democratic society. The handicraft economy was not directed at a small, local, and known groups of wealthy families. Instead, producers, themselves participating in this society without rigidly defined classes, developed an array of strategies to produce commodities for many people of middling wealth, a few people who were very rich, and a majority who were poor. Handicraft producers marketed their products to take advantage of the consumer continuum.

In this type of economy, brand names became an important means of differentiating similar products produced by different people. Producers would attempt to gain advantages over other producers by labeling their product in some fashion and then by having that product consumed by "discriminating" people, whether wealthy or not. Producing strategies rested on turning out distinctive products in sufficient quality to obtain and maintain a good reputation. As several people have noted, the very success of this economy to supply the commodities desired by buyers worked against its changing quickly in the nineteenth century, when Western influence began (Crow, 1937; Hamilton, 1977). The Chinese economy was already consumer oriented, and it already supplied what the consumers wanted.

These differences between the European and Chinese preindustrial economies is captured in the surprise of the Spaniards who travelled to China in the sixteenth century. They found the main streets of the city "entirely devoted to trade and artisans' shops" (Braudel 1981:544). Regarding this location Father de Magaillans observed,

> This custom serves public convenience, because a good part of the streets in our towns [in Europe] are lined with the houses of wealthy people; and one is thus obliged to go a very long way to the market or the ports to obtain necessary articles, while in Peking--and it is the same in all the other towns of China-- everything one could want to buy for maintenance, subsistence and even for pleasure, is to be found at one's doorstep, because these small houses are shops, taverns or stalls (quoted by Braudel 1981: 545).

266

Late imperial China was a consumer society, and it was physically laid out that way, not unlike Western societies have become today.

Conclusion

Consumerism is an important, but rarely studied aspect of most economies, the late imperial economy included. Most research on both traditional and modern economies emphasize production. Factory owners and their relations with workers, the influence of landlords and local communities on peasant agriculture, the familial foundation of proto-industrialization--these are now familiar topics for historians, anthropologists, and sociologists to study. Less frequently researchers investigate distribution, usually through studies on ethnic merchants groups. Although forming half of the supply and demand equation, consumption, however, is almost never studied. Production, and occasionally distribution, is the stuff of books, consumption the content of footnotes.

The reasons for this omission are understandable. Production, on the one hand, is believed to be theoretically more significant and is empirically more well defined. Consumption, on the other hand, is more difficult to study and does not seem theoretically so significant. People produce in ways that researchers can document, but consumption is accomplished in innumerable, often ephemeral acts and is scattered among untold transactions.

Most analysts, therefore, implicitly reduce the economy to production and distribution. Premodern agrarian economies, such as that found in late imperial China, are often equated with peasant agriculture (e.g., Huang, 1985). Recent studies of proto-industrialization broaden the characterization a bit, by including peasant handicraft manufacture (e.g., Feuerwerker, 1985). But these efforts still do not shift the emphasis from production. When applied to premodern economies (e.g., Skinner, 1977; Smith, 1976) central place theory further adds a distributive dimension. But consumption is still left out.

This preoccupation with production has two major shortcomings, both of which we have addressed in this paper. First, the obsession with production artificially separates the processes of production and consumption. Both processes are embedded in a social order and are simultaneously carried out by the actions of knowing, and socially involved participants[13]. These are the strategies of productions, and they rest upon social, as well as economic, calculations. Many analysts, however, rather than seeing an interdependence between the two, make consumption the logical consequence of production; consumption follows production in time, and thus is caused by it. This causative equation, however, negates the fact that producers calculate what they make and how they make it according to what they perceive the probability of consumption to be.

The second shortcoming of most conceptions of consumption is their psychological bias. Relegating consumption to subjective individual decisions--to a consumer psychology--is somewhat like reducing a language to individual decisions about what to say. Although in some instances that equation may be useful, for most purposes it is simply inaccurate.

Consumption, like language, is a form of symbolic communication, the form and content of which is not reducible to the individual actor. Both are social phenomena par excellence. Mary Douglas (1979) has also made this point in a related, but much more general context. The significance of this paper, however, is to show that the symbolic values embedded in market commodities need not be construed as being simply an function of capitalist production or a result of a consumer psychology created by factory owners manipulating symbols for their own profits. In late imperial China, consumerism existed without capitalism. Consumerism of all types is directly related to social structural variables, and the structural parameters of any specific society creates an affinity for particular strategies of production. In late imperial China, the manufacture and use of commodities bearing brand names fit the fluid social structure that China gradually developed during the last millennium of the empire.

Notes

In addition to conference participants, the authors also wish to thank E.L. Jones, Man-houng Lin, Kwang-Ching Liu, and Ben Orlove. They each read one or more drafts of this essay and generously offered us their comments. We are, however, responsible for the oversights that remain.

1. For more discussion on this definition of brand names, see Coles (1949).

2. The Chinese imperial economy was, of course, highly developed from a very early time and, at least during the Sung dynasty (960-127A.D.), this development superficially resembled capitalist (cf., Hartwell, 1966).

3. Recent research on medieval markets (e.g., Berger, 1980; Hilton, 1985; Biddick, 1985) show greater market penetration into the countryside than previously believe, but they do not fundamentally alter Schechter's characterization.

4. The economic literature on brand names is largely confined to marketing research (e.g., Pilditch, 1970). There are, however, relevant economic studies about product differentiation. Economists (e.g., Scherer, 1970: Chamberlin, 1950) have investigated theoretically the conditions producing product differentiation. According to Scherer (1970:324), brand name differentiation occurs when producing firms "strive to differentiate their goods and services from rival offerings." Given this competition, firms rationally plan strategies to create products that consumer will buy.

5.   It might seem inappropriate to include the generic qualities of a product in a discussion of brand names. But a standard discussion of brand names (e.g., Coles, 1949: 66) makes it clear that manufacturers and distributors, when they are able to do so, seize upon true or supposed generic qualities of products as a means to promote those products. In this sense generic qualities take on the dimensions of brand names.

6.   The analogy to modern wine production is appropriate. Usually wine is sold under a producer's label, but occasionally, if a selling firm is large enough or prestigious enough, it will market wine under its own label. Moreover, consumers choose a type of wine and a brand name of wine believing full well that the generic characteristics of that wine vary by both the brand name and the type, this in addition to the year of harvest.

7.   Lai and Hamilton (1986) discuss the widespread distribution of brand name products in more detail than is possible in this location.

8.   The chief discussions of the research on the spirit of capitalism are found in editions issued by Zhungguo remin daxue (1957) and by Nanjing daxue (1980). Also see Liu Yongcheng (1979; 1982).

9   For recent discussions of this issue, see Feuerwerker (1984), Rowe (1984, 1985), Myers (1980), and Hamilton (1985).

10.   For discussions of the agricultural role in Western capitalism, see Jones (1968, 1974) and Clarkson (1985).

11.   Crow (1937) gives many examples of Chinese consumerism from the early twentieth century. Hamilton (1977) gives some for the imperial period.

12.   For a discussion of the artisan economy of the Tang period, see Twitchett (1966, 1968). For the commercial transformation that occurred in the Sung, see Shiba (1970) and Ma (1971).

13.   See Granovetter (1985) for a theoretical discussion of the structural embeddedness of economic activity.

References

Baker, Hugh D. R.
1979 *Chinese Family and Kinship* (New York, Columbia University Press).

Bastid, Marianne
1985 The Structure of the Financial Institutions of the State in the Late Qing.
Pp. 51-79 in S.R. Schram, ed.,*The Scope of State Power in China*
(Hong Kong, The Chinese University Press).

Berger, Ronald M.
1980 The Development of Retail Trade in Provincial England, ca. 1550-1700.
The Journal of Economic History 40 (1, March) : 123-128.

Biddick, Kathleen
1985 Medieval English Peasants and Market Involvement. *The Journal of
Economic History* 45 (4, December): 823-831.

Borden, Neil H.
1947 *The Economic Effects of Advertising* (Chicago,
Richard D. Irwin).

Braudel, Fernand
1981 *The Structures of Everyday Life* (New York, Harper
& Row, Publishers).

Cellini , Benvenuto
1948 *The Autobiography of Benvenuto Cellini*, trans.Symonds, John
Addington (New York , Doubleday & Company , Inc.)

Chamberlin, Edward H.
1950 *The Theory of Monopolistic Competition* (Cambridge, Harvard
University Press).

Chandler, Alfred D. Jr.
1977 *The Visible Hand : The Managerial Revolution in American Business*
(Cambridge , Harvard Univ. Press) .

Chang , Chung-li
1962 *The Income of the Chinese Gentry* (Univ. of Washington Press).

Chao, Kang
1977   *The Development of Cotton Textile Production in China.* (Harvard Univ.
       Press).

Chao, Kang
1986   *Zhongguo Jingji Zhidu Shilun* [History of Chinese economic institution]
       (Taipei, Lianjing Chuban Shiye Gongsi).

Chen , Yuan
1984   *Chaye tongshi* [The general history of tea] (Beijing ,Nongye
       Chubanshe) .

Ch'u, Tung-tsu
1969   *Local Government in China Under the Ch'ing* (Stanford University
       Press).

Chuan , Han-sheng and Kraus, Richard A.
1975   *Mid-Ch'ing Rice Markets and Trade : An Essay in Price History*
       (Harvard University Press).

Chuan, Han-sheng
1979   Qing Kangxi nianjian Jiangnan ji fujim diqu demi jia [The prices of rice in
       Jiangnan and neighboring areas during the Kangxi period (1662-1722)]
       *The Journal of the Institute of Chinese Studies of the Chinese University
       of Hong Kong* , X, no.1 , 63-103.

Clarkson, L. A.
1985   *Proto-Industrialization : The First Phase of Industrialization* (London,
       MacMillian).

Coles, Jessie
1949   *Standards and Labels for Consumer Goods* (New York: Ronald Press.)

Crow, Carl
1937   *Four Hundred Million Customers : The Experiences--Some Happy, Some
       Sad --of An American in China, and What They Taught Him,* (New York:
       Harper and Brothers)

Davis, Alec
1967   *Package and Print, The Development of Container and Label Design .*
       (New York: C.N. Potter.)

Deng , Zhicheng
1926   *Godongsuoji .* (Reprinted.)

Douglas, Mary and Baron Isherwood
1979   *The World of Goods* (New York, W. W. Norton & Company).

Dutton, H. I.
1984   *The Patent System and Inventive Activity During the Industrial Revolution, 1750-1852* (Manchester, Manchester University Press).

Ewen , Stuart
1976   *Captains of Consciousness* (New York , McGraw-Hill) .

Feuerwerker , Albert
1984   The State and the Economy in Late Imperial China . *Theory and Society,* 13, 3 , 297-326.

Feuerwerker , Albert
1985   Qing Economic History and World Economic History.(A Paper Prepared for the Symposium on the occasion of the Sixteenth Anniversary of the founding of the First   Historical Archives of China, Beijing).

Fox, Richard W., and Lears, T.J. Jackson, eds.
1983   *The Culture of Consumption: Critical Essays in American History 1880-1980. (New York: Pantheon Books.)*

Fu, Yiling
1957   Mingdai Jiangnan shimin jingji shitan [Exploratory essay on the urban economy of the Kiangnan area during the Ming dynasty] (Shanghai Renmin Chubanshe) .

Fu, Yiling
1980   *Ming Qing shidai shangren ji shangye ziben* [Merchants and commercial capital in Ming Qing China] (Beijing , Renmin Chubanshe).

Girling , F.A.
1964   *English Merchants' Marks : A field survey of marks made by Merchants and tradesmen in England between 1400 and 1700* (Oxford University Press).

Granovetter, Mark
1985   Economic Action, Social Structure, and Embeddedness. *American Journal of Sociology* 91: 481-510.

Gugong bowuyuan Ming Qing danganbu comp.
1978   *Qingdai dangan shiliu congbian* [The source materials on Qing history] (Beijing , Zhonghua Shuju) .

Hamilton , Gary G.
1977   Chinese Consumption of Foreign Commodities: A Comparative Perspective. *American Sociological Review* 42: 877-891.

Hamilton , Gary G.
1985   Why No Capitalism in China? *Journal of Developing Societies* 1: 187-211.

Hartwell, Robert
1967   A Cycle of Economic Change in Imperial China: Coal and Iron in Northeast China, 750-1350. *Journal of the Economic and Social History of the Orient* 10: 102-159.

Heuser, Robert
1975   The Chinese Trademark Law of 1904 : A Preliminary Study in Exterritoriality, Competition, and Late Ch'ing Law Reform. *Oriens Extremus* 22 no.1: 183-210 .

Hilton, R. H.
1985   Medieval Market Towns and Simple Commodity Production. *Past and Present* 109 (November):3-23.

Ho, Ping-ti
1954   The Salt Merchants of Yang-chou: A Study of Commercial Capitalism in Eighteenth Century China. *Harvard Journal of Asiatic Studies* 17:130-168.

Ho , Ping-ti
1964   *The Ladder of Success in Imperial China* (New York, John Wiley and Sons).

Hohenberg, Paul M., and Lynn Hollen Lees
1985   *The Making of Urban Europe 1000-1950* (Harvard University Press).

Huang , Philip C.C.
1985   *The Peasant Economy and Social Change in North China* (Stanford Univ. Press).

Huang , Wei & Xia , lingen comp.
1984   *Jindai Shanghai diqu fangzhi jingji shiliao xuanji* [The source materials on economic history from the Modern Shanghai gazetteer] (Shanghai Renmin Chubanshe).

Jiangsu sheng bowuguan [Jiangsu provincial museum], ed.
1959   *Jiangsu sheng Ming-Qing yilai beike ziliao xuanji* [Selected Ming-Qing epigraphic materials from Jiangsu province], (Beijing, Sanlian Shuhu).

Jones, E. L.
1968   Agricultural Origins of Industry. *Past and Present* 40 (July): 58-71.

Jones, E. L.

1973   The Fashion Manipulators: Consumer Tastes and British Industries, Industries, 1660-1800. Pp. 198-216 Louis P. Cain and Paul J. Uselding, eds., *Business Enterprise and Economic Change* (Ohio, The Kent University Press).

Jones, E. L.
1974   *Agriculture and the Industrial Revolution* (Oxford, Basil Blackwell).

Kuwayama, Yasaburo
1973   *Trade Marks & Symbols* (Van Nostrand Reinhold Company).

Lai, Chi-kong & Hamilton, Gary G.
1986   Jinshi Zhongguo shangbiao yu quanguo dushi shichang. [Trademark and national-urban market in late imperial China] *Proceedings of the Conference on Regional Studies of Modern China* (Taipei , Institute of Modern History , Academia Sinica) .

Lai, Xinxia
1984   *Jicwanglu* [Selected works of Lai Xinxia] (Tianjin , Nankai Daxue Chubanshe) .

Lamley, Harry J.
forth- Lineage and Surname Feuds in Southern Fukien and Eastern Kwangtung coming under the Ch'ing. In Kwang-ching Liu, ed. *Orthodoxy in Late Imperial China* .

Lei , Chuanzhan
1984   Lei Yunshang he ciushenwan. *Gongshang jingji shiliao congkan* 4 , 230-4 .

Levy, Howard S.
1967   *Chinese Footbinding* (New York, Bell Publishing Co.).

Li, Hua
1980   *Ming Qing yilai Beijing gongshang huiguan beike xuanbian* [Selected Ming-Qing epigraphic materials on Trade Guilds from Beijing](Wenwu Chubanshe).

Li , Renpu
1983   *Zhongguo gudai fangzhi shigao* [A draft history of the premodern Chinese textile industry] (Hunan, Yuelu Shushe) .

Lin, Manhong
1985   *Qingmo shehui liuxing xishi yapian yanjiu : gongjimian shi fenxi* (The study on the fashion of opium consumption in late Qing society: the supply side analysis (1773-1906)] (Unpublished Ph.D. Dissertation, Guoli Taiwan Shifan Daxue [National Taiwan Normal University]).

Liu, Guoji
1982 Woguo shangpin guanggao shihua. [history of Chinese commercial advertisement] *Qiusuo* (Hunan) 2 , 64 .

Liu, Yongcheng
1979 Lun Zhongguo zibenzhuyi mengya de lishi qianti. [On the historical preconditions for the sprouts of capitalism in China]*Zhongguo shi yanjiu* : 2, 32-46.

Liu, Yongcheng
1982 *Qingdai qianqi nongye zibenzhuyi mengya chutan* [A preliminary study of the sprouts of capitalism in agriculture in the early Qing period] (Fuzhou, Fujian Renmin).

Liu, Zhiqin
1984 Wanming chengshi fengshang chutan [A preliminary study of fashion in late Ming cities]. *Zhongguo wenhua* [Chinese Culture] (Shanghai, Fudan Daxue Chubanshu) 1: 190-208.

Lockridge, Kenneth A.
1985 *A New England Town* (New York, W.W. Norton).

Lopez, Robert S. & Raymond, Irving W. eds.
1955 *Medieval Trade in the Mediterranean World* (Columbia University Press.)

Ma, Laurence J.C.
1971 *Commercial Development and Urban Change in Sung China, 960-1279.* (Ann Arbor, University of Michigan, Department of Geography) .

Marchand, Roland
1985 *Advertising the American Dream : Making Way for Modernity, 1920-1940* (California , Univ. of California Press) .

McKendrick, Neil, John Brewer and J. H. Plumb
1982 *The Birth of a Consumer Society: The Commercialization of Eighteenth-century England* (Bloomington: Indiana University Press).

Meinhardt , Peter
1971 *Inventions Patents & Trade Marks* (Gower Press Limited).

Meyer, Roger D.
1986 Cigarette Artistry: Packaging Images. In *The Free China Review* 36, no.2, 13-19 ; 36, no.3, 22-29 .

Ming Qing Suzhou gongshangji beike ji [Selected Ming-Qing industrial and commercial epigraphic materials from Suzhou]
1981   (Jiangsu Renmin Chubanshe).

Mokyr, Joel
1977   Demand vs. Supply in the Industrial Revolution. *Journal of Economic History* 37 (4, December) : 981-1008.

Myers, Ramon H.
1980   *The Chinese Economy, Past and Present* (Belmont, California: Wadsworth).

Nanjing daxue lishixi Zhongguo gudaishi jiaoyanjiushi [Nanjing university history department, Chinese history teaching and research Group]
1960   *Zhongguo zibenzhuyi mengya wenti taolunji, xubian* [Essays on the sprouts of capitalism in China], (Beijing, Sanlian Shudian). 2.

Nanjing daxue lishixi Ming-Qingshi hanjiushi, ed.
1980   *Ming-Qing zibenzhuyi mangya yanjiu lunwen ji* [A collection of essays on the sprout of capitalism in Ming-Qing] (Shanghai Renmin).

Nishijima, Sadao
1984   The Formation of the Early Chinese Cotton Industry. pp. 17-77 In Linda Grove and Christian Daniels eds., *State and Society in China: Japanese Perspectives on Ming-Qing Social and EconomicHistory (University of Tokyo Press).*

Orlove, Benjamin S.
1986   Barter and Cash Sale on Lake Titicaca : A Test of Competing Approaches *Current Anthropology* 27, 2 (April).

Pan Rongsheng
1758   *Dijing suishi jisheng* (Beijing Guji Chubanshe reprinted) .

Peng Zeyi
1983   Qingdai qianqi shougongyi de fazhan . [The development of handicraft industry in early Qing period] In Nanjing daxue lishixi Ming-Qingshi hanjiushi, ed. 1983.*Ming-Qing zibenzhuyi mangya yanjiu lunwen ji* [A collection of essays on the sprout of capitalism in Ming-Qing] (Jiangsu Renmin) .

Piditch, James
1970   *Communication by Design : A Study in Corporate Identity* (London, McGraw-hill).

Polanyi, Karl, Conrad M. Arensberg, and Harry W. Pearson, eds.
1957   *Trade and Market in the Early Empire* (Chicago, Henry Regnery Co).

Qian, Yong
1979   *Luyuan conghua* (Zhonghua Shuju reprinted) .

Quanguo Mingte chanpin [Famous native products in China]
1982   (Shanxi Renmin Chubanshe) .

Rowe, William T.
1984   *Hankow : Commerce and Society in a Chinese City: 1796-1889*,
       (Stanford Univ. Press).

Rowe, William T.
1985   Approaches to Modern Chinese Social History. Pp. 236-296 in Olivier
       Zunz, ed., *Reliving the Past: The Worlds of Social History* (Chapel
       Hill , The University of North Carolina Press).

Sabel, Charles and Zeitlin, Jonathan
1985   Historical Alternatives to Mass Production: Politics, Markets and
       Technology in Nineteenth Century Industrialization. *Past and Present*
       108 (August) : 133-176.

Sabloff, Jeremy A. and C. C. Lamberg-Karlovsky, eds.
1975   *Ancient Civilization and Trade* (Albuquerque, University of New
       Mexico Press).

Schechter, Frank I.
1925   *The Historical Foundations of the Law Relating to Trade-marks* (New
       York : Columbia Univ. Press) .

Scherer , F. M.
1970   *Industrial Market Structure and Economic Performance* (Chicago, Rand
       McNally and Co.).

Shanghai beike ziliao xuanji [Selected epigraphic materials from Shanghai],
1980   (Shanghai Renmin Chubanshe).

Shen , Guansheng
1983   *Shangbiaofa qiantan* [The introduction of the trademark law] (Falu
       Chubanshe) .

Shiba, Yoshinob
1970   *Commerce and Society in Sung China* (Ann Arbor, University of
       Michigan, Center for Chinese Studies).

Skinner, G. William
1964-65 Marketing and Social Structure in Rural China. *Journal of Asian Studies.4 (1):3-43.*

Skinner, G. William
1976   Mobility Strategies in Late Imperial China : A Regional Systems Analysis. In Smith , Carol A. ed. *Regional Analysis* (Academic Press) 1, 327-64.

Skinner, G. William
1977   *The City in Late Imperial China* (Stanford University Press).

Skinner, G. William
1985   Presidential Address: The Structure of Chinese History *Journal of Asian Studies* 46 2: 271-92.

Smith, Carol A. ed.
1976   *Regional Analysis* , 2 Volumes, (New York : Academic Press).

Song, Rulin comp.
1817   *Songjiang fuzhi* (Taiwan , Chengwen Chubanshe reprinted) .

Taub, Richard P.
1974   *American Society in Tocqueville's Time and Today* (Chicago, Rand McNally).

Tocqueville, Alexis de
1969   *Democracy in America* trans. Mayer, J. P. (New York Doubleday) .

Twitchett, Denis S.
1966   The T'ang Market System. *Asia Major* (n.s.) 12:202-48.

Twitchett, Denis S.
1968   Merchant, Trade, and Government in Late T'ang. *Asia Major* (n.s.) 14 : 63-95.

Wiens, Mi Chu
1976   Cotton Textile Production and Rural Social *Transformation in Early Modern China ."The Journal of the Institute of Chinese Studies of the Chinese University of Hong Kong* , 7, 2: 515-34.

Wiens , Mi Chu
1980   Lord and Peasant, The Sixteenth to the Eighteenth Century. *Modern China* 6 (1 January) : 3-39.

Wu, Cheng-ming
1985   *Zhongguo Zibenzhuyi Yu Guonei Chichang* [Chinese Capitalism and Internal market] (Beijing , Zhongguo Shehui Kexue Chubanshe) .

278

Xiao, Shitai & Zheng Boxia
1982 *Zhongguo tutechan Chuanshuo* [The story of Chinese native products] (Shanghai wenyi Chubanshe) .

Xu, Zhongyuan
1827 *Sanyi Bitan in Biji xiaoshuo daguan* [Collected works of notebooks and novels] (Jiangsu Guangning guji reprinted) .

Yang, Hongyuan & Zhao , Junqiu
1984 *Beijing Jingji Shihua* [The stories of Beijing economic history] (Beijing Chubanshe) .

Ye, Mengzhu
1981 *Yueshibian* (Shanghai Guji reprinted) .

Yue, Songsheng
1980 Beijing Tongrentang de huigu yu zhanwang . [The history and the future of Beijing Tongrentang] *Gongshang shiliao* (Wenshi Ziliao Chubanshe) 1: 152-74 .

Zeng, Zhongye
198 *Zhongguo jiuzhi* [The history of the Chinese wine] (Beijing , Zhongguo Luyou , 1980) .

Zhao, Lian
1980 *Xiaoting zalu* (Zhonghua Shuju reprinted) .

Zheng, Li
1979 Qingdai de jingji dangan shiliu . [sources on Qing economic history] *Gugong bowuyuan yuankan* (Beijing) 3: 59-64 .

Zhongguo renmin daxue Zhongguo lishi jiaoyanshi [Chinese people's university, Chinese history teaching and research group]
1957 *Zhongguo zibenzhuyi mengya wenti taolunji* [Essays on the sprouts of the capitalism in China] (Beijing, Sanlian Shudian).

Zhou, Mi
1980 *Wulin Jiushi* (Zhejiang Renmin Chubanshe) .

Zhou, Zhihua
1971 *Zhoungguo zhongyao shangpin* [The important commodities in China (Taipei , Xuesheng).

Zhu, Guocai
1983 *Zhejiang Mingchan Qutan* [The famous native products in Zhejiang] (Beijing , Zhongguo Luyou Chubanshe) .

CONSUMPTION OF HOUSEHOLD PRODUCTION TIME: BRIDGING THE GAP BETWEEN THEORY AND EMPIRICISM

Vicki Schram Fitzsimmons and Jeanne L. Hafstrom

Introduction

Becker's (1965) article on a theory of the allocation of time has stimulated a great deal of interest in time allocation to non-work activities. In this article, he discussed the allocation of time to non-work activities and thus brought attention to the importance of the use of time by the household sector. Becker's theory is of particular interest to us for two reasons. First, he treated the cost of time on the same level as the cost of market goods; that is, time is a resource which has value in the same way that market goods have value. Second, he incorporated "productive" consumption into household decision-making analysis as a suggested application of his theory. He recognized that households do not spend time only to consume goods and services but also use their time to produce goods and services for household consumption. In this way, time is both a consumption and production activity, and time spent in household production has value in its own right. This is an important consideration to families making choices about labor force participation. In spite of these strengths, Becker only summarized implications about empirical phenomena and attempted ". . . little systematic testing of the theory. . . ." (p. 495).

Others have attempted empirical testing related to time use in non-work activities. Empirical studies to date have included primarily economic variables. These have provided some explanation for housework time expenditures. But a large, unexplained variance in wife's housework time remains (see, for example, Hafstrom and Schram 1983; Nickols and Metzen 1978). This unexplained variance suggests that a gap exists between Becker's theory and wives' actual time spent in household production. We feel that the Becker-type model is useful but needs to be expanded beyond the confines of economics and used with non-economic variables to explain more fully the time that wives spend in household production. The purpose of this research is to expand the Becker model in an attempt to bridge the gap between the predictions of this theory and empirical data on wives' household production time.

Becker's model of time allocation

In his model of time allocation, Becker suggests that husbands' consumption of time in household production increases as wives' efficiency in the market increases. Wives' increased labor force participation, which reflects increased market efficiency, implies that husbands respond to their wives' increased labor force participation by doing more work at home. Recent time-use studies, however, indicate that this reallocation of husbands' time is not occurring on a widespread basis (Robinson, Yerby, Fieweger, and Somerick 1977; Sanik

281

1981). More recent findings indicate that husbands now spend more time in child care (Pleck 1985) and food preparation and dishwashing (Sanik 1981) than previously. Pleck (1985) claims that a cultural shift is evident today because husbands' involvement is occurring regardless of wives' employment status.

Becker's model also suggests wives' consumption of time in home production decreases as their efficiency in the market increases. Time spent in market work is not available for use elsewhere. Therefore, a proportionate decrease in wives' household production time might be expected when they allocate time to market work. This trade-off is likely because income from market work could be used to purchase goods and services previously produced in the home.

Wives' time allocations

Employed wives spend less time in household production than non-employed wives but not in proportion to their hours in the labor force (Robinson 1977; Walker and Woods 1976). Instead, employed wives spend less time in leisure, sleep, and volunteer work. The overall result is that employed wives spend a greater share of their available time in work activities (market and non-market work) than any other group, including employed husbands. This lack of a proportionate decrease in household production time for employed wives has sparked much research interest.

Why do wives continue to spend so much time in household production? Based on Becker's reasoning for the division of labor within the family, economists would argue that wives continue to allocate a larger share of time to household production activities than husbands, because they are relatively less efficient in the market (i.e., earn relatively less income than their husbands). Although this is a plausible explanation to economists for the time consumption patterns in families, this explanation is less than satisfactory for those with a broad social science perspective.

Theoretical considerations

We scrutinized Becker's model in an attempt to understand the gap that was evident between the predictions of his theory and actual time allocation of wives. This gap seems to stem from (1) the narrow view of economic returns alone rather than the inclusion of broader, social-psychological returns and (2) the adherence to one household utility function to the exclusion of individual utility functions.

Narrow View of Economic Returns

In his model of time allocation, Becker indicates that households allocate time to maximize family utility, or satisfaction. Limited resources are available to the household (e.g., time, energy, money, skills), but unlimited needs and wants exist. The household can choose to spend its resources in many different ways. For example, more time can be spent working in the labor force and less time producing goods at home. The income from market work could be used to purchase more convenience goods and hire more services to replace lost household production. Alternatively, more time could be spent in household production and less in market production.

To maximize its utility, the household allocates resources to get the highest level of returns possible. In Becker's model these returns are goods and services. This narrow view of possible returns is not surprising because economists tend to focus on easily quantifiable returns. However, utility theory, in its broadest sense, also includes satisfactions or enjoyment as possible returns.

The use of only economic returns to explain time allocation to household production activities overcomes many measurement problems that plague non-economists. However, economic variables are not sufficient to realistically explain household production time use within the family. This is the point where many economists and other social scientists part company. Economic explanations fail to include relationship patterns and individual satisfaction-dissatisfaction responses to household production time allocation observed by anthropologists and family and consumption economists concerned with understanding the total, not just economic, welfare of families. Despite apparent shortcomings, some researchers have cited Becker's model as useful. Geerken and Gove (1983) feel this model is the most appropriate economic theory for studying time use allocations. Gerner and Zick (1983) found that utility maximization, subject to a resource constraint, helped to explain time use in households.

Adherence to one household utility function

Nevertheless, there are individual utility functions which must be considered within a family or household, and a single family utility function cannot be assumed (Ferber and Birnbaum, 1977). Thus, a woman will allocate her time to different activities in order to maximize her utility. This time allocation may benefit her directly or indirectly. That is, a woman may do things that directly benefit other family members; their increased utility indirectly adds to her satisfaction. She can spend time preparing meals for her children which directly affects the children's health and welfare. Indirectly, she benefits by feeling that she has fulfilled her mother role. Or, she can suffer a decrease in her individual utility and allocate her time only to maximize family utility. This suggests that factors other than the traditional economic variables of wage rates, time spent in labor force participation, and family size are influences on consumption of time in household production.

283

Broader models bridging the gap

Some researchers have investigated time allocated to household production, including housework, using broader models somewhat related to utility maximization. Hendrix, Kinnear, and Taylor (1984) drew upon a model of social interaction to develop their hypotheses about wives' housework time expenditures. Their model suggests that constraints exist due to previous choices made to maximize utility; these constraints somewhat determine time allocations to various activities. For example, time already allocated or committed to market work constrains or limits the time which is available for household production. Thus, market work determines the amount of time spent in household production activities by constraining the amount of time available. Given various constraints that exist, there are other motivating factors that determine individuals' differential time allocations to various activities. These motivating factors consist of intrinsic gratification, extrinsic rewards, and support for own role perception. In other words, these factors are returns which furnish some sort of utility to the individual making the time allocation.

Nickols and Metzen (1978) also identified constraints on time inputs to housework as part of their conceptual framework in the study of housework time use. Further, they specified that there are pressures toward greater time inputs to housework which may result because more time is needed. A larger family would produce more household work and would be a pressure toward more time expenditures in housework. Nickols and Metzen also identified facilitators of housework activity which affect housework time use because they make the tasks easier or replace part or all of the housework activity. A higher family income enables the family to purchase goods and services to make housework easier or to replace housework activity of the homemaker. These pressures and facilitators seem to be parallel to the motivating factors in the Hendrix, Kinnear, and Taylor (1984) study. Like constraints, pressures and facilitators are related to utility maximization. Pressures for the wife to spend time in housework result in increased family utility but can increase or decrease her individual utility. Facilitators, on the other hand, directly affect the wife's utility by helping to decrease the amount of time needed for housework or to make it easier.

Both Becker's model and that of Nickols and Metzen have implications for research on consumption of non-market time which Becker (1965) indicates may be more important to economic welfare than that of working time. The Nickols-Metzen conceptual framework is more appropriate than Becker's model because of its utility maximization properties for both the individual and the family and the possibility for inclusion of both economic and non-economic variables. This makes it superior to Becker's model in that it can be used to help bridge the gap between theory and empiricism.

In our study, then, the general hypothesis is that the number of hours a married woman spends on household production is a function of pressures toward greater time inputs to household production, constraints on time inputs to household production, and facilitators of time inputs to household production. All of these factors maximize her utility or her family's utility. Rationale for variables used as measures of pressures, facilitators, and constraints in this study are presented in the next section.

Rationale for study and related literature

Housework and household production measures

Stafford (1983) criticizes Becker's model of time allocation because his definition for home production includes leisure. His definition is not the common one used and is inconsistent with Reid's definition. In 1934, Reid defined household production as ". . . the unpaid activities carried on by and for the members of the family . . . which provide goods contributing to the manner of living desired" (Reid 1934: 6, 12).

Consistent with Reid's definition for household production, measurement includes a broad range of activities performed in the home. For example, household production time includes " . . . time in activities from meal preparation, indoor care and maintenance, laundry, and child care to outdoor cleaning and repairs, gardening, and shopping" (Schram and Hafstrom 1984: 286). For this definition, a comprehensive array of household production activities is required such as that available in the 1975-76 Study of Time Use data collected by the University of Michigan Survey Research Center.

Other data sets are more limited in the data collected, thus restricting the definition of the dependent variable used. In one study, respondents reported the number of hours they usually spent each day of the week on housework such as preparing meals, cleaning the house, and doing other types of necessary work in and around the house and yard (Hafstrom and Schram 1983). This definition is broader than that used by Nickols and Metzen (1978) who defined housework time as cleaning, meal preparation and clean-up, laundry, and financial record keeping. Housework time, then, is a narrower definition than household production. Researchers need to indicate the definition used but do not always do so. Drawing conclusions from studies using these different definitions should be done cautiously.

Pressures toward greater time inputs to household production

Pressures include family size (Schram and Hafstrom 1986; Schram and Hafstrom 1984; Hafstrom and Schram 1983; Nickols and Metzen 1978), wife's chronic health condition (Schram and Hafstrom 1986; Hendrix, Kinnear, and Taylor 1984; Hafstrom and Schram 1983), enjoyment of household production (Hendrix, Kinnear, and Taylor 1984), and household production values, such as feeling a neat house is important (Maloch 1963). Family size is an indicator of the amount of household production needed. A person with a chronic health condition could need to spend more time than others doing an activity. On the other hand, someone with a chronic health condition might actually spend more time in household activities as a way of reciprocating for another household member's contribution to other family resources. Enjoying household production activities and feeling that a neat house is important can increase time spent in them. A person tends to spend more time doing things that are enjoyable and highly valued.

Another source of pressure could be related to the perceived homemaker role. For example, a woman may feel that because she is the wife and mother she should be the one to do certain household production tasks. She, also, may feel the homemaker should do the major share of household production. No studies were found which investigated attitudes about household production roles specifically. Some studies have investigated general role attitudes in relation to housework time of spouses, but the results have been inconclusive (see Pleck 1985, for a review of these studies). It is possible that measurement of these attitudes is the contributing factor to the mixed findings.

Facilitators of household production

Facilitators include family income (Schram and Hafstrom 1984; Hafstrom and Schram 1983; Nickols and Metzen 1978), use of household help (Schram and Hafstrom 1984), number of times husband eats out and number of times wife eats out (Schram and Hafstrom1984), number of hours husband is employed (Nickols and Metzen 1978), and wife's perceived energy spent on housework (Hendrix, Kinnear, and Taylor 1984). Higher income enables the homemaker to purchase convenience goods and services to replace her household production time, thus providing the needed goods and services but freeing her to allocate her time elsewhere. Household help can be purchased or meals can be eaten away from home. Husband's labor force participation is a constraint on his time, but fewer hours that he spends working outside the home facilitate the homemaker's household production because he can allocate some of his time to this activity. More energy spent is likely to reduce the time needed for the task.

Another type of facilitating factor is household management skill; this is a measure of specific strategies used which decrease time spent in household production. Although several have noted the importance of this factor, little research has been done in this area (see, for example, Nickols and Fox 1983; Strober and Weinberg 1980). One such strategy is doing two tasks at the same time which decreases overall time spent in household production.

Constraints on time inputs to household production

Time already allocated or committed to other activities is a major constraint on the time available for household production. The number of hours the homemaker spends participating in the labor force is the largest determinant of the hours spent in household production or housework (Schram and Hafstrom 1986; Schram and Hafstrom 1984; Hendrix, Kinnear, and Taylor1984; Hafstrom and

Schram 1983; Nickols and Metzen 1978; Robinson 1977; Berheide, Berk, and Berk 1976; Walker and Woods 1976).

Data and sample

Source of data was the 1975-1981 Time Use Longitudinal Panel Study from the University of Michigan Survey Research Center. Data utilized were collected in 1981 as a follow-up of a 1975-76 study. The "synthetic week" data were used in this study. The synthetic week was created for each adult respondent and spouse, who supplied data for three of four waves of interviewing, for a set of derived measures.

Cases with substantial amounts of missing data (1440 minutes or more of time in the synthetic week) were excluded from analysis. Data were collected from 620 respondents in the 1981 survey, and the sample was reduced to 493 respondents for the retained synthetic week sample.[1]

Because of the nature of this study, the data also were limited to families in which both the husband and wife were present. This further reduced the sample size used in this study to 246 respondents for 1981. Listwise deletion of missing data resulted in a final sample of 237. Characteristics of the sample reflect the larger family size and higher income often associated with the older mean age reached by respondents by 1981 (Table 1).

Major limitations of this study include panel loss and sample-selection criteria which resulted in a smaller sample size in 1981. However, these data provide enough interesting time utilization and related information to allow us to test the proposed model. No attempt is or should be made to generalize these findings to wives and their families in the population as a whole.

Method

Multiple regression analysis was used to test the model for household production of wives. The dependent variable was constructed from the data available. Time was spent in a breadth of household production activities which ranged from housework and food preparation to repair of furnishings and equipment to shopping and care of family members. This provided the basic data to use in building a broad household production variable. Thus, the dependent variable was a combination of the respondent's assessment of the amount of time spent in each type of activities referred to above. Each was measured in terms of the number of minutes per week spent in that activity. Wives averaged 34.61 hours per week spent in household production using this broader definition.

Information about scales used and coding of the independent variables can be found in Table 2. These variables were entered into the multiple regression equation. Correlation coefficients indicated that none of the independent variables were too highly related to include in the same regression.[2]

Results and discussion

Results of the regression analysis for respondent's household production time are shown in Table 3. The strongest variable, significant in explaining the variation in wife's household production time, was the number of hours she spent in the labor force. As wives increased the number of hours spent in the labor force, they decreased the time spent in household production activities. This indicates, as Becker suggests, that a household member will allocate time between activities, household production and labor force participation in this instance, to maximize family utility. The number of hours the husband spends in the labor force also was significant at the .01 level. Wives increased time in household production as husbands spent more time in the labor force. This trade-off between husbands' labor force time and wives' household production time is another indication that households allocate time of individuals in order to maximize family utility. This finding also is in harmony with Becker's assumption that household members affect each others' allocation of time which happens in a rational way. Increase in husbands' time in the labor force would indicate, following Becker, a decrease in wives' efficiency in the market. Because this study deals only with female household production time, there are unanswered questions on how wives' efficiency in the market affects husbands' household production time allocations.

Another significant time-related variable was the amount of time the wife eats out per week. Eating out results in less pressure for household production, and wives decreased the number of hours spent in household production as they increased the amount of time spent eating out. Although time spent in household production activities is the focus of our study, similar time trade-offs between labor and leisure or sleep and volunteer work, for example, would be expected to maximize family utility in the Becker sense. Credence is given to this by the decrease in wives' household production time accompanied by the wives' increase in time eating out.

Other significant relationships supported the Nickols-Metzen model. A positive management orientation, such as doing two things at once, also resulted in less time expenditure. This type of activity is a facilitator because it is a more efficient use of time in household production. Wife's feelings about energy she has for keeping up with day-to-day responsibilities reached the .05 significance level. This positive relationship indicates that the less energy and effort wives felt household activities took, the more time they spent in total household production. This, too, is a pressure toward more household production time.

Household help, health limitations, family income, family size, and husbands' eating out were not significant. Thus, it would appear that these variables add little toward explaining the amount of time spent in household production when household production is broadly defined. Feelings about household production activities and attitudes of wives toward various activities, although not significant, were close to the .10 significance level.

Sumary and implications

In comparing these findings to the conceptual model, hypothesized relationships were found for variables representing all parts of the model. Economic variables, such as those included in a strict Becker model, were important predictors. Thus, the relevance of a Becker-type model for the study of household production time was confirmed. Non-economic variables, predicted from an expanded model like the Nickols-Metzen one, were important also. This helps in understanding why wives' household production time is not reduced proportionately with increases in labor force participation.

The major constraint we found was not with the Nickols-Metzen model but with the data available. For example, data measuring household production attitudes, values, feelings, and management orientation were limited in the data set we used. Because the primary purpose of the survey was to investigate time-use patterns, it is questionable whether the household production attitudes, values, feelings, and management orientation were explored adequately. To meet these concerns, we suggest an in-depth study of household production with a combined survey and observational approach. One advantage of this approach would be that management techniques people use and of which they may not be aware could be identified. This would enable us to teach others these successful techniques so they can make more informed time-use decisions.

We hypothesized a positive relationship for household production feelings (enjoyment of housework) with household production time. We found a negative relationship instead which indicates that a person spends less time doing an activity that is enjoyed. It is possible that enjoyment increases time inputs originally, but greater time inputs eventually result in greater efficiency at the task with accompanying decreases in time expenditures. An in-depth study could help to clarify this relationship. Another consideration in understanding this relationship is the measurement of the dependent and independent variables. On the one hand, the broader definition of household production was used for the dependent variable while the narrower definition of housework was used for the independent variable. A different finding might result if the dependent variable were housework time.

In a different study (Hafstrom and Schram 1986), we investigated the relationship between enjoyment of shopping and time spent in shopping and found a positive, significant relationship. Shopping is considered part of both housework and household production so we expected similar results. However, the attitudes about a specific activity might not generalize to the whole set of activities regardless of how defined. We suggest additional study of attitudes in specific activities in relation to the time spent in those specific activities.

Earlier, we raised the issue of definition of the dependent variable and cautioned against comparing results of studies using a housework definition and those using a household production definition. We pointed out that some researchers do not indicate the measures they are using for the dependent variable which makes comparisons even more difficult. This definitional problem needs attention, especially as researchers from several disciplines are pursuing research in this area. Many studies use the housework definition which may not accurately reflect men's contribution to the household; this is of particular concern in relation to conclusions about changing sex roles within the household.

Previously, we found that family size was significantly related to time spent in housework and household production; others have found this relationship as well. However, this variable was not significant in the present study. This may be a result of using a much broader definition for household production in this study than others have used. Also, the families were older than the sample we used in previous studies. Perhaps older children participate in more household production activities as they get older. Or, there may be less work needed if they are frequently away at school, work, or other activities.

The area of household production continues to suggest more research questions for study. We have provided some answers and suggested several avenues for future study, especially within an interdisciplinary framework and with the use of a Becker-type model of time allocation. Such an approach should continue to narrow the gap between theory and empiricism.

Notes

1. The data utilized in this article were made available by the Inter-university Consortium for Political and Social Research. The data for TIME USE LONGITUDINAL PANEL STUDY, 1975-81 were originally collected by F. Thomas Juster, Martha S. Hill, Frank P. Stafford, and Jacquelynne Eccles Parsons of the Survey Research Center, Institute for Social Research, The University of Michigan. Neither the collector of the original data nor the Consortium bear any responsibility for the analyses or interpretations presented here.

2. Based on previous research and small correlations among independent variables, it was assumed that the direction of causation would not be a problem in this research. Although income might be expected to determine the number of times eaten out, for example, less than ten percent of the variance in the variable, number of times eat out, was explained by the income variable.

Table 1

Mean Selected Characteristics of Sample

Characteristic	
Number of persons in family	4.33
Age in years (wife)	44.72
Family income in dollars	32,557
Labor force hours/week (wife)	16.34
Labor force hours/week (husband)	34.11

Table 2

Independent Variables and Scale

Wife's Household Production Time	Scale
Wife's labor force time (C)	Hours/week
Husband's labor force time (P)	Hours/week
Wife's time eat out (F)	Minutes/week
Husband's time eat out (F)	Minutes/week
Total family annual income 18 categories (in 1981 dollars (F))	$2000 to $35,000+
Family size (P)	Actual number
Regular household help (F)	No, yes
Wife's feelings about household activities (P)	10 points[a]
Wife's health limits (P)	4 points[b]
Wife's general role attitudes (P)	5 points[c]
Wife's household production attitudes (P)	Yes, No
Wife's household production values (P)	3 points[d]
Wife's management orientation (F)	3 points[e]
Wife's energy/effort (F)	10 points[f]

Note. (P) stands for pressure, (C) for constraint, and (F) for facilitator.

[a]Dislike a great deal (0) to enjoy a great deal (10).

[b]Excellent (1) to poor (5).

[c]Strongly agree (1) to strongly disagree (5).

[d]Very important (1), somewhat (3), not very important (5).

[e]Most of the time (1) to hardly ever (3).

[f]No energy and effort put into an activity (0) to all energy and effort put into an activity (10).

Table 3

Multiple Regression of Household Production Time (n=237)

Independent variables	Coefficient	Beta	F-Ratio
Labor force hours (W)	-0.5538	-.644	162.20**
Management orientation	-288.8577	-.211	19.29**
Time eat out (W)	-1.1061	-.210	14.86**
Labor force hours (H)	0.1187	.148	9.24**
Energy/effort	44.0173	.096	4.19*
Household production feelings			
Household production attitudes	38.1852	.079	2.55
General role attitudes	19.3956	.071	1.94
Family size	33.2515	.050	1.10
Total family income	-.0027	-.054	1.07
Household production values	16.4103	.021	0.24
Time eat out (H)	-0.0921	.010	0.15
Health (W)	19.3956	.010	0.05
Household help	-21.1466	-.009	0.03

Constant = 2159.08
$R^2 = 0.558$
$R^{*2} = 0.531$
$F = 20.07**$
df = 14 and 22
$*p < .05. **p < .01$

References

Becker, Gary S.
1965   A Theory of the Allocation of Time.*The Economic Journal*
        September:493-517.

Berheide, C. W., S. F. Berk, and R. A. Berk
1976   Household Work in the Suburbs: The Job and Its Participants.
        Pacific Sociological Review 19:491-517.

Ferber, Marianne A., and Bonnie G. Birnbaum
1977   The `New Home Economics': Retrospects and Prospects.*Journal
        of Consumer Research* 4:19-28.

Geerken, M., and W. R. Gove
1983   *At Home and At Work: The Family's Allocation of Labor.* Beverly
        Hills, CA: Sage Publications.

Gerner, Jennifer L., and Cathleen D. Zick
1983   Time Allocation Decisions in Two-Parent Families. *Home
        Economics Research Journal* 12:145-158.

Hafstrom, Jeanne L., and Vicki R. Schram
1986   Husband-wife Shopping Time: A Shared Activity? Urbana,
        IL: University of Illinois, *Department of Family and
        Consumer Economics, Working Paper* Series No. 122, 33 pp.

Hafstrom, Jeanne L., and Vicki R. Schram
1983   Housework Time of Wives: Pressure, Facilitators, Constraints.
        Home Economics Research Journal 11:245-255.

Hendrix, Philip E., Thomas C. Kinnear, and James R. Taylor
1984   Time Expenditures in Consumption Activities: Issues and
        Empirical Evidence. Unpublished manuscript.

Maloch, Francille
1963   Characteristics of Most and Least Liked Household Tasks.*Journal
        of Home Economics* 55:413-416.

Nickols, Sharon Y., and Karen D. Fox
1983   Buying Time and Saving Time: Strategies for Managing
        Household Production. *Journal of Consumer Research* 10:197-208.

Nickols, Sharon Y. and Edward J. Metzen
1978   Housework Time of Husband and Wife. *Home Economics
        Research Journal* 7:85-97.

Pleck, Joseph
1985   *Working Wives/Working Husbands.* Beverly Hills, CA:
       Sage Publications.

Reid, Margaret G.
1934   *Economics of Household Production.* New York: John Wiley.

Robinson, John P.
1977   *How Americans Use Time: A Social-Psychological Analysis* of
       Everyday Behavior. New York: Praeger.

Robinson, John, Janet Yerby, Margaret Fieweger, and Nancy Somerick
1977   Sex-role Differences in Time Use. *Sex Roles* 3:443-458.

Sanik, Margaret Mietus
1981   Division of Household Work: A Decade of Comparison--
       1967-1977.*Home Economics Research Journal* 10:175-180.

Schram, Vicki R., and Jeanne L. Hafstrom
1986   Family Resources Related to Wife's Time Inputs to Housework.
       Journal of Consumer Studies and Home Economics 10:235-245.

Schram, Vicki R., and Jeanne L. Hafstrom
1984   Household Production: A Conceptual Model for Time-use Study in
       the United States and Japan.*Journal of Consumer Studies and Home
       Economics* 8:283-292.

Stafford, Kathryn
1983   The Effects of Wife's Employment Time on Her Household Work Time.
       Home Economics Research Journal 11:257-266.

Strober, Myra H., and Charles B. Weinberg
1980   Strategies Used by Working and Nonworking Wives to Reduce Time
       Pressures. *Journal of Consumer Research* 6:338-348.

Walker, Kathryn E., and Margaret E. Woods
1976   *Time Use: A Measure of Household Production of Family Goods and
       Services.* Washington, D. C.: American Home Economics Association.

HOUSES AS CONSUMER GOODS: SOCIAL PROCESSES AND ALLOCATION DECISIONS

Richard R. Wilk

> ... relatively large and well appointed house room is, even in the lowest social ranks, at once a "necessary for efficiency," and the most convenient and obvious way of advancing a material claim to social distinction. And even in those grades in which everyone has house room sufficient for the higher activities of himself and his family, a yet further and almost unlimited increase is desired as a requisite for the exercise of many of the higher social activities.
>
> Alfred Marshall, *Principles of Economics*, 1891:144-145

Introduction

Marshall's view of housing still goes right to the heart of what makes housing and the built environment an important anthropological topic. No artifact is so clearly multifunctional, simultaneously a utilitarian object of absolute necessity, and an item of symbolic material culture, a text of almost unending complexity. In every house the economic, social, and symbolic dimensions of behavior come together. This may be why the analysis of housing has had such a wide appeal in disciplines as diverse as social psychology, folklore, economics and engineering. Anthropologists themselves have shown a new willingness to consider the house as a key artifact in understanding the articulation of economic and social change during economic development.

From the perspective of our own society, surrounded by houses of all shapes and sizes, where wealth and luxury are synonymous with housing, this seems obvious and commonplace. The television show "Lifestyles of the Rich and Famous" and journals like "Architectural Review" are odes to the home as a shrine and symbol of wealth. But just as clearly, there are societies where all the houses look alike, even though all people are not alike. Perhaps then, the assumption that there is something natural and obvious about spending on the house and home as a marker of prestige is ethnocentric. Why the house instead of something else?

A number of anthropological approaches attempt to place the house in a theoretical context which answer this question by relating housing to social, economic, and psychological variation and change. For example, a utilitarian approach that views the house partially as a workspace links changes in the elaboration of houses to changes in the kinds of work done in the household (Braudel 1973:201). Or if the house is seen as a reflection of how all household activities are organized and divided, then the shape of the house will change as activities are modified, differentiated, or recombined (Kent 1983, 1984). An even more utilitarian perspective relates the form of the house to climate, technology, and the kinds of building materials that are available (Duly 1979).

For others, the house is a reflection of the psychological and ideological processes of builders and inhabitants. Following a common sociological view that the consumption of goods functions to create and articulate personal and social identities, Cooper (1974) sees the house as an elaborate personal facade. Glassie stresses the generational design grammar of designers (1975), while Errington sees the house as a cosmological text, reflecting world view and religion (1979, see also Rapoport 1977, Cunningham 1973, Fernandez 1977). A more semiotic view relates house form to culturally-specific definitions of privacy, territory, and personal space (Altman and Chemers 1984). Rapoport views the home as codified culture, a patterned set of cues to proper behavior that he calls a "system of settings" that channel action and meaning (1982). Following these models, changes in value systems, cultural codes, and cosmologies will cause changes in house form.

Other authors argue persuasively that the house is a reflection of social relationships, symbolizing or passively reflecting social status and differentiation (e.g., Chapman 1955, Lawrence 1982, Donley 1982), or the kin relations between members of different households, or between households and the community (Rodman 1985a, 1985b). The house may have great significance in defining or stating ethnic or political affiliations, and it can also be an indicator of social differences within the household itself (Wolf 1968).

In the empirical analysis of why housing styles change or remain the same, these multiple interpretations (and I have by no means covered the full range) face us with a dilemma of priority. How can we judge the relative importance of psychological, cultural, social, and utilitarian factors in determining the shape of the built environment? The theories I have cited each make analytical and interpretive arguments about causality that cannot be judged against each other, or tested with a particular data set. I suggest that the best escape from this analytical problem lies in a refocussing of research orientations and methods. First we should focus research on actual human decision-making about housing in greater ethnographic detail, and secondly we should explode the analytical category of housing as some kind of unique artifact category.

Because the construction and use of a house requires much time, labor, and resources, it always entails choices, negotiations, disagreements and compromises about the allocation of resources to accommodate different household members' needs through design, or selection from a range of options. These choices about the use, reuse, modification and disposal of material goods conventionally fall in the economic category of consumption. Viewing houses as a consumer good, the product of patterned and constrained choices and decisions, provides a workable starting point for unravelling the multi-faceted nature of the built environment. This focus on individual choices falls within the category of "actor-based models" advocated by Orlove (1980).

A complete theory of housing must link housing closely to other important realms of human action, because decisions about housing are intertwined with so many other kinds of decisions. The house is a part of a larger social field, and the decision to buy or build or modify a house is made as part of other social and personal decisions. In Anglo-American culture, decisions about the house are related to those about cars, clothing, furniture, career changes, social mobility, income prospects, the stability of marriage, the age of children.[1] In other cultures relationships with kin, local political conditions, the fertility of the soil, ethnic boundaries or stereotypes, may all be considered in the same context, at the same time, as a part of the decision about the house. Such a complete ethnographic description is beyond the scope of the present paper. Here I will select several connections between housing and other economic and social realms of society in order to demonstrate the utility of a consumption-decision-making approach.

The house as a consumer good

Treating the built environment as a product of consumption decisions means that the focus of research must be the human actors themselves and the processes by which people balance various options. The assertion made is that culture does not shape houses in some abstract or even direct fashion; people shape houses. In doing so they are informed by cultural knowledge and they act within cultural constraints, but always in the context of a dialectic between cultural rules and actual behavior that allows both to change. As Rutz (1988: 4) says,

> The causal arrow between culture and choice goes in both directions. An important part of consumption activities, therefore, concerns the introduction of new goods and the disappearance of existing goods as old meanings are attached to the former and new meanings define the existing groupings.

Therefore, to understand the process of decision-making, we do not have to build a grand overarching theory of the complex balance of function and aesthetics, meaning and social role. Instead we must study the factors that affect human decisions involved in buying, designing, building, altering, demanding, selling, and destroying houses, to see how people themselves achieve a balance through an interaction of cultural knowledge and pragmatic action. From this perspective, changes in housing come about through changes in that balance.

Housing decisions are only intelligible in the context of other kinds of decisions. While housing is a special cultural realm and a highly important category in many societies, decisions about houses are linked to many other kinds of choices, pragmatic and otherwise. Labor that is spent building or modifying a house is labor that cannot be spent in other ways. That labor represents an allocation decision, a choice to devote labor to the house instead of making pottery, relaxing in the shade or attending a ritual dance. Similarly, goods traded for housing materials or money spent on the house or furnishings, represent another allocation decision, a choice among the many different things that could have been obtained. Housing is therefore conceptually the product of allocation decisions that conventionally fall in the analytical category of consumer behavior. The fields of sociology, marketing, and economics have recently been developing a set of concepts for understanding household decision making that can be useful in understanding variability in the built environment.

The economist Gary Becker has proposed an econometric model of how households allocate resources (1981, also Becker and Lewis 1974, Barnum and Squire 1979). This model has been criticized for its overt formalism, and for its assumptions that households have a "joint utility function" (meaning the household can be treated as a single entity with interests in common) rather than individual utility functions for each member (Folbre 1984). This debate has focussed attention on the economic interactions within the household, complementing sociological debates on the power relations between household members in relation to their participation in the labor market or in household labor (Safilios-Rothchild 1972, Hartmann 1981, Rodman 1972, Friedman 1984, Hareven 1982, Curtis 1986). The household itself is depicted as a unit in which each member has different interests, power bases, and goals, which are reconciled through complex processes including negotiation and coercion.

The study of decision processes within the household have been almost exclusively the province of consumer research. While much of this work has been preoccupied with the issue of husbands' and wives' relative power and influence in decision-making (see Ferber and Lee 1974, Davis 1976), a recent anthology includes broader and more sophisticated approaches (Roberts and Wortzel 1984). Recent anthropological discussions of decision-making tend to treat decisions as individual events where a choice is made between discrete and definable options (see critique in Orlove 1980 and Nardi 1983). Otherwise they tend to treat decisions through input-output analysis, defining the environmental conditions and cognitive classifications that make particular decisions rational and understandable. Consumer researchers, in contrast, have begun to treat decision-making as an ongoing process in which the outcome of one decision affects the inputs to the next (Bonfield et al.1984). Credibility in future decisions, for example, can be affected if a husband or wife makes a serious mistake. Consumer researchers are also are willing to consider cases in which the goals of the household are ill-defined, and the range of choices is imperfectly known (Park 1982). Some interesting work has also been done on the strategies used by household members to influence decisions, including bargaining, threatening, offering rewards, and monopolizing information (Spiro 1983).

Park (1982) brings many of these elements together in an analysis of how husbands and wives in American middle-class households interact in the process of deciding on a house to purchase. He maps out both spouses' decision-criteria as a formal "decision plan net" with different kinds of criteria ordered in a sequence.[2] He then compares the decision plans of husbands and wives at different points during the decision-process, observing the ways that agreements are reached. He concludes that the main heuristic in the decision process is one of conflict-avoidance, or what he calls "muddling through." In the end, the goal of purchasing an acceptable house is subordinated to the need to maintain an acceptable marital relationship.

Anthropologists have been curiously silent on the general topic of how households make economic decisions. They have considered fertility decision-making within the household (Nag et al. 1978, Nardi 1984), the patterns of conflict and cooperation between and among members of households and kin groups (eg. Lamphere 1974, Wolf 1968), decisions to divide or dissolve households (eg. Carter 1984), and the ways that households balance resources, production and consumption during the developmental cycle (in a literature considering the work of Chayanov 1966). A general problem is the difficulty of gathering detailed data on the intimate details of household relationships and decisions. Too often, normative descriptions and post hoc generalizations are substituted for the messy descriptive details. A serious problem has been a lack of conceptual tools, like those used by consumer researchers, for describing and discussing what actually goes on within households. A promising approach is discourse analysis, used by Watson-Gegeo and Gegeo (1983) to draw out details of household and family decisions from taped discussions between household members. However, only a very small number of discussions can be analyzed by such intensive interpretive techniques.

I suggest, however, that anthropological analysis of household decision-making is essential for understanding variability in the domestic built environment. We need to look both at the relationships within the household that affect decisions, and at the relationship between the household and larger social entities like lineages or communities. By looking to the general processes of allocation and distribution within the household, it will be possible to understand housing as it is socially and culturally enacted.

Case study: Kekchi Maya economy and housing

The Kekchi Maya of southern Belize have a population of about 5,100 people scattered among 24 villages that range in size from 5 to 110 households, with a mean population of about 210 persons. They are relatively recent immigrants from the Alta Verapaz region of Guatemala, where a much larger Kekchi population remains.[3] Culturally the Kekchi are like most other highland Maya in having cognatic kinship, compadrazgo, and rotating civil-religious cargos.

While the Kekchi have been involved peripherally in a market economy for 350 years, today many Kekchi in the more isolated southern Belize villages pursue a subsistence economy, with a small cash income from selling pigs and crops. In these southern areas the average household income is less than US

$150 per household per year. This small income is spent almost entirely on household goods like kerosene, candles, and soap, on foods like flour, sardines, and lard, on luxuries like liquor, coffee, cigarettes, and soft drinks, on basic agricultural tools, and on clothing for the family. Many purchases are made from travelling Kekchi peddlers who carry goods from the Guatemalan highlands on their backs.

In the Kekchi communities in the northern part of the Toledo District, on the expanding network of primary and secondary roads, cash incomes and economic inequalities are greater. Non-Indian farmers hire some Kekchi as seasonal laborers, but the major sources of income are the production of rice, beans, and to a lesser extent corn and pigs, for sale to the government and in the small local market. Starting about 1980 marijuana cultivation has become a major source of income for farmers in several villages; in such a small and cash-poor economy this influx of money has had a tremendous impact.[4] Some Kekchi entrepreneurs have also built small retail shops, and have engaged in trucking and wholesaling enterprises. It is this emerging elite group that has dominated the marijuana trade as well. A slowly improving educational system has opened up some avenues for Kekchi to join government service, to become salaried schoolteachers, church workers, or clerks in the villages or in the nearby district center of Punta Gorda. Lastly, a few Kekchi have begun seasonal wage-labor migration to other parts of the country, and a very few (especially young men and women) have moved to Belize City and joined the ranks of the urban poor.

I selected three Kekchi villages for fieldwork between 1978 and 1980. Santa Teresa, with 21 households, is located in the southern zone away from any road, and has the lowest average cash income of about $140 in 1979. Aguacate, on the boundary between southern and northern zones, is on the terminus of a dry-season road, and has been involved in cash-crop production on a moderate scale beginning in 1970. For the purpose of this paper we can consider Aguacate to be a transitional community, moving over the last 20 years from a southern subsistence economy towards a northern cash-based economy. In 1979 the 31 Aguacate households had cash incomes ranging from $28 to $357 with an average of $220. Indian Creek was founded in the early 1970s alongside the major highway north, and had 59 households in 1979. For a sample of ten households, 1979 income ranged between $103 and $967 with a mean of $485. Short return visits were made to the three communities, and others in the area, during 1984 and 1985, and changes in housing styles were noted.

Houses and consumption

For the Kekchi, like other Maya groups, the construction of a house is a socially and spiritually important event marked by ritual (Vogt 1969:71-91). The Kekchi house in southern villages like Santa Teresa is built entirely of natural materials gathered in the forest around the village. The household members cut and erect the upright posts, beams, and wall materials, while a village communal work group gathers vines for tying, and palm leaf for thatching, and then meets to erect the roof in two working days (cf. Farriss 1984:135). Houses vary in size, depending on the amount of labor the household can devote to building the framework and walls; this amount in turn depends on seniority in the kinship system and on the number of close relatives living in the community (see Wilk 1984). An average of 28 person-days of construction labor are provided by the community, and another 25 to 30 person-days (and a large pig to feed the groups) are spent by the household itself. Depending on the size of the community, a Kekchi man will donate between four and 12 days a year to others to help them build. In the more remote villages, there is no cash expense required in building a house or furnishing it.

Houses in transitional Aguacate are like those of southern villages. They range from 25 to 112 square meters (sides are about three times as long as the ends) in area, with a mean of 54.5. An interior partition often marks a rough functional division of the house into a kitchen at one end and a public area with benches and the household altar at the other, with a storage area in between. Household members sleep throughout the house in hammocks that are stored overhead during the day, and other specialized activity areas are lacking. In Santa Teresa and other southern zone villages some households use an old house next door as a kitchen and storage area, doubling their domestic space for a couple of years until the roof is beyond repair.

Southern village houses must be re-thatched about every five years, and rebuilt completely every ten. People move housesites frequently, as relationships with kin and other villagers change (house locations are used an average of 6.1 years before abandonment though they may later be reused by the original household or by new residents). Household location and orientation is a sensitive indicator of the state of relations between households. People on good terms with each other tend to live close by, and sometimes groups of kin form informal neighborhoods.

While households may vary greatly in their relative wealth and status within the community, the uniformity of housing expresses the prevalent ideology of equality, enacted also in the ideology of communal land tenure.[5] With increases in cash income in northern villages, changing consumption patterns have emerged. While foods and other consumables are increasingly in demand, much of the new cash income is channeled into the purchase of vehicles, consumer durables (e.g. radios, televisions), housing, and furnishings. While in the southern villages all houses are virtually identical in materials and style, in the north there is a diversity of housing.

Aguacate, in transition between the two zones, still practices subsistence farming. While cash incomes are much higher than in Santa Teresa, housing patterns are identical. Wage labor within the community is absent, and communal work groups still build houses that are essentially identical. Money that is not spent on basic foodstuffs, clothing, and tools (both agricultural and kitchen), is spent mostly on personal consumer goods, items that they consider individual rather than household property. About the only common consumer good that is considered household property rather than that of individual household members is a radio or tape player.

In a sample of expenditures for 10 Aguacate households in 1979, of a mean $242 spent, an average of $130 was spent on taxes, tools, lime, basic foods, kitchen equipment, and clothing, about $14 went for expenses related to children's schooling, and the remainder went for a wide variety of consumer goods including a lot of cosmetics, luxury foods, toys, alcohol, cigarettes, items of personal adornment (mostly clothing not worn on a daily basis, like running shoes and decorative hats), and a few major items like musical instruments, bicycles, shotguns, and radios. No expenditures related to housing were recorded except for $7 spent on a small kitchen table used for making tortillas, and a few dollars spent by two households on nails for the construction of household altars.

Indian Creek is among the poorest communities in the northern zone, but even there, average cash incomes are more than double those of Aguacate. Larger communities like San Pedro Colombia have incomes at least double that of Indian Creek. In all northern zone villages a significant number of villagers receive cash income from shopkeeping, and from relatives who are working in jobs outside the community. A disproportionate amount of the cash income goes to men rather than women (as has been observed often in developing countries, Nash 1983). While in the more remote communities men and women share income from sale of pigs, and women have their own sources of cash, women are increasingly relegated to the domestic, subsistence sphere in the northern villages.

While some of the increase in cash income is spent on personal consumer goods and on consumables, most of it is invested in the house and furnishings. For most, this investment takes the form of substituting purchased construction materials for gathered ones,[6] within the context of the traditional Kekchi house. House plan remains the same, but cut boards are used for walls, corrugated metal replaces thatch in patches or on part of the house, concrete covers the dirt floor, and bedding, kitchen utensils, and other furnishings are upgraded or added. The use of space within the house does not change very much. There seems to be a trend towards less flexibility in the use of interior space that results from substituting furniture like chairs, beds, and tables for hammocks hung from the rafters, since the furniture cannot be put away during the day.

Of 25 houses in Indian Creek that were mapped in 1980, 9 were built entirely from gathered materials in the same shape and style as those in Aguacate and Santa Teresa. I noted a few subtle changes, as in the substitution of wire for split vines and bark strips in some fastenings in the frame and thatch. The average size of these 9 houses was close to that observed in Aguacate. Of the remaining 16 houses, 6 had whole or partial replacement of thatch with corrugated iron sheeting, 12 had cut lumber instead of split boards for part or all of their walls, four had raised hearths on tables rather than the traditional floor-hearth, three had windows with shutters, and three had whole or partial cement sealing of the floor. Those houses with some "improvement" averaged about 15 square meters smaller than those that were built from gathered materials; the occupants were sacrificing space because of the cost of materials. In the two households for which I have expenditure data during the time of house construction (both had board walls and partial tin roofing), 48% and 65% of household cash income over a two year period was spent on the house, as well as some savings from previous years.

For those with larger or more reliable income the major step is to a non-Kekchi style of house. This is a simple two or three room wooden house raised off the ground on pilings, with an iron roof, often with an exterior kitchen in a thatch hut. This style of house is common among all of the ethnic groups of rural Belize, and can be built with a cash outlay of about US $900. In 1979 in Indian Creek there were two of these "creole" style houses in the community, one occupied by a Mopan Maya schoolteacher and the other by a Kekchi Protestant preacher from another village. In 1985 the number had risen to 5, and several more were under construction.

The very wealthiest Kekchi in the most prosperous northern villages, people with salaried jobs or income from marijuana, have begun to hire masons and build concrete block houses in a style common in the well-to-do northern parts of Belize.[7] Striking contrasts can now be found in the richest villages, where large cash incomes have allowed a few Kekchi to build three-story concrete block houses with two-car garages, balconies and electricity, while their old thatch house still stands in the back or front yard, used as a pig pen or occupied by poorer relatives.

The increase in cash income above the level of about US $300 per year, then, has led to a change in the kinds of goods purchased. This change cannot be accurately described as a shift from necessities to luxuries (as is often presumed). Rather, a large percentage of cash income has always been expended on luxuries and consumer products regardless of income level or community type, but they have been personal luxuries--clothes, jewelry and the like. When incomes rise above a certain threshold, cash is reallocated to household luxuries and consumer goods; items like the house and furnishings that belong to the household as a corporate entity rather than to its individual members. The increased cash income could be allocated directly to individual luxuries and consumables like motorcycles, extravagant clothing, jewelry, cosmetics and foods, but for most people this is not done, with few exceptions.[8]

Instead, the main household expenditures besides those on the house itself, are on the provision of medical care and educational opportunities for children. Sending a child to high school in Belize is a costly enterprise, and in several Indian Creek households it required over 45% of annual cash income. I argue that this investment in the children is functionally equivalent to expenditure on the house and furnishings, in that it is shared consumption rather than personal consumption. Children, like the house itself, are the joint product and property of all household members (this is obviously not true in most unilineal societies, where children are considered to belong principally to the kin group of the mother or father).

Seen in this way, the shift in housing patterns and allocation that accompanies greater participation in the cash economy is not a shift from spending on necessities to spending on consumer goods. Rather, there is a drastic change in the kinds of consumer goods that money is spent on. Housing and education replace personal adornment and personal consumption; investment in household property replaces investment in individual property. The cultural context of choice remains the same, but the outcomes of decision-making are quite different given a change in the economic environment and the social relations of production. I will next detail some of the links between specific outcomes (houses) and specific social and economic changes.

Household decisions and the community

Kekchi housing has undergone drastic changes, and these changes are closely related to the degree to which different Kekchi communities are participating in the cash economy of Belize. The question of how and why participating in a cash economy should lead to drastic changes in housing has been left open. I believe that this shift can be explained best at two levels: 1) the relationship between the household and the community, and 2) the relationships within households between its members. At both levels the general processes of economic change in Kekchi communities affect the decisions made by households, and it is patterning in these decisions that will now be outlined.

Kekchi community structures in more remote areas are similar to the type defined by Wolf (1957) as "closed corporate", while those in more accessible locations are much closer to the "open" type. The southern villages, however small, have miniature cargo systems of rotating, ranked political/religious offices. Village fiestas, featuring ritual dances, periodically drain a good deal of money out of the community. Presented as politically egalitarian to the outside world, the village is in fact dominated by several related core families, often descended from the original founders of the community, though they may be divided into rival factions (Howard 1977).

These communities have a strong corporate identity which is partially based on the kinship relations that link almost every household. Kinship being at best a weak "glue", cohesion of the villages is also a product of the practice of communal land tenure,[9] and the use of communal work groups in agricultural production. All adult males belong to labor groups of 12 to 25 men who clear, plant, and harvest each farmer's field in rotation. With the existing technology and crop mix, and with the very short dry season (the only time when fields can be cleared and burned), membership in the village labor group is a matter of economic survival as well as a symbol of community identity (cf. Farriss

1984:256-285). Dependence on the community allows households to be quite independent of their close kin, and neolocal nuclear family households are the norm. Ties between kin tend to be fragile, and neolocal residence is quite common, as is mobility between villages.

In this subsistence-farming system, competition between households within the village can be extremely disruptive. It is partially ameliorated by the formal system of rotating leadership in the cargo system, and is blunted by the inability of any household to accumulate or own land or other productive resources. The major ideological element of village morality is a fierce ethic of egalitarianism, and obligatory generosity. Fairly common for this kind of community in Latin America is a complex of envy, fear of envy, and witchcraft accusations, which serve as a means of social and economic control (cf. Gregory 1975). Obligatory aid and unbalanced reciprocity (codified in normative statements like "we are all a family" and "we must help each other like brothers") are reinforced by fear of envy and witchcraft, with the result that little accumulation of property takes place. The sum is a system of strong social constraints on consumption.

Housing standards fall under the community ethos of equality. Deviations from standard practice are not accepted, and I was told repeatedly that anyone who built a house with a tin roof or other foreign material would have their house burnt down (and several examples were cited). The house, in other words, is a supreme symbol of community membership (and by extension of ethnicity), and uniformity of housing is enforced (Wilk 1983). What happens within the household is not ordinarily a matter of community concern. This attitude towards the house has been observed in a number of societies that constrain individual competition and stress collective institutions.[10]

In communities where cash-cropping and wage labor play a larger role, the ethic of community equality and the cohesion of the village is much weaker. Households with a source of income outside the village no longer depend so heavily on the approval or cooperation of their neighbors, and are able to defy community consumption standards. It is usually petty shopkeepers and partially waged workers who find it easier to break with the standards of the community, because they are able to buy the food they need. Often they seek membership in a Protestant sect at the same time that they refuse to participate in fiesta expenditures, village offices, and the communal work groups. No longer able to draw on the village for help in building houses, they use less labor-intensive materials purchased in town. The building of a new house with board walls or a metal roof is therefore both a symbol of rejection on the part of the village, and a symbol of independence on the part of the owner.

The first person in a village to build a house of imported materials is the subject of intense hostility. Unless household members have very close kin ties with other village members they will be forced to leave. As time goes on, however, others may follow the original example, and more houses will be built with purchased materials. This is not to say that the rest of the community disintegrates. Rather, those who continue to depend on subsistence farming maintain a community within a community, maintaining the ethic of equality in housing, in labor exchange, and in leadership. In the meantime, unbridled competition for economic and social position takes place among those households that have "left the fold", and houses become important symbols of success in that competition.

To summarize, there seems to be a close relationship between community uniformity in domestic architecture, and the economic/ecological unity and corporateness of the community (see also Rodman 1985a, Kowaleski *et al.* 1984). When the village economy is penetrated by the cash economy, and some households can survive without the cooperation of the community, they are also freed from the close constraints that the community places on consumption. Houses are both positive and negative symbols of the relationships among households, and between households and the community.

The household and its members

As mentioned above, in subsistence-farming villages, independent nuclear family households predominate. Upon marriage there is a short period of obligatory uxorilocal residence, and after this most couples set up their own separate neolocal household. With little property to inherit, and the community labor group to provide labor when needed during the agricultural cycle, there are few abiding or lasting links between parents and their married children.

The household economy is characterized by generalized reciprocity. All members of the household are involved in productive labor, and the male and female sectors of the domestic economy are poorly differentiated. All household members tend the household's pigs and chickens; all household members work in the fields (though only the adult males work in the communal work groups); all household members fish and gather wild foods. Husbands and wives have small sources of income that are traditionally considered theirs alone (chicken eggs, pottery, and weaving for women, copal incense for men), but the bulk of the cash income is divided up among household members for their own use after essential tools and supplies have been purchased.

The major issues within the household revolve around how to allocate productive labor, an issue which involves many other members of the community, for households cooperate closely with each other in the fields, in child care, and in house maintenance and construction. Negotiations between household members mostly concern work; will the husband work with the wife's father today, or will he go off with his brother hunting? Will a grown up son go to help his grandfather plant corn, or will he stay home and help fix the chicken coop? Conflicts are generally over the quantity and quality of work, not the distribution of the products that result. The constant exchange of labor, food, and household items between households obscures the balance within them.

With the introduction of cash crops and a general increase in cash income, the organization of agricultural labor and production changes drastically. To handle more crops, growing in spatially separated locations at different times of the year, the community work group is ineffective. More labor is motivated through small exchange-labor groups of close kin. Increased competition for choice parcels of land means that family ties and inheritance become important means of gaining access to agricultural land. Groups of close kin also find it possible to pool cash for investment in productive enterprises like shops or trucks. The social result is the formation of extended family households, as sons or daughters stay in their natal household after marriage.

Physically, the settlement pattern of a community engaged in cash crop production reflects the presence of extended family households. Rather than building larger houses, the Kekchi house an extended family by grouping several small houses around a patio (this is an ancient pattern among all Maya peoples). The proximity of the houses to each other reflects the degree of cohesion of the family fairly directly (as observed elsewhere by Yellen 1977:89 and Kramer 1982:139). The individual houses each contain a nuclear family, and are counted by census takers as individual households, though an economic definition of the household would recognize the clusters as the salient economic unit. Unlike subsistence farming communities where houses are dispersed, mobile, and fairly evenly spaced, cash crop farming villages tend to be composed of discrete nucleated patio clusters that are themselves dispersed. The clusters tend to establish a firm sense of place, an association between the extended family and a particular housing site or area that has some continuity over time.

The extended family household is better able to pool labor and resources to cope with the demands of a more diverse economy (Wilk 1984), but the allocation of new kinds of income becomes problematic and complex. When exchanges between household members consist mainly of intangibles, they are complex and multi-stranded (including promises for the future), and it is hard for individuals to draw short-term balances. The goods that are produced and consumed within the household subsistence economy are joint products of everyone's labor, and that labor has no cash value as a commodity. But when labor can be valued on a labor market, when commodity flows can be converted into cash values, relationships can be more accurately judged in economic terms, and cohesive productive units with several adults face difficult allocation problems. A new imbalance enters the domestic economy. Who has the right to decide how to spend money from selling rice? The husband who took it to market? The sons who helped grow it? The wife whose labor fed them while they worked in the fields?

A major problem is presented to the household when younger people, who often have greater opportunities for wage labor because of their education (or because they will accept lower wages), no longer want to contribute their entire income to the common household fund. Households are deeply concerned with keeping their children in the natal household as long as possible, and must strike a balance that allows the younger worker to retain a portion of cash as disposable income.[11] Thus, many young Kekchi men have a great deal (comparatively) of disposable income and they spend most of it on personal consumer goods. But the discussions and arguments that take place within the household reveal the volatility of the collision between household labor values and those of the wage labor market. Most common are violent arguments between brothers; elder brothers are often called upon to stay home and help their father farm, allowing a younger brother to go and seek wage work. The elder brother feels that it is his farm labor that enables the younger brother to eat and go away to work, but the younger brother has cash of his own to spend, while the older brother has none. And the older brother is doing hard, culturally valued work, while the younger one has an "easy" job. Meanwhile the younger brother finds himself marginal to the household economy, but can do no more than toy with the idea of leaving, given the poor long-term employment prospects outside the village. The authority relationships between siblings of different ages are firmly entrenched in the traditional kinship system (cf. Vogt 1969:230, 243), but the norms come under great stress when cash incomes enter the picture.

As mentioned previously, the gender-based division of labor tends to become much more sharply defined in cash-crop producing areas. Women's sources of independent cash income decline in relative importance, while most cash income is brought in by males. Agricultural production of all kinds falls almost exclusively within the male sphere, while domestic maintenance becomes the province of female work groups and individual female labor. The allocation of cash income between the sexes becomes a major problem, as men's labor can be assigned a cash value, and women's labor cannot (cf. Friedman 1984, Evers et al. 1984). When a man earns US $6 for nine hours of work on a farm, how does he value his wife's food preparation, child care and household maintenance? How does she place a value on her services? This kind of thinking and valuation is alien to the Kekchi and is resisted in many ways, yet the problem of what to do with the $6 a day remains: to whom does it belong?

Kekchi tradition places great value on the conjugal family as a joint decision-making unit, in which husband and wife share and cooperate within the bounds of a relatively flexible division of labor. But in villages with higher cash incomes, these ideals come under increasing strain. Family quarrels are very private, but sometimes they spill over into public when violence or drinking is involved. I witnessed a number of violent arguments between husbands and wives immediately after sales of swine, and the topic was always the allocation of the proceeds. How much could the husband keep? How much was she really going to spend on the childrens' books, and how much was she going to give to her mother or spend on jewelry? Several women complained to me that their husbands did not reveal how much cash they had received from the sale of rice.[12] Women often have to draw on their relatives to apply pressure on husbands when they feel that husbands are misallocating cash. But these are extreme cases. On a daily basis the negotiations between husbands and wives about allocation of goods are extremely complex; they invoke the value of labor, goods, and social standing within multiple and changing contexts.

This crisis of allocation is not an unusual situation in developing countries. It is clear that in some ecological circumstances, the household disintegrates as a corporate entity, and single stranded exchange relationships between individual men, women, and children take its place (see Palacio [1985] for a Belizean example). Wage labor may require temporary or seasonal migration by males, with females left behind to run a truncated subsistence economy and raise the children (Gonzalez 1969). The availability of full-time secure wage labor for males or females in the local area also has distinct, and complex, effects on household organization and the division of labor within the household (Laslett 1981).

But in the Kekchi cash economy, the corporate extended family household is vitally important unit in cash crop production, and the pooling of diverse resources in a large household unit is an important source of security in an uncertain and changing economy (cf. Sahlins 1957). Just as the cash income and subsistence goods from men's work are considered essential, so too women's domestic work and children's farm and household labor cannot be replaced by cash. No man can purchase child labor to help on the farm, prepared food, and lodgings in the local community. To keep the household unit together, however, the crisis of allocation must be solved.

The solution adopted by the Kekchi--to put surplus cash into the house and furnishings--is both traditional and pragmatic. Traditional in the sense that the bulk of all production in Kekchi farming, hunting, and gathering has always been allocated to the family as a group rather than to individuals. Pragmatic in a number of ways. First, because allocating cash income to the household as a unit settles the issue of who is to benefit in an equitable and equal way. Everyone gets to listen to the radio, everyone walks on the concrete floor, everyone shares the bittersweet envy of neighbors. Everyone, that is, who remains in the household. And this sharing is a potent device, on the part of the parents, in the struggle to keep children attached to the household after they marry. It is a demonstration that the income they donate to the household is not going to be wasted on rum for father or clothes for mother, but instead it will be spent on permanent improvements that the whole family can use for many years to come, and which add materially to the the family's assets. They will eventually come back to the child through inheritance, if the child remains in the household to assert a claim.

The issue of who makes these allocation decisions and how they are made remains an open one in the Kekchi case. The analysis above was not foreseen during fieldwork, so my data on how expenditures are negotiated are fragmentary. I was privy to a number of volatile discussions between fathers and sons, regarding the disposition of the son's earned income. Using idioms of "respect" (on the father's side) and "fairness" (on the son's), and "helping each other" (on both parts), some fathers negotiated successfully and kept their sons attached to the household. Others demanded too much or spent the son's donated cash in unacceptable ways, and the son left (sometimes to return later). In the latter case, both father and son became, by their own definitions, poorer, for a large household with more than one adult male is almost a requirement for long-term economic success in the economy of southern Belize.[13]

In the process of allocating the bulk of the household's cash income to the built environment, the scene is set for intensification of the ideology of the household and house (cf. Lofgren 1984, Wong 1984). Many of the emotional and cultural loadings which we are used to placing on terms like "home" and "family" can be seen in nascent forms among the northern Kekchi today. The Kekchi are seeing a transformation of their social field from one with the community and kindred as primary units, to one in which the household is the primary unit. The house itself becomes an important tool for identifying, defining, and manipulating these social concepts and maps, and there is clearly feedback between economic, cultural, and social levels during the process of change.

Conclusions

Based on my analysis of the Kekchi case, I predict that investment in communal property, including the home, is a common solution to allocation problems within the household economy in many other cultural settings. Many other aspects of housing, besides the simple amount of household resources invested in it, should be amenable to similar analysis. One implication of the Kekchi example is that housing patterns are causally related to a number of variables in the wider social and economic sphere that are not usually considered terribly important. My explanation for Kekchi spending on housing suggests that key variable for further investigation include 1) the relative value of men's and women's wages, and the state of the labor market, 2) the monetary and cultural value placed on housework, 3) the value of child labor in the home and the marketplace, 4) the degree to which women own and manage property and their own cash, 5) the importance of inherited property for younger generations, 6) the existing system of marriage and residence, and the domestic cycle, 7) the kind of migratory wage labor opportunities that are available.

It is worth noting, in closing, that much of the recent literature on modernization and culture change is concerned with the issues I have listed above (e.g. Beneria and Sen 1982). Adopting a decision-making approach therefore has the potential of bringing discussion of the built environment back to center stage in the study of culture change, innovation, and economic adaptation. By focussing on how household members themselves make decisions about their domestic architecture we can build up a body of empirical data on the cultural, economic, environmental and psychological factors that affect that decision making in different contexts.

Notes

1. *Kidder's House* (1985), a recent best seller, examines the way that the political, cultural, economic, psychological and aesthetic are all involved in the design and construction of a single American house. Would that we had a single ethnographic account of comparable detail from another culture!

2. Park (1982) makes a distinction between three kinds of decision criteria or dimensions. Rejection Inducing Dimensions establish minimum acceptable levels. Relative Preference Dimensions are attributes that are considered desirable but not essential; they increase the weight of an acceptable option. Trade-Off Dimensions can be compensated for if they prove unacceptable in value; for example if a house does not have a large back yard, this can be compensated for if it does have a swimming pool.

3. See Wilk 1981, Howard 1977, and Schackt 1986 for ethnography of the Belizean Kekchi, and Bolland 1986 for a general discussion of Belize.

4. It is very difficult to estimate the amount of money that has flowed in to the Kekchi area from sales of marijuana. The marketing of the product is handled by Creoles, Caribs and East Indians, so the bulk of the money does not go to Kekchi farmers (US $10/lb was the maximum price paid to farmers in 1984). Based on the number of new vehicles and other consumer goods to be seen in the last few years, some farmers are making several thousand dollars a year. See Birdwell-Pheasant (1984) for a discussion of the impact of marijuana income in Yucatec Maya villages in northern Belize. The influx of marijuana money in southern Belize took place after the main period of fieldwork on which this paper is based, so I have few details on how the Kekchi are spending it.

5. While the villages have systems of communal and usufruct land tenure based on custom (and not recognized by Belizean law), in practice the system is manipulated so that particular households and families have choice of the best parcels and locations. In these and other ways the egalitarian ethic is subverted or bent.

6. This is partially a utilitarian response to the increasing cost of gathered materials, for as the forest is cleared and converted to short-fallow agriculture, wood for construction becomes harder to find and has to be carried long distances. It is still cheaper, however, to rent a truck and drive off into the forest and cut wood, than to buy cut lumber.

7. The concrete block house on a concrete slab floor with a corrugated iron roof could be called the new "international" style dwelling, for it is a common aspiration in rural areas throughout the developing world. Rutz (1984) suggests that these building materials are chosen because they

313

substitute purchased inputs for labor time in construction and maintenance, and time is an increasingly valuable item in cash economies.

8. One exception to this rule is among young unmarried men; they have to give a portion of their income to their parents, but whatever is left over is spent entirely on personal consumption. They most often will spend on goods like motorcycles, musical instruments, clothes, wristwatches, and guns.

9. Kekchi land tenure and agriculture are described in Wilk 1981 and 1984. More remote villages are located in Indian Reserves, where individuals are prohibited from owning land, and the village alcalde ("mayor") is responsible for allocating plots each year and collecting a nominal use-fee. Depending on local population pressure and the quality of land available, informal and formal systems of tenure which sometimes approximate ownership are administered at the village level.

10. Summarizing and reaffirming the insights of Duncan (1981:47), Rodman (1985b:271) says

    . . . where a collective orientation prevails . . . The home is an enclosure with no public face, a private place for keeping women and valued goods. In other words, the house is a container of wealth . . .

    The similarities with the Kekchi case are clear, though the definition of "collective orientation" remains problematic in practice.

11. The whole issue of parents and children negotiating over income is part of a larger topic of research. Caldwell's (1981) discussion of how inter-generation flows of wealth change during development is an excellent place to begin.

12. For an excellent comparable case where women are increasingly shunted into an enclosed domestic economy, while men function in a cash economy, with drastic consequences for the household unit, see Weismantel (1986).

13. See Hunt (1965) and Hughes (1975) for comparable cases where a large household is a prerequisite for economic mobility during rapid modernization. Netting (1982) makes the more general point that large households tend to be wealthier than small on a cross-cultural basis, an observation made also by Hackenburg et al.(1984) in a modern urban setting.

References

ALTMAN, Irwin and Martin Chemers
1984   *Culture and environment.* Cambridge University Press: New York.

BARNUM, H. and L. Squire
1979   *A model of an agricultural household.* Johns Hopkins University Press: Baltimore.

BECKER, Gary S. and H. G. Lewis
1974   Interaction between quantity and quality of children. in T. W. Schultz,(ed.), *Economics of the family.* University of Chicago Press: Chicago.

BECKER, Gary S.
1981   *A treatise on the family.* Harvard University Press: Cambridge, Mass.

BENERIA, Lourdes and Gita Sen
1982   Class and Gender Inequalities and Women's Role in Economic Development: Theoretical and Practical Implications. *Feminist Studies* 8(1):157-176.

BIRDWELL-PHEASANT, Donna
1984   Cycles of Powerlessness: Domestic Development and the "Labor Flow" Enterprise. Paper Presented at the Annual Meeting of the American Anthropological Association: Denver.

BOLLAND, Nigel
1986   *Belize: a new nation in Central America.* Westview Press: Boulder.

BONFIELD, E., Kaufman, C., and S. Hernandez
1984   Household decisionmaking: units of analysis and decision processes. in M. Roberts and L. Wortzel (eds.) *Marketing to the changing household.* Ballinger: Cambridge, Mass.. pp. 231-263.

BRAUDEL, F.
1973   *Capitalism and material life, 1400-1800.* Harper and Row: New York.

CALDWELL, John
1981   *The theory of fertility decline.* Irwin Publishers: Homewood, Illinois.

CARTER, A.
1984   Household Histories. in R. Netting, R. Wilk and E. Arnould
              (eds.) *Households: comparative and historical studies of the
              domestic group*. University of California Press: Berkeley.

CHAPMAN, Dennis
1955   *The home and social status*. Routledge & Kegan Paul: London.

CHAYANOV, A.V.
1966   *The theory of peasant economy*. Irwin: Homewood, Ill.

COOPER, C.
1974   The House as a Symbol of Self, in J. Lang, C. Burnette, W.
              Moleski, and D. Vachon (eds.), *Designing for human
              behavior: architecture and the behavioral sciences*. Dowden,
              Hutchinson and Ross: Stroudsberg, Pa., pp. 130-146.

CUNNINGHAM, Clark
1973   Order in the Atoni House. in R. Needham (ed.) *Right and left*.
              University of Chicago Press: Chicago. pp. 204-238.

CURTIS, R.
1986   Household and Family in Theory on Inequality. *American
              Sociological Review*. 51:168-183.

DAVIS, Harry
1976   Decision Making within the Household. *Journal of Consumer
              Research*. 2:24

DONLEY, Linda
1982   House Power: Swahili Space and Symbolic Markers, in I.
              Hodder (ed.), *Symbolic and structural archaeology*.
              Cambridge University Press: Cambridge.

DULY, Colin
1979   *The houses of mankind*. Thames and Hudson: London.

DUNCAN, J.S.
1981   From Container of Women to Status Symbol: The Impact of
              Social Structure on the Meaning of the House. in J. S. Duncan
              (ed.), *Housing and identity: cross-cultural perspectives*. London.
              pp. 36-59.

ERRINGTON, Shelley
1979   The Cosmic House of the Buginese. *Asia*,
              January/February:8-13.

EVERS, H., W. Clauss and D. Wong
1984   Subsistence Reproduction: A Framework for Analysis. in J.
            Smith, I. Wallerstein and H. Evers (eds.), *Households and the
            world economy*. Sage Publications: Beverley Hills. pp.23-36.

FARRISS, Nancy
1984   *Maya society under colonial rule*. Princeton University Press:
            Princeton.

FERBER, Robert and Lucy Lee
            Husband-wife Influence in Family Purchasing Behavior.
            Journal of Consumer Research. 1:43-50.

FERNANDEZ, James
1977   Fang Architectonics. Working paper in the Traditional Arts,
            No. 1. Institute for the Study of Human Issues: Philadelphia.

FOLBRE, Nancy
1984   Cleaning House: New Perspectives on Households and Economic
            Development. Paper presented at the XII International Congress
            of the Latin American Studies Association, Albuquerque, New
            Mexico.

FRIEDMAN, Kathie
1984   Households as Income-Pooling Units. in J. Smith, I.
            Wallerstein and H. Evers (eds.), *Households and the
            world economy*. Sage Publications: Beverley Hills. pp.37-55.

GLASSIE, H.
1975   *Folk housing in middle Virginia*. University of Tennessee Press:
            Knoxville.

GONZALEZ, Nancie S.
1969   *Black Carib household structure*. American Ethnological
            Society, Monograph 48.

GREGORY, James R.
1975   Image of Limited Good, or Expectation of Reciprocity?
            Current anthropology. 16:73-93.

HACKENBURG, Robert, Arthur D. Murphy and Henry A. Selby
1984   The Urban Household in Dependent Development, in R.
            Netting, R. Wilk and E. Arnould (eds.), *Households:
            comparative and historical studies of the domestic group*.
            Berkeley: University of California Press.

HARTMANN, Heidi
1981   The Family as a Locus of Gender, Class, and Political Struggle:
            The Example of Housework. *Signs* 6:366-394.

HAREVEN, Tamara
1982   *Family time and industrial time.* Cambridge University Press:
            Cambridge.

HOWARD, Michael C.
1977   Political change in a mayan village in southern Belize. Katunob
            Occasional Publications in Mesoamerican Anthropology, no.
            10.

HUGHES, Diane
1975   Urban Growth and Family Structure in Medieval Genoa. *Past
            and Present.* 66:13-17.

HUNT, Robert
1965   The Developmental Cycle of the Family Business in Rural
            Mexico. in June Helm, (ed.), *Essays in economic
            anthropology*, American Ethnological Society, University of
            Washington Press: Seattle. pp. 54-80.

KENT, Susan
1984   *Analyzing activity areas: An ethnoarchaeological study of
            the use of space.* University of New Mexico Press:
            Albuquerque.

1983   The Differential Acceptance of Culture Change: An Archaeological
            Test Case. *Historical Archaeology* 17(2):56-63.

KIDDER, Tracy
1985   *House.* Avon Books: New York.

KOWALEWSKI, S., A. Murphy, and I. Cabrera Fernandez
1984   Yu?, Be?e and Casa: 3,500 Years of Continuity in Residential
            Construction. *Ekistics.* 307:354-359.

KRAMER, Carol
1982   *Village ethnoarchaeology: Rural Iran in archaeological
            perspective.* Academic Press: New York.

LAMPHERE, Louise
1974   Strategies, Cooperation, and Conflict Among Women in Domestic
            Groups, in M. Rosaldo and L. Lamphere (eds.), *Women, culture
            & society.* Stanford University Press: Stanford. pp.97-112.

LASLETT, Barbara
1981   Production, Reproduction, and Social Change. in James Short
(ed.), *The state of sociology*. Sage Publications: Beverley Hills.
pp 239-258.

LAWRENCE, R.
1982   Domestic Space and Society: A Cross Cultural Study.
Comparative Studies in Society and History. 24(1):104-130.

LOFGREN, Orvar
1984   Family and Household: Images and Realities: Cultural Change in
Swedish Society, in R. Netting, R. Wilk and E. Arnould
(eds.) *Households: comparative and historical studies of the
domestic group*. University of California Press: Berkeley.

NAG, M., B. White and C. Peet
1978   An Anthropological Approach to the Economic Value of
Children in Java and Nepal. *Current Anthropology*. 19:293-
306.

NARDI, Bonnie
1983   Goals in Reproductive Decision Making. *American
Ethnologist*. 10(4):697-714.

NASH, June
1983   Implications of Technological Change for Household Level
and Rural Development. *Working paper no. 37*, Office of
Women in International Development, Michigan State University.

NETTING, Robert McC.
1982   Some Home Truths on Household Size and Wealth. *American
Behavioral Scientist*. 25:641-662.

ORLOVE, Benjamin
1980   Ecological Anthropology, *Annual Review of Anthropology*.
9:235-273.

PALACIO, Joseph O.
1985   Food, Kin Ties, and Remittances in a Garifuna Village in
Southern Belize. Paper prepared for a symposium at
University of West Indies, Mona, Jamaica.

PARK, C.
1982   Joint Decisions in Home Purchasing: A Muddling-Through
Process. *Journal of Consumer Research* 9:151-162.

RAPOPORT, Amos
1977   *Australian Aborigines and the Definition of Place. in Shelter, sign and symbol.* Paul Oliver (ed.), Overlook Press: Woodstock, N.Y.. pp.38-51.

1982   *The meaning of the built environment: A nonverbal communication approach.* Sage Publications: Beverley Hills.

ROBERTS, Mary and Lawrence Wortzel (eds.)
1984   *Marketing to the changing household.* Ballinger: Cambridge, Mass..

RODMAN, Margaret
1984   Changing Places: Residential Change in Longana, Vanuatu. Paper presented at the annual meetings of the American Anthropological Association, Denver.

1985a   Moving Houses: Residential Mobility and the Mobility of Residences in Longana, Vanuatu. *American Anthropologist.* 87:56-72.

1985b   Contemporary Custom: Redefining Domestic Space in Longana, Vanuatu. *Ethnology* 24(4):269-279.

RODMAN, H.
1972   Marital Power and the Theory of Resources in a Cross Cultural Context. *Journal of Comparative Family Studies* 1:50-67.

RUTZ, Henry
1984   Material Affluence and Social Time in Village Fiji. in Richard Salisbury and Elizabeth Tooker (eds.), *Affluence and cultural survival.* American Ethnological Society: Washington, DC.

SAFILIOS-ROTHCHILD, Constantina
1972   The Study of Family Power Structure: A Review 1960-1969. *Journal of Marriage and the Family* 34:239-244.

SAHLINS, Marshall
1957   Land Use and the Extended Family in Moala, Fiji. *American Anthropologist.* 59:449-462.

SCHACKT, Jon
1986   One god-two temples: schismatic process in a Kekchi village. *Oslo Occasional Papers in Social Anthropology*, number 13. University of Oslo, Norway.

320

SPIRO, Rosann
1983   Persuasion in Family Decision-Making. *Journal of Consumer Research.* 9:393-402.

VOGT, Evon Z.
1969   *Zinacantan: a Maya community in the highlands of Chiapas.* Harvard University Press: Cambridge.

WATSON-GEGEO, Karen and David Gegeo
1983   Shaping the Mind and Straightening Out Conflicts: The Discourse of Karawa'ae Family Counselling. Paper presented at the conference Talk and Social Inference, Pitzer College, Claremont, California. October 1983.

WEISMANTEL, Mary
1986   Wanja--Food and Family in Highland Ecuador, Paper presented at the Annual meeting of the Association for Consumer Research, Toronto.

WILK, Richard R.
1981   Agriculture, ecology and domestic organization among the Kekchi Maya. Ph.D. Dissertation, University Microfilms, Ann Arbor.

1984   Households in Process: Agricultural Change and Domestic Transformation among the Kekchi Maya of Belize. in Netting, Wilk and Arnould (eds.), *Households: comparative and historical studies of the domestic group.* University of California Press: Berkeley.

1983   Little House in the Jungle. *Journal of Anthropological Archaeology.* 2(2):99-116.

WOLF, Eric
1957   Closed Corporate Communities in Mesoamerica and Central Java. *Southwestern Journal of Anthropology* 13(1).

WOLF, Margery
1968   *The house of Lim.* Appleton-Century-Crofts: New York.

WONG, Diana
1984   The Limits of Using the Household as a Unit of Analysis. in J. Smith, I. Wallerstein and H. Evers (eds.), *Households and the world economy.* Sage Publications: Beverley HIlls. pp.56-63.

YELLEN, Jon
1977   *Archaeological approaches to the present.* Academic Press: New York.

MONEY, SEX AND COOKING: MANIPULATION OF THE PAID/UNPAID BOUNDARY BY ASANTE MARKET WOMEN

Gracia Clark

Introduction

Asante market women face heavy and conflicting pressures both to fulfill their responsibilities for cooking, childcare and cleaning, and to earn income to help support themselves, their children and other relatives.[1] Cultural values and rules affect more than the decision whether or not to forgo money income and put more time into unpaid activities, such as cooking. They also construct the task which the actor chooses to perform or not. These values affect not only the amount but the timing and kind of labor Asante women need to perform domestic tasks. Each of these variables contributes to determining the degree and type of contradictions between domestic work and trading (or other occupations).

Domestic work, as unpaid production for immediate consumption, is dominated by the rules and values associated with the consumption of the goods and services it produces. The relations of production of this type of work are closely related, if not identical, to those in which the goods and services are consumed. Rules and values apply not only to the product of domestic labor, but to the relations in which it is produced. Cultural rules place values, for example, not only on the dishes produced by cooking, but on when to cook, who should cook for whom, and the consequences of specific deviations from these stipulations.

Asante domestic relations present attractive complexities in the dovetailing of paid and unpaid working relations. Women provide use values in their domestic work, but expect a financial return. Relations of childbearing oblige women to provide as well as receive money. Flexible residence patterns provide cases of nearly every imaginable combination or absence of coresidence, domestic work, financial assistance and kin or marriage tie. Commercial arrangements for the provision of domestic needs, including cooked food, are varied and popular, but also a focus of tension and controversy. Women's ability to transfer tasks across the boundary between paid and unpaid work, or between various noncommercial relations, is an important facet of their ability to preserve independent incomes and influence in their families and communities.

This paper focusses on cooking because it creates sharper conflicts for women traders in Kumasi Central Market than childcare or cleaning. Guyer suggests that cooking often overshadows childcare as a constraint on women's working lives (1981). She points out the extent to which cultural and technological definitions of meal schedules and dishes vary the length and frequency of meal preparation. She also draws attention to the timing of meals as

323

a key source of conflict with the daily productive cycle. For Asante women, domestic cooking is closely linked to the marital relationship, which can be threatened by significant variations in meal timing and content, or delegation of preparation. The degree and kind of power women have in marriage, compared to kin relations, affect both the degree and kind of compromises women make on domestic work issues.

Social context of cooking and trading

Lineage and marital obligations

Asante cultural patterns presume lineage loyalty and individual achievement for both men and women. Matrilineal traditions remain strong for Asantes, even for urban residents not using lineage land, houses or other property. Women have a secure position in their own lineages, as daughters, sisters and the mothers of its heirs. Their brothers and mothers' brothers take more of the leadership positions, but there are female positions at each lineage and community level. Women retain rights of access to lineage housing and land, administered by lineage elders, before, during and after marriage. Asantes see a major dichotomy between the enduring nature of lineage relations, including motherhood, and the inherently unstable, transitory relations of marriage. They use a proverb to indicate this: "You can get a new husband (or wife), but not a new brother."

Asante couples may continue living separately in their family houses after marriage. In these cases, children live with their mothers but visit their fathers frequently. Married or unmarried, a woman can live and cooperate economically with her mother, brother, maternal uncle, father, or any of a range of female relatives without losing respectability. Couples more often live together when they migrate to a new area, such as the city of Kumasi, where they may not have family-owned housing available. Of the 65% of Asante market women surveyed who were currently married, 59% live with their husbands (38% of the total). Although duolocality, matrilocal on women's part, is certainly compatible with matrilineal organisation, it is also practiced by Ga women in Accra, the national capital (Robertson 1984, p.57).

Living apart gives Asante women more control over domestic task allocation. Married women living separately have more freedom to invite relatives to live with them, or to go live with them. They can also substitute others' labor in cooking and housework with fewer repercussions, or without the husband's knowledge, and more frequently do so (Clark 1984).

Asantes who openly prefer duolocal marriage, both men and women, claim that the social distance it creates makes for a more peaceful, longer-lasting marriage, with greater mutual respect. Specifically, they believe it "prevents quarrels" over use of money, time, and personal movements. Wives are expected to be submissive and deferential in interactions with their husbands. The ideal is easier to maintain when such interaction is minimised. Virtual ignorance of the spouse's amount and sources of income is not uncommon, and sometimes openly recommended.

Market traders' independent incomes and budgets do not set them apart from Asante women in other occupations. As in much of West Africa, Asantes expect spouses to have separate finances and interests. Each pays for certain expenses related to their marriage and children, and both retain allegiance to their own lineages and help support relatives with labor and money.

Asante cultural values reward both men and women for financial success, but also make considerable demands on women for unpaid work. They provide domestic services not only to their husbands, within marriage, but within lineage relations, to their children, mothers and elderly relatives. Women are encouraged to earn as much money as possible, but expected to earn less than men, on average, because of their domestic responsibilities. Women put time into raising children, which reduces their earning ability, and also put money into raising children, which further reduces their capital accumulation.

Asante proverbs and other folk models acknowledge the conflict between unpaid domestic work and income-generating work for women and analyse it in terms compatible with the production/reproduction and exchange/use value dichotomies. For example, men pay twice the assessment of women towards town and lineage expenses. Asantes explained this practice in terms of each gender's responsibility to the lineage: "Men bring money and women bring children to make the lineage strong." This proverb displays the paid/unpaid dichotomy as a division in gender roles, not primarily marital roles, since it also divides brothers and sisters.

Traditional maternal and paternal roles show a parallel division, with mothers providing use values and fathers exchange values. Both parents contribute to the support of the children, but the mother contributes vegetable foodstuffs, usually homegrown until recently, while the father contributes meat, fish and salt, all widely traded in precolonial times. While not necessarily historical, these ideals were reported by Rattray (1923) and Fortes (1970) and confirmed as oral history in recent interviews (Clark 1984).

Contemporary urban Asantes normally purchase both genders' food contributions. As vegetable food prices rise precipitously, consumption of meat and fish, which men traditionally provided, has dropped sharply. An urban Asante woman's maternal responsibility for growing vegetable foods has now become a financial responsibility for a major proportion of family expenses.

Duolocality also reduces the proportion of paternal contributions. Parents living with the children, usually the mother, often end up contributing more towards their medical bills, clothing and school supplies, according to informants.

As budgets contract, bills cannot always be assigned as planned. Parents not physically present are less available when urgent financial crises must be met. Claims on other paternal and maternal male relatives, a traditional alternative, are weakened by deepening poverty and increased geographical mobility.

Asante women's financial duties towards children and other lineage kin shape the conflict between work and home in different directions than for western, middle-class women. Asantes do not experience a direct conflict between income-generating work, on the one hand, and husband and family, on the other. Within motherhood, they see their financial responsibilities as much more primary and inalienable than physical care of their children. Within marriage, financial support, fidelity and marital stability depend more heavily on the wife's own participation in cooking. Children conversely provide a woman's main source of domestic help to eventually release her from cooking and childcare and enable her to continue working full time. To some extent, this situation creates a contradiction between motherhood and wifehood.

The financial aspect of the Asante motherly role drives a mother to ensure a steady, high personal income, rather than discouraging her participation in paid work. Although a mother also has the responsibility to provide physical care of her child, including meals, her financial responsibility takes precedence. As one mother explained to me, "Everyone likes children, so they will not let them stay hungry or hurt themselves, but no one would work for them the way I do." An Asante child needs not a mother's care as such but reliable care from a competent person. Less exacting standards of care combine with less emotional significance assigned to physical care to encourage delegation. Personal preparation of food, in contrast, is an essential part of the social purpose food fulfills in marriage.

Cooking and marriage

The important role of personal cooking in establishing and maintaining a marriage means that departures from ideal standards of performance can have severe consequences to the relationship. These dangers tend to compress the gap between ideal, expected and actual meals. This effect, however, appears almost entirely in the evening meal, because the sexual and financial associations of cooking focus heavily on the evening meal.

In the classic Asante duolocal marriage, a wife cooks the evening meal in her own house as a preliminary to visiting her husband for the night at his house. In farm villages and Kumasi alike, dusk still brings a noticeable traffic in children and young to middle-aged women carrying large covered dishes. In polygamous Asante marriages (never coresidential), even-handed rotation in cooking schedules removes the necessity to discuss sex directly.

The sexual connotation of cooking is so strong that Asantes use it as a euphemism as well as a symbol for sex. The ubiquitous street comments from young men of "my wife, my wife" change to "ah, you are bringing me food" for girls carrying even the smallest dish. An older woman trader with a new boyfriend made a great show of departing early to cook for him, complete with bawdy gestures. Another trader denied accepting goods on credit from a male farmer (a type of transaction associated in jokes with sex), by loudly maintaining, "I am not cooking for anyone!" As in many languages, Asante Twi uses the same verb (di) for eating and sex, which has many other meanings of possession, taking, inheriting, etc. It must be reduplicated (didi) to unambiguously mean eating.

"Cooking for" a man seems to take the place that "living with" a man occupies in contemporary United States society, as a trial or quasi-marital relationship. For some Asante couples, it will turn out to be a stage of courtship, formalised eventually through lineage, church and legal rituals. Other similar relationships will be broken off due to incompatibility, or remain informal, with less family and public support. Couples in a relationship including daily cooking accept some degree of public recognition of the relationship and also recognise mutual responsibilities similar to marital roles, although less binding.

Cooking can express either positive or negative sexual feelings. Preparing prompt, attractive, large meals for a husband symbolises respect for conservative standards in other aspects of the relationship. Wives express their satisfaction with a warm relationship by extra care in cooking, just as husbands enjoy giving beloved wives extra gifts. One trader described with gusto how a wife chooses her finest bowl, puts a beautiful fufu in it and arranges the fish to look big and plump. Then she bathes carefully, rubs herself with cream and puts on her good cloth to take the dinner to her husband.

Women also express anger and defiance by persistent carelessness in cooking, or by refusing to cook altogether. This expresses the threat or intention of breaking off the relationship. One group of traders sympathised with a middle-aged friend who had stopped cooking for her husband because of his continual adultery. Since he no longer came home to eat dinner, they argued, it would simply waste the food. Although not endorsing it as ideal wifely behavior, they considered it more appropriate and respectable than taking several lovers, her other reaction. Robertson reports that Ga women similarly stop cooking to signal imminent separation (Robertson 1984, p.183).

This sexual charge means that women not intending separation compete sexually with the evening meal, with hypothetical rivals when none exist. A wife becomes extremely suspicious if her husband loses his appetite, especially in the evening. She will accuse him of eating somewhere else (with someone else), or of not liking her food. She will be more reluctant to delegate cooking to potential sexual rivals, such as housemaids, in case the association proves too strong.

The sexual connotation of cooking also applies to commercial sources of the type of food served at evening meals. Informal restaurants serving these heavy meals to patrons of ordinary incomes are called chop bars. Many are perfectly respectable, but the suspicion persists that the chop bar proprietor or her assistant provides sexual services along with the evening meal, as a wife does. Some chop bars serve alcoholic drinks and are indeed neighborhood centers of partying and/or prostitution. If a man goes for dinner to the chop bar, he may "eat" more than food before he comes home.

Cooking the evening meal is not only linked firmly to sex within marriage, but to the main financial contribution from husbands to wives. The man's regular payment, usually weekly, of a specific sum for buying foodstuffs, called "chop money," distinguishes a steady relationship leading to marriage from a casual affair marked by irregular gifts. Chop money is often the only money a husband gives directly to his wife, to cover his obligation to feed his children and help her. A man should pay rent or school fees, but he does so directly, and gives money or clothes to the children themselves. In poor families, where up to 90% of total income goes on food, chop money is the only money he gives to either wife or children.

The wife must pay for any expense related to cooking from this chop money, or supplement it with her own earnings. Several traders emphasized that their chop money was not enough to buy food for the family meal, as it should, or even for their husbands' own food. Robertson remarks on the prevalence of inadequate chop money for Ga women as well (Robertson 1984, p.192). Asante traders mentioned that either sexual competition or pride could lead women to provide higher quality, more ample meals to husbands at their own expense. Low or irregular chop money may reflect the husband's sexual disinterest, which a wife may prefer to conceal (see also Robertson 1984, p.190).

A wife also bears the cost of any substitution for her own unpaid labor in cooking. If she buys more expensive semi-processed foods, she makes up the difference. If a relative or maid does the cooking, any food, clothing, gifts or wages received comes from the wife's pocket. If her own daughter does the cooking, the father is already supporting this child. Her chop money remains intact, although the family may be forgoing income from the child's possible employment.

The connection between cooking and financial support is so strict that any interruption in cooking duties usually stops it. This contradicts the husband's ideal responsibility to support his children, since they obviously continue to eat. In several cases, men who married a second wife simply paid the previous amount of weekly chop money alternately to the wife cooking that week. Men often suspend payment of chop money completely when they travel or migrate abroad, contributing only occasional gifts or clothing.

The tight connection between cooking, sex and finances also links sexual and economic conflicts. A suspicious wife experiences economic and sexual jealousy simultaneously. She fears sexual rivals will be spending money she would otherwise receive for her children. In itself no trivial complaint, the expression of economic outrage on behalf of the children is considered to show more self-respect and propriety than voicing sexual jealousy. Robertson reports similar attitudes among Ga women (Robertson 1984, p.189). A man likewise complains more publicly of his wife's laziness in cooking than of her infidelity or dissatisfaction, that may have motivated it.

In order to enjoy the full sexual and economic benefits of marriage, Asante women must adjust their cooking practices. Marriage does not require new ideal cooking patterns, even for the evening meal, but makes widely accepted ones more rigid. Inflexibility in itself, however, creates conflicts with trading for married women that others can avoid. Higher preparation standards eliminate marginally qualified substitute cooks and increase total labor time. Using semi-processed foods like sliced and powdered vegetables in a husband's meals reduces the distinction between home cooking and the dreaded chop bar. Preparing lighter meals or fufu substitutes also weakens the contrast, since these items are often purchased for lunch or snacks. Meal timing, a critical point in the conflict between trading and cooking, is also a critical quality standard in the context of marital fidelity (see also Robertson 1984, p.183). If the evening meal is late, the waiting husband may be tempted to visit the nearby chop bar out of hunger alone.

Women still cook outside marriage, but the gap between ideal and actual meals can widen without serious repercussions. When women feed themselves or their children, they can pay less attention to correct preparation and timing and resort more to quick dishes or snack foods. One exhausted young mother never cooked when her husband travelled, since "we eat anything."

Marriage means wives cook more carefully, not more often. Cooking rates remain at about 60% before and after marriage age, until middle age, when children take over. During this same period, however, women steadily reduce their personal performance of other domestic chores (Clark 1984). Women traders delegate cooking less often than childcare, partly because maids old enough to cook present more of a sexual threat.

Problems with the ideal

Interference with trading

Cooking close to ideal standards not only subtracts more hours from the working day, but limits the kind of trading women can do. In Kumasi Central Market, three major categories of traders were found selling most commodities. The *nkwansufo*, or travelling buyers, spend most of their working time on the road. They bring goods from distant supply areas to wholesalers working full time in Kumasi, receiving and reselling their goods. The largest number of market traders retail goods bought from wholesalers or other sources inside or outside the market. They generally have lower capital and income levels than the other types of trader within their commodity groups.

Personal performance of cooking chores is only compatible with retailing, and appreciably hampers even this trading role. Travellers obviously must delegate daily cooking when they are out of town. Specialist travellers are only supported on routes to the more distant supply areas. To compete effectively, they must spend one or two weeks on a trip to fill a truck and reduce transport costs.

The most lucrative trading position in Kumasi Central Market is that of the local wholesalers, who sell to retailers and institutional suppliers. Their whole position rests on their availability in the market during all normal working hours, to receive travellers' goods on arrival and to have supplies available at times more convenient for buyers. While price control and tax enforcement measures made direct enquiries on income levels impossible, business hours could be readily observed. The full complement of wholesalers in any yard arrived before other traders and remained until business had stopped for the day. They showed great haste to return to the yard if they left for any reason. Wholesalers who frequently left early to cook would lose valuable shipments and customers to more reliable colleagues.

Meal timing intensifies the interference between cooking and trading. Ideal meal times conflict directly with the daily rhythm of the market. At breakfast time, traders need to be at the market already, buying their supplies when prices are lowest, as the villagers and travelling traders arrive from the supply areas. The wholesale yards open officially after 6am, but villagers arrive with supplies in peripheral areas well before this. Lunch comes at the peak of rush hour in the market. Traders count on their highest volume of sales from 10am to 2pm, and rarely leave their stalls for any reason. The trading day continues until 5 or 6pm, when the market officially closes. Serving fufu by 6pm means arriving home by 3 or 4pm, and leaving the market at 2pm, after shopping, to stand in line for transport. Fufu substitutes delay this schedule by one or two hours only.

Among food retailers, those who cook buy less goods, even if they have the capital to buy more, to be sure of clearing perishable stocks before they leave. Observed cases of temporary or long-term restriction were confirmed by traders' generalisations. One woman left a buying area with a smaller stock of cassava than her colleagues. They explained, "she can't buy as much because she has to sell quickly to go home and cook, because no one is at home." One young yam trader frequently reduced her prices below the prevailing rate in early afternoon. Market neighbors who did not know her personally commented that "she probably has to go home and cook, so she has to sell quickly." Another trader described the normal working hours in two categories. "Some women have to leave early because they have to go home and cook dinner. Others have children at home, so they can stay until the market closes." Traders openly and frequently attributed their own or others' restricted trading to conflicts with cooking, specifically to the need to leave early. They only rarely mentioned any other domestic task as a reason.

Traders could not resolve such conflicts by doing their cooking in the market. Kumasi Central Market is a highly desirable business location and hence extremely crowded. If a trader had the space food preparation requires in her stall, she would almost certainly sublet it to another trader. Trading requires fairly constant attention, which does not leave time for cooking, especially of a full meal. Family members would not be willing to travel to the market for meals, often requiring costly public transport, and eat in such noisy, public surroundings. In addition, cooking or other fires in the market proper were prohibited after a disastrous fire several years ago.

Women traders also face conflicts with their other major domestic task, physical child care. Like cooking, childcare is not particularly compatible with market trading. Contrary to the pattern suggested by Brown (1970), Bohannon and Dalton (1962) and others, less than half of the Kumasi traders with young children brought them to market (Clark 1984). Traders do not consider the market a safe place for young children, citing evident dangers from disease, accidents and exposure in most market locations. Traders who bring their young children to market under these adverse conditions regret that economic pressures force them to compromise their children's health. Childcare also interferes quite directly with trading. The mother must watch her child constantly and stop to wash or feed it, even at her busiest times, when she needs full attention to maximise sales.

Traders look for a different type of solution to their childcare problems. Working shorter hours or choosing less demanding trading roles does not resolve the conflict, since children need continuous care. Instead, traders go to considerable lengths to arrange for caretakers at home. Even nursing babies are brought to nurse several times daily. When substitute caretakers are unavailable, mothers will move to be near relatives or leave market trading altogether. Actual conflict between childcare and trading is reduced by cultural norms making it much less risky for women to delegate childcare than cooking.

Cultural construction of cooking as a task

To understand the choices facing Asante cooks, not only the relationships and associations of cooking but the tasks themselves must be considered in detail. The traditional Asante meal schedule centers around an evening meal of fufu and soup. For fufu, plantains or tubers are peeled, boiled and then pounded to an elastic lump in a large wooden mortar with a pestle up to six feet long. The elaborate preparation process typically takes two or three hours, depending on skill and the quantity, from peeling to serving. The least elaborate of the soups served with fufu can be prepared while the tubers boil.

Asantes consider fufu not only their favorite and most characteristic food, but the only completely satisfying food. Accustomed to this extremely heavy, slow-digesting dish, many say they cannot sleep properly without eating fufu. Funeral attenders consider themselves to be fasting as long as they refuse fufu, taking only rice or lighter dishes. The only acceptable reason for avoiding fufu is a claim of weak digestion, or doctor's orders for such conditions as ulcers. Although young married women may make fufu to please their husbands, divorced and widowed women with sufficient income and household help also prepare fufu for their own enjoyment.

Asantes' fierce attachment to fufu seems not to have much spiritual basis. Yams, the ritually significant food for harvest festivals and offerings, can be used for fufu, but the rituals use other yam dishes. Yam is rarely used for fufu outside of yam producing areas (not near Kumasi) because of its high cost compared to other starchy staples. In Kumasi and most of Ashanti Region, the usual fufu consists of roughly equal parts of plantain and cassava, adjusted to make the fufu harder or softer, as desired.

Fufu makes significantly more labor demands than other dishes. Traders who substitute flour-based porridge dishes for fufu during the work week explain that they do so to save time. Although these dishes also require about an hour of hard stirring, this is less than half the time for fufu. Grinding vegetables to the fine paste desired for the soups accompanying these starchy staples also takes considerable labor time and energy. This naturally depends on skill and the quantity prepared, but rarely exceeds one-half hour. Only palm-nut soup requires a multistep process of boiling, pounding and squeezing comparable to the fufu process.

The proper Asante diet does include ideal home-cooked dishes for breakfast and lunch, but these are much simpler. The same boiled yams, cocoyams or plantain pounded for fufu are eaten unpounded with stew as *ampesie*, or mashed for *eto*. Neither of these dishes takes more than half an hour to prepare, ampesie being proverbial as fast and cheap. Even ideal standards are very flexible for the noon meal, to the extent that it can be difficult to get respondents to specify what the classic farm family eats. Farm families observed to eat fufu daily eat leftovers, snack on fruit, or roast plantain at their farms during the day.

The ideal Asante meal pattern specifies the time as well as the content of morning and evening meals. Women should rise well before dawn to clean the house, bathe and prepare ampesie before family members leave for the farm. Fufu should be served before dark (6 to 6:30pm), when they return. Technical considerations reinforce the cultural value on prompt evening mealtimes. Preparing a fufu-type meal after dark in a typical compound kitchen with no light or one bulb presents considerable practical problems.

332

Cooking up to ideal Asante standards requires only a moderate amount of skill and training. The limited repertoire of preferred dishes means that a daughter can master them within a year or two of acquiring the needed dexterity and strength. Girls begin grinding vegetables for the family soup at age 6 or 8, although they take longer than older children. The ability to judge proper cooking times and ingredient quantities comes at age 10 or 12, with a year or two of experience. Pounding the fufu requires more strength, and the ability to coordinate closely with another person, turning the lump between each stroke of the five-foot pestle. Care and some skill are needed to achieve the desired smoothness and elasticity. A girl can take charge of the entire process by age 12 or 15, depending on aptitude and interest, but she will need a partner to help pound the fufu.

Without any gourmet traditions, there is little motivation for an adult woman to continue improving her cooking skills beyond this point. Grinding to the desired smoothness and pounding thoroughly depend on conscientiousness more than skill. Maids are considered as skillful as daughters, but expected to take less personal interest in preparing ingredients carefully and economically.

For an urban Asante family, good cooking begins with shopping for the ingredients. Lack of refrigeration makes shopping part of the daily routine of cooking. One shops primarily for the evening meal, since other meals often consist of leftovers or purchased snacks. Depending on the distance between home and market and the degree of transport shortage, the shopping trip can take two or three hours, the same labor time spent cooking. Lower quality, higher priced ingredients can be obtained in less time by patronising small neighborhood markets, streetside stands and passing hawkers.

Shopping makes an important contribution to the final quality of the meal. Considering the limited budget of most traders, the quality and quantity of ingredients bought for the money available determine the taste of the meal as much or more than methods of preparation. Shopping well takes more judgment and perseverance than food preparation. Experience, motivation and personal contacts all improve results, so a shopper may continue to improve in efficiency for many years.

Cooking properly requires more skill and motivation than child care, by Asante standards. Mothers can leave their children in the hands of substitutes with little anxiety, because they are concerned mainly with physical safety, including prevention of accidents, adequate water and food, and cleanliness. Once a toddler can walk and eat, another child of eight or nine can look after it. As long as one child is old enough, the arrangement requires no comment other than "there are children at home."

Childcare, like cooking, requires attention, not mature judgment. Asantes consider older siblings the natural caretakers because of their concern for a child's welfare. They fear a maid may be careless, rather than unskilled, letting the child remain thirsty or hungry or fall into the fire while she falls asleep or gossips with friends. Adult relatives or neighbors in the compound can give advice or take action in an emergency.

In contrast to middle-class US families, Asantes do not consider full day interaction with the mother or another adult essential to normal intellectual and psychological growth. Mothers feel they can ensure the child's moral development by making rules and training it at night and weekends. There is no perceived threat to the maternal relationship, as this centers on the more onerous burdens of financial support and sponsorship, as distinguished by Esther Goody (1982).

Limits to dependence on marriage

The emphasis on maintaining something approaching the ideal meal pattern within marriage seems difficult to reconcile with Asante women traders' frequent departure from those standards, until one remembers the limited dependence Asante women have on marriage itself. Although cooking may be essential for Asante women to secure income from their husbands, they do not ordinarily respond by structuring their lives to attract the maximum chop money. Asante marriage does not create a permanent unit determining the control of resources, so women cannot afford to depend on it. Women who depend on their husbands' incomes are not only "soft" or unambitious, according to women traders, but bad mothers, since they do not take care to provide a secure future for their children.

Market women refer constantly to the possibility of divorce or widowhood when advising financial independence. Children do not inherit from their fathers, if any property exists, and in case of sudden death a man may not have made the customary premortem gifts to them. Paternal relatives ideally should take over the father's financial and moral responsiblities, but they may be hard pressed to support their own children. Paternal support usually dwindles in case of divorce, or even when the father travels temporarily to another town or country, to occasional gifts or payment of school fees.

Illness, bankruptcy, or simple poverty can prevent a father from adequately supporting children even when he lives with them. A contracting economy in Ghana means most families cannot survive on a single income in any case. Men acknowledge this and value their wives' contribution. A wife feels justified in resisting demands for domestic services which threaten her earning power and will challenge her husband to replace the lost income. A good father would also feel ashamed to satisfy his vanity and convenience by keeping his wife at home at the expense of his children's food or higher education. Both men and women admit that economic independence gives wives more say in family decisions. Women consider this a positive and men a negative effect. It does not give women more control over their husbands' actions or income, because of their separate budgets. Instead, women get more autonomy to take decisions unilaterally, with their own money. Many Asantes feel strict financial separation strengthens or protects marriages by "preventing quarrels" over how to spend money.

Asante women do not depend on marriage ties for access to their children, as in some strongly patrilineal societies. Children belong to their mother's lineage, so women do not fear losing them at divorce. Children also have strong ties to their father and his immediate family, who should support them until adulthood, but these are more personal and spiritual. Lineage relations arise from the fact of birth, not the choice of marital partners.

On the other hand, marriage is still an important part of an individual's life condition. Women expect to be married for most of their adult lives, and value the companionship and sexual satisfaction to be found in marriage, as well as financial support. Like Ga women, Asante women traders referred first to economic reliability in discussing good husbands in general (Robertson 1984, p.182). However, an older woman referred to "coming during the day to sit and talk with you," the same woman who continued feeding her aged husband because he had been generous when he was earning. Another described an early marriage in which "we were like twins. We went everywhere together, even to the same church." It seems that Asante women value intimacy in marriage, but do not necessarily expect it. This could be related to the fact that young girls are not expected to be virgins at marriage, but to enjoy several years of pre-marital freedom partly used to attract and test a worthy spouse. Several informants commented that they had heard that US women commonly married at 18 or 19, which they considered cut this period of enjoyment too short.

A long-lasting marriage, not necessarily the first, carries considerable prestige. It reflects credit on both husband and wife, who presumably had the good sense to pick a suitable partner, behaved well enough to satisfy them, and were themselves desirable enough to motivate good behavior. Women also realize that they have a better chance within marriage to have many children and get substantial support for them. However, having children, rather than marriage, is the social and spiritual necessity. A bad marriage, which is not providing money, companionship or sex (and therefore children) is worse than no marriage at all. Asante market women often consciously debate and decide how to balance competing claims from husband, children and personal ambition. One onion trader, recently divorced, declared "onions are my husband." She had committed herself to trading as an alternative to remarriage, considering it a more reliable source of support for herself and her children. The majority, with more confidence in their husbands or less in their trading success, negotiate compromises which balance financial and domestic pressures. Success in their womanly roles both requires and is demonstrated by such negotiations.

Compromises between trading and cooking

Commercially prepared food

The variety and sheer quantity of commercially prepared foods available testifies to the willingness of substantial numbers of women to compromise on ideal standards, despite the consequences. Women traders use a variety of commercial relations to resolve the conflict between trading and cooking. Women buy ready-to-eat food consumed at meals, or buy semi-processed foods. They also provide subsistence and wages for maids or foster children. These strategies use the woman's money to substitute for her labor time. Clearly, women are not only willing to compromise, but able to use the time saved to earn the necessary money.

A large amount of ready-to-eat food is sold in markets, residential areas, and at worksites such as office and industrial districts. These mainly substitute for the meals to which the loosest ideal standards apply. Bread, gruel, kenkey (a steamed dumpling) and other light snack meals are the most common breakfast and noon meals. Both farm and urban families rarely prepare these meals at home. Even when family members remain at home all day, they purchase lunch from roadside vendors or wandering hawkers.

For the evening meal, labor time can be reduced by purchasing semi-processed foodstuffs. Sliced and powdered vegetables sold in the market short-cut the most laborious steps of popular Asante soups and stews. These lack the fresh flavor of home-prepared vegetables, and may conceal substandard produce or outright adulteration. Either fresh or dry vegetables can be machine ground on order for a small fee, although not to the optimal smoothness. Women also substitute other dishes for fufu as a labor-saving strategy, although this is difficult for actively married women. The amount of flours and pre-mixed doughs for such dishes carried in the market is in itself evidence of some degree of compromise.

Purchases of cooked food by themselves and their families allow women to work a full day in many occupations, including farming and trading. Women can make the early start essential to make the day worthwhile, or catch the low prices. Husbands and older children can buy lunch at school or work, instead of returning home. Children five or seven years old, too young to cook for themselves, can be left alone at home with lunch money to buy from trusted vendors. Toddlers and young children accompanying their mothers can find appropriate snacks throughout the day, as she can. They may benefit from more frequent snacks, which they need, than their mother would cook herself, if she were at home.

Market traders themselves depend on cooked food sellers for their noon meal in the market. Providing snacks and meals for the 20,000 traders attending Kumasi Central Market daily is a small industry in itself, supporting hundreds of hawkers and chop bar workers. Travelling traders depend even more heavily on cooked food sellers in markets and village roadsides, while on the road. The sexual connotations of cooking to order make it difficult for women travellers to patronise chop bars or make arrangements for meals with local women as male travellers do.

Purchasing meals or snacks relieves time pressures, but increases pressure on a women's income. However, some consumers maintain that street food is less expensive than home cooked meals, partly because they usually purchase less elaborate dishes than they cook. Economies of scale can be considerable for commercial food preparation, in expensive fuel as well as labor time. In addition, men and working children pay for their own lunches bought away from home, when a home-cooked meal would come from the mother's chop money. In these cases, a woman can substitute someone else's money for her unpaid labor.

Commercial food preparation not only allows the consumer to transfer her time to paid labor instead of unpaid, but allows the producer to turn that unpaid task into a paid one. The cooked food industry provides full-time employment for women who cannot find substitute child caretakers and therefore can only leave home for a few hours at a time. They can use their home location, utensils, and family labor to generate income they control, turning consumption resources into production assets.

Although cooked food preparation is distinct from market trading, in many cases the option of cooked food sales reproduces women as market traders. Traders who cannot find or afford domestic substitutes may leave the market temporarily for home-based occupations such as this. They can earn sufficient income to provide basic family needs while unable to trade, instead of consuming their capital. When circumstances improve, their trading capital still exists. If successful, they can preserve their capital against inflation or even increase it. Cooked food sellers also develop relationships with foodstuffs suppliers in the market, who extend them goods on short-term credit. Such clientships and credit reputations can be used in retail trade when they return to the market.

The advantages to Asante market women of using commercially prepared food seem substantial, and they do make substantial use of it. The process has stopped short of taking over the evening meal, however, despite the range of commercial alternatives available and used for other meals. This is because the cultural constraints on using both short-cuts and substitutes in meal preparation are especially strong for that meal. The sexual and financial significance of cooking the evening meal personally within marriage effectively inhibits women from using the available options.

Substitute cooks

Instead of purchasing foodstuffs prepared or processed elsewhere, women can use their income to support dependents to cook for them at home.

This reduces or eliminates losses in quality of ingredients, preparation, or meal timing. Mothers may keep daughters home for cooking who might otherwise be gainfully employed, as hawkers, for example. Foster children or adult relatives living in the same household may cook, in return for subsistence, gifts and future assistance (often unspecified). Market traders also hire unrelated, usually live-in, helpers, referred to as maids. The wages, clothing, and parting gifts these young or adolescent girls receive are usually so small compared to food prices that subsistence support is again the main expense.

Women get most of their assistance in both cooking and childcare from their own children, especially daughters. Adult kin give surprisingly low levels of aid in these urban families. Tables 1 and 2 show that children steadily but gradually take over tasks as women grow older. Age of the mother proved a more reliable indicator of personal task performance than number of children, although the two were closely correlated, as expected (Clark 1984). This confirms observations and interviews indicating that the age of the oldest child was the critical factor, whether later births were frequent, delayed, or the children died.

Daughters represent no sexual threat to their mothers, because of incest rules, but still represent a minor compromise on quality. No daughter will prepare food for her father quite as carefully as for her husband, although she may be a better cook than her mother by age 16. Women living separately from their husbands can even conceal the extent to which children cook. As women turn over cooking to their daughters, they also gradually reduce their emphasis on further childbearing and sexuality. Eventually, many "retire" from marriage by ceasing to visit their husbands and cook for them.

One middle-aged trader had fulfilled the ideal that children take complete charge of the household. Her nine children, aged 3 to 26, lived with other relatives in a house built by her deceased maternal uncle. The oldest, a daughter, had left home to live with her husband. When she became pregnant, her mother convinced her to quit her white-collar job and move back in. Younger sisters and a maid did most of the physical work and cared for the baby, who never came to market. The mother said proudly that she did nothing at all at home, and spent most of her non-trading time at her husband's apartment. Of course, relations between parents and children extend far beyond the exchange of domestic services. Asantes value their children highly for the lasting respect, affection, obedience and ritual support they give, both in childhood and as adults. Parents expect financial support in later life, just as financial support is an important part of their parental responsibilities. But they expect short-term as well as long-term reciprocity. Boys as well as girls help with cleaning and errands, and boys will cook and care for younger siblings if no girls are old enough.

Helping with domestic tasks brings children in closer contact with adults, which may bring them more food and financial sponsorship in much the same way as closer domestic ties gain more support from husbands for wives.

Helpfulness is an important criterion for judging a child's good character and intelligence, and also his likelihood of long-term reciprocation of investments like school fees. There is little assumption of equal treatment of siblings of differently perceived character or capacity.

Children can affect decisions about their future by showing more aptitude and interest in trading compared to cooking, for example. They can also transfer their attentions to neighbors, teachers, or other adults offering higher potential or immediate rewards. Conversely, parents who conspicuously neglect their children face a kind of retribution when they ask for help in old age.

Just as children are not completely dependent on the good faith and resources of their birth parents, women are not completely dependent for assistance on their own childbearing experience. Among Asantes, fostering the children of relatives is acceptable and common. This often involves exchanging children between related households so that each has enough resident older children to take care of the young ones and handle cooking and cleaning. Many Kumasi Central Market traders themselves came to live with relatives in Kumasi or elsewhere during their own childhoods. Such foster children make ideal substitute cooks. Fostered girls are rarely potential sexual rivals, since the extensive Asante incest prohibitions rule out intercourse with any known relative of wife or husband.

Kumasi traders foster in useful children, particularly girls, much more often than they foster out their own. Traders had sent only 10% of their children to stay with relatives for any reason. They find it relatively easy to attract school leavers or uneducated girls from rural homes with the excitement and job prospects of city life. Sex ratios at young ages for Kumasi in the 1960 and 1970 censuses show a considerable excess of girls, who probably came to do domestic work. Traders today show relatively little use of trading assistants compared to domestic help (Clark 1984).

The foster parent of such a girl provides short-term reciprocity in the form of living expenses, pocket money and some clothing. Foster children frequently do not attend school when own children do so, or attend less prestigious schools. However, the foster parent should sponsor the child with training and/or capital for eventual employment when she reaches maturity. A foster child also develops bonds of reciprocity with her young cousins, as if they were her own young siblings. The level of reciprocity depends on the closeness of the relationship and the goodwill of the foster parent. The treatment given to distant, poor relatives can be difficult to distinguish from that given well-treated maids. When the child has no living parents or the foster mother no living children, intense bonds may be formed.

Adult kin naturally cooperate most often when they live in the same house, either in the lineage house or by deliberately moving in together. Adult sisters most frequently share childcare when one has to stay home to take care of her own children. It takes relatively little effort to care for extra children with one's own. The working sister contributes extra food, the labor of her older children, or sometimes supports a maid. Adult sisters or cousins usually cook separately, even when they live in the same house. They borrow ingredients or watch the pot for each other, but reciprocate with the same type of help. Adult daughters sometimes cook for their fathers or mothers, but under different \conditions than as a child. They receive more explicit reciprocity in property or housing rights than child helpers.

Mothers give very little domestic help to their mature daughters, in either cooking or child care. Asante society gives relatively high prestige to elderly women, and relatively little to physical childcare or cooking. Older women still capable of trading or community leadership will devote their time to this. The short period during which a grandmother is too feeble to go to market, but strong enough to pound fufu or look after young children, is not likely to coincide with the domestic labor shortage of more than one of her daughters. Grandmothers are more likely to take a child into their household to be cared for by other residents, or to receive an older child to take care of their own domestic needs.

As an alternative to foster children and adult relatives, traders can seek commercial domestic help from maids. Some women traders say they prefer not to incur the long-term, indeterminate obligations associated with accepting help from kin. They also complain that kin have their own ideas about how to raise children and take more authority over them.

Unrelated maids are recruited through hometown connections, friends, and sometimes near-strangers. Short and long-term remuneration vary drastically at the employer's discretion, but commonly include both monthly payments and the promise of some kind of training or capital at maturity. Maids very rarely attend school, since their main work is to attend to childcare or other chores which cannot be postponed until after school hours. Older own children or foster children still contribute to cooking and cleaning after school.

The sexual conflicts surrounding cooking come to a head with maids. Unlike fostered relatives, maids have no incest prohibitions on sexual relations with the husband. Popular comic books and women's magazines present the recurrent theme of the unfortunate career woman who leaves the maid at home alone with her husband, to provide a hot meal. One might expect maids to be more common when spouses live separately, reducing contact between maid and husband. In fact, women living with their husbands use maids more often, perhaps because they cannot so freely invite kin to live with them (Clark 1984).

Some women try to eliminate the problem by taking very young maids, as young as seven years old. The child is expected to be more obedient and loyal to the family and learn its ways. On the other hand, a teenage maid is more useful, and can handle more responsibility and skilled tasks such as cooking. The maid's family also wants her at home as she matures, to prevent sexual victimization by employers, or making bad friends in the street. The occupation is considered unsuitable for an adult, and especially for a married woman.

Cycles of compromise

The overwhelming reliance on own children for assistance makes the developmental cycle an appropriate explanatory framework for domestic strategies. Assistance from the extended family is available primarily to unmarried and younger women, who have fewer children. Maids become most important in the 35-44 age group, when women have the most small children. They are also critical to the woman wishing to send her own daughters to school. Women over 45 for the first time begin reporting leisure time at home (Clark 1984). At this age women may be withdrawing from their marriages, as they have completed childbearing. They may stop visiting and cooking for their husbands altogether, or may be more willing to share these duties with a co-wife.

Competition between trading and domestic work intensifies because peak demands in both areas come at nearly the same point in the developmental cycle. Around age thirty, a typical Asante women would have four or five children. The oldest, if a girl, cannot yet take major responsibility for domestic work at age eight or ten (assuming two-year spacing). At the same stage, a woman maintains a close relationship with her husband because she still wants several more children. She maintains higher standards of cooking and cleaning at this time to cement the relationship. She more often lives with him now than earlier or later in the marriage, reducing her access to help from her own kin.

Financial pressures also peak for mothers in their thirties, as children grow and progress in school. These motivate women to work even more in the market, not to withdraw under domestic pressures. The age group 25-34 is the largest among women traders in Kumasi Central Market (Clark 1984). Rising expenses leave even less money to support dependent kin or maids.

The extended family gives surprisingly little help to this age group, when women need it most. Adult kin primarily help older and younger women. Young women can often add their first child to their mother's childcare arrangements at weaning, and continue eating with her. Middle-aged or older women can support an adult daughter or niece to cook for them, while she looks after her own children. This relationship naturally removes the younger woman from the traders' sample, but allows the older woman to expand her trading operations.

The domestic bottleneck halfway through the childbearing years defines a kind of dual career structure for Asante women traders. The two ideal types following are well represented in case studies, while other traders fall in between. The ambitious young woman begins trading energetically as early as age ten or twelve. She takes advantage of her early childlessness to prepare for later responsibilities. Less ambitious women avoid strenuous trading as long as their carefree condition allows.

As a teenager, a serious young woman concentrates on trading instead of seeking gifts from boyfriends. She aims to acquire enough experience and build enough capital by the time she marries and has her second or third child that she can afford to take in extra dependents to care for them. This enables her to intensify trading as her financial pressures mount, and perhaps send her own daughters to school.

But young girls have few immediate financial needs to force them to settle down to regular work. Many do so only after the birth of their first or second child, in response to the financial demands of motherhood. These demands grow quickly, so they can save little from their limited starting incomes to finance any domestic help. This limits their careers to small-scale retailing or home-based trading, such as cooked food sales. Their standard of living depends more on their husbands' contribution. If lucky in their choice of husband, their personal domestic commitment increases this income.

Cooked food purchase and maids enable women in between these ideal types to bridge dangerous gaps in the daily routine or developmental cycle which might otherwise disrupt their trading careers. Purchased breakfasts and lunches give women traders the flexibility to fit their daily schedule to their trading needs. Traders know they can buy food occasionally for the evening meal if an emergency delays their return from the market or a trading trip. Maids also provide a kind of social insurance in case women temporarily lack sufficient resident kin and daughters, even though only a small minority of households include maids at any given time. Commercial domestic services used in low overall amounts play an important part in maintaining women's businesses because they provide crucial flexibility. Independent incomes thus become even more important to women, in preserving these strategies as viable options.

The small amount of support given by adult kin and neighbors likewise provides disproportionate benefit by adding another degree of flexibility. Without formal or steady arrangments, kin help out in emergencies such as illness or distant funerals. Neighbors provide similar informal help, to a lesser extent than kin. Only a few women had made arrangements to leave children with a neighbor, and these involved stricter financial reciprocity than with kin. However, emergency backup from neighbors permits women to leave children as young as seven home alone. This mutual aid gives Asante traders an advantage over, for example, Yoruba traders in Nigeria, who live with co-wives they do not trust to feed their children during the day (Sudarkasa 1964).

Such emergency and short-term resources reduce the potential impact of personal crises on a trader's business. A short illness, the illness of a close relative or a sudden collapse of childcare arrangements need not result in rupture of business relations and loss of capital. Risky business ventures also need not create a domestic crisis, if the mother is called away. By reducing total risk levels significantly, these options make worthwhile the heavier investment of time and money essential to profitable wholesale enterprises. They contribute equally to the survival of very low-capital enterprises, for whom a small loss can easily bring complete bankruptcy.

Conclusion

The types of compromise Asante market women make between the demands of cooking and trading can be traced to the nature of the social relations in which the task is imbedded. In the first place, the type and cost of accepted compromises emerge as critical items in the ideal and pragmatic cultural rules defining the task. Flexibility in timing, menu and the person cooking is a particularly influential factor in determining the degree of effective conflict between cooking and trading. The cost, both monetary and social, of deviating from the preferred pattern provides another measure of effective flexibility in cooking patterns. Social costs vary markedly for married and unmarried women, because cooking takes place in different relationships for them. The type and degree of power women have in the relevant relationships is the major determinant both of directions of compromise available and their cost.

As expected, quality standards are important to the task definition and its compromises. Since meal timing is a prime source of conflict, one would expect compromises on the issue. As a quality standard, however, it is relatively rigid because of its marital context. Menu choices and the level of skill in preparation they require also involve quality evaluations. They do not simply set the number of hours the woman or her substitute must put in, but limit or expand the number of qualified substitutes.

Compromises using substitute cooks, however, raise additional questions. Even when preparation skills and time are equivalent (and therefore the resulting meal), the imbedding relationship may be threatened or changed. Rules concerning substitutes do not just say yes or no, but who can be used, and when. The cultural rules discouraging Asante women from using substitutes for husbands' meals specify the consequences, in loss of sexual and financial fidelity. These consequences can be avoided or minimised by choosing substitutes in appropriate kin and age categories, and by developing alternative sources of income. This kind of pragmatic rule has a strong impact on women's behavior, whether in obeying or compensating for it, but results in a large proportion of cases deviating from the pattern of first preference.

It is not always obvious which social relationship has this position of governing the compromises made on a specific task or issue. With cooking, the meal consumers include children, adult kin, friends and women themselves, as well as husbands. Consideration of the costs or consequences of stopping task performance or exercising other available options is needed to uncover the limiting factors. For Asante women, compromises in cooking have consequences mainly to marital, not maternal relations. The degree of autonomy women have in the marital relationship thus defines their effective options with respect to the task itself.

When levels of flexibility in domestic work patterns are high, women can choose arrangements for domestic task performance that eliminate or dramatically reduce conflicts with trading. Cleaning tasks, including laundry, offer an extreme example of flexibility, for comparison with cooking. They take up, in total, an equivalent amount of time to cooking, but were omitted from this analysis because they interfere so little with income-generating work. Cleaning tasks come in small units and can usually be done at any time. The value structure related to them allows women to involve a wide range of helpers, including boys and girls of various ages. This enables women to minimise both financial and social costs, by using relationships within which they have a good deal of control.

Cooking, the most difficult task for women traders to manage, is associated closely with marriage, a relationship within which Asante women have relatively little control. Their matrilineal position mainly enables them to consider leaving a marriage, rather than to modify relations within it. They can minimize their relations with their husbands, through duolocal marriage and financial independence, but those relations remaining are still characterised by deference and subordination. Asante men continue to earn higher incomes than women, on average, motivating women to seek access to a male income, even at some cost.

Asante women's independent social and economic resources enable many to avoid the domestic demands of marriage, either by financing compromises or by leaving the marriage. Since divorce is not catastrophic, they can risk damaging the marital relationship in favor of their commitment to trading. Access to kin and commercial cooking aid also increases their ability to meet these demands without destroying the labor/finance budget. Individual women's strategies depend on the balance between the estimated size and reliability of all three kinds of resources: from the husband, lineage kin or children, and the trader's enterprise.

Note

Fieldwork in 1978-80 was supported by the Overseas Development Administration (UK), International Economics Division. Rural fieldwork in 1980-82, done under contract to the International Labour Office, provided supportive and comparative data. The content of the paper does not necessarily reflect the opinions of these funders. Jane Guyer and Claire Robertson kindly provided very helpful comments on an earlier draft of this paper.

1.   This paper is based primarily on 16 months of field work with market traders in Kumasi Central Market, from 1978-80. Kumasi is the second largest city in Ghana, with a population of about a million. Observations and interviews with traders, male and female, and their neighbors and relatives covered the interaction of trading and domestic responsibilities.

A 600-case sample survey of the market also included questions on domestic work and residence patterns.

The traders studied do not strictly represent all Asante women and certainly have chosen specific strategies for domestic work to accommodate their trading, but data on traders' family backgrounds analysed elsewhere (Clark 1984) shows that they are not from special trading families, or from an unusual economic or social position. It is unlikely that they have unusual ideas about ideal and acceptable practices in domestic duties and finances. Their ideas accord with marital and kin roles described much more fully by earlier ethnographers (Rattray 1923, 1927, 1929; Fortes 1969, 1970; Bleek 1975, 1976). Interviews then and later with Akan farmers and food processors confirmed these ideas as widely accepted models.

Figure 1

ASANTE MEAL PATTERN
NATURE AND RIGIDITY OF IDEALS

	breakfast	lunch	dinner
ideal dishes	ampesie and kontommere stew	eto or ampesie leftover	fufu and soup
actual dishes	kenkey and fish, tea and bread, porridge, rice	wide variety of snacks or dishes	fufu or starchy substitute
acceptable times	5-10am	11am-3pm	6-7pm
timing flexibility	moderate, tied to work schedule	high	low, tied to sex
labor time	low	none	high 2-3 hours
interference with trading	low	minimal	high
social context	co-residence or street vendor	workplace	husband, if married, otherwise kin
risks of substitution	low	none	high, if married
commercial food relations	high	total	low

346

Table 1

COOKING

Usual Cook for Household (Percentages)
by Age of Respondent

| | | Age of Trader | | | | |
Cook	0-14	15-24	25-34	35-44	45-54	Over 54
Self	57	70	69	45	33	25
Adult Kin	29	16	4	0	6	19
Child	14	11	21	45	58	50
Maid	0	1	5	10	3	6
Purchased	0	1	0	0	0	0
Total	100	100	100	100	100	100

Table 2

CHILDCARE

Primary Child Minder in Household (Percentages)
by Age of Respondent

| | | Age of Trader | | | | |
Minder	0-14	15-24	25-34	35-44	45-54	Over 54
Self	0	30	24	26	9	0
None	25	17	13	30	30	0
Child	0	13	21	13	44	50
Own Kin	25	28	6	0	9	25
Maid	0	2	11	17	0	0
Other	50	9	25	14	9	25
Total	100	100	100	100	100	100

References

Bleek, Wolf
1975 *Marriage, Inheritance and Witchcraft*. Leiden: Afrikastudiescentrum.

1976 Sexual Relationships and Birth Control in Ghana: A Case Study of a Rural Town. Uitgave 10, *Afdeling Culturele Anthropologies*, Antropologisch-Sociologisch Centrum, University of Amsterdam.

Bohannon, Paul and George Dalton, eds.
1962 *Markets in Africa*. Evanston, Northwestern University Press.

Brown, Judith
1970 A Note on the Division of Labor by Sex. *American Anthropologist* 72:1073.

Clark, Gracia
1984 The Position of Asante Women Traders in Kumasi Central Market, Ghana. Ph.D. thesis, Department of Social Anthropology, University of Cambridge.

Fortes, Meyer
1969 *Kinship and Social Order*. London, Routledge and Kegan Paul.

1970 *Time and Social Structure*. London, Athlone Press.

Goody, Esther
1982 *Parenthood and Social Reproduction*. Cambridge University Press.

Guyer, Jane
1981 The Raw, the Cooked and the Half-baked: A Note on the Division of Labor by Sex. *Working Paper* No. 48, Boston University, African Studies Center, 1981.

Sudarkasa, Niara (then Gloria Marshall)
1964 Women, Trade and the Yoruba Family. Ph.D. thesis, Department of Anthropology, University of Michigan, Ann Arbor.

Rattray, R.S.
1923 *Ashanti*. Oxford University Press, London.

1927 *Religion and Art in Ashanti*. Oxford University Press, London.

1929 *Ashanti Law and Constitution*. Oxford University Press, London.

Robertson, Claire
1984 *Sharing the Same Bowl*. Indiana University Press, Bloomington.

EXPENDITURE AND INTRAHOUSEHOLD PATTERNS AMONG THE SOUTHERN BOBO OF BURKINA FASO

Mahir Şaul

In this article I present an analysis of monetary expenses in a village in western Burkina Faso; this provides a basis for discussing the implications of relations regulating the use of labor between the sexes and age groups. The majority of the people in this village produce most of the food which they consume, but in recent years exchanges mediated by money have become crucial even for fulfilling obligations within the family. The analysis of monetary transactions provides a clearer understanding of the contributions of different types of actors within the production unit and offers unique clues to the forces of transformation within the community. As in many parts of West Africa, adult dependent members in village households have a sphere of personal economic activity parallel to that of the head of the household and also possess some money that they decide how to spend. The patterns of spending, however, are different for different types of actors. I focus in this article on the respective shares of heads of household, married women, and junior men in various types of expenditure, and I indicate factors that account for differences in spending.

Some of the expenses are for immediate consumption. Differences in these expenses may reflect the normative obligations of various social positions (such as dissimilar roles for the sexes, or privileges and obligations attached to age groups and to certain offices), unequal access to cash, and the varying preferences of individuals; these factors are all tied to each other. Some other expenditures represent productive investment, the most notable of them, isolated here for special consideration, being farm expenses and trade. Whereas differences in immediate consumption, especially personal consumption, can largely be taken as an index of variance in wealth, differences in productive expenditure are among the causal factors of such variance. Because of the nature of the data I do not deal with the category of savings, and capital accumulation is part of the discussion to the extent that it is reflected in investment spending. This study confirms that integration into a wider regional monetary economy provided an important stimulus for differentiation; this point is brought into greater relief at the end, by considering the veterans separately from other heads of household. This integration has also played a role in relations between genders and other positional groups within the household. The descriptive discussion here is largely anchored around a set of graphs that present the data in summary form. A conclusion at the end recapitulates the major findings and offers an interpretation.

Relations within the household

The interest in intrahousehold patterns (relations between groups of actors defined by gender and age within the household) grows from a critique of the notion of household. The household, defined simultaneously as a unit of production and of consumption, is one conceptual tool that has proved invaluable for both economic theory and sociological work aimed at collecting quantitative information in rural societies. Generally it is conceived as consisting of a conjugal core of a man, his wife or wives, and children; it may be extended by incorporating the spouses and offspring of the children, or by including individuals affiliated in other ways, all of whom pool resources for agricultural work and distribute managerial tasks for the common benefit of the members. This notion is inspired by a commonly held view of the organization of premodern European peasant communities (for an evaluation by a historian of Europe see Sabean 1983). There are many difficulties in applying such a definition to certain field situations, and at times a new conceptualization of the basic unit of analysis becomes necessary. It is an ethnographic commonplace now that in many societies in Africa we find that production, consumption, and accumulation define different sets of people (for a classic description see Richards 1939:165-183). Also, it has always been known that in many noncapitalist, non-Western societies, conjugal units that appear to have some autonomy in certain facets of production are linked to each other in other facets; important flows of goods and productive resources occur between them that can seriously mislead the researcher if not taken into consideration at the level of observation or theory (see, for example, Lewis 1981). More recently, some researchers have stressed another point that is perhaps of greater theoretical and practical importance: Individuals who collaborate closely in the joint projects of the family-derived unit frequently have also diverging, or even conflicting, perspectives of their personal projects. In certain situations, the most significant social categories cut across the conjugal based household units.[1] As far as I can identify, this growing awareness has three more or less independent sources in recent scholarship. It may be useful to outline them before presenting my data.

One of them is the research tradition that followed Radcliffe-Brown. Especially a group of anthropologists at Cambridge conceived social structure as a system of positions, which are envisioned as collections of rights and duties, privileges and responsibilities tying individuals to one another. As corporatist as this position has at times assumed to be, it had the potential of bringing the individual to the fore as the elementary unit of observation, because social groups are constituted around jural relations between persons, the prototype for which is the dyadic link. The domestic domain as well as the politico-jural, economic, and religious domains are made up of relations of husband and wife, parent and child, sibling and sibling (e.g., Fortes 1969, chapters 5 and 6). One of the themes that came out of the ethnography inspired by such an orientation is that in many African societies a joint conjugal estate, as found in Europe and elsewhere, does not exist. Spouses own property separately, retain rights to their own earnings, and the goods which they accumulate throughout their lifetime may devolve differently in the case of men and women (Goody 1962, 1976). The contributions that different members of the family are supposed to make to the maintenance of the family can be formulated as norms of some precision imposing upon them obligations vis-à-vis specified others.

As we know, this approach to society has been widely criticized for being possibly responsible for a static understanding of social relations (Leach 1961); it can be taken to imply that an autonomous and arbitrary moral order generates the organization of society (Worsley 1956). Relations, expectations of others' behaviors, and norms change over time following changes in the wider social and material environment, and in dialogue with them. Today we are more keenly aware of the negotiations that go on at the interpersonal level, through which norms are validated or rejected (Barth 1966). Nevertheless, after the excitement and disillusionment created by transactional models, we feel the need to emphasize that these negotiations do not take place among isolated individuals, or separately in each kinship or productive unit. Sanctions are attached to norms giving them thus a social character, asserted by the use of force or by other means of coercion. Internalized moral convictions and spiritual ideas are again social in character, not subject to random variability among individuals. This means that the individual has to bring a set of wider social relations into each act of conformity or non-conformity, and negotiation can take place only at the level of large numbers of individuals who are similarly situated. Although in daily life isolated acts affect the relationship between two persons, significant social changes can take place only at the aggregate level. These changes can be conceptualized as the result of bargaining between categories of people over specific issues, even though these categories may not be visible in other contexts, nor permanent. Seeing social life as partially defined by rights and obligations remains a fruitful approach to ethnographic description when it is accompanied by the awareness that those are not necessarily permanent, and that individual actions can be accounted for at various levels of explanation.

The second source for the current concern in intrahousehold patterns is the feminist literature of the recent decades. The resurgence of a vigorous feminist movement in Europe and North America provided a wider audience for ideas questioning the assumption of identity of interests within the conjugal unit, and of the special relevance of altruism for its constitution (Rapp, Ross & Bridenthal 1979; for an insightful recent feminist commentary on Africa see Roberts 1984). These challenges have been brought at the level of universal analytical categories and not at that of a specific socio-historical order. Thus they have contributed to sharpening the diagnostic sensibilities of observers and interpreters alike. The particular relevance of these ideas for the West African ethnographic scene, however, is worth emphasizing.[2]

The third source to be mentioned here is the work of some French anthropologists who started to write in the 1960s. Influenced by Marxist ideas, Meillassoux first formulated the view that relations between women and men, and between elders and juniors provide a crucial dimension in understanding the social and economic constitution of some African societies (1960, 1972). Dupré and Rey, among others, took this idea one step further and postulated that the divergence of interests crosscutting kinship units can result in conflict and opposition (1968). While the wider theoretical significance of this discovery remained a question of lively debate among the original formulators, the lesson filtered to various sorts of anthropology in the English-speaking world and contributed there to the growing interest in intrahousehold observations and across kinship unit conceptualizations.

Women and men, elders and juniors are differently endowed with primary resources as a result of the definition of their social identities within the wider sociocultural system. These identities appear to individuals as a datum, part of the intersubjective world preexisting them. The situations which individuals encounter are always novel, as they are only partly related to cultural definitions. Nevertheless individual strategies frequently remain strongly shaped by prior identity definitions. Not only are rights to land, types of productive and leisure activities considered suitable, and means of gaining access to accumulated goods prescribed in varying degrees of precision and flexibility, but also access to labor and therefore to one's own and others' time is circumscribed in the same way. In this analysis, I try to identify these constraints as guides to interpret the patterns revealed in the data.

The context of the research

The data used in this paper were collected in Bare, a large Bobo village of about 1,900 residents in western Burkina Faso. The Bobo language, spoken by about 120,000 people, is assumed to be an early branch off the Mande stock. Though recognizable as a single language which contrasts with surrounding speech communities, it consists of several major dialects including in turn numerous subdialectal variant forms, some of which are barely mutually intelligible. These communities also display great heterogeneity in custom and social organizational principles. The village of Bare is in the southern limit of the Bobo speech area, some 30 km. southeast of Bobo-Dioulasso. The southern Bobo have been in contact with the Jula for a long time and have been peripherally incorporated into their polities, especially through ties with the Zara center in Bobo-Dioulasso (see Le Moal 1980 for these populations). Their distinctive social organization is based on autonomous village communities, made up of members of several clans which are tied in ritual complementarity and exchanges. The basic features of this organization continue to the present, even though village autonomy has gradually eroded since incorporation by the colonial administration. The population of Bare, as those of many surrounding villages, possesses a classic double decent system, whereby corporate patrilineages and matrilineages regulate land and movable property respectively. Today they are known for having remained refractory to monotheistic religions, most notably to Islam. Many predicaments of the colonial period, however, apply to them with particular strength, and gradually they have also been drawn deeply into the Western monetary economy.

The climate in the area is typically Sudanic. In most years it receives more than 1100 mm. in total rainfall, a good portion of which comes in a small number of torrential thunderstorms. It is very hot and dry from March to May, hot and wet from June to September (*santu* 'rainy season'), and mild and dry from November to January (the harvest season).

Most agricultural wage work is provided by various teams of youth groups or women who charge a set fee per day of work, and use the proceeds for collective projects at the end of the season. Individual daily wage work is very rare in the village (it is not, however, unheard of, because a few village men who live now in the city but maintain fields in the vicinity may occasionally resort to such employment). The rareity of daily money wages among villagers is due to a number of factors, an important one among them being the necessity for dependent members to spend most of their working hours during the farming season in the fields controlled by the head of the household. Labor contracts for individuals generally take the form of long term relationships and involves the temporary incorporation of the employee in the household of the employer.

Bare is notable especially because it sent a large number of conscripts and volunteers to the colonial and later independent army. Consequently, there are a relatively large number of pension receivers today. This makes it an affluent village, but it is about average for the western region of the country in terms of response to recent development efforts and with respect to agricultural production. The money that pension receivers bring in also contributes to the active trade life in the village.

The survey

After completing a detailed census of the village, enumerators started to administer the questionnaires to a random sample of 33 farming groups, during the last week of September 1983. In May 1984 collaboration with a larger project (carried out jointly by the Center for Research on Economic Development, University of Michigan, and International Agricultural Programs, University of Wisconsin) made it possible to hire new personnel and to extend the duration of the survey until the end of the year; at this time 18 more farmers and their households were added to the sample, bringing the total to 51. Because I found it useful to have more cases from the upper rungs of the agricultural scale, the names of the new sample members were drawn from a list of major farm operators in the village that was provided by the leaders of the *Groupement Villageois* (voluntary precooperative village development cell collaborating with the ORDs[3]). The questionnaires were administered until January 1985. At the writing of this article, however, only data up to the end of June 1984 have been coded and processed, so that only these could be used for the discussion. It is possible that the results will look slightly different when the full set of data is taken into account.

During the survey, all adult members of sample households (adult was defined as 18 years or older) were interviewed once a week. The amounts recorded are the ones reported to have been spent as money by the people in the sample. We have not changed them and we have not imputed cash values to transactions involving other goods. Exchanges in the nature of gifts, non-monetized flows, and the distribution of home-produced food are kept outside of this discussion, except in cases in which they become immediately relevant for explaining patterns of expenditure. As in all similar studies, the accuracy and representativeness of the information reported here should be of great concern. If there are systematic biases in reporting on the part of sample members, I would expect them to derive from selective underreporting. My belief is, however, that these data do reveal some general trends in the village except where I explicitly indicate otherwise. Questions on expenditure could be expected to produce more reliable results than those on income because the former topic is less sensitive. The numerical results have also been submitted to checks by comparison with information collected by conventional ethnographic practices in a regular fieldwork situation. The sociological analysis underlying the treatment of data is also generated by ethnographic work, but this analysis is used here as complementary, since the results could not have been generated without the use of systematically administered questionnaires. The data constitute an independent and, for present purposes, basic source of information.

Types of expenditure

In this section I describe the major types of expenditure in Bare, and the categories into which they have been aggregated. Figure 1 presents the distribution of expenses by adult members of all sample households for the nine-month period covered here. The dry season regroups data for the months January through April. This post-harvest period is marked by greater availability of leisure time and an abundance of grain. People have more money because of sales of crops, gathered products such as shea nuts and locust beans, and processing activities, such as cooking, brewing, making shea butter or sumbala (fermented locust beans) for women, and harvesting of beehives, cutting firewood, and wood, iron work and other artisanal activities for men. These months are also large cash outlay periods because this is when festivals and funerals take place. The farming season has been defined here to cover the rainy season when planting and hoeing take place and the period of harvests in the early part of the dry season; it includes data for October through December in 1983 and May and June in 1984. Total expenditures for the 33 families in the initial sample go from a maximum of 1,180,000 F CFA in January down to 280,000 F CFA in December.[4] For 16 households in the initial sample, the month of largest expenditure is January, for four others it is February, for five it is March, and for two April. March, January, and April are also close seconds in many of the cases. That is, for more than 80 percent of the households in the initial survey, money is primarily spent in the dry months. This heavy concentration of spending in the post-harvest months is disguised in the figures presented here, because the group of high income families were added in June. This month thus came to represent 36 percent of the total sum of expenditure. This anomaly should be kept in mind when interpreting the figures given here.

354

The category of Farm Expenses includes purchases of hoes and other agricultural tools, the most important being draft animals, plows, and associated equipment; inputs such as fertilizers, insecticides, and seeds; wages paid for farm work and expenditures for work parties; and sums paid to reimburse loans taken from the ORD for agricultural inputs. The aggregate amount spent on all these items is moderate, but its distribution is very uneven. As will be discussed below, the bulk of it is accounted for by very few farmers buying large ticket items such as draft animals and plows.

Animals include fowls, goats, sheep, pigs, and cattle purchased for herd building. Raising chickens and guinea fowls is a common activity not only for some heads of household, but also for women and young men. The birds are often killed in sacrifices by heads of household, and sold by others. They are sometimes referred to as the *portefeuille* of the villager, because they constitute a means to keep one's savings until a need for money arises. They are usually sold to outside traders rather than to fellow villagers, but some villagers buy birds too; prospective raisers frequently have to obtain them in the market because their flocks are exhausted by use in rituals, in sales or by epidemics. Goats are a major form of wealth in the village. Until recent times individuals were not allowed to own them; this restriction also applied to most other forms of wealth, including currency. Matrilineages possessed large herds managed by their elders. This pattern has changed today, but goats are still matrilineally inherited and mostly used for sacrifices. Sheep are rare. Pig rearing represents a new type of entrepreneurial activity in which some heads of household engage. These animals are usually sold to outside traders. The cattle belonging to villagers are kept in four combined large herds--each of which contains from 60 to more than a hundred heads--managed by a few settled Fulani elders of the village. Cattle also used to be subject to control by corporate groups, but starting in the 1950s some individuals from the village, especially army men, were able to accumulate personal wealth in this form. They were also able to rally support in favor of changing inheritance norms to allow them to hand over a large part of this property to their sons. Some heads of household in the sample own cattle, either inherited or purchased. During the survey period no one indicated to us that they had bought cattle for herding, but this is one of the delicate issues with which we had to deal. The evidence we have about cattle purchases may need to be treated with reserve, but without cattle expenditure on animals appears to be low.

In Figure 1, the column for Trade Goods represents an investment category. It includes all the goods bought with the intention of resale for a profit. Although trade at a very small scale may be widespread, the major part of the aggregate sum is the result of the activity of a few traders in the sample. It represents the turning over of their capital, the goods thus brought in to the village corresponding to a good proportion of the expenditures made by others. The primary trade items are bottled beer, soft drinks, wine, and other liquors; cereals for processing and resale; manufactured goods such as cigarettes, candy, matches, sugar, kerosene, gas; honey, condiments including dried fish, shea butter, sumbala, and many other food-related products traded by women.

The category Food Grain includes only what has been purchased for consumption by family members. Although some rice was purchased, most of the total is accounted by sorghums, millet, and local cowpeas. Meat and Fish expenses are low. The most common are for dried fish purchases. Some of this fish is produced in the village late in the rainy season, when some farmers engage in fishing in rivers and water pools near their farms. An important part, however, is bought from traders who attend the weekly market or from village traders who bring it from the outside. In the villge there are no regular butchers and most meat sold is provided by hunters. It is purchased primarily by elders, who store it smoked for major festivals. A few people in the village sell cooked meat for immediate consumption, but this was tabulated as a Prepared Food.

The Condiments column in Figure 1 represents expenses for salts, spices, bouillon cubes, oil, sumbala and shea butter (which may be produced in the village or brought from the outside), vegetables and gathered leaves, and peanuts used in sauces. Money spent for having the grain ground at the mill has also been added here. Amounts spent on various cakes and fritters sold by women in the marketplace, noodles, wheat flour, bread, fruits, candy, milk (both imported in cans from Europe and sold fresh by Fulani women) and so on have been separately aggregated as Prepared Foods in Figure 1, but because the amounts in question are proportionately very low, they have been added to the Condiments column in some of the other figures below.

The major Building expenses are for houses and granaries. Most houses are built modestly with local materials, and the greatest cost is wages for a fellow mason or expenses for a work party. People nowadays commonly buy locks for the doors; the use of corrugated metal sheets for the roof is also spreading. Two or three decades ago army men started to build expensive houses with laterite bricks mortared and plastered with cement, iron doors and windows, and a metal roof. Some twenty such houses exist in the village, but none was under construction by members of the sample during the survey. The most important items in the Buildings and Durables category are kettles and other kitchen utensils, motorbikes, and bicycles. Repair expenses related to these latter, guns (for hunting), transistor radios, and turntables are also included here.

The column labeled Consumer Goods includes expenditures made by consumers on items enumerated in Trade Goods. What distinguishes these goods is that they are manufactured goods coming from the city. Batteries, medicines, cigarettes, and coffee have been included here. The category Beverages includes expenditure on local brews--sorghum beer, fermented honey water (*base*), and less-important fermented drinks made out of wild products--as well as bottled beer, carbonated drinks, wine, and liquor. Clothing includes spending on jewelry and shoes as well. There is one tailor in the village, but most clothing items are purchased either from itinerant traders in the weekly market, or from the city. The column for Taxes includes not only head and animal taxes, but also and more importantly the contributions made to social projects imposed by the village. The Bobo have a strong community organization, and frequently money is collected for self-imposed joint projects. Contributions to funds that may be permanent or temporary are sometimes assessed by the household, sometimes by the age class, sometimes by the individual. The age classes can also be mobilized for generating resources to pay their members' share in various village projects. In the period covered here, one frequently mentioned reason for contribution was the building of a youth house. The share of state taxes is low partly because of noncompliance, but in 1984 the tax liability of villagers was totally removed by the government of Captain Sankara. Expenses involved in having issued official documents such as licenses, identity cards, or for fiscal stamps have also been aggregated here.

Expenditures for ritual celebrations, festivals, sacrifices, as well as the minor expenses involved in marriages and the baptism of some Christians have been included in the category Rituals. The major component here is funerals, within which one could distinguish burial ceremonies, "wet" commemorations early in the following dry season, and "dry" memorials organized on a village and lineage basis (usually at the end of each dry season, but which in the custom of Bare take place after the first rains, in the month of May). Most ceremonial expenses are incurred by heads of household, but other individuals participate by making contributions to corporate bodies. They may also engage in small private ceremonies for personal objectives.

As elsewhere in Africa, education is one of the main avenues for upward mobility in Burkina Faso, and many adults strive to educate at least one of their children or young relatives. Bare, which was in close contact with the colonial center through army conscripts, forced labor, and relations with the family of the canton chief in Bobo-Dioulasso, was in a position to take advantage of formal educational opportunities quite early. Many of those who have been educated in the past have selected a military career. Today some parents ask relatives in the cities or in salaried employment in coveted positions to take charge of the education of one of their children. A primary school that recruits every other year has been opened in the village in 1974. Parents who have a child there incur only minor expenses for school supplies such as chalk. At secondary level, students admitted to government boarding schools receive not only free education, but also a good scholarship, which is perceived as a salary and transforms the young person psychologically into a civil servant. There were two young men in this position from the first class to have graduated from the village school, while a third one was admitted to a Catholic seminary. For those who cannot pass the entrance exam, there is now the option of attending one of the private secondary schools in the city, which besides being less creditable are very expensive. A few young men from the village were attending such institutions, but most of them were under the care (sometimes provided grudgingly) of relatives in the city. One parent in the sample, an army veteran, paid 55,000 F CFA for the tuition of his son in the city and this sum accounts for 60 percent of the Education column in Figure 1.

Socioeconomic differentiation and intrahousehold patterns

Figure 2 presents the distribution of expenses for the month of June 1984, broken down for heads of household, women, and dependent adult men. This is done separately for large farm and small farm households in order to see the effect of heads' wealth on the shares of the categories of actors. Large farm households have been defined as units where the head of the household cultivates himself a farm of 6 ha. or more. Many of the farmers in this first group were added to the sample when it was enlarged, but a few were part of the initial sample selected randomly. In turn, some of the newly added farmers had to be included in the second group, because even though ambitious and "progressive" in attitude, they farmed less than 6 ha. In its final form, "large farm households" includes 20 production units. With the exception of an important matriclan and patrilineal elder who is the head of a household organized along customary lines, all of them are interested in newly introduced farm technologies, and their production decisions are guided by the desire for greater involvement in the market. The remaining 31 households, labeled "small farm" in contrast to the ones above, are more heterogeneous. Among them there are two important households of traders including individuals who possess large amounts of cash even though they are average farmers. Two other unusual households consist of men living alone. One of these men disappeared from the sample when, in the dry season of 1984, he decided to seek wage work in the city and gave up farming for one season (he returned to it later in 1985). The rest of the households have varying membership and farm sizes, all of which, however, from the perspective of the head cover a smaller area than those in the first group. With the exception of the few households included in the small farm group but having members with high monetary incomes and herds (such as traders or veterans), the distinction between the two groups also corresponds to differences in wealth.

The total expenses aggregated for all households in June 1984 were about 3,350,000 F CFA, 44 percent of which was spent by members of the 20 large farm households. Furthermore, more than half of the rest (1,103,540 F CFA) is accounted for by the trade transactions of women in only two of the small farm households. If this trade activity is excluded, the expenditure of the 20 large farm households for the month of June 1984 is about twice that of the 31 small farm households.

One of the major differences between the two groups appears in farming investment. Small farm operators made less than a quarter of the total expenditure in this category. What accounts for the large aggregate among large farm households in this column is the purchase of plows, draft animals, and associated equipment by five farmers. Four of them already possessed plows, but added a second or third pair of animals to their belongings. Several factors contributed to this trend. In 1984 several members of the village group received for the first time agricultural credit from the ORD for the purchase of draft animals, but they had to put down 50,000 F CFA to be able to take advantage of it. In this year, the price of cattle also went down due to factors related to the regional export

358

economy and political developments. Some farmers who had money (especially some pension receivers) benefited from this development by buying draft animals with private funds. Two other larger farm operators spent relatively large sums (47,000 and 35,000 F CFA) on fertilizer, labor, insecticides, and other operational farm expenses. In contrast, among small farm households only one purchased oxen and a plow, and this case accounts for more than 40 percent of the aggregate spending on farming in this group. This farmer already possessed a pair and displayed all the characteristics of the large farm operators among whom he was listed by the leaders of the *Groupement Villageois*, but he had, at the time of the survey, only a moderate area under cultivation.

It may be worth reminding that expenditures on farming and farm size are not related here to possession of land. Land is not commoditized, and any household could bring more of it under cultivation by using customary means of access. For members of lineages deprived of permanent cultivation rights on sufficient land, these means include the free borrowing of land from other lineages in the village that are more favored in this respect. Most of the farms in the large farm group in the sample were established on borrowed land (see Şaul 1987). Investment in farm inputs is not a result of access to land but a primary variable in explaining farming scale.

Most farm purchases are made by heads of household, followed by dependent men (mostly married sons), and then by women. Interestingly, women's share in farm investment is larger among small farm households. It may be that women in wealthy households feel less compelled to engage in food production. But one consequence is that in wealthy households the farming resources appear to be concentrated to a larger extent in the hands of the head of the household. It should be remembered that women's farm production activity is not limited to growing vegetables for home consumption. Although nonstaple crops such as peanuts, cowpeas, and red sorghum dominate women's agricultural endeavors, there are also some relatively large women producers who hire labor for their personal fields, rent plows, and sell most of their harvest. The personal fields of the largest woman farm operator in the sample added up to more than a half hectare. Whether in large farm households lesser involvement in personal farming provides women with free time that they can use in processing, collection and trade is a question that can only be answered elsewhere because it requires different types of analysis.

Within Bare, trade life is dominated by women. Although in a few of the large farm households some women and men engage in modest but visible retailing activity, all of these pale to insignificance in comparison to the commerce of the women in the two trading households that are part of the small farm group. One of these households is headed by a settled Fulani who is an army veteran, and the trader is his single wife, a Zara woman born and raised in Bobo-Dioulasso. The value of trade goods she declared to have purchased in June come to 815,000 F CFA. Between husband and wife, they possess more than 80 heads of cattle, the largest number in the village, but I could not determine how many each one of them own (many people in the village believe they all belong to her). These animals are tended in a large herd (including animals belonging to other villagers) that the husband manages; the considerable responsibilities of this herd may explain the relatively modest farm size of the husband. Nevertheless, his farm is highly productive, and both spouses have other sources of income as well. The woman is a medium-sized regional trader who collects grain to store, who buys shea nuts for a trader in Bobo-Dioulasso for a commission, and who owns the mechanical grain mill of the village. Her brother is a trader in Bobo-Dioulasso with whom she has many types of partnerships. Although her trade activity alone accounts for 43 percent of the aggregate expenditure for the month by all small farm households, my enumerators and I shared the belief that the scale of her activity was even greater than what the figures she gave us suggest.

The second trade household is headed by a Zara man who has been established in the village since his youth. The Zara make up one of the trading communities in western Burkina; they speak the same language as the Bobo, but believe themselves to be of recent Mande ancestry and are now Muslims. Today it is especially their women who universally engage in trade. All but one major trader woman in the village were Zara. Many trading Zara women move frequently in order to spend different periods of the year in different villages as dependents of households they choose as temporary bases. Because of this, the household of this man included, in addition to his three wives, many women who spent only part of the year in the village. He himself, in addition to farming, undertook some artisanal activities and raised sheep, but did not do any trading. Therefore, his spending accounts for only about 4 percent of the aggregate for the household. The women's trade goods purchases for June amount to more than 213,000 F CFA. The two trade households together account for 93 percent of the trade related expenses among small farm households, and 86 percent of that for all households in the sample. The June figures may slightly underrepresent the extent of other women's involvement in trade, because for women in regular farming households the most important trade activities are brewing, processing condiments, and cooking in the market, all of which generally take place in the post-harvest season. But it is clear that their relative share would have been small even if the whole year were to be taken into account.

Many young men living as dependents of older heads are attracted by the prospects of trade, especially when they have the possibility of obtaining starting capital from a relative who has a regular salaried job. One such man accounts for the third largest value of trade goods expenditure among the households of the sample (28,000 F CFA). The only head of household in the sample who had a somewhat important trade activity in June was a man who sells cooked meat regularly. A few other heads sell kerosene and one or two other staple products intermittently. Outside of the sample, there is one villager who owns a store/bar and who is considered a trader, and two others among the settled Fulani of the village who are a mechanic and a tailor, respectively.

Purchases of food grain are high for small farm households (the highest item of expenditure when trade is excluded), whereas they are negligible for large farm households. This is not surprising, but note that these data are coming from a village that is moderately productive by national standards and, on the aggregate, is able to supply large quantitites of grain to the market. The figures on food purchases thus confirm that the grain surpluses that reach the market are not contributed by relatively equal shares from all rural households, and there is a clear distinction between those whose farming scale is geared towards market sales and the others. Some households purchase small amounts of rice, in order to break the monotony of the diet, and because in the rainy season the price differences between the generally less expensive sorghums and rice (especially the broken rice that is locally produced in a few irrigated perimeter schemes in the region) are reduced or even reversed. But even among small farm households, the purchase of cereals in the rainy season is not universal; 60 percent of these households either did not buy any or bought only negligible amounts. Many of those who bought more than one sack (100 kg.) are the few former army men who rely on their pension to supplement their farm income. The largest single purchasing household is that of the settled Fulani man and trader Zara woman. During the survey, care was taken to distinguish between purchases of grain for trade and purchases of grain for consumption, but it is possible that in this household some of these purchases were actually intended for resale. Part of the difference in quantity purchased, however, is attributable to the fact that the head of the household was not able to grow all the grain needed. This case actually provides a striking example of the need to look at intrahousehold relations to better understand some aggregate patterns: In this house, while the wife was a regional-level grain trader who stored relatively large quantities in her storehouse, the husband purchased grain to fulfill his obligations for the family.

Although the norm is that grain is provided by the head of the household, especially during the farming season when all household members work on his fields, dependents also buy some. Women buy grain because their contribution to consumption in the household is not limited to providing condiments and vegetables for the sauce. Even in the high farming season when they are spending most time in the joint fields managed by the head, they may also have to cook supplementary meals for themselves and for their children, sometimes using their own grain. Dependent men occasionally buy grain that, like their personal production, is meant to supplement their own nuclear families' needs.

Meat and fish, like oil and condiments, are primarily provided by women for meals taken by the whole household. After the cereal harvests, the head of the household distributes some grain to his wives and to other adult dependents. This is considered to be his contribution for those expenses, but generally it covers only a small portion of them. Women can sell this grain and use the money for later purchases or for their own trade. They can brew the grain and sell the beer. They can also keep the grain and exchange it for condiments with the traders of the village, as the need arises. Women supplement this income not only with many other trade and processing activities, but also grow their own vegetables and peanuts for sauce, make their own shea butter, and ferment their own locust beans. When there is a ritual occasion, heads of households contribute the sacrificial animals, which may eventually be shared to some extent by the other members of the family. These animals, however, usually are not purchased, as they come from their flocks. Even when they are purchased, this expense would not always show up in the Meat and Fish category as it may be tabulated as a ritual expense.

As might be expected, the households of large farm operators spend more on meats, oils, and condiments (about twice as much for a smaller number of people). What would be less evident without having the data is that in these households the heads make a larger contribution for these purchases. These expenses are normatively assigned to women, but as the monetary income of the head of the household increases, he may start to participate more importantly in them. Breaking it down in a different way, heads of large farm households spent 3 percent of their income on meat and fish while those of small farm households spent only 1 percent, in June 1984. Women in large farm households also spend a larger proportion of their income on meat than their counterparts in small farm households, whereas for condiments the ratios are about the same for both men and women in the two groups. All meat purchased by men, however, is not for immediate consumption; some of it is reserved for ceremonies. Many men make extensive use of traps in their fields, occasionally hunt small animals, and may also purchase whole or part of animals hunted by others. This meat is usually smoked in which form it can be preserved for more than a year. In this way elders accumulate considerable quantities of game for use in major festivals. Meals prepared on such occasions are sometimes cooked and consumed ceremonially, but the distribution of shares follows precise customary lines that discriminate against younger dependents and women. For example, in 1984, in Bare and some surrounding villages there took place the initiation of boys to the Do cult, an event which occurs once every six years. In order to be accepted, each candidate has to contribute, among other things, a jar (of about 15 to 20 liters) full of smoked meat. In the past, this was supposed to be hunted or trapped by the boy. Today, in many cases most of this meat is bought little by little by the boy's mother or father during the preceding year. The meat and the other produce collected for the occasion are divided among the senior age classes officiating in the ceremony, whose members then distribute it among themselves. The young men and women see very little of it, unless an elder in the family decides to share some of his lot with his immediate relatives.

Expenses for buildings and durables constitute one of the most pronounced differences between the two groups, but it is not possible to detect all of this in Figure 2, because there was no construction in June 1984, except for two large farm households that had granaries built in anticipation of the coming harvest. Most other large expenditures were for motorbikes, bicycles, and related repair work. Two large farm households bought secondhand motorbikes, while others bought parts and paid for service. Most spending on such large ticket items takes place naturally in the post-harvest season. A good portion of the aggregate for this month is due to the purchase of pots, pans, bowls, large ceramic vessels, and other cooking utensils. Whereas the pans needed for cooking meals are bought primarily by women, the largest vessels are frequently purchased by men. Often they do so, not for their wives but for their sisters, as most movable property among the southern Bobo belongs to matrilineages. This pattern is changing in the village, and there are a few instances of men who buy large beer pots for their own household, to be transmitted at death to the household of their sons. It is, again, of interest to note that in the large farm group most expenditures included in this column were made by heads of household, whereas in the small farm group they were made by women and dependent men. Among the latter they represent mostly costs of bicycle repairs and radios by young men (in one case the building of a room), and the purchase of cooking utensils by women. The pattern points to the fact that in the small farm group, for small out-of-pocket expenses young men may possess more disposable cash income than their elders.

A similar pattern is revealed between large and small farm households in the category of manufactured consumer goods. Actually, the figures here can be taken as an index of wealth. The difference between small farm and large farm groups is attenuated by the inclusion of the two wealthy trading households among the former, these households accounting for 45 percent of the value of this column. If these are not included, the per-person expenditure of large farm households on consumer goods of urban origin is five times that of the nontrading small farm households. Men dominate the picture in this category, but in small farm households, dependents--both men and women--have a proportionately larger role.

Spending on beverages is relatively high even in this month of hard work and restraint. These purchases account for about 4 percent of the aggregated total for the month. Not surprisingly, large farm households spend more than the rest, but the largest single sum (21,475 F CFA) is found in this case in one of the households included in the small farm group, headed by an exuberant veteran. If this atypical instance is excepted, most households in this group spent between 1,000 F and 2,000 F CFA, whereas in the large farm group most expenses are in the range from 2,000 F to 8,000 F CFA. In both groups there are a few households that spent only negligible amounts on drinks, but this is the second category in which households are most consistently represented, following that of farm expenditure. Bottled beer accounts for most of the total, but spending for wine, carbonated drinks, and anise liqueur (pastis)--for which the veterans acquired a taste while in the army--are also important. These drinks are dispensed both by the several women traders of the village, the most important of whom are in the two sample households, and by the aforementioned village bar. Local sorghum beer and fermented honey water represent a small share of these expenses, partly because these drinks are not as available in the rainy season when women have less time to brew. Female and male dependents make a visible but small contribution in both groups. They rarely drink bottled beverages, preferring the cheaper local brews. On the aggregate, women appear to control very considerable sums of money, but this is concentrated in the hands of a few women. Most of the rest, even when they turn around more money than their men, can dispose of less of it for personal consumption because of their obligations to contribute food and cloth to the household. Their attitude also supports the common local stereotype that women are careful managers who do not indulge very much in personal consumption.

The situation is somewhat different with regard to clothing. The share of heads of household is small for both large and small farm households. Women and dependents are generally assumed to be responsible for clothing themselves and their children and make 56 and 67 percent of the clothing purchases for the two groups respectively. The disparity between the aggregate figures for large and small farm households is, however, remarkable. The former spend almost four times more per person than the latter. Dependent men on small farms account for a larger share of their column compared to those in large farms, but this is because their heads' share is almost negligible; otherwise not only the absolute amounts they spend on clothing but also its proportion to their total spending (which is 6 percent) is smaller than that of large farm dependents (28 percent). What facilitates these high expenditures by both men and women in the large farm group is that they receive a share of the agricultural production in the form of gifts from the head of the household after the harvest. This can amount to several *tines* (20-liter cylinder) of sorghum for wives and mature sons of prosperous farmers. The lack of integration in the domestic unit becomes relevent here too, because especially women can receive such gifts not only from their husband but also from brothers and other matrilineal relatives, and can be in a favorable position thanks to the latter even if their own farm group is not highly productive. But it often occurs that in households where there is difficulty in meeting subsistence needs, women, even if they receive generous post-harvest gifts, have to reserve most of them for later use in the year, either as food or to exchange against condiments. In contrast, wives of more prosperous farmers and young men of all groups can afford to sell a large part of these gifts immediately to be able to buy garments and jewelry.

The category for Tax expenditure cannot be expected to reveal a convincing pattern in one month. Six heads of household declared to have paid their taxes for past years. Only one of them was in the small farm group and this was the settled Fulani married to the Zara trader. Contribution for community projects were not represented in this month, while other fiscal payments were insignificant.

Expenses subsumed under the category of Ritual are higher than would be expected if one considers that June is not in the festival season. The aggregates are accounted for by large expenditures made by a very small number of households. Among small farm households, the settled Fulani farmer killed an ox, while the head of the Zara household killed a sheep, the occasion for both being burials. These two trading families practically exhausted the ritual spending in their group. Among the heads of large farm households three have killed cattle, and a few other households have made smaller expenses, also for burials. The killing of cattle, especially for burials, is not strictly a religious requirement for traditionalist Bobo; in the old days few individuals possessed cattle. Today, part of the slaughtered animal can be sold or reserved for another occasion. Actually, three of those who killed cattle are among the few in the village who are Muslims. Killing an animal is a way of asserting preeminence. We will have a chance to come back to this question when discussing Figure 5.

Expenses for education display the skewed pattern discussed with respect to Figure 1. The veteran villager who paid the large sum for the tuition of his son did so in June, so that this item dominates the category for small farm households. Eleven other parents spent small amounts of money for their children in the village school. Although the sums are small, it is significant that seven of them are among the large farm households.

Expenditures by season

Figure 3 aggregates the amounts spent during the whole nine months separately for heads of household, women and dependent men. This figure basically confirms the results derived from data covering the month of June. It brings out more clearly that women, taken together, use more money than dependent men, but if the money revolving in trade (for which only a few individuals in the sample are responsible) is excluded, heads of household as a group have higher levels of expenditure than anybody else. Both heads of household and dependent men spend proportionately more on durables, manufactured goods of urban origin, and beverages, whereas women spend most of their money on condiments and clothing, for which they have family obligations. Dependent men's highest consumption expenditure is for clothing (their own), followed very closely by beverages. Clothing, for young men and women, is the focus of status competition, a common but intriguing evolution considering that the population of this area defined itself primarily by its refusal to wear any clothes until as recently as thirty years ago. Heads of household spend most on beverages, farm expenses, and consumer goods, and the burden for ritual expenditure is also clearly on them.

Figure 4 shows the distribution of expenses by season during the nine months, separately for heads of household, women, and dependent men. As discussed earlier, the limitations of the data set included in this analysis reduces the usefulness of this comparison, but one can discern a pattern complementary to what has been said above. Expenditures in the dry season are higher for dependent men, and (when trade is excluded) for women as well. Because the farming season figures cover a significantly larger number of individuals, one has to discount this factor in the columns; the figures for the dry season would be considerably higher in proportion to the rainy season if the comparison was restricted to the same households. But the difference in spending between the seasons is less evident in the case of heads of household. Their high farming season total can be explained in large part with the important farm expenses made by the few heads who were added to the sample in June. The pattern may also show that household heads' access to money is less seasonal than that of the rest. Some of them have higher levels of monetary income and are able to reserve part of it for later use, while a few of them, as in the case of veterans, receive income evenly distributed throughout the year. The contrast in seasonality between heads and other members of households will certainly be less pronounced when the whole set of data is taken into account, and the overall pattern is likely to be high dry season expenditures for all groups across the board; but the seasonal fluctuations faced by different types of household members is worth emphasizing. In the cash-scarce farming season, most men (including poor household heads) and women have to have recourse to forms of petty consumer credit for the most indispensible purchase items. This is the time when women engage most frequently in an unfavorable exchange with village traders to obtain condiments in return for grain that may have to be taken out of the daily ration for household consumption given by the head, and it is widely believed that in the same period some heads of household themselves enter into different types of dependent relations with grain buyers in order to receive access to credit.

The veterans

The veterans largely overlap with the group of large farm operators. They have been singled out among heads of household because of their privileged access to money from sources that are extraneous to the farming economy. In terms of consumption they display consumer preferences that represent "urban-modernized" tendencies; they are pacesetters for new trends and also provide a strong market force shaping the enlarging (even though still very limited in comparison to cities) supply of manufactured goods in the village. Of the 12 veterans in the sample, only seven receive pensions, but the others also have above-average wealth because of savings achieved during service or because of skills learned in the army that helped them find employment after their years of service. The experience is also important because of influences on world views and consumption habits. Veterans are somewhat older than the other heads of household; they have an average age of 56 whereas the average for the whole sample is 50. They are also more homogeneous in terms of age; it ranges from 47 to 64. There are a few others who, because they are brothers or sons of a deceased serviceman, continue to receive a pension through the wife who has survived him. These people have not been included here because the way the payments are divided and controlled among the relatives could not be determined with precision. This phenomenon is interesting in itself and worthy of further study, because it seems that regulations of the colonial army provided support for the weakening of matrilineal groups as corporate entities by tying a man's monetary income to his conjugal group and agnatic relatives and increased the motivation in such cases for insisting on leviratic arrangements.

Because the veterans are all heads of household, Figure 5 can profitably be compared with the relevant bars in Figure 3. It becomes immediately evident that farming expenses are very large in the present case. Former servicemen are among the farmers who made repeated attempts to use new farming techniques. They have often become mediators with administrative bodies and have provided new role models as farmers. This choice has not been free of disappointments and setbacks. Some former servicemen still complain bitterly about the indifference and even latent hostility they encountered in the village when they attempted to use animal traction for the first time. One veteran lost several animals under suspicious circumstances. He was particularly eloquent in self-criticism and declared that if he were to start all over again he would choose to open a bar instead of trying to engage in improved farming. In practice, however, most veterans hesitate to take a course of action that would cut them off from agriculture, and even this person, so bitter in his reflections, decided in 1984 for the fifth time to replace his dead animals with a new pair rather than using the important sum of money for something else. This attitude towards farming can only be understood within existing social relations regulating access to labor. The veterans came back as household heads already controlling the large labor force of their compounded family, apt to grow further by marrying young wives or absorbing dependents of deceased elder relatives. This presents an advantage for establishing a growing farm.

The former servicemen have an ambigious position in the community. Traditionalist elders often talk of them as introducers of foreign ways disrupting the harmony of social life and as an important factor in the abandonment or weakening of old institutions. In contrast, former servicemen have remained attached to many of the traditional ways, especially in spiritual matters. Most of those who had converted to Islam during their service years slid back to local practices upon their return. Changes that are more difficult to document, however, may be taking place in this respect too. New secret society cults originating in Minianka and Bambara country have spread among the southern Bobo, as elsewhere in western Burkina, in the colonial period. Former servicemen were often the leaders in village initiatives to acquire such cults or were of critical importance in their successful completion thanks to the broad network of acquaintances acquired during the years of service. The spread of these cults put some strain on the authority of traditionalist elders, who found it difficult to amass through traditional channels the formidable monetary and other resources necessary for such mystical acquisitions.

Former servicemen returning to their native village have also remained committed to the customary land-holding system which revolves around patrilineages. This allows them access to as much land as they can farm. They have also retained tight control over the labor of dependents in their households. The control wielded by many rich heads of household is actually tighter than in most other households, because it is facilitated by the additional power money provides. Veterans are starting to replace traditionalist elders as heads of lineage segments, and the tension between the latter and the younger veterans seems to be

367

decreasing in intensity. Three of the veterans in the sample are also elders of important matrilineal and patrilineal segments. One of them has been able to take full advantage of this in order to create the largest farm in the sample, 27 ha. farmed by the members of his crowded household, which includes three generations--all under the unrelenting authority of the elder--as one single production unit.

The large spending on food grains in Figure 5 reveals that there are also a few older veterans who take the option of maintaining a small-scale farming activity while maintaining a high level of consumption thanks to their pension. Farming provides in such cases only part of the needs of the household, which starts to approximate economically the model of urban consumer units. But it is also in such households that one finds the few adult dependent men who engage in trade with a little capital that they have acquired independently.

The high expenditures on durables, manufactured consumer goods, and beverages by veterans reflect the pattern of high income individuals. High expenditures on rituals and on education are relatively even more pronounced. Ritual expenditure points partly to a strategy of status acquisition in a community in which the veterans find themselves in the ambivalent position of both innovators and supporters of traditions. It can also be said that the community is willing to grant the veterans the new roles they are developing for themselves only at the expense of the burden of new responsibilities. This is the obligation to provide larger shares in festivals and community projects, thus contributing more importantly to the constitution of the social order as well as to the consumption level of fellow villagers, especially other elders. Cultural resources are thus perhaps mobilized to distribute part of the new concentrated wealth within the community. But who knows if this is not also a mechanism for the consolidation and furtherance of new stratification patterns, as they thrust themselves and find new life in agricultural production. The emerging new patterns of differentiation in rural Burkina Faso can be discerned in the expenditure data of Bare, and the veterans with the interstitial role they play between the money economy and the village community provide the paradigm for a new stratum of farmers.

Conclusion

If capital of full-time trader women is excluded, most cash in Bare is in the hands of heads of household. But dependent members of households are also involved in the money economy and make both consumption and investment expenditures. No group is totally cut off from any sector in the village life, but commitment to them shows considerable variability. In terms of consumption, heads of households spend proportionately more on personal consumption goods and rituals; women spend more for food and clothing. In terms of production, men spend more on farm expenses, whereas women prefer trade. Trade life is, however, strongly dominated by a few specialized women. The consumption preferences of women can be traced to their normative obligations within the household; many of them are also relatively poor in terms of cash and cannot engage in the purchase of nonessential items. The difference between men and women in terms of productive strategies can be related to access to labor. Elders are privileged in agriculture because they control a good part of the work time of household members; they have in turn the obligation to provide most of the grain consumed. But many heads of household also find plenty of room to engage in production for sale using household labor. When they have access to money, they often find it profitable to enlarge their farming scale beyond what is needed to provide subsistence food. This preference is also related to factors outside the household and the village economy, as prices and other elements of the national grain market have an influence upon them. But the difference within the household in terms of opportunities is also important.

Women also may have access to some labor, especially when they get older, that of their sons and daughters, sons-in-law, and brothers. But this is limited, as these individuals have their primary responsibility towards other individuals. The time that women spend on household chores decrease only late in life. They usually prefer to engage in activities that allow them to profitably use stretches of time available to them without obligating them to make a year-long commitment in order to receive a return. Most wives in farming households adopt a strategy of differentiation trying to fill several niches: collection of wild products, retail trade, processing and cooking activities for sale, and a little personal farming, mostly to avoid buying condiments, but often also to generate a little cash. Although a few women show determination and considerable success in their personal farming, the vocation of most successful women is trade; but at larger scales this is extremely time-consuming as well. It is significant that all of the full-time women traders of Bare were born in the city (Bobo-Dioulasso), and came to the village in relatively mature age as a result of marriages of their own consent. They contribute to the farming endeavors of their husbands relatively little, because of his small farm size, but complement the needs of the household by providing more grain to it with the proceeds of their trade. They also maintain a different ethnic identity.

Dependent men are in an intermediate position. Like married women, they prefer to engage in trade when they can obtain initial capital. They also engage in cutting wood and, when they have more skills, in services such as masonry. Because they are free of many obligations that women have, they can use a greater proportion of their income for personal consumption. In some poor households, they actually appear to afford more daily spending on small consumption items than the head of the household. Many young men who inherited a constituted household and modern farm implements at the death of their father have become some of the most dynamic farmers in the village. It is likely that dependent young men who engage primarily in trade now will return to a full agricultural vocation in their later years, when they control a larger amount of labor in their own household. Perhaps the few who become exceptionally successful in trade may quit the farming community, but generally for young men the way out of farming is to find regular salaried employment in the city.

If additional cash resources were to become available, it is likely that most heads of household would increase their farm investment as well as their personal consumption, of durables such as bicycles and motorbikes (which in part need also to be considered "farm investment") and of nondurables such as beverages and clothing, whereas most women would probably try to increase their participation in trade. Some wealthy heads of household contribute to a larger extent to expenses that are normally left to women, such as certain food items, clothing and education, raising thus the welfare level of the group. In such domestic units, however, men often also control a greater proportion of the productive capacity of the group, and the "household" comes much closer to be what we understand by the term in its Western context.

The critical variable in this whole discussion is the claims of different social identities on each other's labor. At the time when crops were not offered regularly in the market and most of the wealth resulting from farm production was controlled by corporate groups, differences between the genders and age groups consisted of differences in consumption and in labor contributions justified directly by norms stipulating the distribution of food and tasks within the community. Monetization has increased particularly in the last 30 years, but is not spreading in all social arenas because the labor arrangements within the productive unit remain largely unchanged. This is creating the possibility for one set of actors (the heads of households) to harness the labor they control to respond to the stimuli provided by the market, especially when they can bring into it resources from the outside. Their superiority is thus acquiring an economic base it did not possess before, and their privileges are also translated into the consumption of purchased goods. The same development is drawing women increasingly toward trade, but this can be achieved only at a small scale. The possibilities revealed in the normative structure (such as the freedom to engage in many kinds of productive activities) remain unfulfilled for dependent members because relations regulating labor within the household constitute a more fundamental level and conditions responses to the market.

Notes

Field research was undertaken in 1983 and 1984 with funds provided by the National Science Foundation, the Wenner-Gren Foundation for Anthropological Research, and the Research Board of the Graduate College, University of Illinois at Urbana-Champaign. The Research Board also provided subsequent funding for the analysis. The writing was completed during my tenure as a fellow of the Center for Advanced Study at the University of Illinois. In addition to these institutions, I would like to express my gratitude to my enumerators, especially Sanou Feneme Eugène, Sanou Desiré, Sanou Soungalo; to the villagers of Bare, and to the many friends who helped in Bobo-Dioulasso. I would also like to acknowledge the stimulating discussion by participants following the presentation of this paper at the SEA meeting in Urbana, the patient commentary by Benjamin S. Orlove on an earlier draft, and the editorial assistance of Barbara E. Cohen.

1. A good critical review of the literature relevant for these issues has been provided by Guyer (1981).

2. One bridge from the feminist literature to social sciences was Ester Boserup's celebrated *Woman's Role in Economic Development*, which had as large, if not larger, an impact in anthropology as in sociology, agricultural economics and other social sciences, but is now somewhat superseded by the work it inspired. At present, many views deriving from this perspective have found official backing in development aid circles, as evidenced, for example, by the creation of the Women in Development Office in USAID.

3. ORDs (*Organismes Régionaux de Développement*) are decentralized rural development coordination organizations under the Ministry of Rural Development. They provide extension service and are involved in the distribution of modern farm inputs and credit.

4. The CFA frank, the common currency of several Francophone West African states, is tied to the French frank by the guaranteed conversion rate of 1 FF=50 F CFA and floats in international markets with it. In 1984, one dollar USA fluctuated around 400 F CFA.

Figure 1

TYPES OF EXPENDITURE
October 1983-June 1984

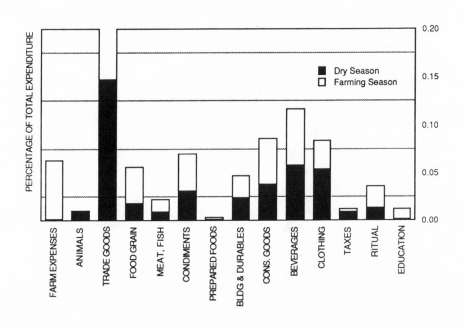

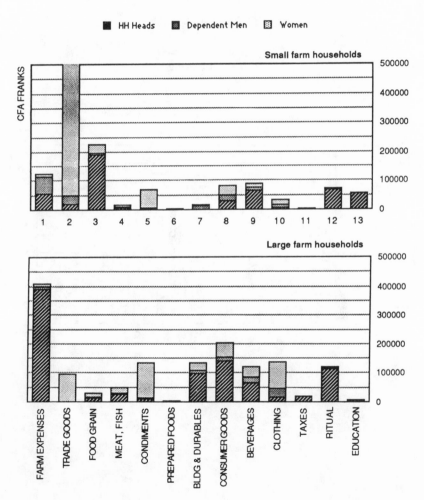

Figure 2

GENDER, ROLE, AND TYPE DISTRIBUTION OF EXPENDITURE
June 1984

■ HH Heads   ▦ Dependent Men   ⊞ Women

Small farm households

CFA FRANKS

500000
400000
300000
200000
100000
0

1 2 3 4 5 6 7 8 9 10 11 12 13

Large farm households

500000
400000
300000
200000
100000
0

FARM EXPENSES
TRADE GOODS
FOOD GRAIN
MEAT, FISH
CONDIMENTS
PREPARED FOODS
BLDG & DURABLES
CONSUMER GOODS
BEVERAGES
CLOTHING
TAXES
RITUAL
EDUCATION

Figure 3

AMOUNTS SPENT
October 1983-June 1984

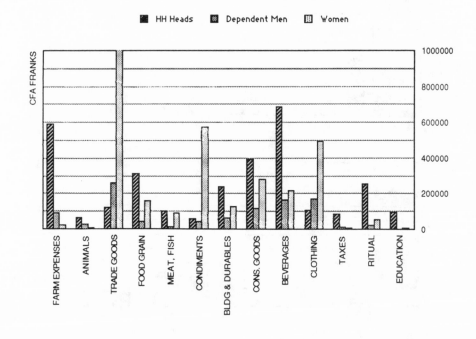

Figure 4

DISTRIBUTION OF EXPENSES BY SEASON

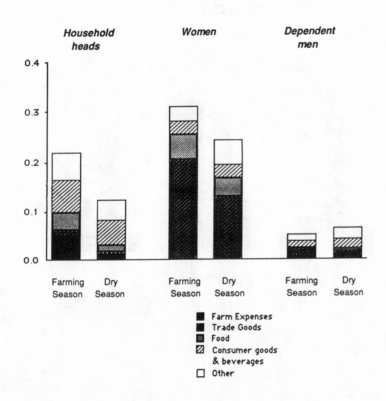

Figure 5

SPENDING BY VETERANS

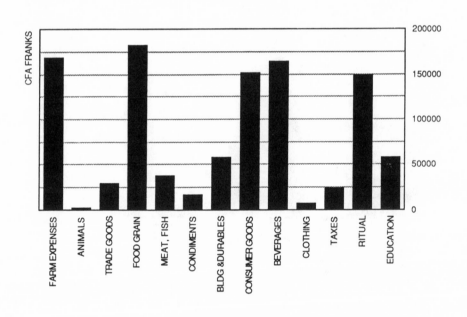

References

Barth, F.
1966 *Models of Social Organization.* Royal Anthropological Institute, Occasional Paper No. 23.

Boserup, Ester
1970 Woman's Role in Economic Development. New York: St. Martin's Press.

Dupré, Georges, and Pierre Philipe Rey
1968 Réflexions sur la pertinence d'une théorie de l'histoire des échanges. *Cahiers Internaitionaux de Sociologie* 46: 133-162.. There are several translations into English, among which: Seddon, D., ed., *Relations of Production*, 1978, pp. 171-208.

Fortes, Meyer
1969 *Kinship and the Social Order.* Chicago: Aldine.

Goody, Jack
1962 *Death, Property and the Ancestors.* Stanford: Stanford University Press.

1976 *Production and Reproduction: A Comparative Study of the Domestic Domain.* Cambridge: Cambridge University Press.

Guyer, Jane I.
1981 Household and Community in African Studies. *African Studies Review* 24:87-137.

Leach, E. R.
1961 *Rethinking Anthropology.* London: Athlone Press.

Le Moal, Guy
1980 *Les Bobo: Nature et Fonction des Masques.* Paris: ORSTOM.

Meillassoux, Claude
1960 Essai d'interprétation du phénomène économique dans les sociétés traditionnelles d'autosubsistance. *Cahiers d'Etudes Africaines* 4:38-67. English translation in Seddon, D., ed., *Relations of Production*, 1978, pp. 127-157.

1972 From Reproduction to Production. *Economy and Society* 1:93-105.

Rapp, R., E. Ross & R. Bridenthal
1979 Examining Family History. *Feminist Studies* 5(1):174-200.

Richards, Audrey
1939 *Land, Labour and Diet in Northern Rhodesia.* London: Oxford University Press.

Roberts, Pepe
1984   Feminism *in* Africa: Feminism *and* Africa. *Review of African Political Economy* no. 27/28:175-184.

Sabean, David Warren
1983   The History of the Family in Africa and in Europe: Some Comparative perspectives. *Journal of African History* 24:163-171.

Şaul, Mahir
1988   Money and Land Tenure as Factors in Farm Size Differentiation in Burkina Faso. In *Land and society in contemporary Africa*, S. P. Reyna and R. E. Downs, eds. University Press of New England. In press.

Worsley, P. M.
1956   The Kinship System of the Tallensi: A Revaluation. *Journal of the Royal Anthropological Institute* 86:37-75.

GENDER AND LOW-INCOME HOUSEHOLD EXPENDITURES IN JAMAICA

Barbara Diane Miller

Poverty, gender, and the issue of spending patterns

As economic anthropology moves ahead with a concern for the study of consumption, it must bring with it advances in the anthropological study of gender dynamics in the household. Recent work in other disciplines is beginning to demonstrate that the gender of those who earn, of those who make decisions about expenditures, and of those who receive allocations within the household, often makes a decisive difference. Cultures pattern the income level of male and female workers, the priorities about how earnings will be spent, and the ways in which consumption occurs. The internal differentiation of households along gender lines affects consumption at every stage. In this chapter I examine only one of the possible gender lines within the household--the structure of household headship--and how it affects the level and pattern of household expenditures. The setting is Jamaica, where male dominance in the public and household economy is less extreme than in most other parts of the developing world and where, often, it is the females who are the economic backbone of the household, particularly in the low-income class.

Evidence from diverse parts of the world shows that female-headed households more frequently live in poverty than joint male-female households (Garfinkel and McLanahan 1985 on the US; Saldert 1984 on Bangladesh; Kossoudji and Mueller 1983 on Botswana; Kaufman 1982 and Kaufman and Lindauer 1984 on El Salvador; Rakowski 1984 on Venezuela; Merrick and Schmink 1983 on Brazil). The factor promoting poverty among female-headed households is generally said to be the lower income-earning ability of a female head of household compared to a male head. Thus, the gender of the head of household is supposedly related to the level of income and expenditure of a household. A related body of thought concerns the composition of household expenditures. Some scholars have written that female-headed households have distinctly different expenditure patterns than male-headed or joint male-female headed households (Dwyer 1983; Folbre 1984; Kaufman and Lindauer 1984; Brown 1975). All authors agree that, in general, female-headed households spend larger proportions of their budgets on "basic needs" than do households not headed by a woman. There are disagreements as to whether the reasons for differential expenditure patterns between the household types are due to women's greater concern with household welfare (Dwyer 1983; Brown 1975), or because one source of women's income is often loans and transfers, and such money tends to be used for basic needs rather than luxuries (Kaufman and Lindauer 1984).

379

In this chapter I explore these two areas--expenditure level and expenditure composition--using detailed data on 145 low-income households in Jamaica for 1983-1984.[1] This data set provides much more detailed information on household expenditures than has so far been examined in relationship to gender of household head. I first discuss the results of the analysis of expenditure level and then expenditure composition by the two household types. In conclusion, I review the areas where the Jamaican data fit the general theories and the areas where they do not, and I speculate about the reasons for these findings.

General characteristics of the sample households

The 145 sample households comprise nearly 1,000 persons. More than half of the households are in the rural areas where average household size is 6.1 persons, slightly less than the 6.7 average in the urban areas(Table 1). This average household size is larger than figures derived from an all-Jamaica survey conducted in 1975 which gives an average of 4.5 persons (*Statistical Institute of Jamaica*, 1986).[2]

Although household size in the sample is larger in urban than rural areas, the ratio of children to adults is lower in urban (.80) than rural areas (.97), a phenomenon which corresponds with the larger number of earners per household in the urban subsample (1.4) than the rural subsample (1.2). Also consistent with other reports on the poor, the survey population has a higher percentage, 50 percent, of female-headed households in the urban areas than in the rural areas, 36 percent (Buvinic et al.1978).

It is noteworthy that in both the urban and rural subsamples, average household size is lower in female-headed households than in female-male households. Corresponding with this fact are the higher child/adult ratios in female-headed households and the lower number of earners per household. The higher dependency ratio of female-headed households than joint-headed households is statistically significant in the urban subsample.

Expenditure levels

Mean weekly expenditures (including savings) for the entire sample are J$102.13, ranging from a minimum of J$21.03 for one rural household to a maximum of J$248.51 for one urban household.[3] On average, low-income urban households in Jamaica spend more money a week than low-income rural households, a phenomenon found throughout most of the developing world (van Ginnekan 1976). No doubt some of this difference is due to consumption of own-produced food in rural farming households, but the bulk of the disparity is probably caused by a lower "standard of living" overall in the rural areas.

The average weekly expenditure per household for all female-headed households in the sample compared to all female-male households is nearly the same: J$104.70 as compared to J$100.21. When we look at the urban and rural subsample, a greater difference in expenditure levels appears between the two household types with female-headed households having lower expenditures than female-male households in the urban subsample but higher in the rural subsample. This urban-rural difference is interesting and consonant with the general belief that the poorest female-headed households worldwide are found in urban areas. Nevertheless, even this difference is not statistically significant. Thus, in this sample we cannot say on the basis of expenditures that female-headed households are clearly poorer than joint female-male households.[4]

This brief excursion into examining the degree of poverty by household type cannot be taken as a conclusive demonstration that female headship is not a cause of household poverty in Jamaica. The major weakness in my argument is that expenditure level alone excludes other measures of welfare and thus may be a bad indicator of poverty. Especially important considerations excluded are capital wealth, such as home and animal ownership, and own-production of food. If one were to assume (though I have no evidence on which such an assumption could be based at this time) that female-male households more often than female-headed households own their homes and thus avoid paying rent, are more likely to own goats or chickens, and are more likely to produce food in home gardens, then female-male households would no doubt have an "income" advantage.

Other evidence points to a likelihood in a gender gap in income in Jamaica that should be considered. Statistics on the "labor force" can rarely be taken at face value (Dixon 1982), but they do provide suggestive evidence for male-female differences. In Jamaica, in 1984, more employed females worked shorter numbers of hours per week than employed males (Statistical Institute of Jamaica 1985:80). The total labor force was about 525,000 males and 410,000 females at the time of the survey. Numbers of males and females employed by parishes are revealing. In the parish of Kingston, which is largely urban, numbers of employed males and females are nearly equal, being different by only a few thousand less females than males employed. In some of the most rural parishes, nearly twice as many males as females are employed (Statistical Institute of Jamaica 1985:46-48).

Although more males are employed than females and work more hours, and more employed males are found in higher income groups than employed females, the disparity is far less than in most developing countries. According to another source presenting worldwide national statistics on female adult literacy, in Jamaica more adult females are literate than males, and the female-male rate is the second highest in the more than 200 countries listed (Sivard 1985:22-23). In sum, the labor force and literacy statistics hint that female-headed households may not necessarily be poorer than joint female-male households, and that the gap between the two household types should not be as great as in countries where women's access to literacy and employment are more restricted.

Expenditure composition

The growing literature on poverty and female-headed households provides an interesting hypothesis that in female-headed households expenditure patterns will be more devoted to "basic needs" than in joint female-male households (Guyer 1980; Dwyer 1983; Kaufman 1982; Kaufman and Lindauer 1984; Brown 1975). The rationale behind this hypothesis, while not detailed in the studies I have reviewed, seems to be that women are more domestic/child-oriented in their expenditure strategies, while men might be more public/display-oriented in their expenditure strategies. In a female-headed household there is no permanent male present to divert household resources for nondomestic purposes.

Related to the possible gender-differentiated expenditure priorities is the issue of income/expenditure control within the household. In joint female-male households where all income is pooled and expenditure decisions are made only by the senior female, then the expenditure strategies may resemble those of female-headed households. But where males and females keep partially or wholly separate budgets, then a portion of household expenditures may be male-biased.

Exploration of cross-cultural data on this subject is beginning to produce a range of variation in income pooling and decision-making (Dwyer 1983), but no study as yet has combined good data on household income control dynamics and expenditure patterns. The Jamaican expenditure data examined here provide more insight into the details of how much money is spent for what items than to the everyday household dynamics which directly determine expenditure patterns. By examining the nature of expenditure compositions in relation to the two basic household headship types (female-male or female-headed), we can only infer what role headship plays in decision-making.

Analyses in this area rarely define with precision what they mean by basic needs, but food and housing are usually the key expenditure categories discussed. Such gross categories as food and housing may well include expenditures for items not generally considered basic needs such as cookies and rent for a fancy flat. In this low-income population, however, expenditures on such luxury items are probably quite small for most households. I have therefore calculated expenditure shares--percent of the weekly budget--allocated to eleven gross categories per household (Table 2).

Food expenditures

As expected, according to a law formulated more than a century ago by Ernst Engel, food constitutes the largest share for all households. Differences in mean food shares by household type do not appear to be great, but the T-test reveals a significant difference in the rural subsample where female-headed households spend more on food (Table 2). Before examining nonfood expenditures in Table 2, we should turn to a detailed examination of expenditures on food. I first present the results of the analysis of food expenditures divided into categories defined by the International Labour Office (ILO), and then I look at some individual food items.

The ILO uses ten categories: bread and cereals; meat and fish; fats and oils; milk, milk products, and eggs; fruit and vegetables; sugar, jams, and confectioneries; meals outside the home; non-alcoholic beverages; alcoholic beverages; and other foods. I have placed the low-income survey food items in nine of the categories, excluding "meals away from home" since the survey did not include a separately coded entry for such expenditures (Appendix B). School lunches, for instance, are an especially important expenditure item for urban Jamaican households with school-aged children, but unfortunately this item was coded as "miscellaneous school expenses" which might include books, paper, or other nonfood items and thus cannot be included as a food variable with complete confidence.

In Table 3 expenditure shares in the ILO categories are provided for the sample households stratified according to headship. Within the urban subsample, visible differences exist for meat/fish and alcoholic beverages, for which female-male households spend larger shares than female-headed households, but these differences are not statistically significant. In the rural subsample, a major difference appears in the share for fruit/vegetables toward which female-male households allocate 9.2 percent of their budget while female-headed households allocate 12.5 percent; the T-test shows this finding to be significant at the .01 level. This difference may be the result of a greater amount of own-production of fruits and vegetables in joint-headed households as compared to female-headed households (future examination of the survey data on own-production, will help illuminate the strength of the hypothesis).

Nonfood expenditures

Mean shares for housing visibly differ in the hypothesized direction. Female-headed households in both the urban and rural subsamples spend larger shares on housing than joint female-male households, but the T-test did not reveal these differences as significant. In the urban subsample, however, near-significance was reached (T=.06).

One might argue that alcohol and tobacco are clearly not basic needs. In this sample population, expenditures on alcohol and tobacco are surprisingly low, compared to expenditure shares on these items reported from an island-wide Jamaican survey and from surveys on other developing country populations (Bird and Miller forthcoming). In these data, expenditure shares on alcohol appear very different between the two household types in the urban subsample, but the T-test does not find the difference significant. Significant differences do appear for tobacco expenditure shares in the urban subsample. Far too little is known about the social patterns of drinking and smoking in Jamaica to allow for any conclusions to be drawn on the basis of these findings. The strongest statement that can be made is that, in this sample at least, no suggestion of female-headed households spending more on alcohol or tobacco can be made.

Education for children is highly valued in Jamaica. Education shares (for school fees, uniforms, and school lunches) in the urban subsample are but not in the rural subsample. In the urban areas, school costs are much higher than in rural areas where very little can be spent on school by any households.

One could consider transportation costs in Jamaica as a basic need that allows adults to get to work via the heavily used, island-wide minibus system and that provides for much urban-rural travel which constantly redistributes people and goods from Kingston to "the country" and back again. Somewhat higher transportation shares are found in female-male households than female-headed households which may reflect the fact that joint-headed households generally comprise more earners than female-headed households.

I also tested for possible significant differences in expenditures on individual items by household type (Table 4). The items which the T-test revealed as having different expenditure shares for the two household types contrast markedly in the urban and rural subsamples; there is only one shared item. The results in Table 4 clearly demonstrate a basic needs orientation of female-headed households, but in the urban areas it is a package of needs relating to children's education while in the rural areas it is starchy and filling foods. Female-male headed households are characterized by higher expenditures on preferred and prestigious foods and goods such as sardines, condensed milk, and oil for fried cooking. Most interestingly, expenditures on illness-related transportation are consistently higher in female-male headed households in both the urban and rural areas. It is perhaps possible that the presence of a male affects the nature of illness, such as beatings, which are acutely in need of treatment and thus require a taxi rather than walking or waiting for a minibus, but this is a mere conjecture at this point. Further analysis of the data on incidences of ill health in the survey households may help in the understanding of this intriguing finding.

Highest-expenditure items

I next compare a ranking of the ten highest-expenditure items from the 90 coded items (Table 5). Within the urban subsample, the ranking is very similar for both household types with the top five items (which account for nearly one-third of total expenditures) being identical: bus fares, rent, chicken, shoes, and beef. Four other main items are all shared, though in different order: bread, rice, fish, and "partner group" which is an informal, rotating savings group generally used by women. Cooking oil is in the list of top ten for female-male households but not for female-headed households while electricity appears in the list for female-headed households.

384

In the rural subsample, nine out of ten of the items are in the top ten of both household types, but the ranking is not as consistent in the urban subsample. Only the first two items are both the same rank: chicken and shoes. Fish is tenth for joint-households but third for female-headed households. One could perhaps argue that sugar and cooking oil are "luxuries," and these two items do rank higher in female-male households than in female-headed households. The unshared items are "miscellaneous food purchases" in female-male households and rent in female-headed households. In the former case, I cannot say exactly what items constitute "miscellaneous food purchases" because that variable is a catch-all for food items for which we had no assigned code. It can include such things as meals eaten out as well as Milo, a chocolate milk drink sometimes mixed with white rum and a favorite beverage of men. It is interesting that in urban female-male households "miscellaneous food purchases" constitute only 1.4 percent of total weekly expenditures.

From Table 5, it is apparent that nearly half of all expenditures go toward what could be considered basic needs items, and that there is little difference in the priorities given to these important items between the two household types. It is possible, however, to select a few other items from the 90 coded items that could be termed "luxury goods" in order to see if any differences appear (Table 6). Item-by-item, major differences in the means do not appear. The total "luxuries" share is lower in female-headed households than female-male households, however, and may indicate some pro- luxury pressure on the budget from males. Cosmetics is the only clearly separable female luxury and its share is negligible and consistently so in all household groups. In all, these "luxury" items constitute a small proportion, less than 10 percent, of the total budget. When one considers, however, that something as valued as children's education consumes only about 2-3 percent of the budget, then these "luxuries" take on more importance.

Conclusions

Many other writers have found marked differences in the degree of poverty and expenditure patterns between female-male headed households and female-headed households. This analysis of data from a low-income sample in Jamaica does not indicate marked differences in poverty as measured by expenditure level between the two household types. Two possible reasons can be proposed for this result, one having to do with gender and survey methods and the other concerning gender and the Jamaican economy.

First, the methodological issue. Our interviewers were carefully instructed to try their best to ensure that expenditures of all members of the household were recorded on the daily record sheets. Our key informant always was, however, the female head of household. It was she who oversaw the recording of data on the sheet, either writing down the information herself or

385

having a literate child do the writing. There has been no empirical research in Jamaica, as far as I know, of the extent of pooling and nonpooling of incomes in Jamaica, or about who makes the decisions about expenditures. But I am sure that at least some men do not share their incomes completely with their spouses, nor do they tell their spouses everything about how they have spent their money. A few households in the survey dropped out because the woman's male partner did not like the idea of the survey after it had gone on for a few weeks. One can imagine that a "male underground household economy" of unknown proportions may exist and that men's expenditures on beer, dances, and women friends would be a major part of that separate budgetary domain.

Thus, the fact that these data do not exhibit dramatically different expenditure levels for the two household types of Jamaica may be a function of not having the full complement of data on male expenditures in joint female-male households. This explanation must hold some truth, but how much I cannot say. I am worried, however, that it does not help us much in comparison to the findings of other studies that have found differences. Why would other studies, based on less intensively gathered data often from one-shot interviews, have succeeded in obtaining fuller data on total household expenditures than this survey? A careful review of the data bases and findings of the other studies is certainly in order. I am not yet convinced that the data are so female-biased that the lack of differences between the two household types is completely a methodological artifact.

The second explanation, which I favor although I believe that the first possible explanation cannot be totally discounted, concerns the role of women in Jamaican society and within the household. Compared to many nations of the world where women's economic and social roles are tightly circumscribed, such as in North India and the Middle East, women in Jamaica are far less discriminated against. Jamaican women are very active as workers and earners, and low-income Jamaican women are nearly as likely to find employment than men. As in the wider society, women's role in the household is visibly important. Much research has shown that those who earn money have a greater say in the disposition of household income than those who do not earn. In Jamaica, many women earn incomes and thus accrue decision-making power about expenditures. The lack of clear difference in expenditure levels between female-male and female-headed households may, then, be attributable to the fact that lone female heads of households can and do earn incomes and can provide a stable source of income. The presence of a marginally employed or unemployed male actually lowers the per capita income of a household.

In this chapter, I also sought to discover differences in the expenditure compositions of female-headed and joint-headed households. Item-by-item statistical testing did reveal some differences that seem to make intuitive sense, but they were not necessarily the differences that the theories about female-headed households being pro-basic needs might have been predicted. In the rural areas, female-headed households spend higher shares on starchy foods, while in the urban areas female-headed households spend more on children's education. It is obvious that decision-makers in the different household types are influenced by the varying constraints and opportunities in the rural and urban areas and are strategizing with household resources in significantly different ways than their counterparts in joint-households.

The lack of more clear differences in expenditures for basic needs such as food and housing versus nonbasic needs such as alcohol can perhaps also be explained by the dominant presence of women in the household budgeting process. Men may want to spend on "luxuries" and nondomestic items, but either they are not allowed to do so, or they must do so secretly and without interfering overmuch in the main concern of the female household head in providing for food and shelter for all members and investing for some future security through saving and children's education.

This study is no doubt affected by a female bias in the reporting of expenditures, but that is because, in this Jamaican population, expenditures are in fact strongly biased toward the items that females think the household should buy. One would no doubt find a rather different picture in societies that are strongly patriarchal rather than somewhat matriarchal like Jamaica. The Jamaican situation could be very usefully compared to other cultural regimes where women's voices are less strong and basic needs perhaps more often subverted for male status-vying and nondomestic affairs.

Notes

1   Data were gathered in conjunction with the Jamaica Tax Structure Examination Project of the Metropolitan Studies Program, The Maxwell School, Syracuse University. The project is funded by the Agency for International Development. Carl Stone, of the University of the West Indies, supervised the data collection. Bruce Riddle and Sam Poikail of the Metropolitan Studies Program assisted with data analysis. For further information on the survey methodology, see Appendix A.

2   It appears that the survey under-represents one-person and two-person households and thus over-represents larger households. Nonetheless, the overall usefulness of the data is unimpaired by this demographic sampling flaw.

3   At the time of the survey, US$1 was equal to about J$3.50.

4   I have also computed mean weekly expenditures on a per capita basis and subjected the means by household type to the T-test. Again, no significant differences were revealed in expenditure level.

TABLE 1

SUMMARY CHARACTERISTICS OF FEMALE-MALE AND FEMALE-HEADED HOUSEHOLDS IN THE LOW-INCOME SAMPLE

| | Urban | | | Rural | | |
	Female-Male	Female-Headed	Total Urban	Female-Male	Female-Headed	Total Rural
Number of Households	33	34	67	50	28	78
Average Household Size	7.2	6.3	6.7	6.2	5.9	6.1
Child/Adult Ratio	.69*	.91*	.80	.98	1.04	.97
Number of Earners	1.5*	1.3*	1.4	1.3	1.1	1.2
Mean Weekly Expenditure Per Household	J$130.96	J$119.56	J$125.17	J$79.93	J$86.67	J$82.34
Mean Weekly Expenditure Per Capita	J$ 20.31	J$ 21.97	J$ 21.16	J$13.77	J$17.07	J$14.96

*Significant difference in means at or above the .05 level, using the T-test.

SOURCE: Low-Income Household Expenditure Survey data.

TABLE 2

MEAN WEEKLY EXPENDITURE SHARES (PERCENTAGES) PER
HOUSEHOLD, BY CATEGORIES, URBAN AND RURAL
SUBSAMPLES, AND HOUSEHOLD TYPE

	Urban		Rural	
	Female-Male	Female-Headed	Female-Male	Female-Headed
Number of Households	33	34	50	28
Food	54.8	51.4	61.9*	63.8*
Alcohol	1.5	.4	.9	1.1
Tobacco	1.2*	.6*	1.4	1.5
Dry Goods & Clothing	9.1	8.0	11.0	12.3
Housing	8.7	11.6	4.1	5.9
Fuel	5.0	5.8	3.7	4.6
Transportation	10.2	9.0	6.0	5.1
Health	.6	.6	1.8	1.1
Education	2.6	3.8	2.6	1.6
Entertainment	.8	.8	.3	.1
Other	6.0	8.6	6.6	3.2
Total[a]	100.5	100.6	100.3	100.3

----

*Significant difference in means at or above the .05 level, using the T-test.

[a]Totals may not add to 100 due to rounding.

SOURCE: Low-Income Household Expenditure Survey data.

TABLE 3

MEAN WEEKLY EXPENDITURE SHARES (PERCENTAGES) IN ILO FOOD CATEGORIES BY URBAN AND RURAL HOUSEHOLD TYPES

	Urban		Rural	
	Female-Male	Female-Headed	Female-Male	Female-Headed
Number of Households	33	34	50	28
Bread/Cereals	19.7	20.9	23.9	22.2
Meat/Fish	32.2	30.1	31.7	34.2
Fats/Oils	6.7	6.0	8.2	7.5
Milk/Eggs	11.3	10.1	10.8	9.3
Fruit/Vegetables	14.1	15.8	9.2*	12.5*
Sugar/Sweets	5.4	5.5	7.5	6.6
Nonalcoholic Beverages	3.4	4.0	3.0	2.6
Alcoholic Beverages	1.5	.5	1.3	1.3
Other Foods	5.3	6.4	4.1	3.3
TOTAL[a]	99.6	11.2	99.7	99.5

---

*Significant difference in means at or above the .05 level, using the T-test.

[a]Totals may not add to 100 due to rounding.

SOURCE: Low-Income Household Survey data.

TABLE 4

T-TEST RESULTS FOR PER HOUSEHOLD EXPENDITURES ON
INDIVIDUAL ITEMS BY HOUSEHOLD TYPE[a]

	Female-Headed Households Spend More	Female-Male Headed Households Spend More
Urban:	school uniforms school books	sardines cooking oil condensed milk cigarettes stout illness-related transportation
Rural:	fish green bananas plantains breadfruit sugar syrups	pork illness-related transportation

---

[a]All results are significant at or above the .05 level.

TABLE 5

TEN HIGHEST-EXPENDITURE ITEMS, BY URBAN AND
RURAL SUBSAMPLES, AND HOUSEHOLD TYPE

		Urban		
Rank		Female-Male		Female-Headed
1	bus fares	J$ 12.91 (9.9)[a]	bus fares	J$ 10.60 (8.9)
2	rent	9.40 (7.2)	rent	10.11 (8.5)
3	chicken	9.02 (6.9)	chicken	8.35 (7.0)
4	shoes	6.29 (4.8)	shoes	4.28 (3.6)
5	beef	5.67 (4.3)	beef	4.30 (3.6)
6	bread	4.44 (3.4)	partner group	4.05 (3.4)
7	rice	4.19 (3.2)	bread	4.02 (3.4)
8	fish	3.85 (2.9)	rice	3.66 (3.1)
9	partner group[b]	3.60 (2.7)	fish	3.50 (2.9)
10	cooking oil	3.41 (2.6)	electricity	3.44 (2.9)
	Total Weekly Expenditure	J$130.96 (47.9)		J$119.57 (47.3)

		Rural		
1	chicken	J$ 6.91 (8.6)	chicken	J$ 8.06 (9.3)
2	shoes	4.36 (5.5)	shoes	5.40 (6.2)
3	bus fares	4.19 (5.2)	fish	4.65 (5.4)
4	rice	3.60 (4.5)	rent	4.50 (5.2)
5	bread	3.49 (4.4)	bus fares	3.91 (4.5)
6	sugar	3.28 (4.1)	rice	3.73 (4.3)
7	cooking oil	3.01 (3.8)	bread	3.49 (4.0)
8	miscellaneous food items	2.71 (3.4)	beef	3.38 (3.9)
9	beef	2.70 (3.4)	sugar	3.12 (3.6)
10	fish	2.66 (3.3)	cooking oil	2.97 (3.4)
	Total Weekly Expendiutre	J$ 79.93 (46.2)		J$ 86.67 (49.8)

[a]Percentage of total weekly expenditure.

[b]Partner group is an informal, rotating savings group whereby several persons regularly deposit money with a chosen leader and then withdraw fixed amounts by turn.

SOURCE: Low-Income Household Expenditure Survey data.

392

TABLE 6

MEAN WEEKLY EXPENDITURE SHARES (PERCENTAGES) PER
HOUSEHOLD FOR "LUXURY" ITEMS, BY URBAN AND
RURAL SUBSAMPLES, AND HOUSEHOLD TYPE

| | Urban | | Rural | |
	Female-Male	Female-Headed	Female-Male	Female-Headed
Salt fish	.8	.7	1.2	1.1
Tinned beef	.2	.3	.4	.5
Sardines	.4*	.2*	.5	.5
Tinned mackerel	.5	.5	.8	.7
Buns, pastries	.3	.3	.3	.3
Sugar syrups	.4	.4	.3*	.6*
Condensed milk	2.5*	2.0*	3.1	2.5
Soft drinks	1.2	1.1	.7	.7
Ice cream	1.1	.6	.7	.8
Patties[a]	.1	.1	.1	0
Cosmetics	.1	.1	.1	0
Cinema	.3	.3	0	0
Games, sports	.1	.3	.1	0
Dances	.2	0	0	0
Gambling	.3	.2	.1	0
Total "luxuries"	8.5	7.1	8.4	7.7

*Significant difference in means at or above the .05
level, using the T-test.

[a]Patties are a meat-filled pastry generally bought
ready-made.

SOURCE: Low-Income Household Expenditure Survey data.

393

APPENDIX A

The low-income household survey

In planning the details of the survey, several general hypotheses served as guideposts. First, rural-urban differences in expenditure levels and composition were expected, so the survey was designed to include a large number of households in both urban (including small towns) and rural areas. Second, expenditure patterns differ according to expenditure level such that poorer households spend higher percentages of their budget on food than better-off households. Thus, the survey needed to include a range of low-income households from the poorest to the upper levels of poverty. Third, household size and composition affect both the level and the pattern of expenditures in that large households may have "economies of scale" in certain expenditures, and households with many children will have more child-specific expenses such as school fees.

Unit of analysis

In view of the relatively fluid boundaries and functions of Jamaican households, it was not easy to define the basic study unit, let alone to classify it. Although a fairly precise definition of a "household member" was used in the study (a person was a "member" if he or she ate three or more meals a week and/or slept three or more nights a week in the household), it was difficult in some cases to apply the rule stringently and judgment had to be exercised by the interviewers concerning borderline cases.

Defining a household "head" is also not a simple matter (Harris 1981; Massiah 1983). I adopted a very simple classification which separates households in which there is an adult female with no permanently co- resident male partner as "female-headed" from households containing a co- resident female and male married either legally or by common-law, designated "female-male headed." This division tells us nothing about the nuances of who earns more money or makes more of the important household decisions in joint households, but at least it does separate the clearly female-only households from those where the possibility of male influence on expenditure levels and composition exists.

Sampling design

The households included were selected by purposive sampling (Miller and Stone 1985; Ward 1983) to include a range of low-income households. Communities were first selected on the basis of prior knowledge of general population distribution on the island. More importantly, the sample areas were deliberately chosen because they have a large concentration of low- income households. Within the sample areas, particular households were also selected on a purposive basis to ensure a heavy representation of very low-income households, defined as those in which aggregate earnings (cash or otherwise) of all members were regularly less than J$200.00 per month. In the final sample, nearly half of the survey households fell into this category. The remainder are also clearly low-income by Jamaican standards, falling within the bottom seven deciles of the national income distribution.

The sample is thus representative of various areas of the country, different economic activities, a range of low-income levels, and several household composition patterns. It is not a random sample, however, and therefore subjecting the data to statistical tests is not necessarily appropriate, but I have computed the means for subgroups, and compared means of various subgroups with each other, using the T-test to examine for significant differences between the means.

Data Gathered

Daily expenditures, including cash savings, were recorded for the 145 households for eight months (34 weeks) from November 1983 through the end of June 1984. The daily expenditure sheets were collected and checked weekly by trained interviewers and were supplemented by monthly interviews about household characteristics, income, assets, and other socioeconomic variables. Substantial efforts were devoted in the course of the survey to sorting out and correcting for data inconsistencies and errors. Subsequently, the daily expenditure data were aggregated into weeks for purposes of coding. In total, 90 expenditure variables were recorded, usually including both price and quantity information for each item purchased.

APPENDIX B

Low-income survey food items in ILO categories

Bread/Cereals:	cornmeal, flour, rice, buns, crackers, biscuits, bread, patties
Meat/Fish:	beef, mutton, pork, chicken, fish, tinned sardines, tinned beef, tinned mackerel, saltfish
Fats/Oils:	cooking oil, butter/margarine
Milk/Eggs:	milk, eggs, condensed milk, cheese, ice cream, baby food
Fruit/Vegetables:	bananas, plantain, vegetables, red peas, potatoes, yams, breadfruit, fruit, coconuts
Sugar/Sweets:	sugar, sugar syrups

Nonalcoholic Beverages:	soft drinks, fruit juices, tea, coffee

Alcoholic Beverages:	rum, beer, stout

Other Foods:	seasoning, miscellaneous foods

References

Banskota, Kamal, Stan R. Johnson and Gary Stampley
1985   Food Expenditure Patterns of Households. *Memorandum #2.* Center for National Food and Agricultural Policy. Columbia, MO: University of Missouri-Columbia, Department of Agricultural Economics.

Bird, Richard M. and Barbara Diane Miller
Forth- The Incidence of Indirect Taxes on Low-Income Households in coming   Jamaica. *Economic Development and Cultural Change.*

Brown, Susan E.
1975   Lower Economic Sector Female Mating Patterns in the Dominican Republic. In Ruby Rohrlich-Leavitt, ed., *Women Cross-Culturally:Change and Challenge.* The Hague: Mouton. Pp. 149-162.

Dixon, Ruth B.
1982   Women in Agriculture: Counting the Labor Force in Developing Countries. *Population and Development Review* 8(3):539-566.

Dwyer, Daisy Hilse
1983   Women and Income in the Third World: Implications for Policy.*International Programs Working Papers*, No. 18. New York: The Population Council.

Folbre, Nancy
1984   Household Production in the Philippines: A Non-neoclassical Approach. *Economic Development and Cultural Change* 32(2):303-330.

Guyer, Jane
1980   Household Budgets and Women's Incomes.*Working Paper* No. 28. Boston, MA: Boston University, African Studies Center.

Harris, Olivia
1981   Households as Natural Units in Kate Young, Carol Wolkowitz, and Roslyn McCullagh, eds., *Of Marriage and the Market:Women's Subordination in International Perspective.* London: CSE Books. Pp. 49-68.

Kaufman, Daniel
1982   Social Interaction as a Strategy of Economic Survival among the Urban
        Poor: A Theory and Evidence. Unpublished doctoral dissertation,
        Harvard University.

Kaufman, Daniel and David L. Lindauer
1984   Income Transfers within Extended Families to Meet Basic Needs: The
        Evidence from El Salvador.*World Bank Staff Working Papers*, Number
        644. Washington, DC: The World Bank.

Massiah, Joycelin
1983   *Women as Heads of Households in the Caribbean: Family Structure and
        Feminine Status.Paris:* UNESCO.

Miller, Barbara D. and Carl Stone
1985   The Low-Income Household Expenditure Survey: Description and
        Analysis. *Jamaica Tax Structure Examination Project, Staff Paper* 25.
        Syracuse, NY: Syracuse University, Metropolitan Studies Program.

Rakowski, Cathy A.
1984   Production and Reproduction in a Planned, Industrial City: The Working-
        and Lower-Class Households of Ciudad Buayana, Venezuela. *Working
        Paper* #61. East Lansing, MI: Michigan State University,Office of
        Women in International Development.

Saldert, Carola
1984   Female-Headed Household in Rural Bangladesh. Report from a Minor
        Research Task, January-February 1984. Development Study
        Unit,Department of Social Anthropology, *Working Paper*. Stockholm,
        Sweden: University of Sweden.

Sivark, Ruth Leger
1985   *Women: A World Survey*. Washington, DC: World Priorities.

Statistical Institute of Jamaica
1986   *The Labor Force 1985*. Kingston: Statistical Institute of Jamaica.

Statistical Institute of Jamaica
1986   *Household Expenditure Survey: Report on Household Expenditure
        Surveys 1975-1977*. Kingston: Statistical Institute of Jamaica.

Wasylenko, Michael
1986   The Distribution of Tax Burden in Jamaica: Pre-1985 Reform.*Jamaica
        Tax Structure Examination Project Staff Paper* No. 30.Syracuse, NY:
        Syracuse University, Metropolitan Studies Program.

397

HOUSEHOLD BUDGETARY STRATEGIES IN URBAN MEXICO: MEDIATING THE INCOME-CONSUMPTION NEXUS

Stephen A. Lorenzen, Arthur D. Murphy, and Henry A. Selby

Introduction

While pursuing a developmentalist approach to modernization, most governments in the Third World have also used subsidies to raise the real wages of workers by reducing the cost of basic consumer goods. The importance of these subsidies to the well-being of the average household and to political stability can be seen in those governments' resistance to International Monetary Fund demands that subsidies be eliminated. What Third World leaders recognize is that, with an almost flat wage structure for the majority of workers (Rocha 1982), the only place households have any control over their standard of living is through measures which free income for use on nonessential consumer goods.

Here we will consider the major alternatives open to the Mexican urban population for increasing consumption possibilities through the control or elimination of expenditures. That is, we will investigate the output side of the household budgeting equation, focusing on strategies for economizing to achieve an acceptable level of well-being.

Measuring and comparing levels of well-being

The objective here is not to develop measures of well-being, but to assess the options available to households to broaden their consumption possibilities by budgeting their limited resources and so produce at least a minimally acceptable living standard. From this perspective, assessments of welfare cannot be separated from notions of vulnerability to a variety of socioeconomic forces or from the extent households have been successful in constructing shelters against adverse economic circumstances. Such shelters allow some latitude in current expenditure decisions, facilitating greater budget flexibility. The latter is important to households when the social and economic environment is undergoing change.

Thus, relative well-being should be conceived not simply in terms of real income or real expenditures, but also in terms of real consumption possibilities under a variety of circumstances. The latter often hinge on the degree of control households can exercise over basic subsistence needs such as food and shelter. For many households (especially among the poor), the maintenance of a viable budgetary pattern and the attainment of a minimally acceptable living standard often depend upon avoiding certain types of expenditures. Welfare, therefore, cannot be judged simply in terms of total household income without reference to household size, nor can it be ascertained from raw consumption/expenditure data. Some attention must be paid to the structure and content of expenditures.

Because of economies of scale in consumption, using simple per capita income or consumption as a measure of the relative welfare of individuals or households may prove misleading. An alternative measure is offered by the notion of residual or discretionary income, i.e., what remains after expenditures for basic subsistence. Discretionary income--defined for purposes of this paper as real household income less expenditures for food, housing, utilities, medical care, and property taxes--is an indicator of the latitude a household has to spend income in accordance with its own preferences. This is not to say that added expenditures on food or other basics would not be preferred by some households, given incremental increases in income. However, overall food expenditures do tend to be inelastic with respect to income (i.e., a given per cent change in income leads to a proportionately smaller change in food consumption), as reflected in the portion of income expended on food by households at different income levels.

This concept of discretionary income may be used in a number of forms: As real pesos per capita, the utilization of discretionary income as an indicator of welfare differs somewhat from the focus on actual consumption per capita in the work of such analysts as Musgrove (1980: 249-66) and Chenery et al. (1974) at the World Bank.[1] The more conventional approach implicitly assumes that consumption expenditures are homogeneous, that they are a generic "good." Concentrating on discretionary income, by contrast, shifts the emphasis from spending per se to the degree of latitude available to households for spending beyond basic subsistence expenditures. The latter concept directs attention to the strategic alternatives open to families for fulfilling their needs as they interpret them. The primary drawback to the use of per capita measures, even in this more limited case, is that economies of scale in the joint consumption of discretionary items such as clothing, private forms of transportation, entertainment, and recreation are ignored.

Alternatively, discretionary income may be viewed as a proportion of total household income, rather than as absolute monetary units. This approach has the drawback of ignoring per capita considerations and failing to differentiate between the absolute amount of discretionary income represented by, say, 20% of a 10,000 peso income and 20% of a 5,000 one. Nonetheless, if gross incomes are segmented by levels such as quintiles, considering discretionary income as a proportion of total income across income levels should highlight key strategic alternatives faced by households commanding different resource endowments. In addition, the inverse of discretionary income as a proportion of the total, i.e., the proportion of income consumed by major subsistence expenditures, provides valuable analytical insights into the tradeoffs faced by urban Mexican households.

A brief example will clarify the essential difference between the more conventional focus on consumption expenditures and the strategic view emphasizing the degree of latitude available to the household after basic subsistence expenditures. Marta, a vendor in Oaxaca, earns the minimum wage and has no alternative options for shelter save a run-down rented apartment in a vecindad in the city's center. Although inexpensive by U. S. and Mexico City standards, the two rooms with no sanitary facilities or running water consume 25% of her household's income. As a result, expenditures for housing, food, and other basic subsistence items reduce her discretionary income, limiting her household's choices with respect to such items as entertainment, clothing, and education. We can contrast Marta's situation with that of Roberto, who also earns the minimum wage as an unskilled construction worker in Oaxaca. Roberto, however, took part in a land invasion a few years back, and although he does not have legal title to his lot, his housing costs are only 10% of his household's income.

The options open to Roberto are greater than those for Marta. He can either save, invest, or consume his residual income. Like other lower-income families, he would probably spend his residual income on consumer goods. A total consumption measure of welfare would rate both households equally. The discretionary income measure, by contrast, would capture the greater range of choices available to Roberto's household by its shelter strategy.

The data

This paper is based on a combination of ethnographic and empirical research carried out in urban Mexico between 1972 and 1985. Our work first began with field research in Oaxaca, Oaxaca, in 1972, with additional long-term fieldwork in Ciudad Netzahualcoyotl, Mexico, beginning in 1982. In addition, we have done short-term fieldwork in Reynosa, Tamaulipas, and Hermosillo, Sonora. The empirical data is from a study of urban households carried out in conjunction with the *Instituto Nacional para el Desarrollo de la Vivienda y de la Comunidad Rural* (INDECO) in the years 1977 through 1979.

As part of its program to use oil revenues in the 1970s to reduce the cost of housing for workers in the nonregulated sectors of the economy, the government of Mexico, through INDECO, undertook a study of the housing conditions and needs in urban Mexico. The foci of the study were the intermediate cities of the nation. The cities surveyed provide a reasonable sample of the broad geographic, economic, and cultural diversity of Mexico, and for that reason we feel it is possible to combine this data with our ethnographic work to make some statements about the Mexican urban household.[2] In order to ensure representativeness within each city, a two-stage sampling method was used. In each case the interview was with the adult head of household or spouse. The total sample size was over 9200 households. The socioeconomic survey instrument used was closed-ended and contained over 200 items. Of particular interest to us here are the questions which dealt with household-level incomes and expenditures (Murphy 1979).

Household income distribution in the INDECO sample: an overview

In dealing with issues relating to welfare, the following analysis employs the somewhat arbitrary categories of quintiles. Some analysts define poverty in terms of the two lowest quintiles of per capita consumption (Musgrove 1980; Chenery et al. 1974). Others, dealing with the INDECO survey data from Mexico, have employed ranges of the legal minimum salary current in each region (Murphy et al. 1984; Selby et al. n.d.). The latter assume the minimum salary is inadequate even for a single-person household. Thus the cut-off point between the "destitute" and the merely "poor" is 1.8 legal minimum salaries. The threshold for the "elite" segment of the population, as defined by total household income in minimum salary units, is 4.8. This latter point is consistent with the minimum income considered adequate by the Fund for Housing (FOVI) of the Mexican government for obtaining private credit (Selby et al. n.d.).

The legal minimum salary at the time of the surveys in each of the cities varied from 1794 to 4860 pesos monthly, with that in the Federal District representing something of a middling benchmark at 3600. Thus the upper limit for the first quintile in real pesos corresponds roughly to just under one minimum salary unit (see A-1).[3] By way of comparison with the schema citied above, the 1.8 minimum salary threshold between the "destitute" and "poor" occurs at the 55th percentile. The upper end of the latter category extends to the 90th percentile. Consequently, by this definition the lowest 55 percent of the population are destitute, while the next 35 percent are poor. Only the upper 10 percent are relatively comfortable.

Household budgeting strategies

Relative levels of money earnings, however, do not provide a very reliable guide to living standards without a knowledge of necessary budget outlays, and especially as to the extent of discretionary control over such outlays. In the analysis which follows, the focus will be on budgetary options as they relate to discretionary income per person. In other words, the overall question to be addressed is how, with given levels of money income, households may most effectively translate those funds into acceptable living standards by gaining a measure of control over basic budgetary outlays, thereby increasing discretionary income.

This is not to say that basic subsistence items such as housing or health care are not "goods." The point is rather that for poor households a strategy of "expenditure avoidance" with regard to such basic goods is both rational and widely practiced. In this way consumption of discretionary goods may be enhanced, while at the same time the household is afforded a wider margin of security against economic adversity. The basic strategy is one of risk avoidance in conjunction with consumption enhancement (see Lorenzen 1986: ch.6).

By way of analogy, this conceptual strategy might be compared to the "permanent income hypothesis" popularized by Milton Friedman (1955; see also Branson 1972). In it, current expenditures for consumption are a function of "permanent," as opposed to "transitory," income. The former is conceived as the expected value of an income stream extending into the future. The basis for the expected value of permanent income is one's past experience, human capital, etc. In our case it would mean that households would attempt to reduce the cost of basic goods such as food and rent to the degree that their current incomes are below what they consider normal, given their level of human capital. On the other hand, if their current income is above what they expect over the long term, the range of choices open to the household increases. For example, if a son or daughter in a household living in two rooms gets an unexpected job with The Party during a campaign year or with the local anthropologist, the "windfall" income may be used to add another room to the house or purchase such other discretionary goods as new clothing, consumer durables, or entertainment.

Control over the household budget is conditioned by an interwoven set of factors--e.g., total household income, number of members, position in the domestic cycle--none of which can be clearly separated from the rest. For example, while food might be considered to take precedence over other expenditures, the level of food purchases may be varied in accordance with other immediate needs. Relatively low-income households with high dependency ratios and access to cheap housing may spend more freely on food, formal medical treatment, or more "discretionary" goods and services. On the other hand, the same households compelled to pay high rents may have to cut back in these areas by decreasing the amount of meat in the diet, using folk remedies rather than a doctor, or removing a child from school.

The distribution of real peso expenditures on the five basic expense categories in the INDECO sample offers some insight into the underlying dynamics of common expenditure patterns (see A-2). Food and utilities represent standard out-of-pocket expenses, the former commanding by far the largest portion of income. The proportion of households reporting positive monthly expenditures for housing, health care, and property taxes, by contrast, is less than 50 percent in each case. Fifty-four percent reported paying no taxes, while 59 percent claimed no monthly housing expenses, and 67 percent reported no health care outlays. Clearly, the key to whether or not many households are able to enjoy tolerable levels of discretionary spending power, despite relatively low levels of money income, may lie in the avoidance of such basic expenditures.

Food and utilities

Not surprisingly, the food burden is heaviest at lower income levels, averaging over 60 percent in the bottom quintile (see A-3). However, food expenditures are subject to considerable manipulation, allowing many households a good deal of latitude either to express their preferences or to cut back in the face of adversity. In other words, to a much greater degree than other major categories, food expenditures exhibit a relatively consistent relationship to income and household size. Consider, for example, the following functional relationship:

$E^f = a + bY + H^n$, where
    (1) E^f is the natural log of real food expenditures;
    (2) Y is the natural log of total real family income; and
    (3) H^n is the natural log of household size.

The coefficients corresponding to the independent variables in the above equation, estimated from the INDECO sample with ordinary least squares regression techniques, are:

$E^f = 4.3666176 + .34433992Y + .24125781H^n$
    $(t = 51.59)$ $(t = 36.33)$ $(t = 13.69)$

The adjusted coefficient of determination (R^2) pertaining to the preceding estimate is .179.

Estimated values of the total, average, and marginal expenditures for food derived from the preceding regression equation indicate that at the median income of some 5600 real pesos per month, the marginal cost to feed an additional member ranges from a high of 200 pesos per month for a household with three members to a low of around 60 pesos per month for a household with 12 members. At the median household size of 5, for example, the estimated marginal food cost of an additional member is roughly 100 real pesos per month, or about 3 percent of the minimum salary in the Federal District at the time of the INDECO survey (see Lorenzen 1986: 225).

It would seem that, for the bulk of the urban Mexican population, the marginal cost to feed an additional household member, in terms of basic subsistence, is minimal. From the perspective of individual household heads, this result underlines the rationality of investing in "human capital" in the form of numbers of offspring, assuming future benefits in terms of financial security and supplemental income in later years.[4] As long as the costs associated with such reproductive activity are low compared to the potential benefits--both monetary and nonmonetary--the inherent rationality remains.[5]

The proportion of income consumed by food does not vary markedly among small, medium, and large households (see A- 4). The critical factor in this regard is the extent to which additional household members are productively employed. Indeed, the drawbacks of large households may be turned to advantages if the household can see to it that more than one member is working.

While most households reported regular expenses for utilities (which include lighting and some form of fuel for cooking and heating), these items are not likely to vary substantially with marginal changes in household size. As a result, food expenditures might be considered the primary variable cost in the household production budget in the short run. The other major subsistence expenditures may thus be conceived as relatively fixed factors.

Health care, housing and property taxes

As indicated above, the majority of the INDECO sample reported making no regular expenditures for health care, shelter, and property taxes. Although health care might conceivably vary with household size, no statistically significant relationship could be identified. To the extent that households do incur regular out-of-pocket expenses for shelter and property taxes, the amounts are not likely to vary substantially with marginal changes in household size, at least not for low-income households in the short run.

For those households reporting some positive monthly expenditures for either shelter or health care, the budgetary burden is especially onerous at the lowest income level (see A- 5). As would be expected, the burden declines substantially as income rises. However, the proportion of households reporting positive health care expenditures rises steadily with income. This result is consistent with ethnographic evidence that modern health care is often inaccessible to poor households (Doyal 1979; Baer 1982; Stebbins 1986).

Health care. Access to health care is often associated with the enjoyment of socioeconomic benefits (*prestaciones sociales*). The latter are basically comparable to the types of fringe benefits provided many workers in the U.S. and generally assume access to health care through the Mexican Social Security System (*Instituto Mexicano de Seguro Social*, or IMSS). Not surprisingly, the incidence of such benefits rises markedly with income level.

The *a priori* expectation would be that socioeconomic benefits offer a degree of protection from the financial impositions of sickness and injury and therefore that average expenditures, either as a proportion of income or in absolute terms, tend to be less when benefits are available. Our results suggest that at both lower and higher income levels health care expenditures tended to command a smaller portion of income in those households which reported having benefits than in those which did not, although the degree of variation was not large. For households of all income levels which incurred positive health care costs, those without socioeconomic benefits reported expenditures averaging 7.0 percent of total income. By contrast, for those units with such benefits, health care expenditures averaged 5.5 percent.

The proportion of households reporting positive expenditures for health care was related directly to income level, while the percent of income expended was inversely related (see A-5). One important consideration in interpreting the behavior of health care expenditures is the fact that, even for those enjoying

405

access to public facilities, these services are not costless. While charges might be judged modest by U.S. standards, they are significant from the budgetary prerpsective of many poor households. Consequently, although access to the system does seem to facilitate increased consumption of health care services, this advantage is not without a concomitant regressive expenditure burden.

Housing and property taxes. The structure of housing expenditures is somewhat more straightforward than that of health care. The latter is especially vulnerable to unforseen and uncontrollable factors such as sudden injury or illness. Housing, by contrast, may often be controlled by simple planning, subject of course to constraints imposed by the local environment. The quest for home ownership has been an important factor in the growth of working-class housing developments and land invasions in the cities of Mexico and elsewhere (see Logan 1984; Velez-Ibañez 1983; Scott 1982). The success of a household in gaining access to housing at little or no cost, either by legal or extralegal means, may be the decisive factor in determining whether the budget is adequate to cover basic expenditures.

Home ownership is relatively constant across income levels, characterizing about two-thirds of the households surveyed. Irregular tenancy is somewhat more common at lower income levels. The percent of legal owners bearing positive monthly expenditures for housing is higher than among irregular tenants (see A-6). For the latter group the proportion of households reporting no monthly housing expenses tends to decline as income level rises. An important factor underlying this result is that a greater proportion of irregular owners had resided in their current locations for a relatively short time, i.e., less than five years (see A-7). At the lowest income levels roughly one-third to one-half of the irregular owners had been in their current locations for under five years. What the data suggest is that for the poorest households, irregular tenancy affords the opportunity of some sort of shelter without the necessity of regular monthly expenditures. By contrast, somewhat better-off households are able to spend more on shelter, either in increased initial cost or in periodic improvements as the flow of earnings allows.

In terms of the proportion of income consumed, a factor which stands out is the lack of differentiation among the alternative types of tenancy (see A-8). While rental appeared to be slightly more burdensome for the lowest income households, the differences were minimal. Nevertheless, viewed in a more dynamic context, renting lacks certain advantages of ownership. For example, rental payments are likely to continue into the foreseeable future, with virtually no hope of a day when the mortgage is paid and housing expenses are more discretionary and limited to repairs or improvements. Thus, the drive for either legal or extralegal home ownership by Mexican households is a drive towards budgetary flexibility as well as long-term security. In the absence of regular payment obligations, ownership often entails the ability to postpone discretionary expenses when economic adversity dictates. Such a strategy does not require that ownership be recognized by the state.

An additional expense closely associated with home ownership is property taxes. Substantial differences in the tax burden exist between households reporting regular as opposed to irregular ownership. The former were roughly twice as likely to pay taxes (see A-9). Furthermore, for those regular owners who did report paying taxes, the burden was about twice as heavy in terms of the proportion of income expended. The avoidance of taxes by the great majority of irregular owners and the relatively small burden represented by these levies on those who do pay represent an additional advantage of irregular ownership.

Quality of life

One major problem with the "expenditure avoidance" approach is the lack of any measure of quality. Of course, conventional consumption expenditure approaches have similar drawbacks, insofar as dwellings of comparable cost are not necessarily of equivalent quality. Here we attempt to shed some light on this problem. Not surprisingly, houses account for the great majority of dwellings in which tenants have ownership rights, whether legal or illegal (see A- 10). Those residences classified as shacks (*jacales*) are somewhat overrepresented among irregular (as compared to legal) owners. The implication is that lower-quality residences may be more common among irregular homeowners.

Irregular owners, however, seem to fare about as well as legal renters with respect to quality, and markedly better than irregular renters (see A-11). Furthermore, recalling that roughly three-fourths of irregular owners avoid the necessity of regular housing expenditures and that the average proportion of income expended for shelter by the remaining one-fourth is much lower than for renters of any type, irregular ownership may still represent the best deal available per peso expended. For low-income households it may represent the preferred alternative.

Implications and conclusions

The objective of the following analysis is to assess the likely impact of the current crisis on major segments of the Mexican population and to compare the implications of alternative budgetary strategies. The logical starting point is the structure of budgetary trade-offs faced by the population at large. Expenditures for food and utilities (over which households have incremental control) represent regular expenditures for virtually all households. By contrast, housing, property taxes, and health care expenses (over which household control tends to be more categorical) were reported by only a minority.

For analytical purposes we will contrast the nature of the budgetary constraints faced by two stereotypical classes of households, homeowners and renters. These two classes may be taken as representing the "minimum" and "maximum" parameters, respectively, of the budgetary options typically faced by

407

the average household in each income quintile. These parameters may be expressed simply as mean percentages of total income expended on the basic items which are a standard part of the budget of each household class (see A-12). What stands out is the critical situation faced by those at the lower end of the income scale. Households in the lowest two income quintiles typically spend over 50 percent of their income on food alone. That most are able to do so while remaining within their limited budgets is due to their ability to avoid expenditures on one or more of the other basic subsistence items.

As indicated previously, the majority of respondents avoided regular expenditures on housing through legal or extralegal home ownership. Taxes are associated with housing ownership and are much more common among regular owners. Thus many families in the lowest income quintile have been able to survive on their limited budgets with some discretionary income for such things as clothing, transportation, and entertainment--as long as injury, sickness, or other emergencies have not arisen--because of the indirect transfer of income represented by the government's tacit approval of irregular land ownership.

A "minimal" budget, consisting only of food and utilities expenditures, consumes an average 72.1 percent of total income in the lowest quintile (see A-12). That such a budgetary structure is both realistic and widespread is underscored by the fact that a majority of home owners reported no regular housing expenditures. Alternatively, renters in the lowest income quintile reported shelter expenses which consumed an average 19 percent of household income, resulting in less than 10 percent of income being left over for discretionary purposes. A health-related emergency or economic adversity might easily unbalance the household budget under such circumstances.

What this suggests is little different from what has been fairly obvious to first-hand observers of life in urban Mexico in recent years. The great mass of the population has exhibited a remarkable degree of ingenuity and perseverance in dealing with an economic crisis which has sharply reduced real wages. Moonlighting seems to have become increasingly common not only among low-income groups, but among middle-class workers struggling to maintain their accustomed living standards (Walsh 1985). For those who have not been able to meet their needs in Mexico, increasing numbers have reportedly ventured into the U.S. in search of employment.

The current budgetary austerity of many individual Mexican households can be conceived as the manifestation, at the 'micro' level, of conventional macroeconomic policies ostensibly aimed at creating the basis for future recovery. Similar policies have been promoted, if not imposed, by the International Monetary Fund (IMF) around the world. Typical recovery packages include anti-inflationary measures, structural reforms to reduce the role of the state in the economy, exchange rate reforms, and trade liberalization. In Mexico, a major component of recent anti-inflationary policy has been a reduction in real wages achieved by restraining wage increases to levels below the rate of inflation. At the same time, attempts to reduce government spending have included significant reductions in subsidies for basic food items and fuel. As we have demonstrated, even in the relatively prosperous period just prior to the current economic crisis households in the lowest income quintiles had precious little discretionary income they could sacrifice for national recovery.

Notes

The authors would like to acknowledge the support of the National Institute for Community Development of Mexico (INDECO-MEXICO); the Institute of Latin American Studies, The University of Texas at Austin; The Rusk Center, The University of Georgia; the University Research Committee, Baylor University; and the Fulbright-Hays program. In addition, thanks are due to Arq. José Ma. Gutiérrez, Ing. José Luís Aceves M., Arq. Ignacio Cabrera, Lic. Diana Luque, Lic. Aida Castañeda, Steve Kowalewski, Laura Finsten, and Jeanie Fitzpatrick for their help. The authors are, of course, responsible for the content of the paper.

1. The per capita measures in this paper consider all household members equivalent consumption units, and the relevant household income figures are calculated on a straightforward per capita basis. This approach is supported by empirical results of Latin American studies reported by Musgrove (1980: pp. 250-51), who cites evidence that the cost of a minimal diet does not vary greatly by age or sex for persons older than five years; and that elasticities of subsistence spending with respect to household size apparently fall within a fairly narrow range from 0.9 to 1.0.

2. Oaxaca served as the pilot study for the project. The survey was designed and tested in late 1976, with the final data collected in 1977. Oaxaca was followed in 1977 by Villahermosa, which was in the throws of its oil boom. In 1978 Reynosa, Mérida, and Delegación Venustiano Carranza were added, and finally in 1979 Mexicali, Querétaro, San Luís Potosí, Mazatlán, and Tampico. In each case an individual from the INDECO-MEXICO office was in charge of the study but engaged local interviewers to carry out the work.

3. The data for this paper are presented as a series of appendices at the end of the paper. The data source for each appendix is the INDECO-Mexico urban study.

4. For a theoretical discussion of the incentives for a household to emphasize quantity vs. quality in its reproductive strategy see Gary S. Becker 1976, Part 6.

409

5.   Alternatively, if the household is conceived as a producer of cheap labor power for the industrial sector, it may be seen to perform this function quite successfully as well (see Portes and Walton 1981, especially chapter 3).

APPENDIX 1
Distribution of Monthly Household Income
by Quintile Upper Limit

Minimum Quintile	Real Mexican Units Pesos	Regional Salary
1	3,240	0.985
2	4,540	1.365
3	6,920	2.000
4	11,330	3.336
Mean	14,240	4.234
Median	5,660	1.667

APPENDIX 2
Quintile Upper Limits of Real Per Capita
Expenditures on Basics (Adjusted Mexican Pesos Per Month)

Quintile	Food	Housing	Utilities	Healthcare	Taxes
1	300	0	30	0	0
2	465	0	45	0	0
3	630	20	70	0	5
4	915	150	115	40	25

APPENDIX 3
Mean Expenditures on Food and Utilities as
A Proportion of Total Household Income, by Income Quintile

Income Quintile	Food	Utilities
1	61.8	10.3
2	54.9	7.2
3	49.9	6.1
4	38.8	4.4
5	24.7	2.9

APPENDIX 4
Average Percent of Total Household Income Expended on Food
by Household Size by Participation Rate in the Economic
Sphere

Size	All	Under 20%	20%-39%	40% and over
1-4	44.3	n.a.	45.5	40.2
5-7	46.9	51.0	46.8	38.6
8+	46.7	54.0	39.9	30.6

APPENDIX 5
Percent of Households Reporting Positive Monthly
Expenditures for Housing and Health Care, and Average
Percent of Income Expended on These Items by Such
Households, by Quintile of Total Real Household Income

Income Quintile	Housing Households	Income	Health Care Households	Income
1	33.8	18.9	25.0	11.2
2	37.8	15.5	33.2	7.4
3	42.5	13.8	34.6	6.4
4	43.5	11.9	32.8	4.9
5	45.2	9.4	41.5	3.6

APPENDIX 6
Percent Distribution of Households by Type of Tenancy, by
Quintile of Real Household Income

Income Quintile	Legal Ownership	Irregular Ownership	Legal Rental	Irregular Rental	Borrowed, etc.
1	42.0	26.0	20.1	5.4	6.6
2	43.1	21.0	24.8	4.3	6.8
3	44.0	22.3	25.5	4.9	3.4
4	47.8	19.6	26.9	2.7	3.0
5	51.9	15.7	28.8	2.4	1.3

APPENDIX 7
Percent of Households Reporting No Monthly Housing
Expenditures & Percent of Such Households Residing in
Current Location for Less than Five Years, by Type of Housing
Tenancy, by Quintile of Real Household Income

Income Quintile	Legal Ownership		Irregular Ownership	
	No House Payment	Under 5 Years	No House Payment	Under 5 Years
1	89.7	17.4	83.3	45.9
2	86.8	18.5	84.9	39.0
3	83.6	18.7	74.3	30.1
4	84.8	18.5	62.6	29.7
5	83.3	16.4	61.4	30.5

APPENDIX 8

Average Percent of Income Expended for Housing by
Households Reporting Positive Housing Expenditures by Type
of Housing Tenancy, by Quintile of Real Household Income

Income Quintile	Legal Ownership	Irregular Ownership	Legal Rental	Irregular Rental
1	17.3	15.0	20.6	17.1
2	15.6	16.1	15.8	10.5
3	12.1	12.5	14.9	10.4
4	12.2	13.1	11.9	8.8
5	8.4	10.4	9.7	6.6

APPENDIX 9

Percent of Home Owners Paying Taxes and Proportion of Total
Income Expended on Taxes by Such Households, by Real Income
Quintile

Income Quintile	Regular Owners		Irregular Owners	
	% Households	% Income	% Households	% Income
All	77.2	3.4	39.9	1.8
1	63.1	6.1	19.3	3.1
2	74.0	3.9	37.2	2.6
3	77.7	3.2	48.9	1.7
4	82.9	2.7	48.6	1.2
5	84.8	2.2	58.5	1.0

APPENDIX 10

Percent of Households by Housing Type, by Type of Housing
Tenancy

Type of Tenancy	Housing Type			
	Shack	Room	Apartment	House
Legal Ownership	5.2	6.1	5.6	83.1
Irregular Ownership	15.8	12.7	1.6	69.9
Legal Rental	3.2	20.3	25.2	51.2
Irregular Rental	8.5	33.7	8.5	49.3
Borrowed, etc.	16.2	25.6	6.1	52.2

APPENDIX 11
Percent of Households by House Type, by Subjectively
Perceived Quality of Housing

Type of Tenancy	Perceived Quality				
	Very Good	Good	Mediocre	Bad	Very Bad
Legal Ownership	11.5	40.6	37.2	9.1	1.7
Irregular Ownership	7.2	33.2	41.2	13.5	4.9
Legal Rental	7.3	35.5	39.3	14.6	3.3
Irregular Rental	2.9	26.2	45.9	19.0	6.1
Borrowed, etc.	4.2	26.7	43.8	22.2	3.1

Note: Quality of housing was rated by the interviewees themselves.

APPENDIX 12
Composite Household Budgetary Patterns Percent of Total
Income Expended on Basic Items by Type of Tenancy by Real
Housing Income Level.

Income Quintile	Food	Utilities	Rental Housing	Owners Total	Renters Total	Health Care
1	61.8	10.3	19.9	72.1	92.0	11.2
2	54.9	7.2	15.1	62.1	77.2	7.4
3	49.9	6.1	14.2	56.0	70.2	6.4
4	38.8	4.4	11.7	43.2	54.9	4.9
5	24.7	2.9	9.5	27.6	37.1	3.6

References

Baer, Hans
1982 On the Political Economy of Health, *Medical Anthropology Newsletter*,14(1):1-2, 13-17.

Becker, Gary S.
1976 *The Economic Approach to Human Behavior* Chicago: University of Chicago Press.

Branson, William H.
1972 *Macroeconomic Theory*. New York: Harper and Row.

Chenery, Hollis, Montek S. Ahluwalia, C.L.G. Bell, John H. Duloy, and Richard Jolly
1974 *Redistribution with Growth*. London: Oxford University Press.

Doyal, Lesley
1979 *The Political Economy of Health*. Boston: South EndPress.

Friedman, Milton
1955 *A Theory of the Consumption Function*. New York: National Bureau of Economic Research.

Logan, Kathleen
1984 *Haciendo Pueblo: The Development of a Guadalajaran Suburb*. University of Alabama Press.

Lorenzen, Stephen A.
1986 *Employment, Earnings, and Consumption Strategies in Urban Mexico.* Unpublished Ph.D. dissertation. AUniversity of Texas at Austin.

Murphy, Arthur D.
1979 *Urbanization, Development, and Household Adaptive Strategies in Oaxaca, a Secondary City of Mexico*. Unpublished Ph.D. dissertation. Philadelphia: Temple University.

Murphy, Arthur D., Alex Stepick, and Aida Castañeda
1984 La articulación de una ciudad intermedic con la economía Mexicana y el efecto sobre los niveles de vida: el Caso de Oaxaca *Revista Interamericana de Planificación*, XVII(71):115-28.

Musgrove, Philip
1980 Household Size and Composition, Employment, and Poverty in Urban Latin America, in *Economic   Development and Cultural Change*, 23(2):249-66.

Portes, Alejandro, and John Walton
1981   *Labor, Class, and the International System.* New York: Academic Press.

Rocha, Alberto García
1982   Wage Differentials in Mexico. In Jorge Slazar-Carrillo, *The Structure of Wages in Latin American Manufacturing Industries.*
        Miami: University Presses of Florida, pp. 157-70.

Scott, Ian
1982   Urban and Spatial Development in Mexico. Baltimore: Johns Hopkins University Press.

Selby, Henry A., Arthur D. Murphy, Ignacio Cabrera, and Aida Castañeda
in   Battling Urban Poverty from Below: A Profile of the Poor
press   in Two Mexican Cities. *American Anthropologist.*

Stebbins, Kenyon Rainier
1986   Politics, Economics, and Health Services in Rural Oaxaca, Mexico, *Human Organization*, 45(2):112-18.

Velez-Ibañez, Carlos
1983   *Rituals of Marginality: Politics, Process, and Culture Change in Central Urban Mexico, 1969-1974.*   Berkeley: University of California Press.

Walsh, Mary Williams
1985   Bitter Bourgeoisie--Mexico's Middle Class Blames Government for Economic Crunch. *Wall Street Journal* (December 30): 1, 6.

416

INDEX[1]

---

1. See also Table of Contents